The Private Pilot's Licence Course

Principles of Flight
Aircraft General Knowledge
Flight Performance and Planning

The Private Pilot's Licence Course

Principles of Flight
Aircraft General Knowledge
Flight Performance and Planning

Jeremy M Pratt

ISBN 1 874783 23 3

Published by

Airplan Flight Equipment Ltd

This book is intended to be a guide to the Principles of Flight Aircraft General Knowledge Flight Performance and Planning element of the PPL course. It does not in any way replace or overrule the instruction you will receive from a flight instructor at a flying training organisation (FTO) or registered facility (RF). No part of this book overrules or supersedes the Air Navigation Order (ANO), Aeronautical Information Publication (AIP), Aeronautical Information Circulars (AICs), Joint Aviation Requirements (JAR) and other documents published by a competent authority; the flight manual/pilot's operating handbook for the aircraft being flown; the pilot order book/flying training organisation or registered facility syllabus; and the general provisions of good airmanship and safe flying practice.

First Edition 1997
Reprinted with amendments and revisions 1998

Second Edition 2001

Third Edition 2004
Reprinted with amendments and revisions 2005
Reprinted with revisions 2006

The Private Pilot's Licence Course
Principles of Flight
Aircraft General Knowledge
Flight Performance and Planning

ISBN 1 874783 23 3

Airplan Flight Equipment Ltd
1a Ringway Trading Estate, Shadowmoss Road, Manchester M22 5LH
Tel: 0161 499 0023   Fax: 0161 499 0298
email: enquiries@afeonline.com
www.afeonline.com

Contents

Introduction

PRINCIPLES OF FLIGHT

The Atmosphere and Properties of the Air pf1-pf6
    The Atmosphere pf2
    Air in Motion pf2-pf5
    Revision pf5

The Four Forces pf6-pf23
    The Four Forces Acting on an Aircraft in Flight pf8
    Mass pf9-pf11
    Thrust pf12
    Lift pf12-pf18
    Drag pf19-pf21
    Balance and Couples pf22
    Revision pf23

Stability and Control pf24-pf39
    Static and Dynamic Stability pf26-pf27
    The Three Planes of Movement pf27
    Stability in Pitch pf27-pf30
    Control in Pitch pf30-pf31
    Stability in Roll pf31-pf32
    Control In Roll pf33-pf34
    Stability in Yaw pf34-pf35
    Control in Yaw pf36-pf37
    Mass and Aerodynamic Balance of the Flying Controls pf37-pf38
    Revision pf39

Trimming Controls pf40-pf45
    Purpose and Function pf42
    Operation of Trimming Controls pf42-pf43
    Types of Trimmer pf43-pf44
    Revision pf45

Flaps and Slats pf46-pf51
    The Flaps pf48-pf50
    Slats, Slots and Air Brakes pf50-pf51
    Revision pf51

The Stall pf52-pf66
    Slow Flight - The 'Back of the Power Curve' pf54-pf55
    Principles of the Stall pf55
    Stall Airspeed pf56
    Factors Affecting Stalling Airspeed pf57-pf59
    Symptoms of the Stall pf59-pf60
    The Stall Recovery pf60-pf62
    Stall Warners pf62-pf63
    Stall Accident Scenarios pf63-pf65
    Revision pf66

Avoidance of Spins pf68-pf75
    Causes of a Spin pf70
    The Forces in a Spin pf71
    Spin Recovery pf71-pf72
    The Spiral Dive pf73

6

      What's It Doing Now?..pf74
      Spin Accident Scenarios..pf74
      Revision..pf75

Load Factor and Manoeuvring Flight...pf76-pf81
      Structural Considerations pf78
      The V-n Envelope...pf79-pf80
      In-Flight Precautions pf80-pf81
      Revision..pf81

AIRCRAFT GENERAL KNOWLEDGE

The Airframe gen1-gen29
      Airframe Configuration..gen2-gen3
      Wing Construction gen3-gen4
      Wing Design gen5-gen10
      Fuselage Construction gen11
      Fuselage Design...gen11-gen12
      Modern Design Concepts gen13-gen14
      Serviceability Checks gen14-gen16
      The Elevator..gen16-gen17
      The Rudder...gen17-gen18
      The Ailerons..gen18-gen19
      Flaps gen19
      Control Locks gen20
      Flying Control Serviceability Checks gen20-gen21
      The Undercarriage gen22-gen23
      Tyres gen24
      Brakes..gen24-gen26
      Undercarriage Serviceability Checks and Handling.................................gen26-gen28
      Revision gen28-gen29

Aero Engines gen30-gen41
      Principles of Piston Engines gen32
      The Four Stroke Cycle gen32-gen33
      Basic Engine Design...gen34-gen36
      Two-Stroke Engines gen37
      Rotating Combustion (Wankel) Engines gen38-gen39
      Supercharging and Turbocharging gen38-gen39
      Engine Designators...gen40
      Revision...gen41

The Fuel System..gen42-gen49
      The Fuel System gen44-gen46
      Fuel Grades...gen47
      Fuel System Serviceability Checks and Handling....................................gen47-gen49
      Revision...gen49

The Induction System...gen50-gen57
      The Induction System gen52-gen53
      Carburettor Icing...gen54-gen55
      Fuel Injection..gen55
      Serviceability Checks and Handling gen56
      Revision...gen57

The Ignition System gen58-gen63
      The Ignition System gen60-gen62
      Serviceability Checks and Handling gen62
      Revision...gen63

The Cooling System gen64-gen67

      The Cooling System gen66-gen67

      Serviceability Checks and Handling gen67

      Revision gen67

The Oil System gen68-gen73

      The Oil System gen70

      Oil Grades gen71

      Serviceability Checks and Handling gen72

      Revision gen73

The Propeller gen74-gen81

      Principles of Propellers gen76-gen77

      The Fixed-Pitch Propeller gen77-gen78

      The Variable Pitch Propeller gen78-gen80

      Propeller Handling and Serviceability Checks gen80-gen81

      Revision gen81

Engine Handling gen82-gen97

      Starting Procedure gen84-gen85

      Starting Problems gen86

      Fire on Start gen86

      Taxying, Power Checks, Take-Off gen87-gen89

      Climbing gen89

      In The Cruise gen90-gen93

      Engine Problem Troubleshooting gen94-gen95

      Descent gen95

      After-landing and Shut Down gen96

      Storage gen96

      Revision gen97

Aircraft Systems gen98-gen111

      Principles of Electrical Circuits gen100-gen101

      Aircraft Batteries gen101-gen102

      Generators and Alternators gen102-gen103

      Aircraft Electrical Systems gen103-gen105

      The Master Switch gen105

      Electrical Failure gen106

      Bonding gen106

      External Power gen107

      Electrical System Serviceability Checks gen107

      The Suction System gen107-gen108

      Suction System Serviceability Checks gen108

      The Pitot-Static System gen108

      The Static Source gen109

      The Pitot Source gen109

      Position and Manoeuvre-Induced Errors gen110

      Pitot-Static System Serviceability Checks gen110

      Revision gen111

Instruments gen112-gen132

      The Altimeter gen114-gen115

      Altimeter Errors gen116-gen117

      Altimeter Serviceability Checks gen117

      The Vertical Speed Indicator (VSI) gen118-gen119

      VSI Serviceability Checks gen119

      The Airspeed Indicator (ASI) gen119-gen120

      Airspeed Indicator Errors gen121-gen123

8

Airspeed Indicator Serviceability Checks..gen123
Principles of Gyroscopes..gen123
The Turn Indicator..gen124
The Turn Co-ordinator gen124
Turn Co-ordinator Serviceability Checks gen125
The Attitude Indicator (AI)...gen125
Attitude Indicator Serviceability Checks..gen126
The Heading Indicator gen127-gen128
Heading Indicator Serviceability Checks gen128
The Magnetic Compass gen129-gen130
Compass Serviceability Checks gen131
Revision..gen132

Airworthiness..gen134-gen141
Aircraft Documents..gen136-gen138
Aircraft Maintenance gen138-gen139
Pilot Maintenance..gen140
Modifications gen141
Revision..gen141

Aeroplane Flight Safety..gen142-gen153
Seat Belts and Harnesses and Seat Adjustment gen144
First Aid Kits...gen145
Fire Extinguishers gen145
Survival Equipment..gen146-gen147
De-Icing Systems gen147-gen148
Cabin Heating and Ventilation Systems..gen148-gen149
Refuelling Precautions..gen150-gen151
Dangerous Goods...gen151
Revision gen152

Operational Flight Safety...gen154-gen161
Windshear, Gusts and Turbulence gen156-gen157
Wake Turbulence gen158
Aquaplaning..gen158
Emergency Exits gen159
Passenger Briefing...gen159-gen160
Revision..gen161

FLIGHT PERFORMANCE AND PLANNING
Introduction
Mass and Balance fpp1-11
Maximum Mass Limits..fpp2-3
Centre of Gravity..fpp4-9
Loading fpp9
Revision..fpp10

Take-Off and Climb fpp12-29
Take-off and Climb Performance fpp14
Forces in the Take-Off Run fpp14-15
Ground Effect..fpp15
The Initial Climb fpp16
Principles of Climbing...fpp16
Climb Performance...fpp16-fpp19
Calculation of Take-Off Performance fpp19-fpp26
Calculation of Climb Performance fpp26-fpp27
Revision fpp28-fpp29

In-Flight Performance..fpp30-fpp41
      Principles of Cruising Flight fpp32
      Power + Attitude = Performance fpp32-fpp34
      Principles of Manoeuvring Flight..fpp34-fpp35
      Rate of Turn and Turn Radius..fpp35
      Cruise Performance..fpp35-fpp39
      Revision..fpp40-fpp41
Descent and Landing Performance fpp42-fpp57
      Principles of Descending..fpp44
      Gliding Performance fpp44-fpp47
      Sideslipping fpp47
      The Powered Descent fpp48
      Minimum Sink Glide..fpp48
      'Stretching' the Glide fpp49
      Controlling the Approach fpp49-fpp50
      The Landing..fpp51
      Ground Effect..fpp51
      Calculating Landing Performance fpp52-fpp56
      Revision..fpp56-fpp57
Runway Dimensions..fpp58-fpp61
      Runway Dimensions fpp60-fpp61
      Revision..fpp61

Appendix 1   Energy Management..fpp63-fpp64
Appendix 2   Wind, movement of the atmosphere and the downwind turn fpp65
Revision Answers..fpp67-fpp75

Editorial

AUTHOR: JEREMY M PRATT

Jeremy Pratt took his first flying lesson aged 14, paid for by weekend and holiday jobs at his local airfield cleaning aircraft and working in the hanger. Later he also worked in the air/ground station of the airfield and in the operations department of an air taxi company. He completed his PPL after being awarded an Esso/Air League scholarship and became a flying instructor at the age of 19. Since then he has taught students for the Private Pilots Licence and associated ratings and also applicants for professional flying licences. He has flown as a commercial pilot in a variety of roles and has also flown microlights, gliders and helicopters. He stays current by instructing and flying himself for business and pleasure.

He has been Managing Director of Airplan Flight Equipment since 1985, is author of the 'Pilot's Guide' series, the 'Questions and Answers' series; and has also co-authored, compiled and contributed to, a number of aviation books and publications.

TECHNICAL ADVISORS:

Bill Stitt – Chief Flying Instructor of Horizon Flying Club, Bill has been a flying instructor for over 20 years and is a delegated flight examiner. He has been training instructors for over 15 years and he is married to a flying instructor: their daughter also flies!

Phillip G Mathews – Chief Flying Instructor of Cotswold Aviation Services, Phil has over 10,000 hours experience of flying light aircraft. He gained his PPL at the age of 17 and went on to achieve an ATPL through the 'self-improver' route. Phil also runs his own business teaching applicants for the PPL and IMC rating technical exams and flies as a commercial pilot.

John C Gibson, Msc – John Gibson is a specialist in the handling qualities of aircraft. In a 40 year career with British Aerospace (formerly English Electric and BAC) he worked on aircraft such as the Lightning, TSR2, Jaguar, Harrier, Tornado and Eurofighter, and has authored a number of publications on handling qualities. In 1991 he was awarded the Royal Aeronautical Society Bronze Medal for innovations in handling qualities analysis and design methods. John Gibson has been a glider pilot since 1947, a gliding instructor since 1966, and is co-designer of the BG.135/SD3 sailplane series; he has flown 46 types of glider and powered aircraft.

Acknowledgments

This book would not have been possible without the invaluable assistance of many people and organisations, including:

Aero Club de Montpellier

ASA, Seattle

Chris Mathews

Derby Aero Club

Flight Safety Bulletin

Imperial War Museum, Duxford

John Nelson

Kelly Instruments

Mark Smith

Mike Rudkin

Museum of Flight, Seattle

Pilot magazine

Ravenair

Rob Taylor, GDi studio

Steve Dickinson

The New Piper Aircraft, Inc. Vero Beach

UK VFR Flight Guide

Wisconsin Aviation

Introduction

"Just what is it that is keeping this thing airborne?"

Rare is the pilot, no matter how experienced, who has not looked out along the wing of an aeroplane and asked this sort of question. The fact that there is no single one-line, easy-to-summarise answer does not help matters. Thus myths grow, half-truths go unchallenged and an air of mystique comes to surround the whole subject of aerodynamics and the principles of flight.

In the first part of this book, aimed at the pilot rather the scientist, the objective is to produce a practical guide to the forces that govern aircraft flight. An applied knowledge of what keeps an aircraft in the air, how to control it and get the best performance from it, should be one of the pilot's most valuable assets. The majority of 'serious' accidents, and a fair percentage of minor ones, are caused by some form of pilot mis-handling; a better understanding of the forces involved, how they interact, and what a pilot can (and cannot) control might lead to fewer damaged aeroplanes. This book is written for the non-mathematician – where the occasional formulae has been included in the text, it is there for illustrative purposes only and not intended to be memorised. Any formulae included are for the benefit of those who have a mathematical mind and to provide a 'proof' of some of the common aerodynamic principles.

Once the basic concepts of aircraft flight have been explored, this book turns to the 'nuts and bolts' of an aircraft and its systems. Again the aim is to produce a practical guide, for the pilot rather than the engineer. In each case what is important is how to check a part or system before flight, to know its features and limitations, to be able to describe faults so that an engineer has a better chance of knowing what is amiss, and also to arm the pilot with some basic 'trouble shooting' skills to deal with things that can go wrong in a flight. Here, it is worth emphasising that purely mechanical failures of any kind in an aircraft are rare – regular maintenance and rigorous checks are designed precisely to avoid unpleasant surprises. A component or system that is about to fail in some way will usually give some warning signs that are clear to anybody with the basic knowledge and awareness of what to look and listen for. Many a pilot has avoided a potentially unpleasant incident by simply heeding a strange instrument reading, reporting a part that does not look right, or even just listening to a nagging doubt that says things just don't *feel* right. The Aircraft General part of this book includes an 'airworthiness' section which details the paperwork that is essential for safe, and legal, aircraft operation. There is no denying that tatty and incomplete paperwork often accompanies tatty and incomplete aeroplanes.

Before ending this introduction, the now traditional disclaimer. In the absence of a suitable 'neuter' noun, the pilot is usually referred to as 'he'. I rely upon the understanding of all readers to insert 'he or she' as appropriate.

This third edition of PPL 4 has been fully revised and incorporates the JAR PPL syllabus, including new and updated material. Of particular note is the increased use of the term 'mass' in place of 'weight'. Further explanation is made within the text, but it is a fact that the term 'mass' is gradually creeping into everyday usage in General Aviation.

The overall aim of this book goes beyond merely passing an exam or completing a course. If the reader can look out along the wing of an aircraft in flight, and feel that he or she has at least a working knowledge of the forces that make controlled flight possible, and where the pilot fits into the larger scheme of aircraft flight, a much greater goal has been achieved.

Principles of Flight
Properties of the
Atmosphere

Principles of Flight
Properties of the Atmosphere

▶The Atmosphere

▶Air in Motion

▶Revision

Properties of the Atmosphere

▶ The Atmosphere

As described in the Meteorology section of PPL 3, the basic parameters of the atmosphere – its temperature, density and humidity – are constantly changing. Indeed, such changes are the elemental driving force shaping the weather. However, in considering the behaviour of air and how it affects aircraft, constant change is a nuisance. So when thinking about aerodynamics and aircraft performance, we assume that standard atmospheric conditions apply – i.e. the International Standard Atmosphere (ISA). To recap, the basic parameters of the ISA are:

Sea-level temperature	+15°C
Sea-level pressure	1013·25mb/hPa
Sea-level density	1·225 kg m³
Temperature lapse rate	1·98°C per 1000ft up to 36,090ft

Based on these figures, the ISA temperature and density can be calculated for any level in the atmosphere. For example, taking the temperature lapse rate as 2°C per 1000ft, it is not difficult to calculate that in the ISA the temperature at 5,000ft is +5°C, calculated by taking the ISA sea level temperature of +15°C and deducting (5 x 2°C). Sometimes aircraft performance parameters are calculated in relation to the temperature deviation between the theoretical ISA temperature at a given level, and the actual temperature prevailing.

As a general rule, the lower the pressure and the higher the temperature, the lower the air density. Reduced air density has an adverse affect on take-off, climb and landing performance. Less dense air implies greater take-off and landing distances and reduced climb rate.

Humidity also has an effect on density; humid air (i.e. air with a high water-vapour content) is less dense than dry air.

Finally, the basic constituents of the dry atmosphere are:

78% nitrogen

21% oxygen

1% other gases (argon, krypton etc.)

These percentages stay largely fixed as altitude increases.

Air totally without moisture is not found outside the laboratory, and water vapour makes up a significant percentage (up to 4%) of a parcel of air found in the real world. The percentage of water vapour the air is holding, compared with the amount it could hold before becoming saturated (when visible water droplets form), is called the relative humidity. If other conditions remain the same, the greater the relative humidity the less the air density.

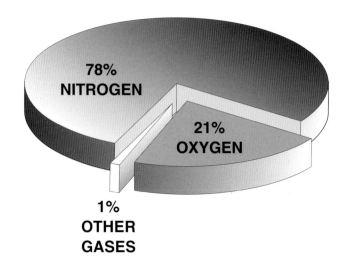

▶ Air in Motion

Air behaves in much the same way irrespective of whether something moves through the air or the air moves past something. So the behaviour of air in a wind tunnel (where air is blown past a stationary shape) is the same as the behaviour of air around a moving object.

Imagine a tube at rest. The tube is experiencing a pressure from the air around it. This pressure is known as the *static* pressure, and is the pressure exerted on all of us by the atmosphere all day and every day. Now let's move the tube at, say, 100kts. There is now an additional pressure caused by the movement of the tube through the air. This pressure is known as the *dynamic* pressure. Dynamic pressure increases as the tube's speed increases, and will also increase if air density is increased. For the mathematically inclined, dynamic pressure is given by:

Half air density x velocity squared

or

$\frac{1}{2}\rho V^2$ (ρ pronounced "rho", is the Greek letter used to denote air density).

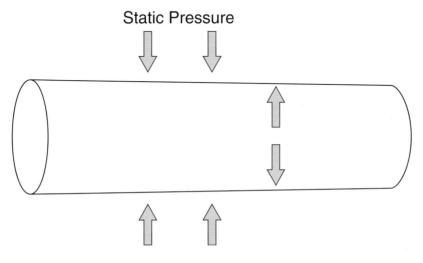

A tube at rest, experiencing static pressure only

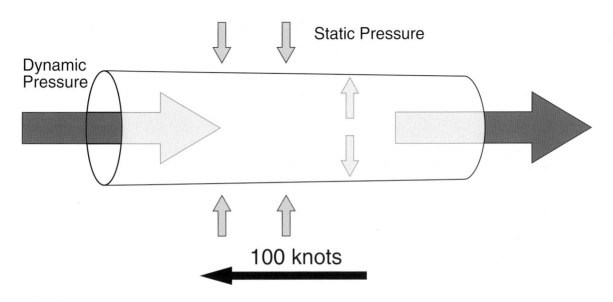

A moving tube, with dynamic pressure and static pressure

One of the properties of air in motion is that static pressure plus dynamic pressure equals a constant. So, if dynamic pressure is increased, static pressure decreases. To see this work in practice, below is a cross-section through a *venturi* tube, which narrows in the middle (making a constriction) then widens again. This venturi is moving through the air at 100kts. At the constriction, the air accelerates to pass through. The increased speed of the air at this point leads to a reduction in static pressure – which is just the opposite of what might be intuitively expected.

If this seems a little far-fetched, try the following experiment. Take two pieces of thick paper or card and bend each slightly in the middle. Now hold the pieces of paper or card lightly together to form a venturi and blow between them. As you blow, the pieces of card will move closer together because the reduction in static pressure is forming a suction. The harder you blow (and thus the faster the airflow through the venturi) the lower the static pressure and the closer together the pieces of card move. Not what you would expect, but it does prove the theory.

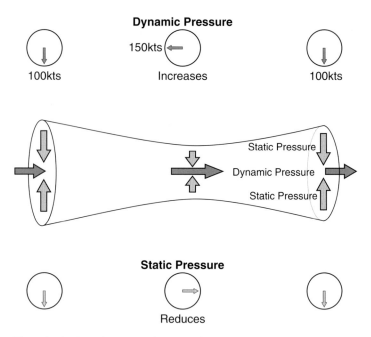

The reduction in static pressure in a venturi

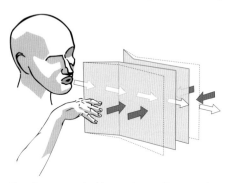

Forming a venturi with two pieces of bent card

This is just basic physics; but what does it have to do with flying aeroplanes? The answer is that the reduction in static pressure described above, and its relationship to air speed, is the essence of *lift* – the force responsible for keeping an aeroplane in the air. It is also a practical example of the much misunderstood *Bernoulli's theorem*. For a practical demonstration, take just one of the pieces of bent card, hold it horizontally close to your lips and blow across the top of it. As the increased speed of the airflow over the surface reduces the static pressure, the card rises up – it is producing lift. The harder you blow (i.e. the faster the airflow speed) the greater the lift produced over the card. The bent piece of card can be likened to a wing, and blowing over it is the same as moving a wing through the air. The airflow over the wing produces lift, and this lift is responsible for keeping an aircraft in the air.

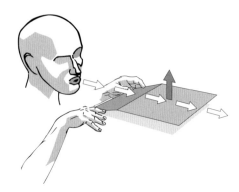

Lift acting across a piece of card

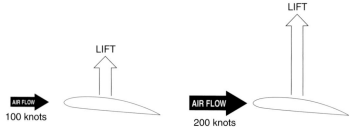

A wing shape produces lift due to the airflow around it. Increased airflow speed means increased lift

A pilot needs to know more about lift, how it is created, and how lift interacts with the other forces acting on an aircraft. Having 'discovered' Bernoulli's theorem, it's time to look at the equally legendary 'four forces'.

▶ Revision

Revision questions are printed at the end of each chapter in this book. The aim of the revision questions is to enable the reader to test their knowledge of the chapter subject, and to help retain the principal elements of each subject.

Attempt these questions once you are satisfied that you have understood and learnt the main points of each chapter, you should aim for a 'success' rate of around 80%.

1   What is the temperature lapse rate in the ISA?

2   In the ISA, what will be the 'standard' temperature at 7000ft?

3   If the actual air temperature at 7000ft is +4°C, how might this temperature deviation from ISA be described?

4   At a temperature of +15°C and a pressure of 1013·25mb/hPa, air density is 1·225kg m3. If temperature is +25°C, but pressure remains at 1013·25mb/hPa, what will be the effect on air density?

5   How does air density vary with humidity?

6   What is the average percentage of oxygen in dry air at 20,000ft?

7   Other than oxygen, what are the two other major constituents of the atmosphere?

8   What is the definition of relative humidity?

9   As dynamic pressure increases, what is the effect on static pressure?

Answers on page fpp67

Principles of Flight
The Four Forces

Principles of Flight
The Four Forces

▶ The Four Forces Acting on an Aircraft in Flight

▶ Mass

▶ Thrust

▶ Lift

▶ Drag

▶ Balance and Couples

▶ Revision

▶The Four Forces Acting on an Aircraft in Flight

There are four main forces that act on an aircraft in flight.

■The *mass* of the aircraft acting straight down towards the centre of the earth.

Mass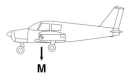

■*Thrust*, provided (in the average General Aviation-type aircraft) by the engine turning a propeller, acting at approximately 90° to the plane of rotation of the propeller.

Thrust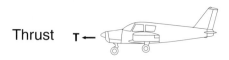

■*Lift*, generated by the airflow around the wings and acting at approximately 90° to the airflow meeting the wings.

Lift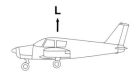

■*Drag*, or resistance to the movement of an object through the air acting behind the aircraft along its flight path.

Drag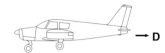

If an aircraft is in straight and level flight at a constant airspeed:

Lift = *Mass* and *Thrust* = *Drag;*

and the aeroplane is said to be in *equilibrium*.

Even at this early stage it is evident that lift and thrust are *good* things which aircraft designers and pilots will try to maximise, whereas mass and drag are *bad* things generally minimised.

To understand more about how and why aircraft fly, and the pilot's role in controlling the process, it is necessary to know more about each of these four forces; and of the four, mass is arguably the most straightforward to comprehend.

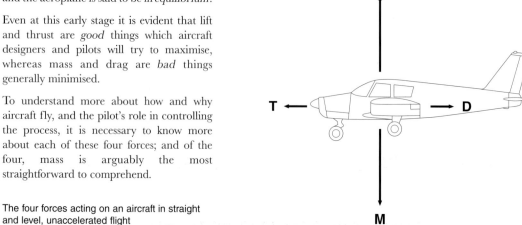

The four forces acting on an aircraft in straight and level, unaccelerated flight

▶ Mass

To start with, think of mass as being equivalent to weight. An 800kg aircraft parked on the ground weighs 800kg and also has a mass of 800kg. Things get more interesting once the aircraft is airborne, but for now visualise the mass of an aircraft as being equal to its weight; the term most non-pilots would use.

If an aircraft had no weight – technically speaking, if it was lighter than air – it would float off the ground. This is just how gas and hot-air balloons work. But in the world of heavier-than-air flying, the aircraft does possess mass, and every gram or ounce of that mass has to be supported by lift (and at times some thrust) for an aircraft to fly. Mass acts directly towards the centre of the earth, making it quite easy to visualise, and is considered to act through a point called the *centre of gravity* of which more later.

An aircraft designer will work hard to make an aircraft as light as possible. On the one hand, the greater the maximum permitted mass, the more scope the designer has to provide for *payload* such as passengers, baggage and fuel; and also for structural strength. On the other hand, greater aircraft mass means reduced performance – so longer take-off and landing distances, slower cruising speeds, reduced range and so on.

In level flight, the aircraft's mass is borne by lift produced from the wings: lift = mass. It follows that a heavier aircraft requires more lift to maintain level flight. One way to produce more lift is by increasing the wing area; clearly a bigger wing can produce more lift than a smaller wing of the same shape. The ratio between aircraft weight and wing area is called the *wing loading*, which is simply aircraft weight divided by wing area. The significance of wing loading is that an aircraft with high wing loading (e.g. a small wing relative to its weight) will have to produce more lift per ft² or m² of wing than an aircraft with a low wing loading.

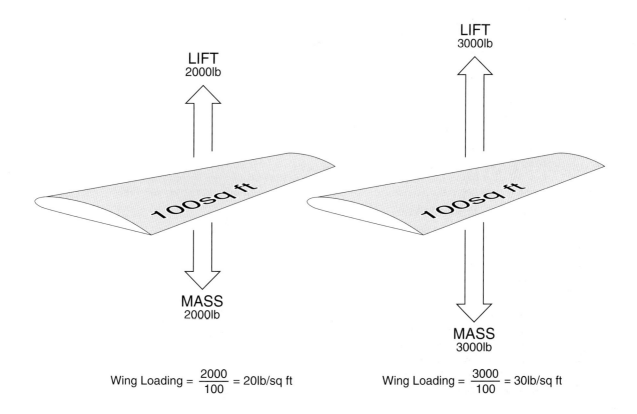

For a given wing area, increasing mass increases wing loading

The table below gives some comparative wing-loading figures for some general-aviation (GA) aircraft and one military machine:

Piper Vagabond
(two-seat tourer, 80kts cruise)   7·8lb/sq ft

Grob 109B
(two-seat motor-glider, 90kts cruise)   9·16lb/sq ft

Cessna 152
(two-seat trainer, 90kts cruise)   10·5lb/sq ft

Cessna 172
(four-seat fixed-undercarriage trainer/tourer, 105kts cruise) 13·8lb/sq ft

Beech Bonanza A36
(six-seat retractable-undercarriage, 175kts cruise)   20·2lb/sq ft

Piper Aztec
(six-seat twin-piston engines, 160kts cruise)   25·1lb/sq ft

MU-2
(seven-seat twin-turboprop engines, 300kts cruise)   58·8lb/sq ft

Learjet 60
(10-seat twin-jet engines, 450kts cruise)   87·3lb/sq ft

Jaguar GR1
(single-seat low-level strike/attack military-jet, 530kts cruise) 135lb/sq ft

The Piper Vagabond with a wing loading of about 8lb/sq ft can get airborne in about 250 metres, and carries two people at 80kts at around 2500ft

The Learjet with a wing loading of nearly 90lbs/sq ft needs around 1650 metres to get airborne, and carries 10 people at 450kts at 43,000ft

This table tends to confirm what designers and pilots already know. As a rule, the greater the payload the aircraft is designed for (and the faster its intended cruising speed) the smaller its wing will be *relative to its mass* – in other words, the higher its wing loading. All other factors being equal, an aircraft with low wing-loading can fly more slowly than one with high wing-loading. This is one reason why aircraft with high wing-loading (such as military fast jets and airliners) often have all sorts of 'high lift' devices so that they can achieve take-off and landing speeds which do not require unfeasibly long runways.

Increased wing loading has certain advantages. The aircraft is less affected by turbulence, giving smoother flight, and the aircraft tends to feel very stable and hence display *low gust response* (e.g. the aircraft does not bounce around too much in bumpy conditions). One downside is that high wing-loading reduces manoeuvrability – it can take a lot of effort to haul the aeroplane around a tight turn for example. More importantly, many pilots make a direct connection between wing loading and the handling characteristics of the aircraft – especially its slow-speed behaviour, such as during take-off and landing. The inference is that aircraft with high wing-loading are more demanding to fly than those with low wing-loading. Taking two examples from the table, the Cessna 172 – weighing 2400lb, with a cruise speed of about 105 kts and a wing area of 174 sq ft – is widely considered to be one of the safest aircraft ever built, undemanding to fly and tolerant of slapdash flying. The 10,470lb MU-2, with a cruise speed of about 300 kts and a wing area of 178 sq ft – just *four square feet more* than the C172 – is considered to be a demanding aircraft to fly and not very tolerant of bad piloting. Of course, even the most docile aircraft will eventually bite back if provoked enough.

The 2400lb Cessna 172, with a cruise speed of about 105kts and a wing area of 174sq ft

Many training aircraft have a very limited practical weight range due to their limited payload capacity. There may be perhaps no more than 200lb (91kg) difference between the mass with near-minimum fuel, one pilot and no baggage, and the maximum permitted mass. If an aircraft has a much greater range of permissible weights, the pilot will notice distinct differences between handling when the aircraft is near its maximum permitted weight as opposed to when it is very light. This is one reason why flying clubs and schools often want a pilot to 'check-out' on a four-seat touring aircraft near its maximum mass, rather than just with it lightly loaded.

The 10,470lb MU-2, with a cruise speed of about 300kts and a wing area of 178sq ft

So far we have interspersed the term 'mass' with the term 'weight'. Now we need to make a differentiation, to understand when mass does not equal weight. We have already established that a 1600lb aircraft on the ground weighs 1600lb and also has a *mass* of 1600lb. However, if the aircraft is flying and is then subjected to an *acceleration* of 2g (for example, by pulling sharply out of a dive) it still has a mass of 1600lb but its weight is now 3200lb. In other words, weight is mass multiplied by acceleration. Under 2g conditions the aircraft effectively weighs 3200lb – the wing loading of the aircraft has been **doubled**, and it will handle and perform accordingly.

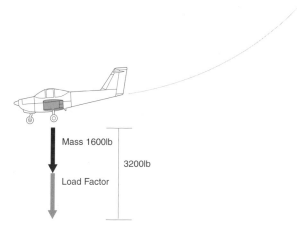

Mass 1600lb

3200lb

Load Factor

An aircraft subjected to an acceleration of 2g (which can also be described as a load factor of 2). If it has a mass of 1600lb in under normal 1g conditions, it now 'weighs' 3200lb

At present most pilots are probably more familiar with the term "weight" than the term "mass". However, the term *mass* is increasingly being used instead of *weight,* and terms such as "all-up mass" are being found in some modern documents, whilst older ones still refer to weight.

The maximum permitted weight (mass) for an aircraft is noted in the Pilot's Operating Handbook/Flight Manual (POH/FM) and may take more than one form (e.g. maximum take-off weight, maximum landing weight, maximum weight for certain manoeuvres etc.). The appropriate limit must be adhered to at all times. The calculation of the weight of an aircraft is detailed in the Flight Performance and Planning section of this book.

WEIGHT LIMITS		
	Normal	Utility
(a) Maximum Ramp (lbs.)	2558	2138
(b) Maximum Weight (lbs.)	2550	2130
(c) Maximum Baggage (lbs.)	200	0

NOTE

Refer to Section 5 (Performance) for maximum weight as limited by performance.

An aircraft's weight/mass limitations in the Pilot's Operating Handbook/Flight Manual (POH/FM)

▶Thrust

Thrust is the force provided by the engine, through the propeller still used on most General Aviation (GA) aircraft.

The principle of the propeller is that it accelerates a mass of air. This creates a fast-moving *slipstream* behind the propeller which can be felt behind an aircraft with its engine running. A propeller blade has a cross-section rather like that of a wing. In fact, a propeller works much like a wing, producing an aerodynamic force when it is rotating, which in this instance is called *thrust*. Turning a propeller faster (by increasing the engine's revolutions per minute or RPM) makes it produce more thrust, just as moving a wing faster through the air makes it produce more lift. However, for various reasons a propeller begins to lose efficiency above 3000 RPM.

The maximum thrust an engine/propeller combination can produce varies with the aircraft's airspeed. A graph of maximum thrust available against airspeed shows that thrust tails off at high airspeeds, due in part to a loss of propeller efficiency. Nevertheless, propellers are a reasonably efficient way of turning engine power into thrust for relatively low-speed aircraft. As a matter of fact, they are still better than jet engines for speeds of about 300kts or less – which is why there are still so many propeller-driven aircraft being produced.

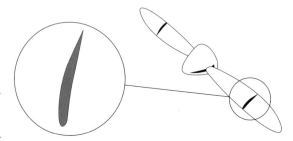

The typical wing-like cross-section of a propeller blade

Thrust is Good, and the designer will try to maximise it, which is not necessarily easy. One way is to fit longer propeller blades, but this increases the risk of having them strike the ground if the clearance between the surface and the tip of the propeller blades (*tip clearance*) is too small. Another way is to increase the number of blades, but this can lead to aerodynamic interference between them. More commonly, designers have opted for more powerful engines. However, this inevitably implies greater weight, not just in the engine itself but its accessories, the extra fuel required and so on. This extra weight in turn reduces performance, so that the real-world benefit of simply using a bigger engine in the same airframe may be disappointing.

To make significant gains in performance, it is necessary to go back to basics. In level flight at a steady airspeed, thrust is equal to drag. So if the designer can reduce drag, the amount of thrust required can also be reduced. In fact, the amount of drag at any particular airspeed could just as easily be described as 'thrust required'. So now we need to know more about drag, and before that we need to know more about lift.

▶ Lift

Let's recap the flow of air around objects. Air is *viscous*, which is the scientific way of saying that it's sticky. Even when it meets an object travelling at a few hundred knots, air will try to follow its contours rather than be scattered in all directions. The viscosity of air is essential in the production of lift, because there is little point in carefully optimising the shape of a wing if the air will not follow it.

Imagine a cylinder placed in an airflow, and viewed side-on. We'll use streamlines to show how the airflow is behaving. Air moving past a stationary cylinder acts pretty much as would be expected. The air splits in two to pass above and below it. Behind the cylinder, the air can no longer follow its contour and so it separates, forming a turbulent wake.

Airflow past a stationary cylinder

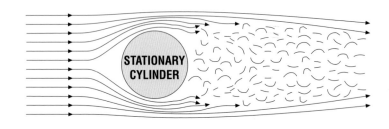

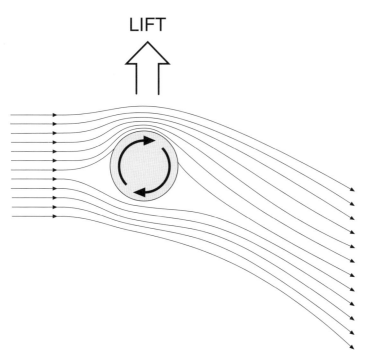

LIFT

The airflow past a rotating cylinder. There is upwash ahead of the cylinder, downwash behind it. Above the cylinder, the faster airflow (increased dynamic pressure) leads to reduced static pressure, which creates most of the lift

Now to set the cylinder spinning. The rotation of the cylinder places a *circulation force* on the airflow: note the *upwash* ahead of the cylinder, the *downwash* behind it and the reduced separation of the airflow. Above the cylinder, the air is moving faster than the general airflow speed. This means that there is an *increased dynamic pressure* and so a *reduced static pressure* above the rotating cylinder where the streamlines constrict – rather like the narrow section of a venturi. This reduced static pressure creates a force acting upwards – *lift*. If the cylinder was free to move vertically, it would rise.

The ability of a rotating cylinder to produce lift is known as the *Magnus effect*. Sporting professionals such as cricket bowlers, baseball pitchers or tennis players put 'spin' on the ball to make it swerve – the lift generated as a result of rotation pulls it off-course. As far as aircraft are concerned, numerous patents have been filed in attempts to produce flying machines in this way although none is known to have succeeded in practice.

Back in the wind tunnel, let's replace the cylinder with a thin plate. This has an almost flat section, which we will incline slightly to the airflow. Now the air acts in much the same way as it did around the rotating cylinder. There is upwash,

LIFT

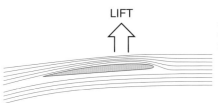

A thin plate inclined in an airflow behaves rather like a rotating cylinder

The thin, almost flat wing of a 1920s de Havilland DH-4M

downwash, and a pressure differential causing lift. So this is a workable wing shape, and many early aircraft had a wing (sometimes called an *aerofoil*) close to a flat plate in cross-section. Many model aircraft still have a flat plate wing, but model builders soon discover that a wing can produce lift more efficiently if it is curved slightly in its cross-section. This curvature is known as *camber*, and it was a pronounced feature of many early aeroplanes. By about 1930, thicker wing cross-sections were in almost universal use which could produce lift even when aligned at a zero or a slightly negative angle to the airflow and they still are today.

A 'cambered' wing, capable of producing more lift than a flat plate

The thick, cambered wing of a 1930s Boeing 80A-1

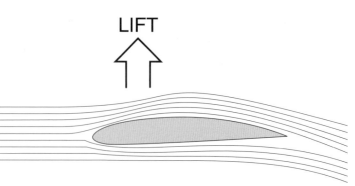

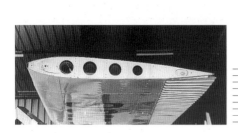

The wing section of a Cessna 152

A thick, cambered wing can produce lift even when set at a zero or slightly negative angle to the airflow

The primary purpose of a wing is to produce lift. Before discussing wings and lift further, a couple of definitions:

The wing *section* is the cross-section through a wing (also known as the *aerofoil section*).

The front of the wing is the wing *leading edge*.

At the rear of the wing is the wing *trailing edge*.

The 'end' of the wing is the wing *tip*.

The area where the wing meets the fuselage is the wing *root*.

The distance from wing-tip to wing-tip (along the wing's length) is the wing *span*.

The distance from trailing edge to leading edge (across the wing's width) is the *chord*.

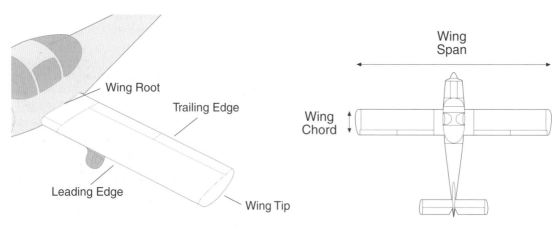

The principal parts of a wing

Wing span and wing chord

Whatever the precise details of the wing's shape, the airflow above the forward part of its section acts very much like the airflow through the constriction of a venturi. This implies increased airspeed, increased dynamic pressure and reduced static pressure. Indeed, it is in this region that the production of lift is greatest in normal flight. And whatever the wing section, lift acts at approximately 90° to the airflow in normal flight.

Lift is greatest where the airflow speed is fastest over the wing, and acts at around 90° to the airflow

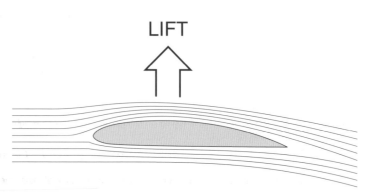

If all other factors remain constant, increased airflow speed – strictly speaking, increased dynamic pressure – means increased lift and *vice versa*. Dynamic pressure is measured and displayed to the pilot in the form of **airspeed.** Since airspeed is within the pilot's control, this is one of the principal ways a pilot can control lift. *Increased airspeed means increased dynamic pressure and so increased lift; reduced airspeed means reduced lift.* Dynamic pressure varies as the square of airspeed:

At Sea Level in the ISA

Air Speed (knots)	50	100	200	300	400	500
Dynamic pressure	8	34	136	305	542	847
(pounds per square foot)						

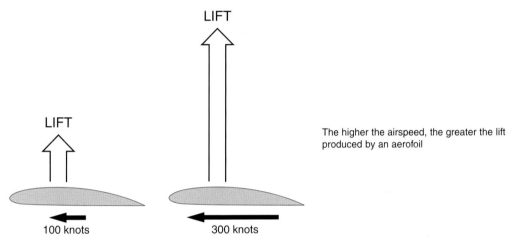

The higher the airspeed, the greater the lift produced by an aerofoil

The other major factor in lift production that the pilot can control is the angle at which the wing meets the airflow. A line drawn through an aerofoil section, from the leading edge to the trailing edge, is called the *chord line*. The angle between the *relative airflow* (the airflow meeting the wing) and the chord line is called the *angle of attack*. For practical purposes, the angle of attack (also known as 'α' – the Greek letter alpha) is the angle between the wing's chord line and the aircraft's flightpath.

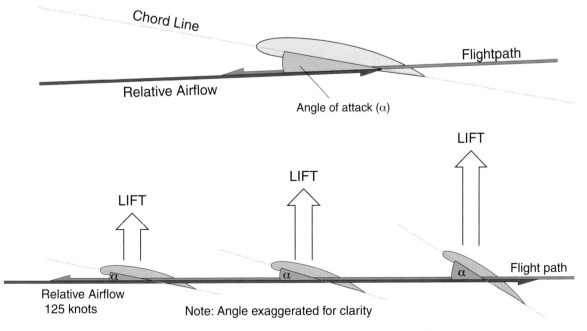

At a constant airspeed (dynamic pressure), increased angle of attack means increased lift – up to a certain point

The efficiency of a wing section in producing lift is expressed as the *coefficient of lift* (C_L) – the higher the C_L, the greater the lift if all other factors remain the same. If C_L is plotted on a graph against angle of attack, the first part of the graph is a straight-line increase; as angle of attack increases, C_L increases. Thus, a pilot can increase C_L by increasing the angle of attack (i.e. by increasing the angle at which the wing meets the airflow). Unfortunately, this only continues up to a certain point, where the C_L 'peaks'. After that, an increase in angle of attack actually leads to a decrease in C_L as the airflow stops following the wing's contours and separates from it. This airflow separation causes a loss of lift which is called the *stall*, and the angle at which this separation becomes critical is the *critical (or stalling) angle of attack*. To be quite clear about this, in aviation terms a stall is the marked loss of lift caused by an excessive angle of attack. It has nothing to do with the engine(s). Gliders can stall just as powered aircraft can. Angle of attack and its control by the pilot is an essential factor in aircraft performance and control.

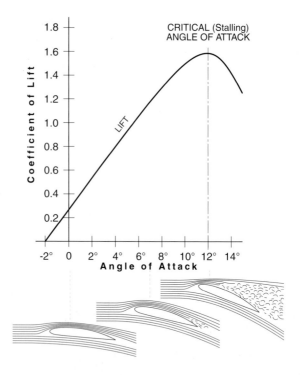

Coefficient of lift (C_L) plotted against angle of attack for a typical GA wing section

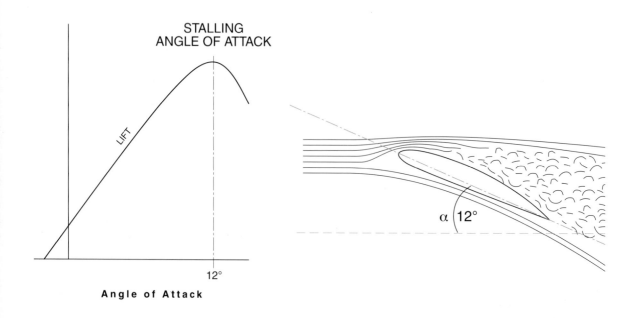

At the stalling angle of attack (12° in this case) there is significant airflow separation from the wing and a marked loss of lift occurs

The distribution of lift across the wing varies with angle of attack. The point at which total lift can be said to be acting on an aerofoil section is called the *centre of pressure*. As angle of attack increases, the distribution of lift is concentrated more towards the leading edge of the wing and the centre of pressure moves forward. It continues to do this with increasing angle of attack until the stall is reached, at which point the centre of pressure moves quickly rearwards. The implications of this are discussed later.

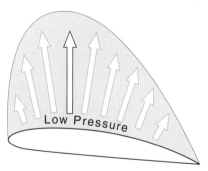

Pressure distribution over a wing and centre of pressure

A trailing edge flap when retracted (up) and extended (down)

The lowered flap of a Cessna 150

Flaps are parts of the wing which can be extended and/or lowered in flight. The most common type of flap is that fitted at the trailing edge of the wing, technically known as a *Trailing Edge* (TE) flap but most commonly referred to as just "flap". Extending and lowering flap generally increases the coefficient of lift of the wing section, so in practical terms the flap allows a wing to produce more lift at slow airspeeds.

To summarise what has been covered so far, the amount of lift produced by a wing is dependent on:

■ the coefficient of lift (C_L) set by the angle of attack and the wing section.

■ the airspeed and density, i.e. dynamic pressure.

■ the size of the wing, i.e. the wing area.

These factors can be put into a formula:

Lift = coefficient of lift x dynamic pressure x wing size.

Which, put into mathematical form, looks like:

Lift (L) = C_L $\frac{1}{2}\rho V^2$ S

where

C_L = Coefficient of lift

$\frac{1}{2}\rho V^2$ = The dynamic pressure

S = The size of the wing

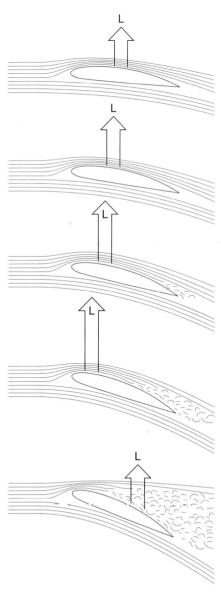

The movement of the centre of pressure with increasing angle of attack

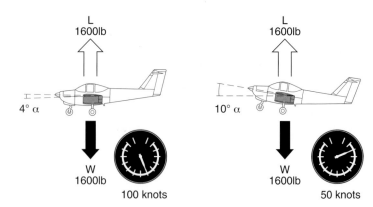

An aircraft flying level at 100kts and 4° angle of attack, and at 50kts and 10° angle of attack

A formula on its own can be a bit daunting and not easy to relate to, so let's take a practical example. In a 100kts cruise, the wing of an average training aeroplane might have an angle of attack ('a') of 4°. In this case a value of 4° equates to a coefficient of lift (C_L) of 0·5, which is a fairly typical value for a conventional slow-speed wing section. From the table of dynamic pressure versus airspeed stated earlier, an airspeed of 100kts at sea level in International Standard Atmosphere (ISA) conditions is equal to a dynamic pressure of 34lb/sq ft. So at 100kts and 4° angle of attack, each square foot of wing is producing (0·5 x 34) or 16lb of lift. If the wing of the aircraft has a total area of 100 sq ft, it is producing (100 sq ft x 16lb) 1600lb of lift. And if the aircraft weighs 1600lb, lift = weight and it will fly level.

Should the pilot slow the aircraft to 50 kts, the dynamic pressure will now be halved to about 8lb. With the same wing area of 100sq ft, the pilot must find a way of increasing the C_L to 2 to maintain level flight. This might be done by increasing angle of attack and lowering flap, for example. But if the required value of C_L cannot be attained, lift will be less than weight and the aircraft will descend.

So, to maintain level flight a pilot can fly at a high airspeed and low angle of attack, or a slow airspeed and high angle of attack.

A couple of incidental points to consider before leaving the subject of lift. At a normal positive angle of attack, the air flowing **below** the wing is said to flow more slowly than the 'free' airflow, leading to an *increase* in static pressure below the wing compared to that outside its influence. It is also important to appreciate that the forgoing explanation of lift, and its reliance on Bernoulli's theorem, is very much the 'classical' theory of lift production and the one on which exam questions are usually based. There are differences of opinion amongst scientists on the subject and while some ascribe lift more to the positive increase in static pressure under the wing, others point to the downwash behind the wing and state that lift is merely a reaction to this downwash in accordance with Newton's laws of motion (every action has an equal and opposite reaction). Whatever view you take, the essential importance of airspeed and angle of attack in lift production is not in dispute.

▶ Drag

Drag is the resistance to the movement of the aircraft through the air. Total drag can be broken down into two principal components: *parasite drag* and *induced drag*.

Parasite drag is a generic term covering the various elements of drag created when any object moves through the air. The disruption to the airflow, and the turbulent wake created, resists the movement of the object and there are several components of parasite drag.

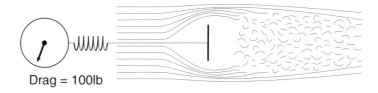

Drag = 100lb

The form drag of a flat plate and a streamlined shape of the same frontal area

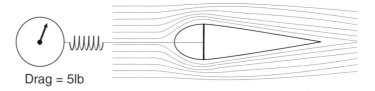

Drag = 5lb

Fairings around the undercarriage legs of this Piper PA-28 Warrior are claimed to add 2-3 knots to cruise airspeed by reducing drag

A key element of parasite drag is *form drag* (also known as *pressure drag*), the resistance caused by the size and shape of an aircraft. Anyone who has tried to carry a large flat object (such as a sheet of plywood) on a windy day will know all about form drag; life becomes much easier if the object is turned sideways on to the wind. In the same way, an aircraft with a large frontal area is presenting a larger 'form' to the air than a smaller aircraft. However, reducing frontal area is not the whole story – the real key to reducing form drag is to minimise the disturbance to the air as the object passes through. One way to achieve this end is to *streamline* the object. Streamlining a rod or tube can reduce its form drag by as much as twenty times for the same frontal area. This is why even relatively slow aircraft often have streamlining of the undercarriage legs, wing struts, pitot heads, bracing wires and so on.

So form drag can be reduced by streamlining. However, there is a drawback, which is that streamlining increases the total surface area of the object concerned. Air flowing over an object is slowed down by contact with its surface – an effect known as *skin friction drag* (or *surface friction drag*). At the surface of an object, the viscosity (stickiness) of the air brings it to a complete stop. Moving away from the surface the airflow speed gradually increases as the effect of contact becomes less marked, until the point where airflow speed is no longer affected by skin friction.

The layer through which this speed change takes place is the *boundary layer*, and over the leading edge of an average wing the boundary layer might be less than a millimetre thick. Incidentally, the existence of the boundary layer is the reason why aeroplanes and even cars need washing from time to time. However fast they fly or drive, the air in immediate contact with the dust and grime at the surface does not move.

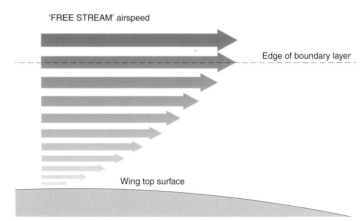

'FREE STREAM' airspeed

Edge of boundary layer

The change in airflow speed in the boundary layer

Wing top surface

Skin friction can be minimised by making the overall size of the aircraft as small as possible – which is another reason why high-speed aircraft often have relatively small wings. Skin friction can also be reduced by making the surface as smooth as possible (by removing rivet heads, gaps, panel edges etc.) and keeping the surface clean and polished. Some pilots claim that giving an aircraft a good polish can add five knots or more to the cruising speed. Now, the composite materials often used in aircraft construction allow a much smoother surface finish than traditional materials, and have significantly reduced skin friction.

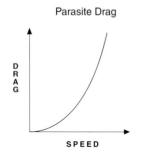

Parasite Drag

DRAG

SPEED

The change in parasite drag with airspeed

There are other components of parasite drag. *Interference drag* is produced where differing airflows meet – for example at the wing root where the wing joins the fuselage. Fairings are often used in 'corners' such as this to reduce the interference effect. *Cooling drag*, described in more detail later, is in essence the drag caused by the need to force air over an air-cooled engine. What all the components making up 'parasite drag' have in common is that they react in the same way to increasing airflow speed. As the aircraft goes faster, parasite drag increases as the square of airspeed. So **doubling** the airspeed leads to a **quadrupling** of parasite drag.

As stated earlier, total drag is made up of two components. Parasite drag is fairly straightforward to comprehend (the faster the aircraft flies, the greater the parasite drag). However, *induced drag* can at first sight seem less understandable because it is created by the production of lift.

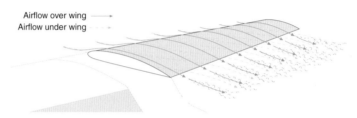

Airflow over wing
Airflow under wing

Small-scale vortices at the trailing edge of a wing

At most angles of attack, there is lower static pressure above the wing than below. The airflow below the wing tends to move out towards the tip and the airflow above the wing tends to move in towards the root. These two airflows meet at the trailing edge of the wing, where they form small vortices of disturbed air. At each wing tip, where the air from beneath the wing 'curls over' to the upper surface, a much stronger vortex is created. These vortices increase *downwash* which is the name given to the area of sinking air behind the wing.

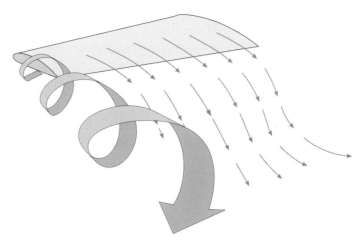

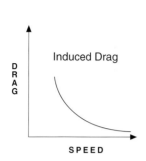

Change of induced drag with airspeed

Wing-tip vortices and downwash behind a wing

This relatively large-scale displacement of air causes a resistance which is known as induced drag. The amount of induced drag is proportional to the coefficient of lift (C_L); the higher the C_L, the greater the induced drag. For a given wing section and shape, C_L increases with increased angle of attack, therefore high angles of attack imply high induced drag. High angles of attack are most often associated with slow airspeed and also with manoeuvring flight. At angles of attack close to the stall, a small increase in 'α' will lead to a large increase in induced drag. For more 'normal' flight conditions, high C_L is associated with slow airspeed. So induced drag increases as airspeed decreases. Induced drag varies inversely as the square of airspeed; **halving** airspeed **quadruples** induced drag.

Induced drag is also known (mostly to aerodynamicists) as *trailing vortex drag*; and the military often call it *lift-dependent drag*.

A graph of induced drag and parasite drag versus airspeed shows a marked increase in drag at the high-speed and slow-speed ends of the scale. This gives the 'total drag' line (i.e. the combination of induced drag and parasite drag) a distinctive 'U' shape. The trough of the 'U' marks the point of minimum drag, and when flying at this point on the 'drag curve' the aircraft will have the maximum range, as discussed in more detail later.

Having established what the four forces are, we will look briefly at how the designer arranges these forces to give the aircraft stability and balance.

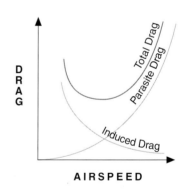

Total Drag
(eg. Parasite Drag + Induced Drag)

The total drag curve for a typical light aircraft

▶ Balance and Couples

The four forces do not all act through the same point, and the couples between these forces effect the 'balance' of the aircraft.

The strongest of the four forces are mass and lift. Mass acts towards the earth through the centre of gravity (CG), and lift acts through the centre of pressure, which is normally found behind the CG. With this arrangement of forces the couple between them produces a residual effect which would pitch the aircraft nose-down. In most aircraft this nose-down pitching effect is balanced by the *tailplane* – in effect a small wing at the back of the aircraft. In cruising flight this tailplane is set to produce lift acting downwards, causing an effect to pitch the aircraft nose-up. The end result is that the downward force produced by the tailplane helps to balance the nose-down effect of the lift/mass couple. If lift is reduced (for example if the wing is taken beyond the stalling angle of attack), the lift/mass couple will tend to make the aircraft pitch nose-down.

In this instance, the horizontal tail is producing a download to keep the aircraft in trim

There is also a couple between the effective lines of thrust and drag. Most often, the thrust line is below the centre of gravity (CG) and the drag line is above it. This means that an increase in thrust will causes the aircraft to rotate around the CG and pitch nose-up, a decrease in thrust will cause the aircraft to pitch nose-down. This reaction to changes in thrust is the norm in most conventional light aircraft, and is logical given that thrust is normally increased for a climb and reduced for a descent.

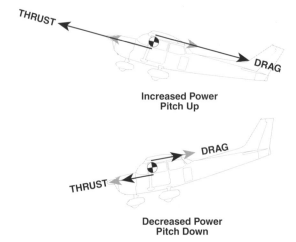

In most aircraft, increasing thrust makes the aircraft pitch up; reducing thrust makes it pitch down

▶ Revision

10.   Aircraft A has a weight (or mass) of 2000lb and a wing area of 90 sq ft, aircraft B has a weight (or mass) of 4000lb and a wing area of 200 sq ft; which has the greater wing loading?

11.   If the RPM of an engine/propeller is increased, what is the effect on thrust?

12.   In normal flight, is the static air pressure immediately above the wing greater, the same as, or less than the static pressure of air unaffected by the wing?

13.   What is the definition of wing chord?

14.   What is the definition of angle of attack ('α')?

15.   What happens if the angle of attack of a wing is increased beyond the point of maximum CL ?

16.   As angle of attack is increased up to the stall, how does the centre of pressure move?

17.   What is the name given to the resistance to the movement of an object through the air?

18.   If 'parasite' drag is 25kg at an airspeed of 60 knots, what will it be if airspeed is increased to 120 knots?

19.   On the graph below, label parasite drag, induced drag and total drag:

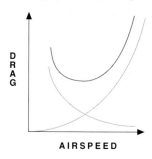

20.   In 'normal' cruising flight, does the tailplane of a conventional aircraft produce an upforce or downforce?

21.   Given a 'conventional' arrangement of thrust and drag forces, what is the pitching effect of reducing power?

      Answers at page fpp67

Principles of Flight
Stability
and Control

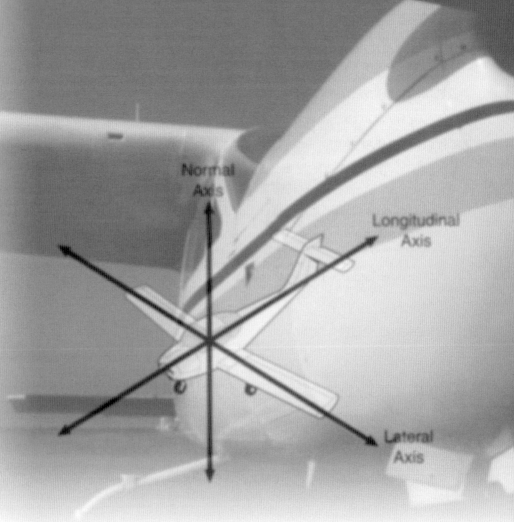

Principles of Flight
Stability and Control

The subject of aircraft stability and control is one where it is very easy to become lost in laborious detail which is dauntingly mathematical. It can also be quite difficult to differentiate between cause and effect, and what means one thing to a pilot may mean something quite different to an aerodynamicist. In this chapter we will concentrate on the practical elements of the subject as a pilot sees them – with apologies to aerodynamic engineers and those with an advanced understanding of mathematics and physics.

▶ Static and Dynamic Stability

▶ The Three Planes of Movement

▶ Stability in Pitch

▶ Control in Pitch

▶ Stability in Roll

▶ Control in Roll

▶ Stability in Yaw

▶ Control in Yaw

▶ Mass and Aerodynamic Balance of the Flying Controls

▶ Revision

| **Stability and Control**

▶ Static and Dynamic Stability

The late Jeffrey Quill, test pilot for the Spitfire, described stability as "The tendency of an aircraft, when disturbed from a condition of steady flight, to return to that condition when left to itself."; an explanation which is difficult to better. This broad definition of stability can be looked at as two elements – *static stability* and *dynamic stability*.

Static stability is a measure of how readily the aircraft tends to return back towards its original condition. For example, if an aircraft which has been in steady level flight is pitched nose-up by a gust, strong static stability will cause it to pitch nose down again without intervention by the pilot. This is an essential component of overall stability and can be described as positive static stability. However, if the aircraft continues pitching down beyond the original condition (level flight), and then swings back up through the original condition and so on, the resulting roller-coaster ride will be uncomfortable and even dangerous. At the other extreme, if the aircraft continued to deviate from its original condition without pilot input, it could be said to have negative static stability – a dangerous situation in most aircraft. If the aircraft remained at its new condition without trying to return to the original, it could be said to have neutral static stability (as found in some aerobatic machines).

Dynamic stability governs the behaviour of the aircraft after the initial static stability response has started returning it towards the original condition. It would be good if dynamic stability stopped the restoring motion as soon as the aircraft returned to its original condition, but what is more likely is that dynamic stability will 'dampen' the effect of static stability. Therefore in the above example the aircraft will move through a diminishing cycle of oscillations in pitch, with smaller and smaller deviations each side of the original condition, until the aircraft settles back to equilibrium. This would be an example of positive dynamic stability.

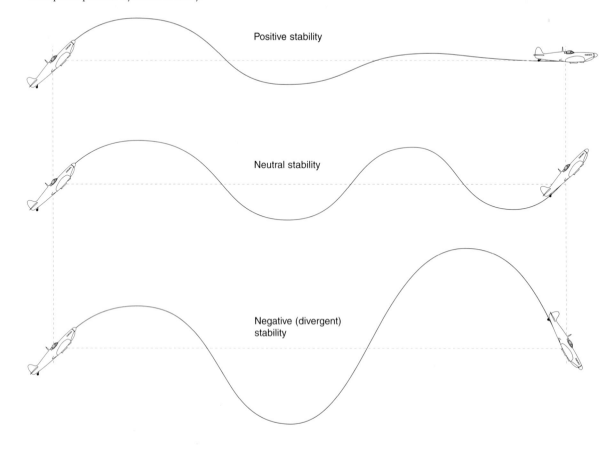

Positive stability

Neutral stability

Negative (divergent) stability

So, positive static stability on its own is no good without corresponding positive dynamic stability. Staying with the original example, once disturbed from level flight an aircraft with positive static stability but poor dynamic stability could enter a series of increasingly large (*divergent*) pitch oscillations until control was lost either in a dive or a climb. In 'flight test' reports, a common test of stability is to trim the aircraft to steady level flight, then pitch the aircraft nose-up until the airspeed has dropped by a certain amount (say ten knots). The pilot then leaves the aircraft to fly 'hands-off' to see how many long oscillations (or *phugiods*) it passes through until the original flight condition of level flight is restored. In general the fewer and more gentle the phugiods, the more stable in pitch the aircraft is considered to be.

▶The Three Planes of Movement

An aircraft can rotate around three axes, each of which passes through the aircraft's centre of gravity:

- *Longitudinal* axis – runs through the aircraft from nose to tail.
- *Lateral* axis – runs through the aircraft from wingtip to wing tip.
- *Normal* (or vertical) axis – runs vertically through the aircraft.

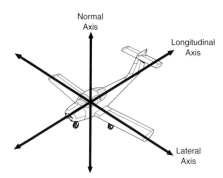

The Longitudinal, Lateral and Normal (vertical) axes

Movement around these axes are known as:

- *Pitching* – around the lateral axis.
- *Rolling* – around the longitudinal axis.
- *Yawing* – around the normal (or vertical) axis.

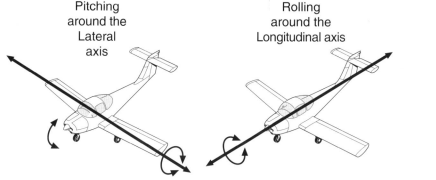

Pitching around the Lateral axis

Rolling around the Longitudinal axis

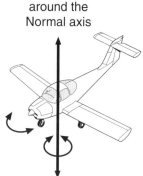

Yawing around the Normal axis

▶ Stability in Pitch

Stability in the pitching sense is known as *longitudinal stability*, and it is this which is usually of most concern to designers and pilots alike. In this book we will refer to longitudinal stability as **stability in pitch**; test-pilots, aeronautical engineers and aerodynamicists should read 'longitudinal' stability where appropriate.

Stability in pitch is achieved by an appropriate arrangement of the lift and weight forces acting on the wing, and on the aircraft as a whole. An 'average' wing is, in isolation, unstable. If a surface generating lift is disturbed from a settled condition (i.e. a particular angle of attack) it will, by itself, continue to diverge away from its original state. For example, if a wing has been flying at an angle of attack of 4° but a gust causes a momentary increase in this figure, the angle of attack will continue to increase. The wing will just tumble over and over once disturbed. Try to 'fly' a rectangular sheet of cardboard, or a model wing without fuselage or tail, and the phenomenon of divergence can be seen quite clearly.

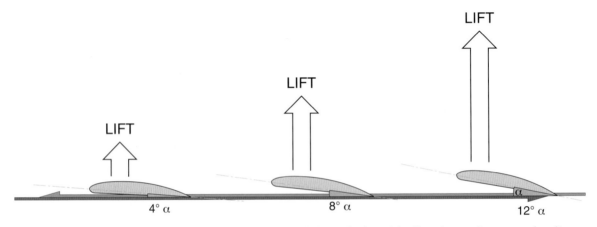

An average wing is, by itself, unstable. If disturbed from a particular angle of attack it will continue to diverge away from it

To overcome this problem and make the aircraft stable in pitch, the usual solution is to place a horizontal tail surface – in effect a smaller wing – some distance behind the main wing. Now, if the wing is disturbed from a steady state as before, there is a change of angle of attack at both the wing and the tail. The change of lift at the wing is *destabilising*, but the change of lift at the tail is *stabilising* because it will tend to restore the wing to its original angle of attack. The force applied by the tail can be called a **moment**, which is the proper name for a force causing a rotation about a point. In any physical system, the total moment is given by (force x distance) and it is an important concept in aerodynamics. To give the horizontal tail sufficient moment to overcome the destabilising effect of the wing, the designer will place it some distance from the wing. The greater the distance, the greater the moment the tail can exert (think of it as leverage). Alternatively, the designer can keep the tail quite close to the wing but make it bigger so that it exerts more lift.

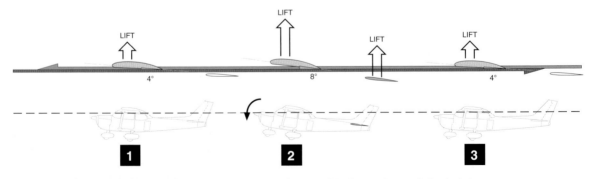

Action of tailplane restores wing angle of attack to original state

In this stable arrangement, the horizontal tail provides a lift force to return the wing to its original angle of attack

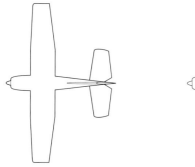
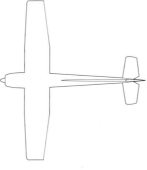

For the horizontal tail to provide the same moment, it can be large and close to the wing, or small and some distance from it

Any aerofoil, such as a wing, possesses a point known as its **aerodynamic centre** (AC). The definition of AC need not concern us, but for any wing section it is a fixed position regardless of angle of attack and it is usually very close to one -quarter of the chord back from the aerofoil leading edge. This position is known variously as 25% of chord or 'quarter-chord'. Any object also has a position known as the **centre of gravity** (CG) through which its mass acts. The CG position is where there is equal mass each side of the point; if you try to balance a pencil horizontally by sliding a finger beneath it, the point at the finger has to be for the pencil to balance level is the pencil's centre of gravity.

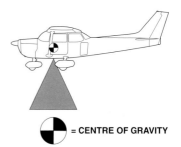

= CENTRE OF GRAVITY

Mass acts through the centre of gravity (CG), the point where the aircraft would balance if you could put a pivot under it

An 'average' wing is unstable because the centre of gravity is usually behind the wing's aerodynamic centre; the further back the CG is from the AC, the more unstable the wing. Indeed, the couple between the AC and the CG defines the wing's stability. The addition of the horizontal tail surface confers stability on the aircraft as a whole, but only as long as the CG remains within a carefully defined range relative to the AC. This concept is vitally important to pilots because the CG position is altered by the payload (fuel, passengers, baggage) of the aircraft. In an average training/touring machine, the CG with just one aviator and a normal fuel load on board will be somewhere very close to the pilot's seat. Lots of passengers and baggage at the rear of the aircraft moves the CG back, and *vice versa*. This movement of the CG may have significant consequences.

The position of the centre of gravity is a major factor in stability in pitch. As the centre of gravity moves *forward*, the aircraft becomes *more stable* in pitch (increased longitudinal stability). Ultimately, as the CG moves further forward, the aircraft will feel very nose-heavy – to the extent that the pilot will be unable to prevent the aircraft pitching nose down, especially at slow airspeed (for example, when landing). If the CG is

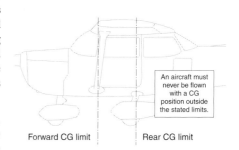

An aircraft must never be flown with a CG position outside the stated limits.

Forward CG limit | Rear CG limit

Permitted CG limits for a typical general-aviation (GA) aircraft

moved rearwards, the aircraft becomes less stable in pitch (reduced longitudinal stability) as the wing's destabilising effect overcomes the stabilising moment of the horizontal tail. If the CG is moved too far rearwards, the destabilising effect of the wing will overcome the stabilising influence of the horizontal tail. This makes it very difficult for the pilot to maintain a given angle of attack. If the CG is moved too far rearwards, the pilot will at some stage simply lose control – probably when the wings reach the stalling angle of attack as the aircraft pitches up uncontrollably. This is not recommended.

From the foregoing, it is clear that knowing the position of the CG and keeping it within defined limits is of critical importance. The Pilots Operating Handbook/Flight Manual (POH/FM) will have a section for calculating the CG position, together with information on the forward and rearward CG limits. These will have been carefully researched by test pilots and flight engineers, and it is an exceedingly foolhardy pilot who flies (or attempts to fly) an aircraft with its CG outside the defined limits. It is worth noting that **most light aircraft cannot be loaded to their full capacity in terms of fuel, baggage and passengers and still remain within their permitted CG range**. There is often a trade-off required between the various items of payload to keep the CG within the defined limits. The calculation of CG is covered in detail in the Flight Performance and Planning section of this book.

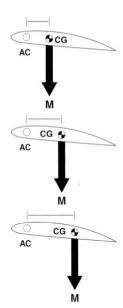

As the CG moves further back from the aerodynamic centre, the wing (and aircraft attached to it) becomes increasingly unstable

The amount of stability the aircraft designer attempts to build into an aircraft will depend largely on its intended role. A touring aircraft will be more stable than an aerobatic aircraft, just as an airliner should be more stable than a fighter. This brings us to the next consideration. Having achieved a certain *stability* in pitch, the aircraft designer has to give the pilot a means to *control* the aircraft in pitch.

▶ Control in Pitch

The conventional method of providing an aircraft with control in pitch is to hinge part of the horizontal tail so that the rear part can be moved up and down. This alters the overall camber of the tail surface and thus the amount of lift (up or down) it will produce. The part of the horizontal tail that moves up and down is called the *elevator*.

When the pilot pushes forward on the control column in the cockpit, the elevator moves down. This change in camber creates lift acting upwards at the tail. The aircraft rotates nose-down around the CG which reduces the angle of attack of the wing. If the control column is pulled back, the elevator moves up. This creates a downforce at the tail, rotating the aircraft nose-up around the CG and thus increasing the angle of attack of the wing.

The horizontal tail and elevator of a Chipmunk

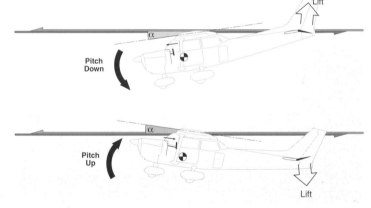

The elevator, controlled from the cockpit control column, controls the aircraft in pitch

The elevators will seem more effective as airspeed increases (because of increased dynamic pressure) and less effective as airspeed decreases. At slow airspeed the elevators feel 'sloppy' and greater control movements are needed to achieve the required result. This change in control force is an important clue to the pilot that airspeed is becoming slow. Changes in power change the speed of the slipstream passing over the elevators (except in the case of a T-tail aircraft, described later). Increased slipstream makes the elevators feel more effective; reduced slipstream makes them feel less effective.

The effect of the thrust and drag forces on pitch control has already been described – in most light aircraft an increase in power causes the aircraft to pitch nose-up, a reduction in power causes it to pitch nose-down. The use of flap also has an effect on pitch control. This is due in part to a change in the drag line, but is mostly because of a change in the downwash passing over the horizontal tail surface. The pitching effect varies between aircraft types. For example, most Cessna single-engined aircraft pitch up quite markedly when the first stage of flap is lowered; in the same situation Piper Cherokees (but not Warriors) pitch nose-down.

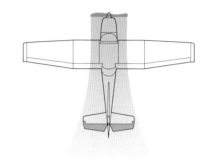

Increased slipstream makes the elevators feel more effective

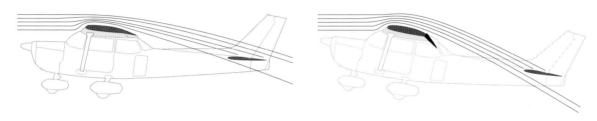

Lowering flap can alter the airflow over the horizontal tail, leading to a pitch up or down

▶ Stability in Roll

Stability and control in **roll** (lateral stability) is inextricably linked with stability in **yaw** (normal stability). It is unavoidable that references to yaw crop up when discussing roll and *vice versa*.

Dihedral angle

5°

Dihedral

The dihedral angle is clearly visible on this Piper PA-28 Cherokee

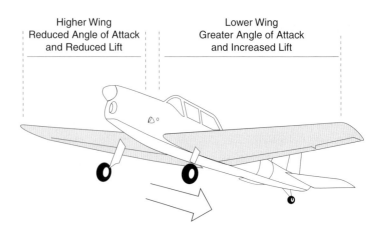

Higher Wing
Reduced Angle of Attack
and Reduced Lift

Lower Wing
Greater Angle of Attack
and Increased Lift

As an aircraft slips towards the lower wing, the lower wing meets the airflow at a greater angle of attack than the higher wing, due to dihedral. Thus the lower wing produces more lift, which rolls the aircraft level

One method to give an aircraft stability in roll is to incline the wings upwards slightly from the lateral axis. This is called **dihedral**, and a typical light aircraft might have a dihedral angle of around 5°. Dihedral works as follows. If the aircraft is disturbed so that it is no longer flying wings-level, the mass and lift forces are no longer directly in line as seen from ahead. The result is that gravity takes a hand and the aircraft will 'slip' towards the lower wing. Due to the dihedral angle, the lower wing is now meeting the airflow at a greater angle-of-attack than the upper. It therefore generates more lift than the upper wing and the result is a rolling moment, restoring the aircraft to wings-level flight.

The small (1°) dihedral angle of a high-wing Cessna 150

The anhedral angle of the wings of the Russian An-124 is quite marked

On high-wing aircraft, the centre of gravity is further from the displaced lift in a sideslip than in a low-wing aircraft, so creating a greater rolling moment to level the wings. This is why high wing designs usually have less dihedral than low wing aircraft. As a matter of fact, the overall design of an aircraft (particularly a large high-wing machine) can give it *too much* stability in roll. In these instances the wings may be angled down from the fuselage – a situation known as **anhedral** – to improve manoeuvrability in roll. Also, many swept-wing aeroplanes have anhedral. Sweeping back the wings produces an effect like dihedral and hence provides stability in roll, thus anhedral can be used to counteract wing sweepback and hence reduce excessive roll stability.

The **fin** (vertical tail) and **tailplane** (horizontal tail) can also aid stability in roll. As the aircraft slips towards a lower wing, the airflow acting on the vertical fin and horizontal tailplane can aid the rolling moment to restore wings-level flight. A particularly high vertical fin with a lot of surface area above the CG is especially helpful in this aspect.

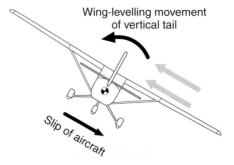

Wing-levelling movement of vertical tail

Slip of aircraft

The effect of the vertical fin in applying a wing-levelling moment as the aircraft slips towards the lower wing

▶Control In Roll

Control in roll is provided by **ailerons**, fitted at the outboard trailing edge of each wing. These move up and down in opposition, thus altering the camber of that section of each wing and so the amount of lift (and drag) being produced at each wing. The ailerons are controlled through the control column. If the control column is moved to the right, the aileron on the right wing moves up (reducing the lift at that part of the wing) and the aileron on the left wing moves down (increasing the lift at that part of the wing). The result is that the aircraft will roll to the right. The aircraft will continue rolling for as long as the control column is held over. It can be said that the primary effect of the ailerons is roll.

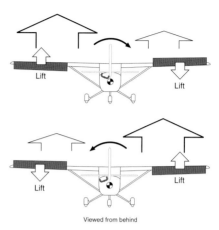

The ailerons, controlled by the control column, make the aircraft roll

When the ailerons are deflected, they not only alter the lift being produced at each wing, but the drag also. Increased C_L normally means an increase in induced drag. So when an aircraft is rolling, the wing producing the most lift (the higher wing) also produces more drag than the lower wing. This drag acts against the direction of the turn, in effect 'skidding' the aircraft out of the turn. This effect, operating in the yawing plane, is known as **adverse yaw**. However, because it is caused by the deflection of the ailerons, it makes sense to consider it at this stage, and we can say that the secondary effect of using the ailerons is yaw.

The most common way to overcome adverse yaw is to use *differential* ailerons, found on virtually all modern aircraft. Differential ailerons are arranged so that when the control column is moved left or right, the up-going aileron moves up through a greater angle than the down-going aileron moves down. Because in effect it increases the angle of attack and hence the lift, it is the down-going aileron which produces the most induced drag. So by moving the ailerons differentially, the

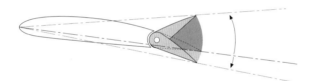

Differential ailerons: the up-going aileron moves through a greater angle than the down-going aileron

Differential ailerons: the up-going aileron moves through a greater angle than the down-going aileron

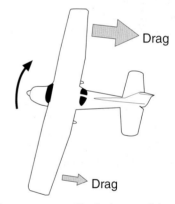

Adverse yaw caused by the increased drag from the upper wing (with the downgoing aileron) causes the aircraft to yaw in the opposite direction to which it is rolling

amount of drag created by each aileron is more closely equalised. The second innovation, also found on almost all modern aircraft, is the *Frise* aileron. This is an arrangement in which a small part of the aileron projects into the airflow below the wing when the aileron is deflected upwards. This creates extra drag on the down-going wing, in turn causing extra yaw in the direction of the turn. Both these design features help to maintain the aircraft in balance (i.e. not slipping or skidding) when there is the greatest aileron deflection – e.g. when rolling into a turn and rolling to wings-level flight.

The ailerons feel more effective as airspeed increases and less effective as airspeed reduces. Ailerons are usually well outside any propeller slipstream and so are unaffected by power changes.

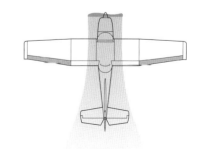

Ailerons are usually outside the propeller slipstream, and so their 'feel' is unaffected by changes in slipstream alone

Much emphasis has been placed on the effect of CG on stability and control in pitch. A similar consideration applies to the lateral CG position and its effect on roll. Imagine a situation where an aircraft with wing fuel tanks has one tank full and another virtually empty – which is *not* good flying practice. Now imagine that the aircraft is loaded with occupants only on the side of the aircraft with the full fuel tank, and that perhaps some heavy baggage is loaded on that side of the baggage compartment too. The net result is that the aircraft will tend to roll towards the heavier side, and considerable effort may be required to keep the wings level or turn in the opposite direction. This will be especially evident at slow airspeed, just after take-off for example.

The effect of loading on lateral CG

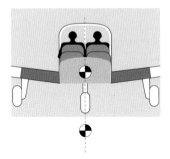
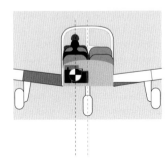

▶ Stability in Yaw

Stability in yaw ('normal stability') is achieved mostly through the **fin** (also known as the **vertical stabiliser**. This is quite simply a symmetrical aerofoil section mounted vertically. In balanced flight with no yaw, the fin meets the airflow head-on. And being symmetrical, it does not produce any significant lift. If the aircraft starts to yaw, the fin is now meeting the airflow at an angle; an angle of attack. Lift is created (in a horizontal plane) and the aircraft yaws around the CG until the fin is meeting the airflow head-on again. This can happen, for example, if an aircraft is not flying wings-level and the aircraft slips towards the lower wing. The effect of airflow upon the fin causes it to yaw towards the lower wing. Left uncorrected, this can cause the aircraft to gradually roll and yaw into a steepening spiral descent. This is often demonstrated in early flying exercises and underlines the interaction between roll and yaw, and thus the effect of aileron and rudder.

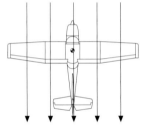

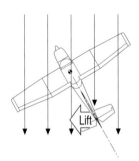

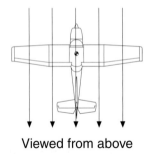

When the aircraft is yawing (skidding), the fin produces a restoring lift force

Viewed from above

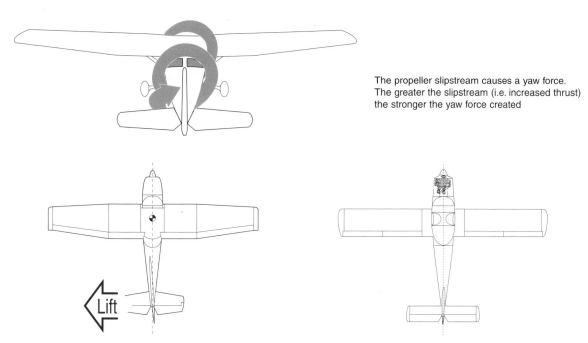

The propeller slipstream causes a yaw force. The greater the slipstream (i.e. increased thrust) the stronger the yaw force created

An off-set fin designed to counter the yaw caused by slipstream

The engine of a PA-38 Tomahawk is angled (off-set) by a few degrees to the right to counter the yaw caused by the slipstream

Stability in yaw is complicated by the effect of the engine and propeller slipstream especially in a single-engine aircraft. The rotating tube of air of the slipstream tends to meet the fin at an angle, hence creating lift and yaw. The greater the power, the greater the slipstream and the greater the yaw created. To reduce this unwanted yaw, aircraft designers sometimes off-set the fin (or the engine) a few degrees. The offset engine of the PA-38 Tomahawk, for example, is quite noticeable. Because these measures are fixed, they are only properly effective at one particular power setting and airspeed (usually those for the cruise). For this reason single-single-engine propeller aircraft tend yaw noticeable in response to changes in power setting. As a general rule, the more powerful the engine, the greater the yawing effect caused by power changes. The effect is most noticeable at high power setting and slow airspeeds.

We have already seen how stability in roll can affect stability in yaw (through adverse yaw). Yaw will also have an effect on roll. If an aircraft is yawed, the differing airflow speeds over the wings and the effect of dihedral will alter the amount of lift being produced by each wing, causing the aircraft to roll in the same direction that it is yawing. Left uncorrected, this can also lead to a spiral descent.

Theoretically, a forward CG increases yaw stability and a rearward CG reduces yaw stability. However, in reality the effect is not significant and movement of the CG location within its prescribed limits has little noticeable effect on stability in yaw.

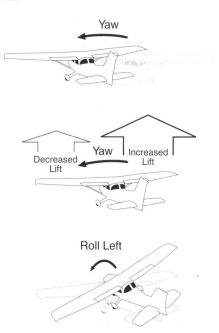

Yaw followed by roll: roll is the secondary effect of yaw

▶ Control in Yaw

The rear of the vertical tail is hinged in a similar way to the horizontal tail, and the control surface thus formed is called the **rudder**. The rudder is operated from pedals in the cockpit. When the left pedal is pressed forward, the rudder moves over to the left. This alters the camber of the fin/rudder combination and generates lift, which acts to rotate the rear of the aircraft to the right about its CG. This motion is called **yaw**, and is the primary effect of the rudder. The amount of yaw is determined by how far the rudder pedal is moved, and pressure must be maintained on the rudder pedal to keep the aircraft yawing. When the aircraft yaws, it will also tend to roll in the same direction even without any aileron input. Thus the secondary effect of the rudder is roll.

The vertical fin and rudder of a C172

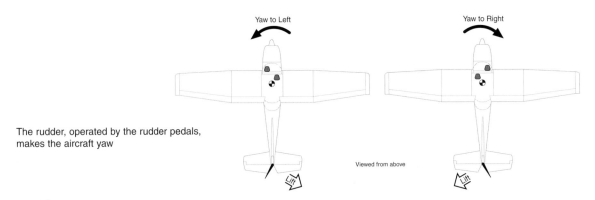

The rudder, operated by the rudder pedals, makes the aircraft yaw

The rudder feels more effective at higher airspeeds, and less effective at slower speeds. Changes in power setting (which increase or decrease the slipstream) also alter the apparent effectiveness of the rudder unless it is somehow placed outside the slipstream (as on some twin-tail aircraft).

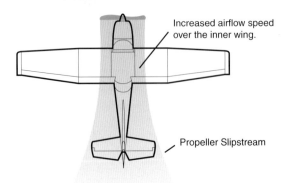

The rudder is usually within the propeller slipstream, and so feels more effective at higher power settings

Changes in power setting tend to cause yaw. Slipstream is not the only force at work, but to the pilot the effect is more noticeable than the cause. At slow airspeeds and high power settings, considerable amounts of rudder may be required to keep the aircraft in balance. Some of the final generation of propeller-driven fighter aircraft, embodying the most powerful piston aero-engines ever built, could literally 'flick' out of control if full power was applied clumsily at slow airspeeds.

Increased Power   **Decreased Power**

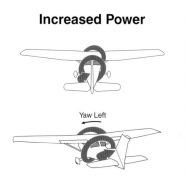

Yaw Left   Yaw Right

If the propeller rotates clockwise (right-hand), the aircraft tends to yaw to the left when power is increased, and vice versa

As a general rule, aircraft powered by American Lycoming and Continental engines (i.e. most modern light aircraft) have propellers which rotate clockwise (right-hand) as seen from the cockpit. With this direction of rotation the aircraft tends to yaw to the left when power is increased, and to the right when power is reduced. Engines with a propeller rotating anti-clockwise yaw in the opposite sense.

▶ Mass and Aerodynamic Balance of the Flying Controls

The pilot should be able to move the flying controls in flight without having to use unreasonable effort, but at the same time the controls must not be so 'light' that the pilot could inadvertently overstress the aircraft with a careless movement of the control column. To this end the designer will 'balance' the flying controls, to provide both ease of movement and progressive 'feel'. To give an idea of what the designer is trying to achieve, the generally accepted ideal ratio of control forces is:

Aileron	:	Elevator	:	Rudder
1		2		4

Thus, the ailerons should be the 'lightest' control and the rudder the 'heaviest'. Not all aircraft achieve this ideal, and that does not make them bad designs, but aircraft with this kind of control harmonisation are often known as a 'pilot's machine'.

As the load factor increases – for example, during a steep turn or when recovering from a dive – the load on the flying controls should increase too, so that the pilot is aware of the loads being imposed on the aircraft and so does not inadvertently overstress it. This is particularly important in the case of the elevators, which are the controls most likely to overstress the aircraft.

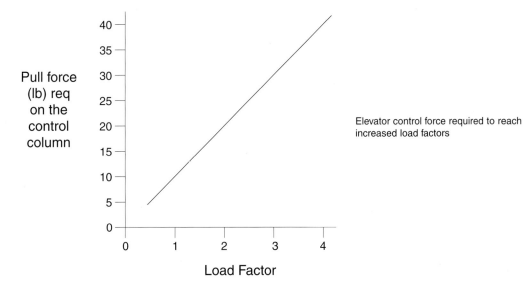

Elevator control force required to reach increased load factors

It is often necessary to give some sort of assistance in the control system to help the pilot move the surfaces and keep the control forces reasonably light under normal conditions. This is often achieved using a *horn balance*. A horn balance is an outer part of the flying control extending ahead of the hinge line so that when the control is moved, the horn balance extends into the airflow on the other side of the hinge-line. The pressure of the airflow on the horn balance aids the movement of the control and reduces the force required to move the control.

A mass balance

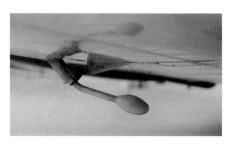

A horn balance on the elevator of a Cessna 172. The area ahead of the hinge line aids the movement of the elevator and also contains a mass balance

A mass balance ahead of the hinge line to reduce control flutter

A mass-balance weight

As well as balancing the flying controls for ease of movement and 'feel', *flutter* has to be addressed by the designer. Flutter is the rapid oscillation of a control surface, felt as a buzz or high-frequency vibration, which may occur at high speed and can have very serious consequences. One solution is to add a weight ahead of the control's hinge line, known as a *mass balance*. This moves the centre of gravity of the control surface forward, preferably to about the position of the hinge line itself, which in principle makes the control less prone to flutter. Use of a mass balance can also be a rather crude way of arranging the weight distribution of the control surface (especially if it is large) so that it is easier to move. In the past, some aircraft had mass balances in the form of large weights placed on struts which were bolted on to the control surface. Nowadays, designers try to avoid external mass balancing because of the drag it creates. Thus mass balances are usually *shielded*, often by placing the weights inside the control and ahead of the hinge line (e.g. within a horn balance).

▶ Revision

22   If an aircraft tends to return to its original condition once disturbed, how can this overall stability be described?

23   What is the name of the axis passing along the aircraft's fuselage from nose to tail?

24   What part of a 'conventional' aeroplane helps achieve longitudinal stability?

25   If centre of gravity (CG) is moved forward, what is the effect on stability in pitch?

26   If an aircraft has 4 seats, a baggage compartment and long range fuel tanks, can the pilot assume that it can be loaded with 4 occupants, maximum permitted baggage and maximum capacity fuel and still be within CG limits?

27   As airspeed increases, how does the apparent effectiveness of the elevators change?

28   What is the purpose of dihedral?

29   In order, what are the primary and secondary effects of aileron?

30   If an aircraft is fitted with differential ailerons, what will the relative positions of each aileron be whilst the aircraft is rolling to the right?

31   If a single-engine aircraft has a propeller that rotates anti-clockwise (left-hand) as viewed from the cockpit, how would it be expected to yaw after an increase in power?

32   What design feature is intended to prevent 'flutter' of flying controls?

Answers at page fpp68

Principles of Flight
Trimming
Controls

Principles of Flight
Trimming Controls

▶ Purpose and Function

▶ Operation of Trimming Controls

▶ Types of Trimmers

▶ Revision

Trimming Controls

▶ Purpose and Function

No matter how carefully an aircraft is designed in relation to control and stability and balance; the range of permissible loads, CG positions, power settings, airspeeds and operating conditions etc. mean that in practice to maintain a desired attitude, balance and performance, some constant pressure on the flying controls (most especially the elevator) is needed. If it was necessary to apply a constant force to the flying controls in this way, flying would soon become very tiring. To alleviate such control forces, some or all of the flying controls may be fitted with a pilot-adjustable *trimmer*. A trimmer usually takes the form of a small control surface (a *trim tab*) fitted to the trailing edge of the flying control surface. This small control surface produces an up-force or down-force of its own and so applies an up or down force to the flying control it is attached to. At its simplest, a trim tab is merely a piece of bendable metal bolted onto the trailed edge of a flying

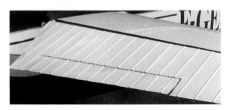

Elevator trim tab on a Cessna 172

control. For a control surface that will need regular in-flight trimming, the trim tab is controlled independently of the flying control by a trim wheel or lever in the cockpit. The pilot alters the angle of this trim tab (in effect a mini control surface) so that it produces lift of its own at the back of the control surface, keeping the flying control at a particular angle to the airflow. A conventional trim tab will maintain a constant position relative to the control surface it is attached to, regardless of any movement of the control surface itself.

▶ Operation of Trimming Controls

In light aircraft, a pilot-controlled trim tab is most often found on the elevator. Finding the correct position of the elevator trimmer is nowhere near as complicated as it might seem. In practice, the pilot only has to do two things:

- select the airspeed required
- move the trim control until no pulling or pushing pressure is needed on the control column to maintain that airspeed.

Aerodynamically speaking, the aircraft will now maintain the desired angle of attack without the pilot having to maintain a constant pressure on the control column. Except for transient manoeuvres such as a turn, it is good flying practice always to fly the aircraft 'in trim'.

Once an aircraft is in trim, its stability in pitch should ensure that it will return of its own accord to the trimmed angle of attack after a minor disturbance in pitch. From the practical point of view, the pilot uses the control column to place the wing at the desired angle of attack, and then uses the trimmer to maintain this angle of attack without constant force on the control column. If a constant **push** force is required, the trim wheel in the cockpit is wound **forward** until the push force disappears. If a constant **pull** force is required, the trim wheel in the cockpit is wound **back** to remove the force. If the trim wheel is moved the wrong way, the control force required will increase. It is tiring to fly an aircraft 'out of trim' because in effect the pilot is fighting against the aircraft's natural stability in pitch – an aircraft allowed to fly 'hands-off' will settle at the trimmed angle of attack. Many pilots underestimate the importance and advantages of keeping the aircraft properly trimmed in pitch. Properly trimming the elevator will remove a great deal of the pilot's workload because the aircraft should now maintain airspeed and performance itself. This enables the pilot to look after other aspects of operating the aircraft. If the aircraft is constantly deviating from the desired airspeed/performance, poor trimming is often the cause.

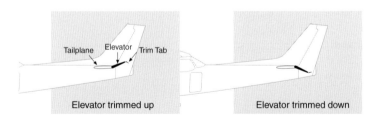

Tailplane Elevator Trim Tab

The operation of a trim tab

Elevator trimmed up

Elevator trimmed down

Although on many training aircraft only the elevator has a pilot-adjustable trimmer, some types have a rudder trimmer control too. To set this, the pilot first uses the rudder to ensure that the aircraft is flying in balance. When this has been achieved, the rudder trimmer is used to relieve any residual load on the rudder pedals.

▶ Types of Trimmer

The most common type of trimmer is the small control surface (trim tab) fitted to the trailing edge of the flying control, operated by a trim wheel or lever in the cockpit. The trim tab acts as a mini-flying control, applying a small amount of lift to set the control surface at a certain angle. For example, to hold the elevator in an 'up' position, the trim tab must normally be selected some degrees down and *vice versa*. Once set, a simple trim tab maintains its position relative to the control surface. The intricacies of this need not worry the pilot, since the trimmer is merely being used to remove control force on the control column or rudder once the desired attitude/airspeed or balance has been achieved.

An adjustable cockpit rudder-trim control

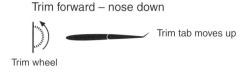

Trim forward – nose down

Trim wheel   Trim tab moves up

Trim back – nose up

Trim wheel   Trim tab moves down

Cockpit elevator trimmer control and indicator of a Cessna 152

Sometimes the trimming function is carried out by a spring within the flying control linkages. The cockpit control works in the conventional way and the feel and effect are much the same (although arguably less precise) as far as the pilot is concerned, but there is no external trimming surface. The venerable Tiger Moth uses this type of elevator trim, as does the slightly more modern Piper PA-38 Tomahawk and some light aircraft (Cessna 172s for example) use trimming springs for the rudder trimmer.

A roof-mounted elevator trimmer control and indicator

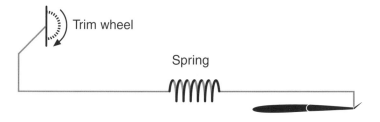

Trim wheel

Spring

The use of a spring to trim an elevator

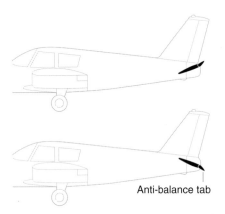

Anti-balance tab

The movement of the anti-servo (anti-balance) tab on the stabilator of a PA-28

An aircraft which has an especially powerful elevator or *stabilator* (described later), may have a specific type of trimmer known as an *anti-balance tab* (sometimes called an *anti-servo tab*). The anti-balance tab operates as a conventional trim tab, but in addition when the control surface is moved, the anti-balance tab moves in the same direction as the control surface, thus increasing the control load felt by the pilot and 'dampening' the movement of the control. Such an arrangement might be used on a particularly powerful control surface to prevent the control force from being too light and thus too easy for the pilot to overstress the aircraft. A balance tab (rarely found on smaller aircraft) works in the opposite sense. The tab moves in the opposite direction to the control surface, assisting its movement and so making the control force lighter.

A bendable trim-tab on a rudder

Some control surfaces (the ailerons on most light aircraft and sometimes the rudder) may also be fitted with trim tabs that are not attached to any trimming control, but instead are merely bent by hand to deflect them as required to balance the force on the flying control. Setting and adjusting a fixed trim tab is essentially a question of trial and error. It will be necessary to make a flight to assess any residual force on the relevant flying control, adjust the fixed trim tab on the ground after the flight, and then repeat the process to see if the desired result has been achieved. The process is best done under the supervision of a qualified engineer.

▶ Revision

33 Is an elevator trimmer used to *change* the aircraft's angle of attack, or *maintain* the selected angle of attack?

34 In order to maintain a given attitude, the pilot has placed the control column so that the elevator is deflected up. If the aircraft has an aerodynamic trim tab, and that trim tab is presently at neutral, which way will the trailing edge of the trim tab be moved to hold the elevator in the desired position?

35 If a cockpit elevator trim wheel is wound forward, will the trailing edge of the elevator trim tab move up or down?

36 When a control surface is moved, how does a conventional trimming control move relative to the control surface?

37 What is the name of the moveable tab, often found at the trailing edge of a stabilator or all-moving tailplane, which is designed to add 'feel' to the stabilator and prevent inadvertent overstressing of the aircraft?

38 How does a servo or balance tab operate?

Answers at page fpp68

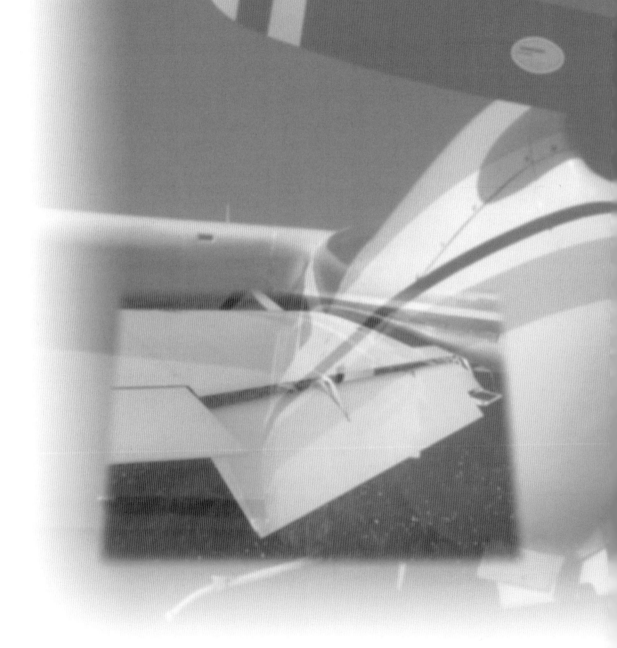

Principles of Flight
Flaps and Slats

Principles of Flight
Flaps and Slats

▶The Flaps

▶Slats, Slots and Air Brakes

▶Revision

Flaps and Slats

▶The Flaps

On a light aircraft, the flaps are sections of the trailing edge of the wing that can be moved and deflected downwards, altering the camber of the wing and hence its lift and drag. The altered downwash behind the wing caused by lowering flaps alters the airflow over the tailplane. This generates a pitching moment, the direction and magnitude of which varies between aircraft types. For example, on the high-wing Cessna single-engined aircraft the initial deflection of flap tends to cause a strong pitch-up whereas on many low-wing Piper Cherokee aircraft, lowering flap causes a nose-down pitching.

Extending flaps usually has a pitching effect. In this instance, lowering flaps on this high-wing aircraft alters the downwash over the tailplane, leading to a significant nose-up pitching movement

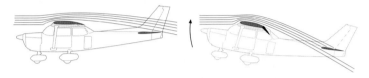

Generally, the initial flap deflection (10-15°) causes a useful increase in lift for a modest increase in drag. As flap is deflected further, lift increases at a lesser rate but drag becomes much more significant.

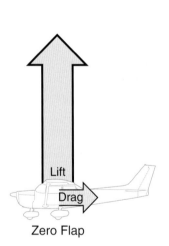

Zero Flap

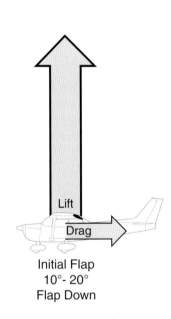

Initial Flap
10°- 20°
Flap Down

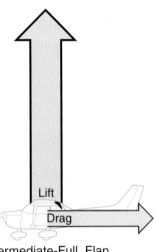

Intermediate-Full Flap
20°+
Flap Down

Changes in lift & drag as flaps are extended

Flaps come in all manner of shapes and arrangements. These are some of the more common designs:

- The *plain* (or *simple*) flap. A section of the trailing edge hinged along its lower edge. Can improve the maximum attainable coefficient of lift ($C_{L\ max}$) by about 50%.

The simple flap of a Piper PA-38 Tomahawk

- The *split* flap. Only the underside section of the wing hinges down. Maximum C_L is improved by up to 60%, but this type of flap also creates more drag than the plain flap.

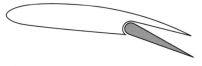

A 'close up' of a split flap of a Hunter (classic jet fighter)

- The *slotted* flap. Similar to the plain flap, but a slot or gap opens up between the flap and the wing as it is deflected. This allows relatively high-pressure air from underneath the wing to flow over the flap, delaying airflow separation and therefore stalling. $C_{L\ max}$ is improved by up to 75%.

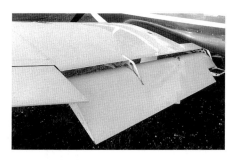

Slotted flaps on a Robin 3000

- The *Fowler* flap. In this design the flap moves rearwards, thereby increasing wing area, before or during lowering. This is a very good method for increasing lift, especially when combined with the slotted flap, and can improve $C_{L\ max}$ by up to 100%.

At 10° extension the flaps of the Cessna 172 have a mostly Fowler action, increasing the wing area

In practice the flap arrangement may include more than one of the above design features. Cessna single-engine aircraft, for example, have a combination of Fowler and slotted flaps. These flaps are generally agreed to be very effective, and indeed are arguably the best fitted to light aircraft. Some very elaborate multi-stage flaps are found on airliners, and complicated arrangements of double or even triple-slotted Fowler flaps in conjunction with leading-edge devices (described soon) can increase the maximum C_L by anything up to 120%. Such complexity is necessary if the wing of a modern airliner, which is chiefly designed to fly at high speed and at high altitudes, is also to produce enough lift to attain landing and take-off speeds which do not require runways many miles long.

Although flaps reduce the stalling speed, most designs used on light aircraft also cause the wing to stall at a more shallow angle of attack. This means that the aircraft will probably stall with a lower nose attitude, but also means that the aircraft can attain the lowest landing speed without such a high nose attitude that sight of the runway is lost, or the tail of the aircraft strikes the ground on landing.

▶ Slats, Slots and Air Brakes

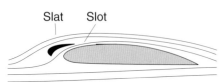

How a slot or slat 're-energises' the airflow over the front of the wing

Slats and slots along the front section of the wing are known as LEDs or 'Leading Edge Devices'. A slat or slot in the leading edge increases lift close to the stall by allowing relatively high-pressure air from just underneath the wing to flow over the wing's upper surface, re-energising the airflow and delaying airflow separation. Slats and slots are capable of increasing $C_{L\ max}$ by 50-60%, and they cause the stall to occur at a higher angle of attack than for a 'clean' wing. A slot is a fixed gap in the leading edge of the wing; a section of leading edge that moves in and out is called a slat.

Spoilers are sections of the upper wing surface that can deflected to reduce lift (and increase drag) on the wing. When used symmetrically, spoilers act as a type of airbrake or 'speedbrake'. In airliners the spoilers also move up to full deflection on landing, acting as so-called lift dumpers. High speed aircraft (such as almost all airliners) can also use spoilers asymmetrically for roll control. Where used in this way the spoiler lies flush with the wing when the control column is central. If the control column is moved to the right (for example), the spoiler on the right-hand wing will rise. This reduces the lift on that wing whilst also increasing drag, causing the aircraft to roll (and yaw a little) to the right. Spoilers are often favoured for high-speed aircraft because in this regime of flight spoilers are a more effective means of roll control than ailerons. Conversely, spoilers can be ineffective at slow speeds. Most aircraft that use spoilers for roll control also have ailerons for use at slow airspeeds; watch the wings of the average airliner on approach to see spoilers and ailerons in action.

Spoilers on an Airbus A320 acting as 'lift dumpers' just after touchdown

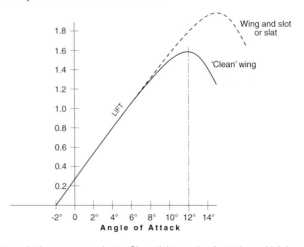

A slot or slat increases maximum CL and the angle of attack at which it occurs

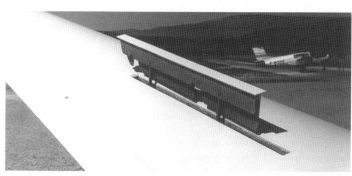

Airbrakes extended on a glider's wing

Gliders, motor gliders and certain light aircraft are fitted with *airbrakes*, whose only function is to increase drag. These normally take the form of flat plates extending vertically above (and occasionally below) the wing, operated by a cockpit control. Glider pilots use airbrakes to achieve precise control of the final approach path, and open them fully on landing to ensure that the aircraft will not float along above the runway.

▶ Revision

39 How does a conventional trailing edge flap alter the maximum coefficient of lift ($C_{L\ max}$) a wing can produce?

40 With trailing edge flap lowered, is the stalling angle of attack greater, lesser or unchanged from that when flap is not lowered?

41 What is the difference between a 'slat' and a 'slot'?

42 How does a slot or slat effect stalling angle of attack?

Answers at page fpp68

Principles of Flight
The Stall

Angle of Attack

Principles of Flight
The Stall

▶ Slow Flight – The 'Back of the Power Curve'

▶ Principles of the Stall

▶ Stall Airspeed

▶ Factors Affecting Stalling Airspeed

▶ Symptoms of the Stall

▶ The Stall Recovery

▶ Stall Warners

▶ Stall Accident Scenarios

▶ Revision

▶ Slow Flight – The 'Back of the Power Curve'

Slow flight is generally taken to be the situation where the aircraft is flying more slowly than the minimum-power-required airspeed, or 'on the back of the power curve' as some pilots call it. For most flight conditions this probably means that the aircraft is within a few degrees of the stalling angle of attack, and for a light aircraft the airspeed will be within 10kts or so of the stalling speed.

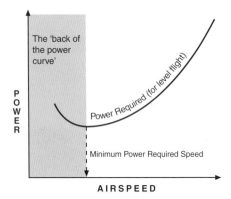

The power-required curve (power-required = drag x airspeed). When flying slower than the minimum power-required airspeed, a **decrease** in airspeed requires an **increase** in power to maintain level flight

When an aircraft is flying faster than the minimum-power-required airspeed (which is around 55 knots in an average training aeroplane) an increase in angle of attack will cause it to fly more slowly. Power can then be reduced to maintain level flight because drag (and so power required) is reduced at the slower airspeed. This makes airspeed and height control simple, and is the sort of behaviour the pilot might intuitively expect. However, once the aircraft is flying more slowly than the minimum power-required airspeed, a speed reduction actually necessitates an *increase* in power to maintain level flight. This is because as high angles of attack are reached, induced drag rises rapidly with even a small increase in angle of attack.

For those not entirely convinced, try the following experiment at a safe height and under the supervision of an instructor. From the normal cruise, move the control column back slightly to pitch the aircraft nose up a degree or two and so increase the angle of attack. As the airspeed reduces, the aircraft will start to climb because at this slower airspeed there is now more power set than that required for level flight. So reduce the power slightly until the aircraft is flying level again. Trim for the new airspeed and power setting. Now repeat the process, gradually reducing the airspeed in steps of 5kts or so. The point will come where a further reduction in airspeed requires an <u>increase</u> in power to maintain level flight. The aircraft is now flying more slowly than the minimum-power-required airspeed, it is now 'on the back of the power curve' and even a small increase in angle of attack leads to a large increase in drag. Any further reduction in airspeed will require still more power to maintain level flight as induced drag begins to build up at the high angle of attack. Ultimately, as the power curve shows, the slowest possible airspeed will be achieved at the highest power setting.

There is another way to demonstrate the practical effect of the power curve. Again, under the supervision of an instructor, from the normal cruise in an average training aircraft, reduce the power setting to around 1900RPM and allow the aircraft to settle at a slower speed – say around 80kts in a C152/PA-28-type machine. This is point A on the power curve opposite, where total drag is largely made-up of parasite drag. After a good lookout, pitch the aircraft nose-up quickly to an attitude a little steeper than the normal climb (in effect significantly increasing the angle of attack) whilst leaving the power untouched. After a very short-lived climb, the aircraft should settle back to level flight – albeit at a much higher nose attitude than before, with a greater angle of attack and hence a slower airspeed. The aircraft is now at point B on the power curve, where drag is mostly made up of induced drag because the wing is operating at a high angle of attack. When tired of mushing through the air in this nose-high attitude, pitch the aircraft nose-down (reducing the angle of attack) and the aircraft will descend for a short while as it accelerates back to the original level-flight airspeed.

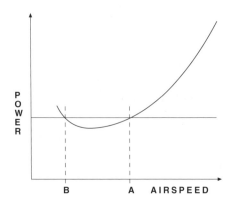

Two points on the power curve achieved with the same power setting but at different airspeeds

The inclusion of 'slow flight' in the training syllabus is intended to reinforce awareness of the issues involved in flying close to the stall; it is not intended to be an everyday flight manoeuvre. Apart from demonstrating the principle that performance is dictated by a combination of power and attitude, slow flight also allows the pilot to explore the 'feel' and handling of the aircraft close to the stalling angle of attack. The flying controls feel less effective and larger control movements are required because of the slower airspeed and therefore the reduced dynamic pressure. Handling is generally 'sluggish' and there is a feeling that the aircraft is 'mushing' through the air. Considerable effort is also required to keep the aircraft in balance, and proper use of the rudder becomes far more important than in normal flight. Even a small change in power requires far more footwork to keep the aircraft in balance as the combined slipstream, asymmetric-blade and torque effects (described later) become more noticeable. Likewise, any aileron deflection – when rolling into or out of a turn, for example – will produce more noticeable aileron drag and adverse yaw. Nevertheless, keeping the aircraft in balance at high angles of attack is very important.

▶Principles of the Stall

The stall occurs when the smooth airflow over the wings breaks down and the airflow largely separates from them, severely reducing the circulation responsible for the creation of lift. The result of this circulation breakdown is a marked **decrease** in lift, and a marked **increase** in drag. For a given wing size and shape, the stall **will** always occur at a given angle of attack. The pilot controls angle of attack through the control column, making the elevators pitch the aircraft nose-up or nose-down, thus presenting the wings to the airflow at a greater or lesser angle. It follows that, as a general rule, a stall occurs because the pilot pulls the control column too far back, bringing the wings to the stalling angle of attack. This basic action is the cause of the vast majority of stalls, deliberate or otherwise.

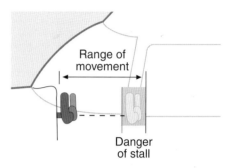

An idealised diagram of the relationship of control column position to angle of attack

One obvious solution might be to limit the rearward movement of the control column, and indeed this has been tried. The problem is that it is not possible to exactly equate control column position to angle of attack; for example, slipstream makes the elevators more effective, so the control column does not have to be moved as far back to achieve a particular angle of attack at high power settings as it does in the glide. Furthermore, at slow airspeeds in particular, limiting the rearward movement of the control column elevator and hence restricting the amount of upward elevator deflection available would mean that on landing, an aircraft would tend to arrive nosewheel (or propeller) first rather than on the mainwheels. The pilot might observe that the aircraft "ran out of up-elevator". The minimum controllable airspeed would also be higher, leading to faster approaches and longer landing distances. All in all, there are several reasons why an aircraft usually has plenty of rearward control column movement – not least to allow for a reasonable CG range – and training and common sense are needed to keep the pilot from stalling the aircraft inadvertently.

Because a stall is caused by presenting the wings to the airflow at too great an angle of attack, it follows that the recovery is made by reducing the wing's angle of attack. If the aircraft is the right way up, this involves pushing the control column forward. It should be stressed here that at the stalling angle of attack, the centre of pressure moves rearwards, and the effect on the lift/mass couple is to pitch the aircraft nose-down. Thus, at the stall, the aircraft usually has a tendency to pitch nose-down already. Nevertheless it is necessary for the pilot to relax any 'up elevator' force on the control column and ensure the control column moves forward in order to reduce the angle of attack. A common technique is to ensure that the aircraft pitches nose-down to about the normal glide attitude. That said, all aircraft behave differently at the stall and the best guide to the stall recovery actions is the advice of the POH/FM and a flight instructor experienced on the type.

Although not covering all possible stalling scenarios, the principles of stalling and stall recovery are no more complicated than the forgoing. Re-read the above and, if you've not already tried it, carry out the 'hand-out-of-car' experiment detailed in Chapter 10 of PPL 1. To summarise, place your hand into the airflow from a moving car, presenting it to the airflow like a wing. Increase the angle of attack and feel the lift force developing. Increase the angle too far and feel the loss of lift and increase in drag that characterise the stall. Now reduce the angle of attack to return your hand to a 'normal' lifting action.

Using your hand and an airflow to create a basic wind tunnel

▶ Stall Airspeed

Because light aircraft do not usually have an angle-of-attack indicator, airspeed is the primary reference for avoiding the stall. The aircraft's Pilots Operating Handbook/Flight Manual (POH/FM) will usually state at least two specific stalling airspeeds, known as V_{s0} and V_{s1}, and these are normally marked on the airspeed indicator. These figures signify speeds at which the stalling angle of attack will be reached *under a very specific set of circumstances*. The specified circumstances in the case of V_{s0} & V_{s1} are usually:

V_{s0} (bottom of white arc on airspeed indicator)	V_{s1} (bottom of green arc on airspeed indicator)
Wings Level Flight	Wings Level Flight
Power Off	Power Off
Maximum Gross Weight	Maximum Gross Weight
Flaps fully down	Flaps fully up
Most forward C of G permitted	Most forward C of G permitted

V_{s0} (Bottom of White Arc)

V_{s1} (Bottom of Green Arc)

V_{s0} (flaps down) and V_{s1} (flaps up) as marked on an airspeed indicator

The airspeed indicator essentially reads dynamic pressure, and dynamic pressure is one of the principal ingredients in the lift process. This means that the under a specific set of circumstances, the stall will occur at the same *indicated* airspeed – i.e. the speed displayed on the airspeed indicator (ASI) – regardless of the altitude.

Indicated stall airspeed at sea level

Indicated stall airspeed at 10,000 feet.

If all other factors remain equal, an aircraft will stall at the same indicated airspeed regardless of altitude

ASI   ASI

▶Factors Affecting Stalling Airspeed

Many factors can affect stall airspeed; here is a brief outline of some of the more common ones:

- Mass. If mass is increased, the aircraft must fly at a higher airspeed for any given angle of attack to produce the increased lift necessary to maintain level flight. Because a given angle of attack is associated with a higher airspeed than for a less heavy aircraft, the stalling angle of attack is reached at a higher speed.

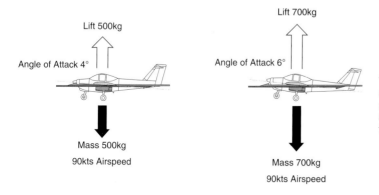

Lift 500kg

Angle of Attack 4°

Mass 500kg

90kts Airspeed

Lift 700kg

Angle of Attack 6°

Mass 700kg

90kts Airspeed

The heavier the aircraft, the greater the angle of attack required at any particular airspeed to produce the same amount of lift, so the stalling angle of attack is reached at a higher airspeed than for a less heavy aircraft

- Load Factor. Increased load factor (such as that caused by manoeuvring flight) increases the stalling airspeed. This is because at any given angle of attack, the airspeed has to be higher to provide the increased lift necessary to support the increased weight caused by the additional 'g-force' or load factor. Therefore the stalling angle of attack is reached at a faster airspeed with extra load factor (to be exact, stall speed increases by the square root of the load factor).

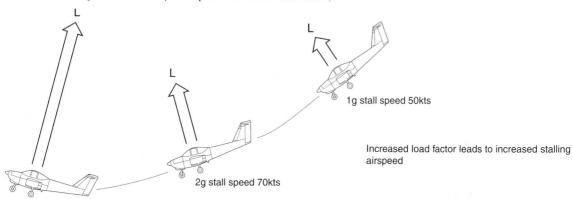

L

L

1g stall speed 50kts

L

2g stall speed 70kts

3g stall speed 86kts

Increased load factor leads to increased stalling airspeed

- Angle of Bank. As angle of bank increases in a level turn, so load factor increases. The steeper the angle of bank, the higher the airspeed at which the stalling angle of attack will be reached.

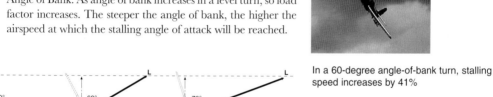

In a 60-degree angle-of-bank turn, stalling speed increases by 41%

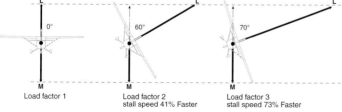

L

0°

M

Load factor 1

L

60°

M

Load factor 2
stall speed 41% Faster

L

70°

M

Load factor 3
stall speed 73% Faster

The steeper the angle of bank in a level turn, the higher the load factor and so the higher the stalling airspeed

■ Power. The more power is used, the slower the stalling airspeed. At the high nose attitude often (but *not* always) associated with the stall, the thrust line is inclined upwards and so acts in the same direction as lift, adding a component to the lift force. The propeller slipstream also increases the airflow speed over the wings, at least in most aircraft, thus making that part of the wing produce more lift than that outside the slipstream.

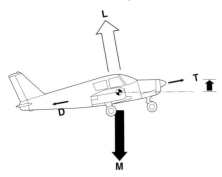

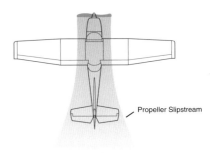

A component of power acts in the same direction as lift at a high angle of attack…

…and faster slipstream creates more lift over the inner wing. Both reduce stall airspeed

■ Flaps. Flaps increase the maximum C_L the wing can produce, meaning that the aircraft can fly more slowly before running out of lift. The effect of flaps varies between different aircraft types and flap designs, but a reduction in stalling airspeed of 5-10kts is fairly standard for a light aircraft. Note, however, that the stall occurs at a reduced angle of attack compared to a 'clean' wing.

Lowering flap increases the maximum C_L attainable, reducing stall airspeed

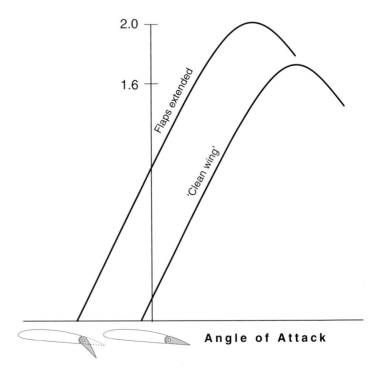

■ Centre of Gravity. A forward CG increases the stalling airspeed. Moving the CG from the rearward limit to the forward limit can increase stalling speed by as much as 5kts in an average light aircraft. The stalling speeds marked on the ASI are normally based on the most forward CG.

Forward CG limit	Rear CG limit	
Stall airspeed 51kts IAS	Stall airspeed 46kts IAS	The effect of CG position on stall airspeed

In summary:

	INCREASED	**DECREASED**
Load Factor	Higher stall airspeed	Slower stall airspeed
Angle Of Bank	Higher stall airspeed	Slower stall airspeed
Power	Slower stall airspeed	Higher stall airspeed
Flaps	Slower stall airspeed	Higher stall airspeed
C of G Rearwards	Lower stall airspeed	
C of G Forwards	Higher stall airspeed	

The stalling speeds marked on the airspeed indicator are, at best, an approximate guide and must be treated with caution. The simple fact is that an aircraft can be made to stall at almost *any* airspeed.

Anything which disrupts the wing's shape – such as ice, frost or damage, – will also significantly affect the aircraft's stalling characteristics, in particular increasing the stalling speed. Even a very thin coating of frost, let alone a covering of snow, can prevent an aircraft getting airborne (and snow will NOT blow off the wing during take-off). Likewise, icing can reduce a wing's performance so much that the aircraft is unable to maintain level flight, even at full power and best-rate-of-climb airspeed.

▶ Symptoms of the Stall

Given that a stall can occur over such a wide range of airspeeds, it makes sense to be familiar with the symptoms of the approach to the stall and the stall itself. The classic symptoms of an approaching stall, not all of which may manifest themselves in every stall, are:

■ Control column well back

■ Abnormally slow airspeed for the manoeuvre being flown, airspeed reducing further

■ Unusually nose-high attitude for the manoeuvre being flown

■ 'Sloppy' and ineffective flying controls

■ Unusual quietness

■ Stall warner operating

■ High rate of descent

■ 'Buffet' of the airframe as airflow detaches from the wing.

In general terms at least two or three of the symptoms above will be present whenever an aircraft approaches the stall. The symptoms will persist up to the stall itself; additionally the stall may be marked by:

■ Increased 'buffeting' felt through the airframe and flying controls

■ Significant increase in rate of descent

■ A nose-down pitching moment, despite the control column being held back (sometimes called the 'g-break')

■ Possible wing drop.

Although there is much emphasis in basic training on recovering from a fully developed stall, it is not necessary to reach the actual pitch-down and/or wing-drop of the stall to get into trouble. Indeed, if the stall is approached gently enough it may be quite difficult to persuade the aircraft to 'g-break' (the point of the aircraft pitching nose-down), despite the fact that the wing is, to all intents and purposes, stalled. This condition, which leaves the aircraft mushing downwards in an almost level attitude (but with an excessive angle of attack and a high rate of descent) in a 'quasi-stall'. This sometimes happens to glider pilots trying to 'stretch the glide' when landing, resulting in the glider hitting the ground with an excessive rate of descent.

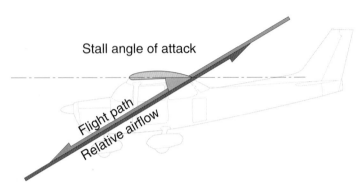

The quasi-stall. Although the aircraft is in a roughly level attitude, its steep flight path means an excessive angle of attack at the wing

In any case, during the approach to the stall the pilot's control over the aircraft is being progressively eroded. The rudder may not be effective enough to counter the yaw from a sudden application of power; the ailerons may not be effective enough to counter unwanted roll. Moreover, it is not unusual for the rate of descent to build up unexpectedly quickly, something which might become noticeable only as the aircraft gets close to the ground. This phenomenon is often responsible for a heavy landing when the pilot fails to maintain a safe airspeed on the final stages of approach and landing.

▶The Stall Recovery

The stall recovery is led with the elevators. By moving the control column forward, the angle of attack at the wings is reduced. This allows the wing to start producing more lift and less drag. By pitching nose-down to the normal gliding attitude, the aircraft should quickly reach the glide airspeed, which is well above the stalling speed. All this is quite simple and undramatic; the only real problem is the loss of height, which is likely to be at least several hundred feet. This is not a problem if the stall takes place at 4000ft AGL, but is far more serious if the aircraft stalls at 400ft AGL. It is worth emphasising that the control column *must* be moved forward to recover from the stall, even if the aircraft has already pitched nose-down. The angle of attack is the angle between the wing's chord line and the aircraft's flightpath. In the stall, even with the aircraft in a level or nose-down attitude, the flightpath is steep enough to exceed the stalling angle of attack – attitude is not the same as angle of attack. The angle of attack actually **increases** as the aircraft pitches down at the stall, because of the rapidly steepening flightpath. The fact that the aircraft pitches nose-down at the stall does not amount to a self-recovery; the angle of attack of the wings still has to be reduced by moving the control column forward.

At the stall 'g-break', the angle of attack is increased by the aircraft's steepening flight path

Steepening flight path
INCREASES angle of attack,
even with the aircraft descending.

To reduce the height loss in the stall recovery, power is applied (normally full power) after the control column has been moved forward. This should arrest the descent and, when a safe airspeed – usually somewhere around the standard climb speed – has been reached, the aircraft can be pitched nose-up to the normal climbing attitude. The use of power in the stall recovery reduces the height loss considerably. Exact figures vary between aircraft types, but most light aircraft can recover from a wings-level stall with no more than around 100ft of height loss if the pilot is alert and in current practice.

The stall recovery becomes more involved if a wing 'drops' at the stall. This is perfectly possible because there is no reason to suppose that both wings will reach the stalling angle of attack at the same moment. Small manufacturing or rigging inaccuracies can make a marked difference, and sometimes a fleet of the same aircraft type may contain one or two individual aircraft prone to drop a particular wing at the stall. However, the most common cause of wing-dropping is unwanted yaw – or, to put it another way, the aircraft was not in balance at the stall. The cure is simple. Use the rudder to keep the aircraft in balance, especially at slow airspeeds/high angles of attack.

If a wing does drop at the stall the instinctive reaction is to correct with aileron. However, it is widely seen as the wrong response. The reason is that the down-going aileron which is invoked when attempting to 'pick-up' the lower wing *increases* the angle of attack on that part of the wing.

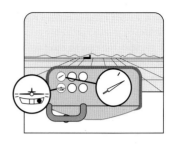

The ideal set-up
to a wing-drop
at the stall

Stalling an aircraft that is out-of-balance is the best way to provoke a wing drop

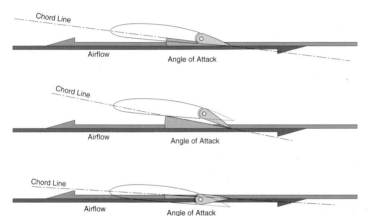

Aileron deflection alters local angle of attack at that section of the wing

This can lead to a significant increase in drag (i.e. adverse yaw) and so the aircraft yaws towards the lower wing – not at all what the pilot expected to happen. The currently 'approved' action if a wing drops at the stall is to use enough opposite *rudder* to prevent further yaw whilst keeping the ailerons central and, of course, moving the control column forward to unstall the wing. Large amounts of rudder to try to lift the lower wing are not necessary; just enough rudder is applied to prevent further yaw towards the lower wing, along with the standard stall-recovery action of moving the control column forward. As soon as the wing unstalls, the ailerons can be used to level the wings.

Whether or not the use of ailerons can actually stall a wing is a long-running arguement between aerodynamicists and pilots; modern thinking is that they cannot. What *is* generally agreed is that while a wing is stalled, down-going aileron on that wing is unhelpful. However, once the wing has unstalled, using the ailerons is the quickest way to level the wings. Most modern training aircraft can be made to 'pick-up' a dropped wing at the stall with aileron, but using the same technique in an older or more advanced aircraft may result in a totally different (and surprising) response. This is why pilots are taught not to use aileron at the stall, it being a well-known fact that in times of stress, pilots (like all humans) tend to revert to the longest established behaviour – which for pilots usually means what they learned in basic training.

The use of rudder to 'contain' a wing drop at the stall is also a matter of contention. One common argument is that it is a counsel of perfection, and there is always the danger that large amounts of rudder at the stall (possibly at the same time as forgetting the importance of un-stalling the wing quickly with forward control column) can make things worse. The British Gliding Association have looked closely at stall recovery and decided that is best simply to leave the rudder alone in the stall itself. Instead, they recommend concentration on 'breaking' the stall by moving the control column forward and then levelling the wings with aileron as soon as the wing is un-stalled. An RAF test pilot noted that this technique worked well with all the 50 powered-aircraft types that he had flown, including a few vintage machines with notoriously bad wing-dropping behaviour at the stall. Powered aircraft pilots can be very conservative, but possibly the time has arrived for a re-think on this question. For now, assume that an instructor's word is law in this matter!

A stall with a wing-drop increases the height loss suffered and several factors increase the possibility of a wing drop at the stall. The use of power can easily create unwanted yaw, especially at slow airspeed. If the propeller turns clockwise as seen from the cockpit (the case in most light aircraft) application of power tends to increase the chance of the left wing dropping. Lowered flaps also make a wing-drop more likely at the stall, because of the altered lift distribution across the wing and the slower airspeed at which the stall occurs. In either case, a wing usually drops because of significant yaw at the stall. The best solution is to keep the aircraft in balance – which is what a pilot's feet are for.

Stalling in a turn also makes a wing drop more likely, but not in the direction one might intuitively expect. In a level turn, the outer (higher) wing has the higher angle of attack, and so is likely to stall first. Thus, in a right-hand turn, the aircraft may well drop the *left* wing at the stall.

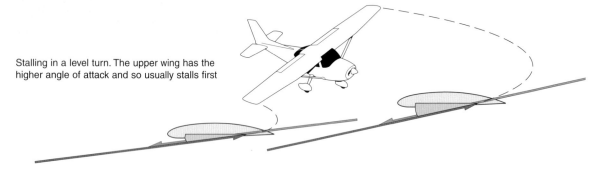

Stalling in a level turn. The upper wing has the higher angle of attack and so usually stalls first

▶ Stall Warners

Because of the possible consequences of an unintentional stall, aircraft designers incorporate devices to warn the unwary pilot that he is approaching the stalling angle of attack. In ancient biplanes, the 'singing' of the wing wires at a high angle of attack was enough to warn a pilot of impending trouble. Today's stall warners rely on the same principle but with a different implementation.

A reed-type stall warner in a Cessna wing leading edge

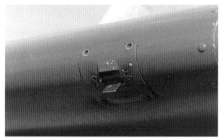

A tab-type (or vane) stall warner

The most common stall-warning device is a small movable tab set into the wing leading edge. At an angle of attack just before the stalling angle, this tab is lifted by the changing airflow. An electrical switch is closed and a horn, clanger or bell is then activated in the cockpit. A few stall warners activate a light, which unfortunately does not have the same attention-grabbing nature. Some Cessna single-engine aircraft have a reed in the wing leading edge. As the angle of attack approaches the stalling angle, air is sucked through this reed and this causes a whistle which becomes increasingly high-pitched as the stall approaches.

A stall strip on the wing leading edge, encouraging airflow separation at high angles of attack – felt as 'buffet'

Along with such devices, 'stall strips' may be fitted to the wing leading edge. These disturb the airflow over the wing at a high angle of attack, and are usually intended to induce a g-break beyond a certain angle of attack. They also tend to increase the buffeting felt in the approach to the stall and so provide additional warning of the approaching stall. Stall strips encourage different parts of the wing to stall before others, of which more when we look at wing design.

Leading-edge stall-warner strip to encourage airflow separation at this part of the wing

▶ Stall Accident Scenarios

'Loss of control' is the most common cause of serious accidents, and in visual flying conditions loss of control virtually always means an inadvertent stall usually followed by a spin (described shortly). Because of the way stalling is taught in basic training, a pilot can sometimes get the impression that it must be almost impossible to stall an aircraft inadvertently. However, stalling an aircraft at 4000ft is very different to stalling at 200ft.

The following scenarios are based on the recurring causes of stall/spin accidents. The words in italics are from actual accident reports.

■ The Steep Turn

'Dived into the ground during a steep turn at low altitude around another aircraft on the ground.'

'Lost control during a turn at about 200ft after take-off....'

'Loss of control while manoeuvring at low level in the vicinity of a village...'

'Aircraft dived into the ground after rolling and yawing after entering a steep climbing turn to the left at about 200ft after take-off.'

'On take-off after a fly-in, the aircraft entered a steep climb combined with a steeply banked turn of 60° or more during which it stalled at about 200ft and crashed.'

There is a common theme in the above accidents. An increase in angle of bank, and the increase in load factor which usually accompanies it, causes an aircraft to stall at a much higher airspeed than a pilot might be expecting. It is very noticeable how quickly load factor builds up as angle of bank increases beyond 60°. At this angle of bank, the load factor is two. At 70° (if the aircraft can manage that in level flight) the load factor is three. So, for example, an aircraft known to stall at 50kts in wings-level flight will stall at an airspeed 41% faster in a 60° angle-of-bank, constant level turn. This is 70·5kts. Increase angle of bank by just a further 10° and in a 70° banked turn, the stall occurs 73% faster than wings-level and the stalling speed becomes 86·5kts.

The lesson is that relatively slow airspeed and steep turns don't mix, especially at low level. A hard-pulling, steep turn just after take-off, or a tight circle right over a friend's house, or a similar stunt in front of a crowd, is one of the surest ways to turn a serviceable aircraft into a scattered pile of wreckage.

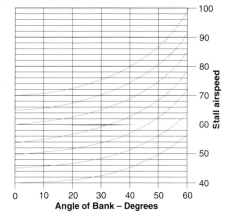

The increase in stall airspeed with increasing angle of bank

■ The Accelerated Stall

'Flew into the ground during low-level aerobatics'

'Lost control during a formation run-in and break' (a 'run-in and break' is a high-speed, low-level pass along the runway followed by steep pull-up and turn).

'...attempted a loop at an estimated height of 500 to 600ft...was seen to flick whilst descending and struck the ground travelling almost vertically.'

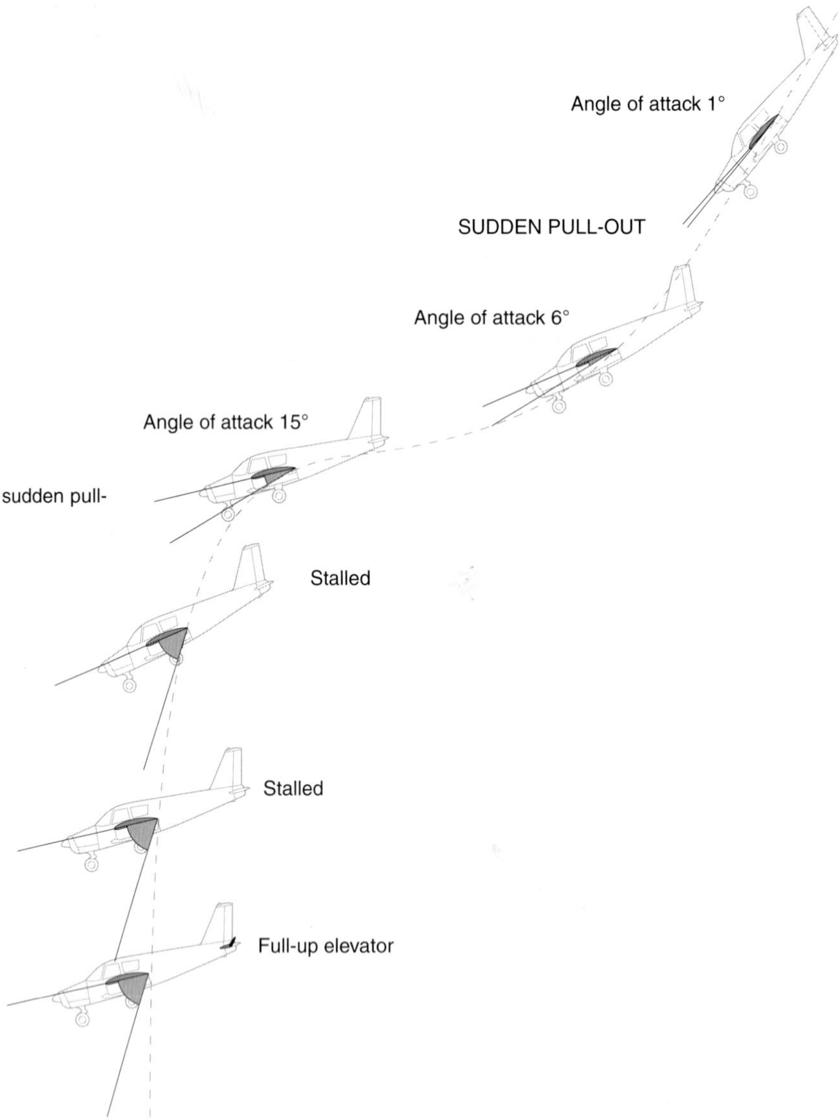

Angle of attack 1°

SUDDEN PULL-OUT

Angle of attack 6°

Angle of attack 15°

An 'accelerated' stall caused by a sudden pull-out from a dive

Stalled

Stalled

Full-up elevator

The effect of load factor on stall airspeed is a standard mathematical formula: the stalling speed increases by the square root of the load factor. So a load factor of two increases stall speed by 41% (1·41) and a load factor of three increases it by 73% (1·73). Because of this mathematical relationship, as load factor increases beyond two the stall speed increases dramatically.

It is the increase in load factor that makes stalling speed in a turn higher than that in level flight. However, it is not necessary to turn to increase load factor. Load factor can be increased simply by pulling back sharply on the control column. Whether such mishandling will break the aircraft or stall it depends mostly on the airspeed.

The common scenario for an *accelerated stall* – a stall caused by increased g-force or load factor – is an aerobatic manoeuvre going wrong at low level. The aircraft is left pointing almost straight down, with the ground rapidly filling the windscreen. The instinctive reaction is to pull back hard on the control column, but this is quite likely to increase the load factor such that the aircraft stalls, even at a high airspeed and nose-down attitude (remember that nose attitude is not directly linked to wing angle of attack). With the wings stalled the aircraft continues more or less straight down, despite – or more accurately because – the pilot is heaving back on the control column with all his strength. In this situation it is fair to say that the aircraft will come down the fastest with the control column right back.

So aerobatics should be practiced at a safe altitude, where there is plenty of room to recover from mistakes.

■ The Departure Stall

> *'After take-off some 8lb below Maximum Take Off Weight, the aircraft maintained a nose-high attitude until it stalled and crashed.'*
>
> *'Aircraft appears to have stalled, possibly when the flaps were raised shortly after take-off...'*
>
> *'During the climb-out after a touch and go the pilot lost control, possibly after the engine had failed, and the aircraft stalled and crashed.'*
>
> *'...aircraft made a low pass followed by a steep climb to about 300ft, when it entered a spin...'*

The *departure stall* describes a stall in the climb shortly after take-off. The cause is often that the pilot tries to make the aircraft climb better by pulling back further on the control column. Despite their name, the 'elevators' **cannot** make the aircraft go upwards any better if the engine is already at full power and the airframe at best climb airspeed. In fact, the increased angle of attack and consequent reduction in airspeed will reduce climb performance. Once the airspeed is below best climbing speed, the further back the control column comes, the worse the aircraft climbs.

The steep nose-up attitude of a departure stall at full power often leads to a very high angle of attack in the stall – angles of attack of up to 70° have been recorded. For this reason it is particularly important to make a positive forward movement of the control column to recover from a departure stall, not just a relaxation of back pressure.

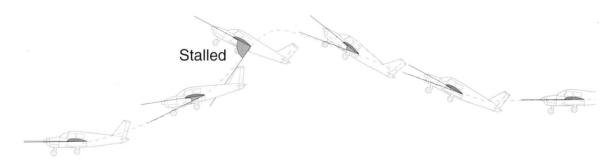

Stalled

The departure stall. Note the very high angle of attack as the aircraft descends in the stall

A stall after take-off can also occur if the flaps are raised at too slow an airspeed, because as flaps are raised the stalling airspeed increases and if power is suddenly reduced (deliberately or otherwise) in a climb, the stall airspeed will also increase. Additionally, the aircraft is likely to 'mush' down, in effect increasing the angle of attack even if a constant nose attitude is maintained.

So pay close attention to airspeed during the climb. The aircraft will only achieve best climb performance at full power and the best-rate-of-climb airspeed. Make any power or flap changes carefully and at a safe airspeed.

The last summary above involves the spin, so it is time to look at this much-misunderstood flight condition.

▶ Revision

43   When flying more slowly than the minimum-power-required airspeed, does a decrease in airspeed require a decrease or increase in power to maintain level flight?

44   What power setting permits the slowest possible airspeed in level-flight?

45   What single action is necessary to recover from a stall?

46   How does the movement of the centre of gravity (CG) effect stalling airspeed?

47   Does airframe icing, such as frost for example, effect stalling airspeed?

48   If stall airspeed is 50 knots IAS at 3000ft, what will it be at 12000ft in the same flight condition?

49   What is a 'stall strip'?

50   If stall speed in level flight is 50 knots, what will be the approximate stalling speed in a 60° angle of bank turn?

Answers at page fpp68

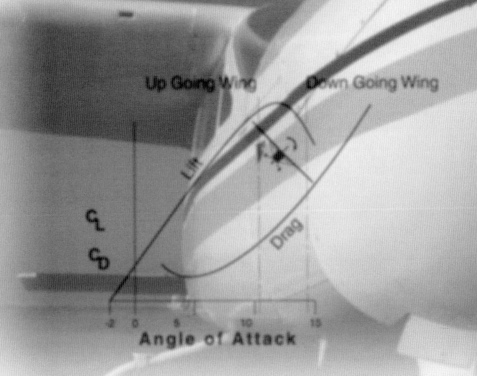

Principles of Flight
Avoidance
of Spins

Principles of Flight
Avoidance of Spins

Principles
of Flight

Spinning is a subject often surrounded by rumours, myths, and a healthy respect. The aerodynamics of a spin are far from simple, and indeed it would be quite possible to devote an entire book to this subject alone. Here we will concentrate on the basics.

▶ Causes of a Spin

▶ The Forces in a Spin

▶ Spin Recovery

▶ The Spiral Dive

▶ What's it Doing Now?

▶ Spin Accident Scenarios

▶ Revision

▶Causes of a Spin

A spin occurs when an aircraft stalls with significant yaw present, and the consequent wing drop allows the aircraft to develop *autorotation*. Autorotation in a fixed-wing aircraft (e.g. not a helicopter or gyrocopter) is a condition where the

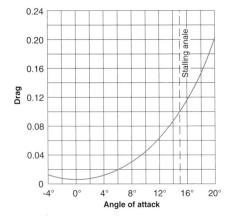

A graph of drag against angle of attack. Note the rapid increase in drag approaching the stall angle of attack

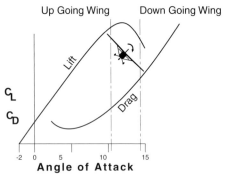

The cause of autorotation

aircraft is rotating of its own accord, without further control input from the pilot. Autorotation is caused by differing angles of attack across the wing at or near the stall. In a spin to the left, the left (lower) wing will have a greater angle of attack than the right. This means that the left wing will be producing both less lift and more drag than the right one. This differential in lift and drag keeps the spin going until recovery actions are taken.

In this case, the right wing has exceeded the stalling angle of attack, and so is producing both less lift and more drag than the left wing which has a lesser angle of attack. This causes both roll and yaw to the right

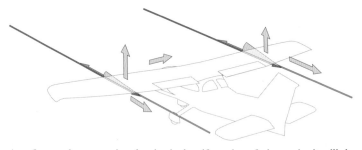

An often under-appreciated point is that if an aircraft does spin, it will do so in the direction of any rudder applied at the stall. Thus, if a pilot stalls an aircraft with left rudder applied, any resulting spin will be to the left.

In a spin the aircraft will be descending vertically (a rate of descent of 6000ft per minute is quite common, even in a light aircraft), yawing at an impressive rate (a complete turn every few seconds or so) and probably also pitching and rolling through each turn. But the major issue is that the aircraft is in a stalled condition, so let's be clear about one fundamental point:

An aircraft has to stall before it can spin. *Prevent the stall and you prevent the spin.*

The forces across the left and right wing that maintain the autorotation of a spin

▶The Forces in a Spin

The traditional arrangement of forces in 'normal' flight conditions are somewhat altered in a spin. Indeed, they are augmented by the *gyroscopic* force, which acts so that a large mass at the extremities of the aircraft (a concentration of weight in the nose and tail for example, or at the wing tips) tends to lead to a flatter spin. Generally, the flatter the spin, the more difficult and prolonged the recovery. The overall shape of the aircraft will also affect spin characteristics. An aircraft with a long wing span compared to the fuselage length will tend to have a slower rate of rotation in the spin than one with a shorter relative wing span. Imagine an ice-skater spinning on ice with arms outstretched; as the arms are pulled in, the rate of rotation speeds up.

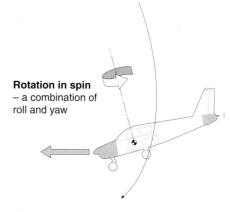

Rotation in spin – a combination of roll and yaw

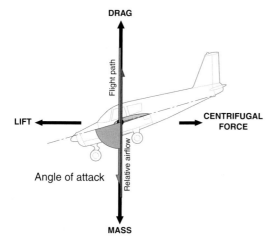

DRAG

Flight path

LIFT

CENTRIFUGAL FORCE

Angle of attack

Relative airflow

MASS

Effect of mass distribution on spin characteristics (mass at nose & tail)

Forces in an established spin

▶Spin Recovery

Because of the height loss involved in a spin and recovery (1500ft for a three-turn spin in an average light aircraft), timely recognition of a spin and correct recovery action is essential. Although the spin is a stalled condition, the recovery actions are different from those of a standard stall recovery.

Because of the changed relative airflow in a spin, the initial recovery action is *not* with the elevators but with the rudder. The first recovery action is to reduce the yaw by applying full opposite rudder against the direction of the spin (i.e. in a spin to the left, apply full right rudder). The control column is then moved forward to reduce the angle of attack, and the spin should stop as the stall is broken. However, that the control column may have to go right to the forward stop, and recovery may not be instantaneous – especially in a well-developed spin. Once the spin stops, the aircraft is left in a dive. The rudder is centralised, and the aircraft can be recovered from the descent. All this presupposes that the throttle is closed, the ailerons are central and the flaps are up.

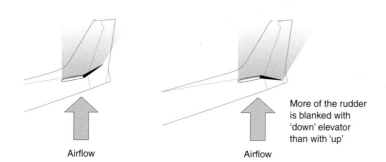

Airflow

More of the rudder is blanked with 'down' elevator than with 'up'

Airflow

How the horizontal tail and elevator can blank the rudder in a spin

To summarise the standard spin-recovery procedure:

- Check **throttle closed** and **ailerons neutral** (flaps up),
- Confirm direction of spin, apply **full opposite rudder**,
- **Move the control column forward until rotation stops**,
- **Centralise the rudder** and recover from the ensuing dive.

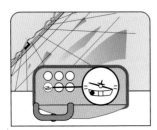

The turn co-ordinator should show the direction of the spin. Ignore indications from the balance ball

It is normally possible to see the spin direction by looking ahead, although the turn indicator or turn co-ordinator should accurately show the direction of the spin too. Ignore indications from the balance ball.

Here it must be stressed that different aircraft have differing spin characteristics and varying recovery techniques. Read the aircraft's Pilots Operating Handbook/Flight Manual (POH/FM) thoroughly (it may recommend a different recovery method from that given above, which will over-ride this general advice) and get a checkout with an instructor qualified on type before even *thinking* about spinning an aircraft.

If the correct recovery actions do not seem to work, there are still several options left. It is worth considering moving the controls to full 'pro-spin', that is stick held fully back and rudder fully in the direction of spin. If by any chance the rudder has been applied the wrong way initially, this should sort it out. If not, re-apply recovery actions. Applying pro-spin aileron (i.e. left aileron into a left-hand spin) in co-ordination with the recovery actions may also help recovery from a spin. If the aircraft still does not recover, it is worth trying to 'destabilise' the spin by moving the elevators fully back then sharply forward, co-ordinated with full and idle power (full power with forward elevator and *vice versa*). Lowering the undercarriage, opening speed brakes and even lowering flaps are also on the list of 'worth a try' options. An old flying manual suggests opening the canopy and standing up – not recommended without a parachute on!

Once again, it is stressed that this general advice is **not** applicable to all types, and with some aircraft might makes things worse. Before spinning, **read** the aircraft's Pilots Operating Handbook/Flight Manual (POH/FM), use the recovery technique it details, and **get a checkout** with an instructor qualified on type. It must also be remembered that specific weight and CG limits for spinning may well apply to the aircraft being flown. It is imperative to know these limits and *abide by them*. A CG aft of (behind) that permitted for spinning may make the aircraft reluctant or even impossible to recover from a spin.

Many aircraft are not cleared for spinning

SPIN RECOVERY

Intentional spins are prohibited in this airplane. If a spin is inadvertently entered, immediately apply full rudder opposite to the direction of rotation. Move the control wheel full forward while neutralizing the ailerons. Move the throttle to IDLE. When the rotation stops, neutralize the rudder and ease back on the control wheel as required to smoothly regain a level flight attitude.

Finally, a large number of GA aircraft (perhaps the majority) are *not* cleared for spinning. There are also several aircraft types – for example, the Piper PA-28 series – where some models are cleared for spinning but others are not. Once again, it is vital to read the Pilots Operating Handbook/Flight Manual (POH/FM) for the individual aircraft and follow its advice.

▶The Spiral Dive

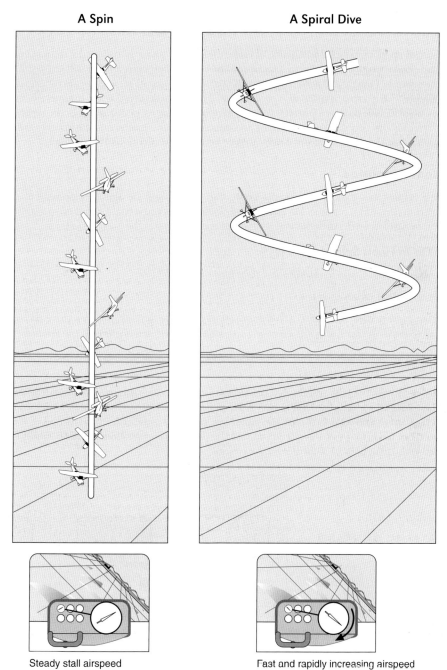

The spin and the spiral dive. In the spiral dive the airspeed increases rapidly

Many modern training aircraft are quite reluctant to spin, which is not necessarily a bad thing. If the spin entry does not go correctly, the aircraft may well end up in a spiral dive. As the name implies, this is basically a steep descending spiral rather than the vertical, rotating descent of the spin. A look at the ASI will confirm whether the aircraft is in a spin or a spiral dive. A rapidly increasing airspeed indicates a spiral dive; an airspeed steady around the stall indicates a spin. An aircraft can normally be recovered from a spiral dive by levelling the wings with aileron and recovering gently from the dive. Reducing power during the pull-out will reduce load factor on the aircraft.

▶ What's It Doing Now?

Spinning is often associated with aerobatics, because an inadvertent spin is one of the likely outcomes of a mishandled aerobatic manoeuvre. This is one reason why an aerobatic course usually starts with some spinning practice.

Should the aircraft end up in a totally unfathomable attitude, the general advice is to close the throttle and centralise the control column and rudder pedals. To quote an experienced aerobatic pilot, most aircraft will cease evil thoughts if the pilot centralises the controls. Gravity and aerodynamics will take over at some stage, and the aircraft should ultimately do something recognisable – be it a spin, a spiral dive or whatever. The pilot can then take the appropriate recovery actions. If doing aerobatics (after suitable dual training), it is worth remembering one particular point. In the event of a manoeuvre going wrong, the wait for the aircraft to do something recognisable – and the subsequent recovery – will be much less stressful if the pilot has had the foresight to put a safe distance between the aircraft and the ground.

▶ Spin Accident Scenarios

Rather like stalling, a pilot can sometimes gain the impression that it must be almost impossible to spin an aircraft inadvertently. Unfortunately, this is not true. We have already looked at several scenarios leading to a stall/spin accident – not least fooling around at low level. An additional scenario to consider here is the 'turn on to finals'

■ The Turn On To Finals Spin

> 'Aircraft appears to have spun in during a low final turn to land...'

> 'Lost control on final approach to land'

> 'While making a very tight, steep and curved approach to land...the aircraft appears to have flicked in the opposite direction to the turn, altering direction through about 180° and diving into the ground...'

How could a relatively simple manoeuvre such as turning on to final approach go so badly wrong? Well, consider this hypothetical scenario.

Turning on to final approach, the pilot realises that the aircraft is going to pass through the extended runway centreline. The airspeed is a bit slow, which the pilot hasn't noticed. He pulls back on the control column to tighten the turn, which increases the angle of attack and load factor. At the same time he applies rudder in the direction of the turn – **not** to balance the aircraft, but to try to 'push' the aircraft around the turn. This application of rudder moves the nose further below the horizon, so the pilot pulls back further on the control column.

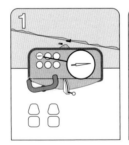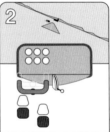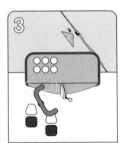

The classic stall/spin scenario during the turn onto final approach

Freeze the picture there and examine it. There is slow airspeed, turning flight, control column well back, and an aircraft seriously out-of-balance – all at low level.

When the stall/spin does happen, it may seem rather innocent and quite unlike the nose-high attitude and rapid roll rate the unfortunate pilot might remember from training. Instead, the stall is almost gentle as the aircraft pitches nose-down despite (in fact, because of) the control column being held even further back. The wing drops in the direction of the applied rudder, i.e. towards the low wing, but the pilot tries opposite aileron thinking that this will level the wings, not realising that what is happening is the incipient stage of a stall/spin accident. It will require considerable self-discipline to make the correct recovery actions – especially moving the control column forward when the nose is already well down. The ultimate outcome will depend chiefly on whether the pilot recognises the situation in time and how much height is available for recovery. But, of course, how much better not to get into this position in the first place...

▶ Revision

51   During the entry to a right-hand spin, which wing has the highest angle of attack?

52   What is the standard spin-recovery procedure?

53   Which cockpit instrument will most accurately indicate the direction of a spin?

Answers at page fpp69

Principles of Flight Load Factor and Manoeuvring Flight

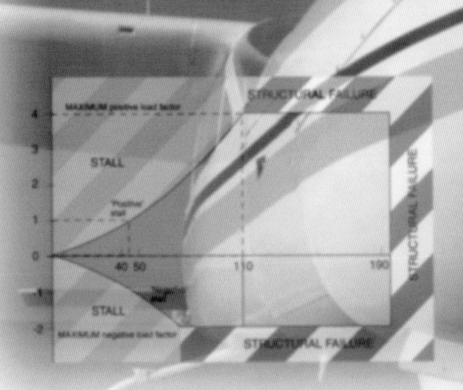

Principles of Flight
Load Factor and Manoeuvring Flight

▶ Structural Considerations

▶ The V-n Envelope

▶ In-Flight Precautions

▶ Revision

Load Factor and Manoeuvring Flight

▶ Structural Considerations

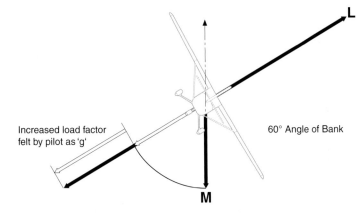

Load factor in a level turn

Increased load factor felt by pilot as 'g'

60° Angle of Bank

M

It is in manoeuvring flight (e.g. steep turns, pulling out of a dive, a sharp pull-up into a climb etc.) that the effect of *load factor* upon the aircraft becomes more noticeable. For example, in a level turn the extra lift needed to counter both the vertical component of mass and provide the force into the turn is felt as *g*, or load factor. There is a direct correlation between angle of bank in a level turn and load factor, as shown below:

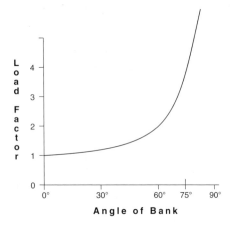

Load factor against angle of bank for a level turn

Increasing load factor has two important implications. As the load factor increases, the angle of attack must also increase to increase the coefficient of lift and hence the amount of lift produced by the wing. So the stalling angle of attack is reached at a higher airspeed than if no load factor was present. In a 60° angle of bank with a load factor of two, the stall airspeed will be 41% faster than in wings-level flight at the normal load factor of one.

The second implication of increasing load factor is the effect upon the aircraft structure. When a pilot subjects the aircraft to extra load factor, the mass multiplied by the load factor gives the effective weight. A level turn at 60° angle of bank imposes a load factor of two on the aircraft, meaning that every part of the aircraft structure is having to bear twice the weight that it was before. Of course, as load factor increases so the stress on the structure increases. An training aircraft will have been through a certification process to confirm that it is capable of withstanding a certain load factor without sustaining damage to the structure, a typical limit being around +3·8. The limit may be less if flaps are lowered and there may be certain mass and CG position limitations before even this limit is safe. Exceeding the stated flight load limit, even momentarily, may have exceptionally serious consequences. At best the airframe may suffer permanent damage but be capable of getting the pilot home – though the aircraft may never fly again. At worst, part of the structure (probably the wing) will fail completely; the implications of which are obvious. If an aircraft is over-stressed, no matter how momentarily or how inadvertently, a gentle return to an airfield and an inspection by an aircraft engineer is a necessity.

FLIGHT LOAD FACTORS

	Normal	Utility
(a) Positive Load Factor (Maximum)	3.8 G	4.4 G
(b) Negative Load Factor (Maximum)		No inverted maneuvers approved

Load factor limits in a POH/FM

▶The V-n Envelope

To prevent the consequences of over-stressing an aircraft, various airspeed and load-factor limitations are arrived at during the certification process by test pilots and engineers using a *V-n* diagram (also known as a *V-g* diagram). Different diagrams are drawn for various aircraft weights and configurations. A V-n diagram based on a 'clean configuration' aircraft at maximum mass might look something like that displayed below.

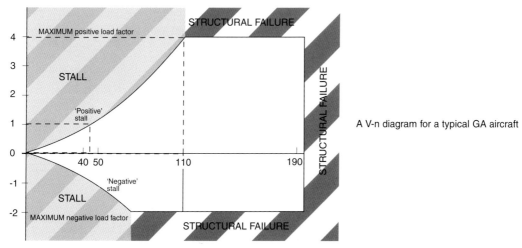

A V-n diagram for a typical GA aircraft

The horizontal axis of the diagram represents indicated airspeed; the vertical axis represents load factor. The curved lines originating from the zero point represent the maximum lift (causing the maximum load factor) that the aircraft can produce at the set airspeed. Increasing load factor beyond this point will stall the wings. The upper curve represents positive load *(+g)* and the lower curve represents negative load factor *(-g)*. At +1g the curve initially represents the wings-level, unaccelerated stalling speed to the point where the aircraft can produce enough load factor, without stalling, to damage the structure. This point on the curve represents the *design manoeuvring speed* (V_A) which is the maximum speed at which full and rapid movement of the flying controls (in particular the elevators) can be made without damaging the structure of the aircraft. Beyond the V_A speed, the horizontal line represents the maximum permissible load factor. The far end of the graph is the maximum speed under any circumstances – the never-exceed speed (V_{NE}). Flight beyond V_{NE} risks structural damage and failure at any load factor.

The limits mapped out by the lines of the graph form an 'envelope'. In essence, flight within the envelope means that the aircraft should be safe from either stalling or structural damage.

Unfortunately V-n diagrams do not usually appear in the Pilots Operating Handbook/Flight Manual (POH/FM) of a light aircraft. In essence a POH/FM is an owner's manual containing the limitations and operating techniques for the individual aircraft and every pilot of the aircraft should be familiar with it. The information gleaned from the V-n diagram is stated in the POH/FM in terms flight load limitations and limiting airspeeds. The limiting airspeeds can be described in terms of the 'V code'.

The common V speeds are:

Vs0 stalling speed in the landing configuration. In a light aircraft this is usually taken as maximum weight, most forward CG, landing gear down, flaps fully down and power off.

Vs1 the stalling speed in a specified configuration. In a light aircraft this is usually taken as maximum weight, most forward CG, landing gear up (if retractable), flaps up and power off.

VFE the maximum speed for flight with flaps extended.

VA the design manoeuvring speed. The maximum speed at which full and sudden flight control movements can be made without the danger of over-stressing the structure.

VNO the maximum Normal Operating or structural cruising speed, only to be exceeded with caution and in smooth conditions.

VNE the Never Exceed speed, not to be exceeded in any circumstances.

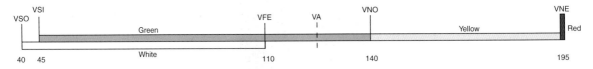

Colour coding of airspeed limitations

Key indicated airspeed (IAS) limitations and ranges are usually marked on the airspeed indicator using a system of colour coding. The following applies to a single-engine light aircraft:

White Arc	Extends from Vso to the flap limiting speed (VFE)
Green Arc	Extends from Vs1 to VNO
Yellow Arc	The 'caution' airspeed range, flight in smooth conditions only
Red Line	The VNE speed

Thus the white arc reflects the speed range for flight with the flaps lowered (the flap operating range); the green arc represents the normal operating range; the yellow arc represents the caution range and the red line represents the never exceed speed.

▶ In-Flight Precautions

To avoid the serious consequences of exceeding the aircraft's flight load limitations, the first requirement is to know the limitations both in terms of maximum flight loads and the various maximum airspeeds such as VA, VNO and VNE. This information is found in the POH/FM already described, and this is the pilot's first stop for reference. The POH/FM will also state the permitted manoeuvres and, just as importantly, any prohibited manoeuvres. Not every aircraft is suitable for flying aerobatic manoeuvres; even if it can be made to fly around an aerobatic figure, there may not be enough structural integrity to ensure that the flight load factors will not be exceeded either in the figure itself or in the recovery.

Once in flight, observing the flightload limitations is mostly a matter of common sense – respect the VA, VNO and VNE limitations and do not attempt prohibited manoeuvres. An aircraft is most likely to be overstressed by pulling back too hard on the control column at too high an airspeed, so as soon the load factor builds up the pilot must be especially aware of the flight load limitations. It is also worth noting that applying roll (via the ailerons) whilst also pulling large amounts of positive 'g' significantly increases the stress on the airframe – especially the wings.

The aircraft may be fitted with a 'g' meter which can be used to check the flight load, but this is fairly rare outside aerobatic aircraft. A 'g' meter shows the flight load value via three needles. One needle is for positive 'g' and 'sticks' at the maximum value attained until returned to zero using a reset button. One needle shows negative G in the same manner and one needle moves to show the current 'g' value. Where a 'g' meter is fitted it is a commonly accepted practice *not* to zero the 'g' meter at the end of a flight. In this way the next pilot to fly the aircraft can see what maximum positive and negative flight load was imposed on the aircraft during the previous flight. As already stated, and whether or not a 'g' meter is fitted, it is essential to have an aircraft properly inspected if it is known or thought to have been overstressed.

A typical 'g' meter, also known as an accelerometer

▶ Revision

54 For a level-flight turn, how does load factor vary with angle of bank; and what is a typical load factor for a level flight 60° angle of bank turn?

55 What does the white arc on an airspeed indicator represent?

56 What does the red line on an airspeed indicator represent?

57 What is the reference given to the maximum airspeed at which full and abrupt movement of the flying controls can be made without overstressing the aircraft structure?

Answers at page fpp69

Aircraft General Knowledge
The Airframe

Aircraft General Knowledge
The Airframe

▶ Airframe Configuration

▶ Wing Construction

▶ Wing Design

▶ Fuselage Construction

▶ Fuselage Design

▶ Modern Design Concepts

▶ Serviceability Checks

▶ The Elevator

▶ The Rudder

▶ The Ailerons

▶ Flaps

▶ Control Locks

▶ Flying Control Serviceability Checks

▶ The Undercarriage

▶ Tyres

▶ Brakes

▶ Undercarriage Serviceability Checks and Handling

▶ Revision

▶Airframe Configuration

For the purposes of this chapter, the airframe is considered as the basic structure of the aircraft – the fuselage and wings – excluding the engine and propeller.

Any average General Aviation (GA) airfield will be home to a wide variety of aircraft designs and configurations for machines essentially designed to do much the same job. If designers had found one optimum light-aircraft configuration displaying clear advantages over all others, virtually all small aeroplanes would conform to this basic shape. Because no such universal ideal has been found, the apron of a busy general-aviation airfield will contain aircraft of many different design shapes and concepts. The most common configurations are shown below:

■ Biplane. An aircraft with an upper and lower wing.

■ Monoplane. An aircraft with a single wing, now the favoured configuration for the vast majority of aircraft.

■ High-Wing. A monoplane with the wing attached over the top of the fuselage.

■ Mid-Wing. A monoplane with the wing mounted at the mid-point of the fuselage.

■ Low-Wing. A monoplane with the wing mounted underneath the fuselage.

■ Canard. A design with the horizontal tailplane placed ahead of the wing rather than behind it.

■ Tricycle Undercarriage. An undercarriage arrangement in which the mainwheels are located underneath the wing or fuselage and a nosewheel is placed under the front of the aircraft. This configuration is generally agreed to be the easiest for ground manoeuvring and handling during take-off and landing, and is found on the majority of modern aircraft.

■ Tailwheel Undercarriage. An undercarriage arrangement in which the mainwheels are located underneath the wing or fuselage and a wheel (or skid) is placed under the tail. This arrangement is still quite commonly used, particularly on modern homebuilt/kitplanes and 'sporting' aircraft. A few aircraft have a *tandem* undercarriage, with wheels under the fuselage centreline and supporting 'outriggers' under the wings.

▶ Wing Construction

The wing is designed first and foremost to provide the lift necessary to make an aircraft fly. However, in constructing the wing the constructor has to make allowance for other factors – for example, the requirement for flying controls such as ailerons and flaps to hang off the wing, and the undercarriage and fuel tanks which may become part of the wing's construction. The wing structure has to able to sustain downwards bending forces on the ground, under the weight of its own construction and any fuel in wing fuel tanks, and upwards bending forces in flight created by lift in 'positive' flight load conditions. The greater the positive load factor, the greater the upwards bending force.

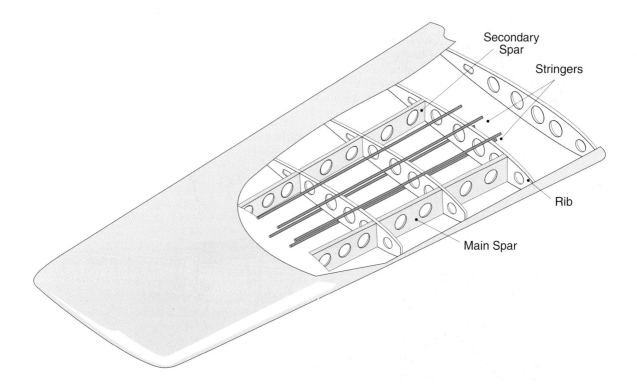

The traditional construction of a wing with main spar, secondary spar, ribs and stringers

In traditional construction, a wing is built upon a basic 'skeleton' structure. The 'backbone' or 'spine' of the wing is the *spar*. This runs the length of the wing, and in cross-section a spar usually has either an 'I' or a box section. Commonly there are two spars: the *main spar*, close to the leading edge, and the *secondary spar* behind it. Running parallel to the spar(s) there are often *stringers*. Attached across the spars and stringers are the *ribs*, which are shaped to give the wing its aerofoil section.

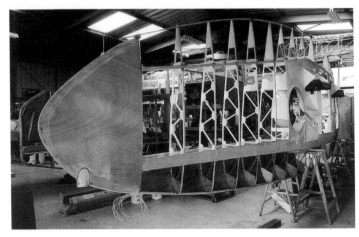

This wooden wing shows quite clearly the main spar and ribs. It is, incidentally, that of a replica Spitfire being built from plans

The basic structure of the spars and ribs then has to be covered. Many older aircraft, and one or two newer ones, have a structure of wood or metal which is then covered with fabric stretched over it. More common is a metal skin covering, riveted to the stringers and ribs. Usually an aluminium alloy, this skin is designed to take some of the loads imposed on the wing, hence the term *stressed-skin* construction. One advantage of this construction is that the internal structure of the wing can be simplified and lightened because it is no longer has to carry all the loads and stresses. Increasingly, light aircraft are following the lead set by gliders in the use of construction materials known collectively as *composites*. The term 'composite' can encompass a very wide range of materials, from the fibreglass or GRP used for many years on wing tips, fairings, wheel spats and so on to modern materials of great strength incorporating boron or carbon fibres. As a rule, composite materials can be easily formed into complex shapes (giving the designer maximum flexibility with wing design) and can be finished to give a very smooth surface, which reduces skin-friction drag. Composites also combine increased strength with reduced weight, and reductions of up to a third compared with aluminium construction are sometimes claimed. Indeed, the strength of composite materials often allow the constructor to remove much of the complex basic structure of ribs and stringers usually associated with metal or fabric-covered aircraft. The type of aircraft construction which carries all or most of the stresses in its outside skin is called a *monocoque* structure. In a *semi-monocoque* structure the strength is in the stressed skin, but it is supported on a structure of formers and stringers to give shape and rigidity.

Early aircraft had to have some form of bracing to add strength to the wing structure. This was particularly true of early biplanes, which had a profusion of wires and struts. Improvements in materials and construction techniques have reduced the need for such heavy, drag-producing items. Most modern aircraft have no external wing bracing, and such a style of construction leads to what is sometimes called a *cantilever* wing. That said, certain high-wing light aircraft such as the Cessna family have a single supporting strut, giving them a *semi-cantilever* wing.

The under-wing strut of a Citabria – a 'semi-cantilever' wing

The multiple wing struts, undercarraige struts and wire bracing of a 1920s Avro 504K

▶Wing Design

When designing an aircraft from scratch, it is the properties of the wing which will define the major performance and handling characteristics. In many ways the wing **is** the aircraft; a wing can be made to fly perfectly well without engines or even a fuselage, but a fuselage or engine without a wing won't even get off the ground. The design of the wing can be a complex affair, with many different factors to consider and inevitable compromises. But because the wing design has such a fundamental effect on the aircraft's performance and characteristics, it is necessary to know something about how a wing is designed.

Firstly, the designer has to consider the primary role for which the aircraft is intended. For most aircraft, the designer will have an idea of approximately how heavy the machine is going to be and how fast it should cruise. With these two points in mind, it is simple to calculate the wing area required to produce the necessary lift to keep the aircraft airborne. The wing area required can then be achieved either by having a long-span narrow-chord wing or one with short-span and wide-chord. Such a measure of the wing's shape is called the *aspect ratio*, which is simply the wing span divided by the average wing chord. A long, thin wing has a high aspect ratio; a short 'stubby' wing has a low-aspect-ratio.

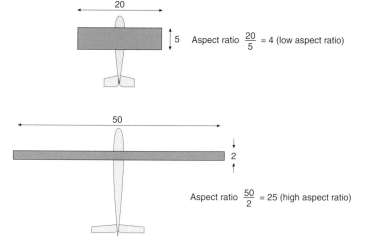

Wings of the same area but different aspect ratios

The low aspect-ratio wing of an F-104 Starfighter

A low-aspect-ratio wing is relatively easy to build, can be made very strong and is aerodynamically efficient at high speeds. A high-aspect-ratio wing displaying the requisite strength can be considerably more difficult to construct, but the increased wing span produces less induced drag (which is primarily caused by the large vortices shed at the wing tips). Induced drag is significant even in the cruise, when it may be 25% of total drag; increasing wing span by 10% cuts induced drag by almost 20%. If an aircraft is operating at the angle of attack for best range (which usually means flying more slowly than the 'normal' cruise airspeed), induced drag is an even greater proportion of the overall drag – in fact about half of total drag. So achieving a reduction in induced-drag of any magnitude is well worth the effort. Gliders spend a lot of time flying trying to achieve a maximum glide range and so their long-span wings are essential for the job they are designed to do. Similar considerations dictate the high-aspect-ratio wings of modern airliners and other high-altitude/long-range aircraft. A longer wing span also gives an aircraft better climb performance, particularly at high altitude. Aircraft mass divided by the wing span gives a figure called *span loading*. The lighter the span loading, the better the aircraft climbs and the lighter the ailerons will feel to the pilot. Taken together, these factors imply that for an aircraft designed to climb quickly, fly high and fast and have long range, a relatively high aspect-ratio wing is required.

The high aspect-ratio wing of a glider

The *planform* shape of the wing, i.e. the wing profile as viewed from directly above or directly below, also affects the wing's (and therefore the aircraft's) performance and handling. The easiest and therefore cheapest wing to build is one with a constant chord (width). Alternatively the wing can be *tapered* towards the wing tips; in other words the chord becomes more narrow as you look from fuselage to wing tip. This effectively increases the aspect ratio (because the average chord is narrower) and may confer certain performance advantages. The oft-quoted example of the advantages of tapered wings is the difference between the performance of the PA-28 'Cherokee' series with their constant chord "plank" or 'Hershey Bar' wing, and the PA-28

A constant chord, semi-tapered and tapered wing planform

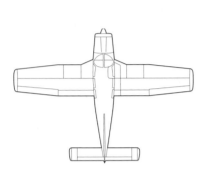

The semi-tapered wing of a PA-28 Warrior

'Warrior' which was developed from the Cherokee but has a semi-tapered wing. There are certainly some performance improvements in the Warrior, but it is often over-looked that the Warrior wing also has 3ft more span than that of the Cherokee. Where the difference in constant-chord and tapered wings is undisputed is in stalling behaviour, which we will look at shortly.

C_L for a 'thick' and 'thin' aerofoil section, note the difference in the change of C_L at the stall

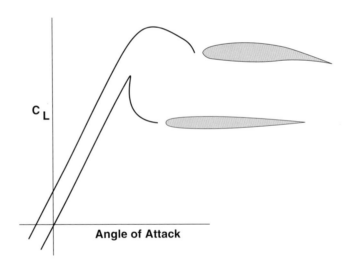

C_L

Angle of Attack

The relatively thick and gently curved aerofoil section of a Jodel wing

The wing section, i.e. the aerofoil shape, is also an important factor in performance and handling characteristics. On early aircraft, thin and cambered wings were common. Advances in design allowed wings to become thicker – not least to increase structural strength (a deeper spar was possible) and to accommodate fuel tanks, retractable undercarriages and so on. As a general rule, thick wing sections without sharp changes in curvature lead to more rounded C_L curves which do not display a marked drop at the stalling angle of attack. This implies docile and safe slow flying characteristics, at the cost of relatively 'draggy' wings with certain performance penalties.

Today, modern materials and computer-aided design are shifting the emphasis back to thinner wing sections with marked changes in curvature near the wing leading edge, especially for relatively fast aircraft. These wing sections give good performance, sometimes at the cost of less forgiving handling near the stalling angle of attack.

A training aircraft is designed to have predicable handling characteristics especially in terms of safe slow-speed handling and a docile stall behaviour with plenty of stall warning. The ideal is a wing on which airflow separation at high angles of attack begins at the rear of the inboard part of the wing. This reduces the chance of unwanted roll (and consequent yaw) developing, and also leaves the ailerons on the outboard part of the wing in clean, unstalled airflow and so still able to provide roll control.

The wing planform has a marked effect on stalling behaviour, and a constant-chord wing approaches the ideal stall characteristics described above. Airflow separation can be arranged to begin at the inner rear part of the wing, giving the pilot warning of the impending stall through the loss of lift and buffeting whilst leaving the pilot with roll control as the outer wing and ailerons remain unstalled. If a wing is tapered, airflow separation tends to begin closer to the wing tips; the more tapered the wing, the more pronounced this phenomenon tends to be. Such a situation is less than ideal, because if the outer wing stalls before the inner, loss of roll control and a sharp wing drop is virtually inevitable.

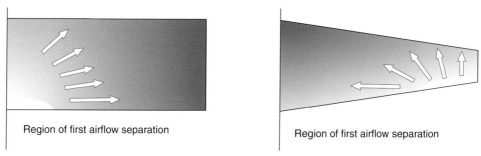

Airflow separation at the stall over a constant-chord and tapered wing

One way to ensure that the stall occurs first on the inboard section of the wing, especially in the case of a tapered wing planform, is to construct it with *washout*. Washout is a twist in the wing section. The wing's *angle of incidence* – the angle between the wing chord-line and the fuselage – is fixed by the construction of the wing and the angle at which it is bolted on to the fuselage. Washout means that there is a greater angle of incidence near the fuselage – the inboard part of the wing – than outboard near the wing tips, so the inboard section of the wing flies at a greater angle of attack than the outboard section. The result is that at high angles of attack, the inner wing will reach the stalling angle before the wing tips. This provides docile stall characteristics and plenty of stall warning.

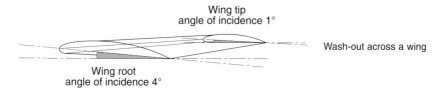

Wing tip
angle of incidence 1°

Wash-out across a wing

Wing root
angle of incidence 4°

As well as washout, the inner wing may have *stall strips* fitted to the leading edge. Stall strips 'sharpen' the leading edge, making airflow separation more likely at that point. By fitting them at the inner portion of the wing, the manufacturer is encouraging the stall to start here rather than further outboard.

Going back to the example of the PA-28 series, the PA-28 Cherokee series with its constant-chord wing has very safe and docile handling characteristics and needs considerable provocation to do stall badly – let alone to spin. The PA 28 Warrior series, with the semi-tapered wing, is not generally as tame in the stall as the plank-wing Cherokees. And unlike most Cherokee models, Warriors and other PA-28s with semi-tapered wings are **not** cleared for spinning.

On a point of interest, *sweeping* the wings also leads to airflow separation starting at the wing tips. Those few light aircraft with swept wings almost always have design features to avoid the stall altogether.

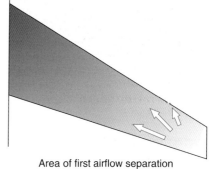

Area of first airflow separation

Airflow separation at the stall over a swept wing

There is one other aspect of wing design (and for that matter overall aircraft design) that has not been covered yet. Look at the aircraft with the 'plank' wing as opposed to that with the tapered wing. Which *looks* better, which *seems* sleeker, which would a pilot *believe* to be more modern, faster? Aircraft design is not just about aerodynamics, it is heavily influenced by marketing too.

Laminar flow | Transition point | Turbulent flow

Boundary layer transition from smooth 'laminar' flow to 'turbulent' flow

Modern design techniques enable the wing designer to make much better use of the boundary layer. The boundary layer is the layer of air passing over a surface through which the velocity slows from the 'free stream' speed, outside the influence of the object, to zero at the surface. The boundary layer over a wing will tend to start as a smooth, *laminar* flow over the leading edge. Laminar boundary layer tends to be quite thin, and to slide easily over the surface in layers, in the way that clean playing-cards in a brand-new pack slide easily past each other. A short way back across the wing, the boundary layer changes to *turbulent;* imagine this as the way that the playing-cards in an old and sticky pack tend to drag past each other. Turbulent boundary layer is a much more disturbed airflow that creates much greater resistance. In short, laminar flow creates far less drag than turbulent, and keeping the boundary layer laminar can improve aircraft performance considerably. Not surprisingly, designers looking for speed and range are very keen on doing this; with suitable sections and smooth surfaces, often achieved with composite materials, they will do their best to encourage laminar flow.

Unfortunately, because a laminar boundary layer slips so easily over a surface, it is also very quick to separate from the surface at the stall. By contrast 'sticky' turbulent boundary layer stays attached much better. So in a high angle-of-attack situation, a turbulent boundary layer is a good thing; it isn't suddenly going to detach itself from the wing without warning, taking lots of lift with it.

Laminar flow is very much the buzz-word in aircraft design – especially in homebuilt and kit aircraft. Furthermore, some modern glider designs (which are mostly far more advanced aerodynamically than powered aircraft) seem to have achieved the ideal of a wing with mostly laminar boundary layer at cruising airspeeds but turbulent flow at high angles of attack near the stall. Perhaps wings for powered aircraft will catch up in time.

Despite the best efforts of the aircraft designer, it is not always possible to design the basic wing in such a way as to persuade the airflow to behave exactly as required. As a result, wings may sprout various appendages and attachments – shaped wing tips, winglets, fences, notches and so on. The most common modifications to a wing are made at the wing tip. Modifying this part of the aeroplane is done with a view to reducing the size of the vortex shed at the tip. This will lead to a reduction in induced drag, which in design terms is a desirable goal.

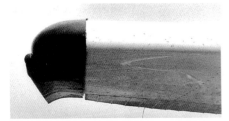

The drooped wing-tip of a Cessna 172

The Hoerner wing-tip of a Piper PA-28 Warrior

The upswept wing-tip (incorporating fuel tip-tank) of a Cessna 340

One simple modification of wing-tip shape is to 'droop' the tip, as seen on some Cessna single-engine aircraft. This droop is intended to shed the wing tip vortex outboard of the tip, which is the aerodynamic equivalent of giving the aircraft a greater wing-span. Conversely, some Cessna twin-engined aircraft have an upswept wing-tip – with the same objective of shedding the tip vortex as far outboard as possible. Some Piper singles have a distinctive 'Hoerner' wing tip; here again the upsweep on the underside encourages the vortex to move out from the tip. None of these devices has a huge effect on overall drag, but they have two distinct advantages to the aircraft manufacturer:

- they *do* seem to have some beneficial effect, and
- they look good, which helps sell aeroplanes.

The order of importance of these points to a manufacturer is open to question.

A later development in wing-tip shapes is the *winglet*. In essence this is a wing tip turned up to the vertical or nearly so. The winglet (occasionally referred to as a *tip-sail*, which describes its purpose well) acts in two ways:

- it has an aerofoil shape, which interacts with the wing-tip vortex to produce a component of lift forward, in the same direction as thrust:
- it causes the wing-tip vortex to be shed at a higher point than would otherwise be the case, reducing the downwash behind the wing and reducing the induced drag.

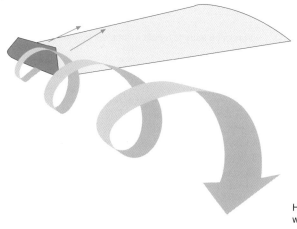

How a winglet interacts with the airflow at the wing tip

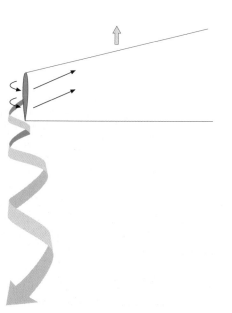

Winglets can undoubtedly give some performance improvements, particularly at slow indicated airspeeds such as during landing and take-off. They also offer benefits when cruising for range at high altitude. This is one reason why they appear on some modern airliners; a one or two per cent reduction in drag becomes significant when an aircraft consumes fuel in terms of tonnes per hour.

The aerodynamic relevance of winglets to a small aircraft is open to question and whether they provide a tangible benefit, or just look good to aircraft buyers is a matter of opinion.

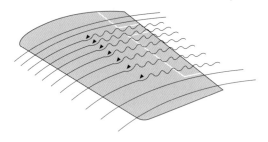

A winglet on a homebuilt Vari-eze

Vortex generators to create a turbulent boundary layer at a specific point

Aside from changing the wing-tip shape, the wing may 'grow' other appendages to encourage the airflow to do what the designer wants it to. *Vortex generators* may be found on the wings of high-speed aircraft. These small vertical plates stir up the boundary layer and create a turbulent flow behind them. At first glance this seems like an odd idea; a turbulent boundary layer creates more drag than a laminar boundary layer. But the turbulent boundary layer is also less prone to separating from the wing – and such separation can lead to high drag. Keeping the airflow attached is essential, especially at high angles of attack, and vortex generators are often placed just ahead of the ailerons or flaps to keep these control working at high angles of attack.

Other devices used to create a vortex which will delay airflow separation include *wing fences*, *vortilons*, leading-edge *notches* and the *saw-tooth* leading edge.

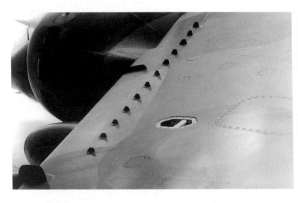

Vortex generators on the wing of a Harrier

Vortilons on the wing leading edge of a Cozee

▶Fuselage Construction

The fuselage has a role quite unlike that of the wing, and so not surprisingly its design and construction are often quite different. In principle, the fuselage of a single-engine aircraft (and some multi-engine ones) has to house the engine(s), the cockpit and cabin, various aircraft systems (possibly including fuel tanks), the undercarriage and usually the tail unit too.

Early aircraft most commonly had a 'box' section for ease of construction. *Longerons* run the length of the fuselage, with cross-bars to provide rigidity, and the whole lot could be covered in fabric. Later, more refined fuselage shapes could be made by using *bulkheads* on to which the longerons and *secondary formers* were attached. As with the wing, metal-skinned aircraft often adopt stressed-skin construction, so that some of the loads and tensions are borne by the fuselage skin. Also like the wing, composite materials allow the construction of a fuselage with a reduced load-bearing internal structure and with the skin carrying a larger proportion of the loads and stresses (a monocoque or semi-monocoque structure). Use of composite materials also gives the designer more flexibility to develop more complex but aerodynamically efficient shapes.

Bulkheads, longerons and secondary formers making up a Beagle Pup fuselage (left) and a Beaufighter fuselage (right)

▶Fuselage Design

Designing the fuselage is usually simpler than designing the wing. The vast majority of single-engine aircraft have the engine and propeller at the front, known as a *tractor* layout. The reverse arrangement, with engine and propeller at the rear, is known as a *pusher*. With the engine at the front, and usually a noseleg underneath it, the cabin comes next. There must be some provision for windows; doors for the occupants and baggage and the appropriate seats and compartments inside. Things tend to get more interesting towards the tail; conventionally there is a vertical surface for the fin (or vertical stabiliser) and rudder, and a horizontal surface for the tailplane (or horizontal stabiliser) and elevator.

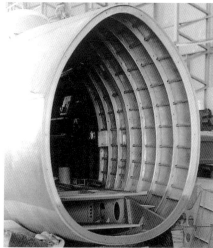

Marketing versus aerodynamics. Note the severely swept fin of this Osprey II amphibian (average cruising speed 90 knots)...

Certain aspects of the rear fuselage give the designer problems. A short fuselage means reduced weight and – because there is less airframe for the air to flow over – less drag. However, the tail surface and controls need to be a certain distance from the CG to provide the necessary stability and control. The principles of leverage and moments arise. In essence an aircraft can have small surfaces a long way from the CG or larger ones closer to the CG to achieve the same effect.

...and by contrast the 'straight' fin Mooney 20, average cruising speed 130 knots

Ventral strakes visible under the fuselage of a TB10 Tobago

Firstly, let's look at the fin (vertical stabiliser). The vast majority of light aircraft have a swept fin. According to the aerodynamicists, there is no advantage whatsoever to a swept fin at light-aircraft speeds. In fact, excessive sweep of the fin can cause problems in spin recovery; depending on the sweep of the fin and the relative position of the tailplane and elevator, the rudder may become 'blanked' or shielded from the airflow. However, it looks good and helps to sell aircraft. Of course, before an aircraft goes on sale, it will have been extensively tested and cleared (or not) to spin, and the tail configuration is the sort of factor a test pilot will take into account. An aircraft with a Certificate of Airworthiness will have undergone more intensive testing than a 'permit to fly' homebuilt or kitplane. But either way, if the POH/FM says the aircraft is not to be spun, don't spin or attempt to spin it.

The rear fuselage may also have vertical surfaces under the fuselage – often called *ventral strakes*. These are usually there to improve stability in yaw, particularly at high angles of attack such as in stall/spin situations.

The tailplane (or horizontal stabilator) and elevator can be positioned at different points on and near the vertical tail. The most common design is the low tailplane. This is simplest arrangement from the structural point of view and tends to prevail. Less commonly, the tailplane may be placed at a mid-point on the fin, although moving it here introduces structural complications, increasing the structure (and therefore the weight) of the tail assembly.

The 'conventional' tailplane of a Cessna 172

The mid-mounted tailplane of a Rockwell Commander 114

The other option open to designers is to place the tailplane right at the top of the fin, giving the so-called *T-tail*. There are one or two good reasons for adopting a T-tail (spin recovery characteristics being one). However, as a package, the tailplane and associated structure usually has to be extensively modified (to no obvious advantage) in order to sit atop the fin. The T-tail has caught on for light aircraft and is now regarded as a passing fashion, less common on aircraft being designed and built today.

The T-tail of a Robin 3000

▶Modern Design Concepts

The majority of production general-aviation aircraft in use today originate from basic designs that can be traced back several decades. The economic and legal factors applying to general-aviation aircraft manufacture favour traditional designs, and in any event production aircraft with radically different design features have tended to be poorly received by business buyers. By contrast, the market for home-built aircraft and 'kitplanes' (where the manufacturer provides major components ready-built) has expanded steadily in the last decades, driven largely by innovative designs. Such machines are readily available to private pilots, and often offer significant performance gains over production aircraft, so some of the common design concepts are worth looking at.

Many modern high-performance light aircraft are designed and constructed to promote the maximum possible laminar boundary-layer flow over the surfaces. A laminar boundary layer causes much less drag than a turbulent boundary layer, and this drag reduction leads to a significant improvement in performance – especially in terms of cruising speed. Composite materials are commonly used, because they are capable of being moulded into relatively complex shapes to encourage laminar flow and can be finished to give a very smooth surface. This in turn reduces skin friction and avoids lumps and bumps which can trip laminar flow into turbulent flow. On the downside, any blemishes on the surface can have an extremely adverse effect on lift and drag. One aircraft type relying heavily on laminar flow was reported to have encountered control problems after flying into rain as a result of water droplets attaching to the skin and breaking up the smooth surface. In another case, an owner unwisely painted wide stripes on the wings of his home-built aircraft; the roughening caused by the paint prevented the aircraft from getting airborne from a 2000m runway. By the same token, some high performance kitplanes have a reputation for unpredictable stalling behaviour as the laminar flow tends to separate more readily and with less warning than turbulent flow. Such quirks are largely dependent on many factors of the aircraft's design, and are yet another reason why any pilot contemplating flying a new aircraft type should pay close and careful attention to the POH/FM and the advice of pilots experienced on the type. A dual check, if possible, is also a good idea.

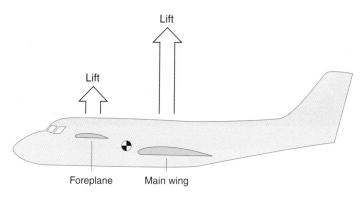

The arrangement of lift and weight forces on a canard

The *canard* design, which involves a lifting surface (a mini-wing or foreplane) ahead of the main wing, is often quoted as a modern innovation – ignoring the fact that the first powered aircraft to fly, the Wright 'Flyer', was a canard! The foreplane of a canard replaces the conventional tailplane. On aircraft configured in the conventional and time-honoured way, the tailplane produces a download in flight due to the arrangement of the lift and weight forces. Because the foreplane of a canard is located ahead of the CG, it supplements the 'positive' lift of the main wing. So in theory the canard can produce more lift and less drag that an aircraft with a conventional tailplane, leading to improvements in cruise performance. In practice, the improvements in performance are not always so clear-cut. Because of the location of the foreplane ahead of the CG, it is de-stabilising. This means that often a canard's CG range is quite limited. The main wing flies in the wake of the canard, which will reduce the lift it can produce and moreover, the foreplane *must* be made to stall before the main wing. If the main wing stalls whilst the foreplane is still un-stalled, the aircraft will inevitably pitch up and recovery may be impossible – not very helpful. The designer will therefore have to look very carefully at behaviour in the approach to stall. 'Fixes' such as setting the foreplane at a higher angle of incidence than the main wing (to ensure that it reaches the stalling angle of attack before the main wing) and limiting the available up-elevator movement may be incorporated. Such measures will tend to lead to 'quasi-stalls', where the aircraft mushes down at a moderate rate of descent rather than entering a full stall. Such behaviour can be interpreted as implying that the aircraft is stall-proof, though in fact virtually all aircraft of this layout have been manoeuvred into stalls – if only by determined mis-handling and loading the aircraft outside permitted mass and CG limits. The 'fixes' used to modify or avoid the stall in a canard invariably increase the stall/minimum-control airspeed, leading to a consequent increase in take-off and landing distances. Most canards are not renowned for particularly good short-field performance.

In the quest for drag reduction, designers look for ways of reducing the surface area of the aircraft because less surface area means less skin friction. One obvious target is the large tail surface of a conventional fin and rudder, and abolishing this leads to the so-called 'tail-less' aircraft. These tend to have swept wings, chiefly because a swept wing increases stability in roll. Sweeping the wing also allows any remaining vertical surfaces to be placed on or adjacent to the wing tips and thereby ensures that they are located behind the CG – as they must be in order to make a positive contribution to directional stability. If the pitch-control surfaces are attached to the wing (as they usually are in a tail-less aircraft) sweeping the wing also places these well behind the CG. One might add that swept wings also have the priceless advantage of looking particularly sleek amongst a crowd of straight-wing aircraft. This is despite the fact that swept wings in themselves display little aerodynamic merit or benefit unless they are attached to an aircraft designed for flight in excess of Mach 0·8 (500kts or thereabouts).

A pusher-propeller

Another reason why the designer might consider a tail-less aircraft is to incorporate a pusher propeller. Having the propeller at the back of the aircraft, pushing the aircraft rather than pulling it as a front-mounted propeller does, has several theoretical advantages. One of the principal benefits of a pusher propeller is that it avoids the extra drag created by the high-speed and turbulent propeller slipstream passing over the fuselage and wings. Of course, it also reduces the contribution that slipstream can make to lift as it passes the wing, and elevator and possibly rudder effectiveness may be reduced. But in aircraft design an advantage gained in one area will often be compromised by drawbacks elsewhere. Pusher propellers are often used in canard and swept-wing designs, where rear-mounted engine can have a beneficial effect on CG location.

A canard Vari-eze, incorporating a pusher propeller, swept wing and no conventional tail (but winglets/fins and rudders at the wing tips)

The foregoing is intended to give a basic grounding in some of the main design concepts increasingly used in modern aircraft design. There is no denying some of the benefits of these innovations, not least when an aircraft powered by a 200hp engine can achieve cruise speeds of close to 200kts – an improvement of at least 40% on more conventional designs with the same powerplant. However, it also has to be recognised that some of these aircraft possess noticeably less forgiving and tolerant handling qualities than those of the average training/touring aircraft, and more restrictive loading limitations. **A thorough check-out and a briefing on individual idiosyncrasies in handling behaviour are essential when converting to any new type**, and never more so than when the aircraft has 'innovative' design features.

▶ Serviceability Checks

The *pre-flight check,* also known as the *walkround,* is the pilot's opportunity to inspect the aircraft structure before flight. During the pre-flight check, the close inspection of sundry ports, drains, hinges and so on sometimes leads to a tendency to forget to look at the overall shape and integrity of the airframe itself – a classic case of not seeing the wood for the trees. The following are some basic danger signs to look for in the airframe structure itself when inspecting an aircraft.

In a metal-covered airframe, the skin almost invariably takes some of the flight loads and stresses imposed on the aircraft. If the aircraft has been overstressed in some way – by exceeding the permitted load factor, for example, or by a heavy landing – this may manifest itself as 'wrinkles' in the skin. Any such signs, no matter how minor, are not to be ignored because they may indicate far more serious damage to the aircraft's internal structure. Metal aircraft may also show signs of corrosion in the form of 'bubbled' and flaking paint. If there is the slightest doubt about any corrosion seen, it should be reported to the operator or an engineer. It is also worth noting that certain ground handling practices (such as pushing down on the tailplane to manoeuvre an aircraft) can result in overstressing the structure if done incorrectly. Many pilots of Cessna single-engine types pay particular attention to the tailplane during their pre-flight inspection for this reason alone.

Metal-skinned aircraft often have drainage holes in the bottom of the fuselage to allow water entering the rear fuselage to flow out. Check that any such drain holes are clear; especially in wet and cold weather, water can get into the fuselage and freeze there, which is not good for the health of the structure. Whilst looking over the aircraft, check for loose or 'pulled' rivets which might indicate overstressing, and ensure that any screws or 'Dzus' fasteners holding on panels, cowlings, fairings and the like are secure.

The generally stained and tatty appearance of this aircraft, and the long grass under it, suggests an aircraft that has not flown for some considerable time

An aircraft, or portions of it, may be covered with fabric rather than metal. Here again, apparently minor wrinkles, looseness, cuts or rips in the covering require further inspection, because they may indicate more serious damage to the aircraft structure. This is an essential point worth reiterating. There have been a number of accidents and incidents where a pilot has discovered minor external damage after striking an obstruction on the ground, and decided to fly again. In at least one such case the result was the in-flight break-up of the aircraft on the subsequent flight. The static strength the designer builds into the structure is designed to cope with a range of expected ground and flight loads (this is often done by loading a structure on a test rig with increasing weight until it fails). However, even a relatively minor collision on the ground can exceed these static strength limits if it afflicts a particular spot or produces an excessive force in a particular direction. Aircraft constructed of wood and fabric are best not left in the open for long periods in wet conditions. If looking over such an aircraft, be especially vigilant for signs for water ingress; amongst many other things, this can lead directly to rotting of the primary structure. This is not desirable.

A Europa motorglider, constructed mostly from composite materials

Aircraft made from composite materials are subject to rather different considerations from those applying to metal/wooden/fabric flying machines. One major problem for an aircraft of composite construction can be *temperature*. Fibreglass is generally considered to be the most sensitive of the composite materials to excess heat – a few hours of direct sunshine on a hot summer day can be enough to make a fibreglass structure lose 25% of its cold strength. This is one reason why composite aircraft tend to be painted in white or very light colours; heat absorption is thereby reduced. Many modern composite materials react better to high temperatures and may be safe to surface temperatures of 70°C or more. However, this is the temperature of the *surface* itself, in direct sunlight this will be much higher than the *air* temperature. If flying an aircraft with a GRP or composite structure, carefully check the POH/FM for the highest air temperature in which the aircraft is certified for flight, this value may be as low as 30°C.

Apart from temperature considerations, stress or impact damage may show on a composite surface as cracks or gashes. These may indicate much more extensive damage to the airframe than might be expected and the previous comments apply. Composite material may also suffer delamination, when one of the layers (plies) of a laminated material separates. To check if an area has delaminated, try tapping it with the edge of a coin. This should produce a clear ringing sound, whereas a dull thud indicates delamination. As with any other aircraft damage, if in doubt ask for an engineer to examine the suspect area before flight.

A universal illness suffered by all aeroplanes irrespective of their construction is so-called 'hangar rash'. This is the usual reason for the scratches, dents and grazes which appear on an aircraft with the passing of the years. Such minor damage is fairly easy to inflict, especially if the machine resides in hanger with lots of other aircraft. Careless manoeuvring, people squeezing past bits of aeroplane and attempts to make just a *tiny* bit more space are all to blame. As a rule, the extremities of the aircraft are most prone to hangar rash – wing tips, leading and trailing edges, the tail, the propeller and spinner. Pay particular attention to these areas during the pre-flight check – and don't be afraid to ask questions.

As a final point, the underneath of the aircraft (especially the underside of the fuselage) often receives no more than a passing glance during the pre-flight check, not least because it is dirty and difficult to get to. For this reason alone, it is worth making a conscious effort to check this area as any problems here may go undetected for a very long time, and certainly longer than elsewhere on the airframe.

▶ The Elevator

In the vast majority of conventional aircraft, control in pitch is obtained via a movable surface (the 'elevator') usually attached to the horizontal tailplane, although in some cases the entire tailplane moves instead. The elevator is controlled by the control column in the cockpit, to which it is linked by a series of cables and pulleys. Pulling the control column back moves the elevator up, altering the camber of the horizontal tail and creating 'lift' downwards. This in turn causes the tail to move down and consequently the nose to move up, as the aircraft pitches nose-up around the centre of gravity (CG). Moving the control column forward moves the elevator down, creating lift up at the tail. This causes the tail to rise and the nose to fall, as the aircraft pitches nose-down around the centre of gravity (CG).

In essence, the elevators allow the pilot to alter the angle of attack of the wings. As such, they are the primary means of preventing the wing from reaching the stalling angle of attack, or recovering from the stall if it occurs. Provided the aircraft is within its permitted CG range, it should be almost impossible for the tailplane and elevator to stall before the wing does. So the pilot always has the means to recover from an excessive angle of attack.

The elevator will be fitted with a trimmer to help the pilot remove excessive control loads in flight. The trimmer is usually in the form of a small control surface (a trim tab) fitted to the trailing edge of the elevator and controlled from a trim wheel or lever in the cockpit. Once set, a simple trim tab maintains its position relative to the control surface. Sometimes, the trimming function is carried out by a spring within the elevator control linkages as found for example on the Piper PA-38 Tomahawk.

The tailplane/elevator combination is the most common method of pitch control. However, it is also possible to engineer a system in which the entire tailplane can move – it is known unsurprisingly as the *all-moving tailplane*, or *stabilator*. This arrangement provides a very powerful pitch control which allows a wide CG range without the need to place the tailplane at the end of a very long fuselage to give the necessary leverage. Indeed, because this method of pitch control is so powerful and tends to lead to overly 'light' controls, a tab at the rear of the stabilator is geared so that it moves in the same direction as the surface which 'damps' the movement of the control and hence provides extra control force. This tab is the anti-balance or anti-servo tab. On the Piper Cherokee/Warrior family, all of which make use of stabilators, the anti-balance or anti-servo tab is also connected to the trimmer control in the cockpit and is also used to trim the stabilator in the conventional sense.

A more rare tailplane configuration is the *butterfly* tail, in which two tailplanes and control surfaces form a shallow 'V' shape. These act as the horizontal and vertical tail and the movable surfaces are interconnected in such a way as to provide both elevator and rudder control. The main

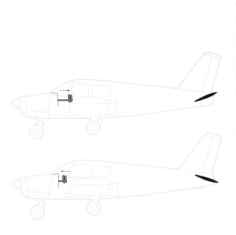

An all-moving tailplane (stabilator)

The butterfly (V) tail of a Beech V35 Bonanza

advantage usually claimed is a reduction in weight and drag, but nevertheless the best-known light aircraft to use this arrangement (the Beech Bonanza) later reverted to the more conventional fin/rudder and tailplane/elevator configuration.

Conventional elevators may make use of both horn balances and mass balances as already described in the 'Principles of Flight' section.

▶ The Rudder

With the exception of the 'V' tail just described, the rudder is always a conventional control attached to the rear of the fin (or vertical stabiliser). The rudder is operated through the rudder pedals. Pressing the left pedal deflects the rudder to the left. The change in camber of the fin/rudder produces lift in the horizontal plane, and the aircraft will yaw to the left around the centre of gravity. Pressing the right rudder pedal yaws the aircraft to the right. As with the elevator, the use of both a horn balance to aid the movement of the rudder and a mass balance to prevent flutter is quite common.

The fin may have a 'fillet' running up to its leading edge, usually referred to as a *dorsal fin*. The dorsal fin improves stability in yaw, particularly in a sideslip. Because in essence the fin is only a wing in the vertical plane, it is quite possible to stall the fin and rudder if its stalling angle of attack is exceeded. In the case of the fin/rudder, such a stall may indeed happen at extreme angles of slip: the pilot will probably first detect a lessening of the foot load on the rudder pedal, followed by the pedal moving to its limit of travel as the rudder 'locks' over at full deflection. A dorsal fin helps to prevent such an occurrence, which is rare in modern aircraft designs in any case.

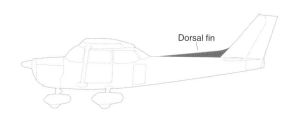

A dorsal fin

The dorsal fin of a Cessna 182RG (RG meaning Retractable Gear)

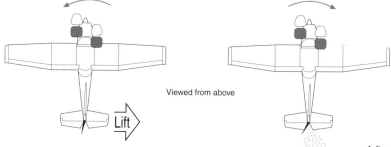

Viewed from above

When the fin/rudder stalls

A fin stall, which will lead to the loss of directional control

The rudder may have a trim tab, or a spring trim in the control linkages, so that the pilot can trim-out high control forces. This may be particularly necessary on a high-powered aircraft requiring a lot of rudder to stay in balance at high power settings and slow airspeeds. More commonly, a light aircraft may have a simple plate attached to the rear of the rudder, which can be bent by hand to deflect the control surface. The adjustment of such a trim surface must be done on the ground and the adjustment is very much a matter of trial and error, making a test flight, then a small adjustment, then checking the effect in flight again. A disadvantage of a 'bendable' tab such as this is that it can only provide trim at one particular airspeed/power combination; at all other times footwork will be required. So setting a bendable trim-tab to counter forces in the climb after take-off will probably mean that constant rudder force is required in the cruise. Most commonly a bendable tab is used to balance control forces in the cruise – because this is what the aircraft spends most of its airborne time doing.

The vast majority of light aircraft have a single fin/rudder assembly on the rear fuselage. A small number of aircraft are *twin-tailed* – that is they have two vertical tails and rudders. Apart from looking a bit different, this arrangement in itself holds no particular advantages or vices from the handling point of view, at least not in the case of the single-engine aircraft.

The twin vertical tail surfaces of a French Broussard

▶The Ailerons

The ailerons, located at the outboard trailing edge of each wing, control the aircraft in roll. Moving the control column to the left causes the left aileron to move upwards (reducing lift on the left wing) and the right aileron to move downwards (increasing lift on the right wing). As a result of this lift differential, the aircraft rolls around its CG to the left.

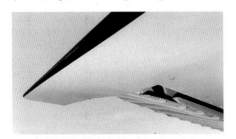

The Frise aileron with mass balance of a Cessna 152

As with the other flying controls, ailerons may have horn balances (although these are quite rare on modern aircraft) and mass balance. The mass balance is more common, because ailerons are more prone to flutter than the other flying controls. It is worth noting here that damage to a flying control, such as an aileron, can be the cause of flutter. Even an apparently insignificant dent or crease on the trailing edge of an aileron has been known to lead to unexpected control problems.

Devices such as differential aileron deflection and Frise ailerons are used to reduce adverse yaw when the ailerons are deflected. Despite these devices, a degree of adverse yaw still tends to occur and is especially pronounced in aircraft with high aspect ratios; sailplanes and motor gliders are particularly prone to displaying the phenomenon on a grand scale if the pilot's co-ordination is less than perfect. The further the ailerons are deflected (i.e. the further the control column is moved left or right) the greater the adverse yaw, but once the ailerons are centralised as the aircraft reaches the desired angle of bank, the adverse yaw will mostly disappear. Although adverse yaw is not a significant factor at cruising speeds in a modern aircraft, in an older aircraft (or any glider) it is much more evident. Adverse yaw (or aileron drag) becomes more important near the stall, when it can encourage an out-of-balance condition which increases the chance of a wing drop. The use of aileron to correct roll near and at the stall has already been discussed. Whether or not using the ailerons really can stall the wing is a matter of contention, but in general the best advice is to control yaw with rudder near the stall and not use aileron to correct roll until the wing is unstalled.

If the ailerons on a light aircraft possess any form of trim system, it will usually be of the 'bendable plate' type and similar remarks to those made in respect of the same device on the rudder apply.

An alternative method of roll control, not often found on light aircraft, is the spoiler (described earlier). For example the twin-engine MU-2 relies solely on spoilers for roll control. This allows the entire trailing edge of the wing to be used for flaps, thus allowing the high-wing loading MU-2 to attain reasonably slow take-off and landing speeds, so improving short-field performance. Spoilers can also be used as airbrakes, as previously described.

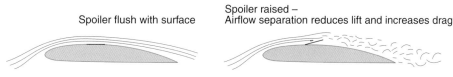

Spoiler flush with surface

Spoiler raised –
Airflow separation reduces lift and increases drag

Spoilers reduce lift and increase drag, making them particularly effective for roll control at high speeds

▶ Flaps

Most (but by no means all) aircraft designs include some form of trailed edge flaps along the wings to improve slow speed behaviour and reduce take-off and – in particular – landing distances. Unlike the three primary flying controls (elevator, rudder and aileron), which are invariably mechanically operated in a light aircraft, flaps may well be electrically driven. The implication is that in the case of an electrical failure, an aircraft with 'electric' flaps (such as most Cessna types) will not be able to use them. Because flaps have such a powerful effect on the wing's lift and drag, the flaps on each wing are interlocked so that they always move symmetrically and so do not affect roll or yaw. Should flaps deploy asymmetrically, they will cause an extremely strong rolling and yawing force which may require full opposite aileron and rudder to counter.

Because of the powerful effect of flaps, the aircraft's load-factor limits are usually reduced when flaps are extended. Also, the extension of flaps and flight with flap extended, will be limited to an airspeed known as V_{fe}. Exceeding V_{fe} with flaps down, or lowering flaps when faster than V_{fe}, can put excessive loads on the flap mechanism. If the flaps are overly abused, especially over a period of time, there is a danger that one will one day fall off the aircraft. The effect on controllability will be even worse than for asymmetric flap deflection, so it is wise not to abuse the flaps and respect the V_{fe} speed.

Slots (permanent gaps in a wing or control surface) are quite rare because although they work well at slow airspeeds, there is a significant drag penalty in the cruise. The slat is a more practical device because it can be retracted flush with the leading edge in the cruise. Slats may move out automatically on a spring at slow airspeeds – the most usual option if fitted to a light aircraft – or may be controlled by the pilot. However, despite their advantages, the weight and complexity of adding slats to a wing means that they are relatively rare on small aeroplanes. One exception is the French 'Rallye' aircraft, whose benign slow-speed characteristics resulting from automatically extending slats have earned it the nickname of the "Tin Parachute".

There are a very limited number of light aircraft fitted with airbrakes in the form of flat plates that extend out vertically from the wing's surface. It is particularly important with these controls that they lock properly in the closed position, as inadvertent operation during a critical flight phase (e.g. just after take-off) could clearly cause a serious problem.

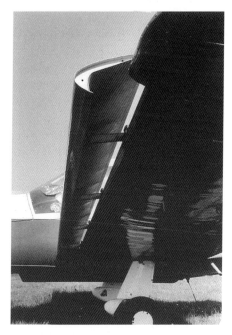

A moving slat (controlled by springs and so extending/retracting automatically) on a Rallye wing

▶Control Locks

Aircraft may be fitted with both internal and external *control locks*. Internal locks should be made physically obvious (for example by including a warning plate that covers the starter switch), so they cannot be missed in the cockpit checks; nevertheless, more than one pilot has tried to get airborne with the internal control locks still in place. External control locks normally have a red flag or streamer to signal their presence, but again a careful pre-flight check and adherence to the aircraft's checklist is the best way to avoid the danger of trying to get airborne with the controls locked solidly in position.

A cockpit control lock will often have a device, such as the plate here which covers the magneto switches and Master Switch, to make it difficult for even the most careless pilot to miss it. Nevertheless, one or two have succeeded

An external control lock on an aileron, unfortunately without a red warning streamer to make it more visible

The control locks are provided primarily to prevent damage to the flying controls as a result of the movable surfaces being banged about by strong winds or jet blast when the aircraft is parked. Use of control locks is highly recommended when an aircraft is parked outside, because the damage that can be caused to control linkages by such onslaughts may not be immediately apparent during a normal pre-flight inspection.

▶Flying Control Serviceability Checks

As part of the walkround pre-flight checks, the condition and movement of the flying controls can be inspected. Being located at the extremities of the airframe, the control surfaces are particularly vulnerable to dents and other damage – so-called hangar rash. Treat any damage found with some caution, no matter how minor it might seem. Seek out somebody suitably qualified to look it over if unsure. If in doubt, shout.

Apart from any visible control-surface damage, check the control for the presence of mass balances if they should be there – it isn't unknown for them to fall off in flight. Also, even apparently slight damage to the trailing edge of a control surface may cause potentially serious flutter, particularly in the case of the aileron. In moving the controls, take great care not to bang them around or force them against the stops. There are usually two sets of control stops to prevent the control being moved beyond its set limits; one is at the surface itself and one somewhere on the cockpit controls. Normally the stop at the surface should be encountered first to prevent excessive control movement. The flying controls are designed to be moved from the control column and rudder pedals, *not* from the outside, and so over-enthusiastic waggling of the surfaces against their stops is the sort of thing engineers don't like. Note also that if the rudder is directly linked to the nosewheel (as it is, for example, on many Piper single-engine types), it will probably not be possible to move it with the aircraft stationary – and forcing it to move may damage the control linkages. Likewise, electrically-operated flaps cannot normally be moved manually from their selected positions.

The underside of the wing and flaps near the main undercarriage can suffer from damage caused by stones and debris thrown up by the wheels. If the aircraft has been operating from a wet, soft surface, there may be a coating of mud on the underneath of the wing and flap. This is not necessarily a cause for major concern, but mud in the control gaps and linkages may freeze at altitude and restrict the movement of the control. Check any drainage holes in the control surfaces. Water can easily get in, especially if the aeroplane has been parked outside in heavy rain, and may even freeze into a solid block. This can have various undesirable consequences.

A castellated nut with cotter pin, properly secured

Mud thrown up on the underneath of a wing and flap

Some parts of the control linkages and hinges may be visible during the pre-flight checks. Where nuts and bolts are used to secure the flying control and its cables or push rods, a castellated nut is often used. This nut is tightened on the bolt, after which a wire or *cotter pin* is passed through a hole drilled in the bolt and turned over. When inspecting this type of arrangement, make sure the locking wire or cotter pin is in place. Otherwise the nut could 'unwind' off the bolt. Control cables may also have turnbuckles for adjusting cable length and tension. Once adjusted, a turnbuckle should be wirelocked and no more than three threads of the terminals should be visible either side of the turnbuckle body.

The flying controls are checked for full, free and correct movement during the pre-starting checks. The elevators and ailerons can be checked for full movement in the correct sense, being usually visible from the cockpit. Likewise the elevator trimmer can usually be visually checked if it is of the trim-tab type. Remember that when the control wheel is trimmed nose-down, the trim tab moves up and *vice versa*. The flaps are normally checked for symmetrical operation (this is particularly important) and to see that any cockpit indicator agrees with the approximate deflection of the flaps. If the rudder is directly linked to the nosewheel and so cannot be checked whilst stationary, it can be checked for full and correct movement during taxying.

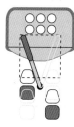

Moving a control 'stick' around the extremes of its movement, simultaneously checking the rudder pedals

During the pre-take-off checks, the emphasis is on the full and free movement of the controls and that the trimmer and flaps are set in the correct take-off positions. A trim tab on the elevator can usually be checked visually to ensure that it is set as required; likewise, the position of the flaps once set for take-off can be checked from the cockpit. The best way to check for full and free movement of the flying controls at this stage is to move the control column/control wheel 'around the box' – i.e. to each extremity of its movement – whilst moving the rudder pedals to their extremes (if possible). This will reveal any blockages, such as those caused by a flightboard on the pilot's lap or the knees of a front-seat passenger.

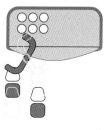

Moving a control 'wheel' around the extremes of its movement, simultaneously checking the rudder pedals

▶The Undercarriage

Aircraft can operate on hard or unprepared surfaces using tyres, on water using floats and even on snow and ice using skis. Here we will concentrate on 'conventional' undercarriage systems incorporating undercarriage legs, wheels and tyres and some form of braking system.

The undercarriage legs are more than simply the means of attaching the wheels to the aircraft. As well as providing enough height clearance to keep the airframe and propeller clear of the ground, there has to be some form of shock-absorption system to cushion the loads placed on the undercarriage – particularly during landing.

There have been many different types of shock-absorption systems used in undercarriages over the years, starting with springs, elastic bungees and simple rubber blocks. Today the two most common systems are *spring leaf* undercarriage legs (such as those used on Cessna single-engined aircraft) and *oleo* undercarriage legs.

In the air   On the ground

The principle of a 'spring leaf' undercarriage leg, which bends to absorb loads

A 'spring leaf'
undercarriage leg

Spring leaf or *spring steel* undercarriage legs are nothing more sophisticated than metal bars or tubes bolted on to the airframe with a wheel at the end. When a force is placed on such a structure, it bends a little – just as a metal ruler or a springboard will bend slightly if you put a heavy weight at one end. When the force is removed, the structure returns to its original shape. The simplicity of a structure of this kind makes it cheap, light and easy to maintain, and it is considerably stronger than it looks!

A tubular steel undercarriage leg that absorbs loads in the same way as a 'spring leaf' type

The oleo-undercarriage leg of a Piper PA-28

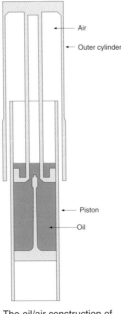

← Air

← Outer cylinder

← Piston

← Oil

The oil/air construction of an oleo

An oleo-type undercarriage leg incorporates a piston and cylinder assembly. In flight, with no load on the oleo, the lower piston end – attached to the wheel – drops down to its full extent. The piston is hollow and filled with oil; the cylinder above is hollow and filled with air. Between the two is a narrow opening. On landing, the aircraft's weight pushes the piston into the cylinder, forcing oil through the small aperture; this transfer of oil under pressure absorbs the landing load placed on the undercarriage leg. As the piston and the oil within it moves up into the cylinder above, the air in the cylinder is compressed. This absorbs the normal taxying loads. The action is not dissimilar to that of trying to compress a bicycle pump. As the air is forced through a narrow opening at the end of the pump, much of the energy (pressure) applied is absorbed and more and more force is needed to compress the pump.

Some aircraft use a combination of the two forms of construction, with spring-leaf undercarriage legs joined by an oleo strut.

An oleo-type undercarriage leg may have *torque links* (sometimes also called *scissors* because of their profile) joining the cylinder and piston halves of the oleo. The torque links keep the wheel straight by preventing the piston, and the wheel attached to it, rotating freely. Without the torque links the wheel could rotate through 360°, which would make for some very interesting landings!

The nosewheel on many tricycle-undercarriage aircraft is steerable, operated from the rudder pedals directly by rods and cables or via linking springs. The requirement to make the nosewheel capable of being steered adds a certain geometric complication to the structure and introduces the possibility of nosewheel *shimmy*. Shimmy is a high-frequency oscillation of the nosewheel in the yawing plane, which usually occurs at certain speeds and is felt as a marked vibration or shuddering through the airframe and rudder pedals. To eradicate nosewheel shimmy, the nosewheel assembly may be fitted with a *shimmy damper*. This is essentially another piston and cylinder assembly which damps out the rapid vibration associated with shimmy. It does not interfere with normal steering.

If the aircraft has direct nosewheel steering (usually through rods or cables linked to the rudder pedals) the angle of the nosewheel is controlled directly by the position of the rudder pedals. This means that when the aircraft is stationary, the rudder pedals cannot be moved at all without using excessive force. This is not recommended. Likewise, at slow taxying speeds the nosewheel steering can be very heavy. If the rudder pedals act on the nosewheel via springs, the full movement of the pedals is still available when stationary. However, some pilots find that once on the move, the 'spring' steering is less precise than when there is a rigid link between the rudder pedals and the nosewheel. Where springs are used in the nosewheel steering system, it is not unusual for the nosewheel to be steerable through a fairly small arc – say 10° either side of straight-ahead – and then castor freely to a greater angle, say 30°.

On some aircraft the nosewheel is completely free-castoring (i.e. not mechanically steered), in which case direction is controlled solely through differential braking of the main wheels.

'Scissors' torque link on a undercarriage leg

The piston and cylinder arrangement of a shimmy damper

The nosewheel of this Cessna 150 is steered via cables and springs from the rudder pedals to the push rods (visible)

▶ Tyres

The tyres on an aircraft have a very different task compared with their counterparts on road-going vehicles. On the one hand they cover a very limited mileage, and in flight they do nothing at all except contribute to drag and weight. Conversely, when they are in use – and especially during landing – the loads they endure can be extreme. The average

tyre on even a light aircraft spins up from zero to perhaps as much as 100mph in the space of a few feet, and simultaneously makes the transition from supporting no load at all to supporting the entire weight of the aircraft. Unsurprisingly, aircraft tyres are quite different in material and construction from those on a car.

The standard 'ribbed' tread of an aircraft tyre

Most modern aircraft tyres have a *ribbed* tread, which amounts to parallel longitudinal grooves in the tyre rubber – a pattern which has been found to be the most effective for grip in aircraft operations. Clearly the tyre has to have enough tread to do its job, and the overall condition and correct inflation are all-important.

One operational consideration regarding tyres is *aquaplaning*, which is considered in more detail later.

▶ Brakes

Apart from a handful of vintage aircraft which have tailskids to slow them down, all land-based aircraft have some form of braking system acting on the main wheels. In principle the brakes work by producing a frictional force within the brake unit attached to a wheel. It is well known that friction produces heat, and in practical terms it can be said that the brakes turn the kinetic energy of a moving aircraft into heat. The harder the braking, the more heat is produced.

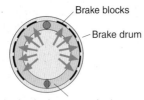

Activating brake presses brake
blocks against brake drum

The principle of a 'drum' brake

The first practical design used on aircraft was the *drum* brake. In this, a brake block inside the drum is pressed against its inner face, creating the friction needed to slow the wheel. A feature of drum-type brakes is the phenomenon of 'fading'. Fading occurs when the drum expands away from the brake blocks as the brakes become hot after prolonged application. This makes braking action less effective which will always tend to happen during very heavy brake application – such as the end of the runway looms up, for example. Variations on the drum brake were used for many years until the speed and weight of aircraft increased to the extent that a new braking system had to be devised.

The brakes used on almost all modern aircraft are of the *disc* type. In this design, a brake disc is attached to the wheel so that it rotates with it. Either side of the disc are brake *linings* or *pads*. When the brake is applied, the pads press against the disk and generate the required friction. Disc brakes are generally acknowledged to be more effective than drum brakes, and do not usually suffer from fading when they get hot.

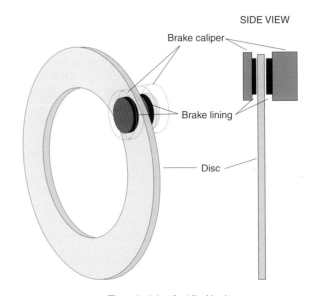

The principle of a 'disc' brake

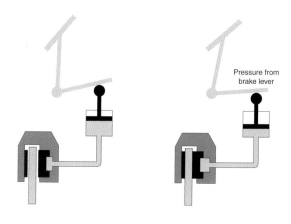

Pressure from
brake lever

A simple hydraulic system, used here to control
the brakes

Whatever design of brake is fitted to the aircraft, the pilot needs some way of activating brakes and controlling the degree of braking action. Although simple cable connections and even compressed-air pneumatic systems have been used for the purpose, the vast majority of aircraft use some form of *hydraulic* system. In the cockpit there will be a 'master' cylinder filled with hydraulic fluid and attached to a brake lever or brake pedal. When the lever or pedal is operated, a piston moves down the master cylinder and creates a pressure in the hydraulic fluid. As fluid is for all practical purposes incompressible, the pressure is transmitted through the system, via fluid pressure in the brake pipes, to the brake unit. Here the pressure acts upon a piston/cylinder assembly and creates a movement to apply the brakes. This system allows the pilot to vary the braking action by varying the pressure applied on the lever or pedal; when the pressure on the lever or pedal is released, the brakes release. A parking brake is normally incorporated in the system. In most instances the parking brake is set by applying the brakes in the usual way, then a valve is operated which traps the fluid in the system, maintaining the pressure on the brake units and holding the brakes on.

The parking brake and locking button of a
Piper PA-28

In the simplest braking systems, a single lever applies the brakes on both main wheels simultaneously, although on some designs if nosewheel/tailwheel steering is applied at the same time as the brakes, there may be a degree of extra braking action in the direction of the rudder applied. So if the rudder is applied to the left, braking on the left wheel will increase to aid the turn. More modern aircraft are almost invariably fitted with left and right brake pedals (usually at the top of the rudder pedals), so the pilot can apply the brakes evenly or apply different pressure to one side or the other. This is called *differential braking*. Differential brakes have many advantages; directional control is easier (particularly when operating in a crosswind), and the use of brake on one side only can give a very small turning circle limited only by the limit of the movement of the nosewheel or tailwheel. If the nosewheel or tailwheel is totally free-castoring, it may be possible to turn in a very tight circle. However, it is all too easy to lock one wheel completely and then turn around it; the resulting pirouette is usually accomplished with the use of a very high power setting and whilst the result is a very tight turn, such treatment is very bad for the landing gear, 'scrubbing' the tyre tread and applying excessive forces to the undercarriage.

Use of toe brake pedals to control braking. Placing your heels on the floor keeps the feet clear of the toe brakes

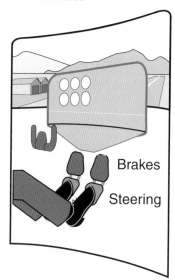

Brakes

Steering

Aside from the dangers of turning around a locked wheel, differential braking has other operational considerations. The most common location for the brake pedals is directly above each rudder pedal – giving so-called *toe brakes*. The brake pedal may be an integral part of the rudder pedal, whereby the entire assembly hinges forward to apply the brakes when pressure is applied at the top half. Conversely, it may consist of a separate pedal above the rudder pedal. In either case, care must be taken not to apply the toe brakes inadvertently when operating the rudder. This is normally avoided by placing the heels on the floor, thereby keeping the feet clear of the toe brakes. This works well unless flying an aircraft such as the Piper Cub which has *heel* brakes – brakes **below** the rudder pedals! The moral is to know the aircraft.

Toe brakes are an optional extra on many light aircraft and are not always fitted, so a fleet of otherwise identical aircraft may contain some individual aircraft with toe brakes, and some without. So, picture a pilot landing one of these fleet on a short runway. It's a well-known fact that humans tend to revert to their established behaviour at times of stress, and it is fairly stressful to be rolling steadily towards some solid obstruction, such as the fence at the end of the runway, whilst frantically pressing the feet forward onto non-existent toe-brake pedals. At times like this, well-meaning advice such as "It's only a Cherokee just like any other" takes on a whole new significance.

▶ Undercarriage Serviceability Checks and Handling

An aircraft's undercarriage is one of the more hard-working and hard-wearing parts of the airframe. Therefore it should receive particular attention during the pre-flight inspection.

When first approaching the aircraft it should be evident whether it is sitting level or seems to be unusually nose-down or leaning to one side. On reaching the aircraft, pushing it at some point such as the inner wing leading edge will indicate whether the parking brake is applied and working properly. Closer up, more of the general condition of the undercarriage leg itself can be inspected. If the strut is a simple steel-spring type, check its overall condition. Does it seem to be distorted or cracked in any way? Don't forget also to check any fairings for condition and security. Look to where the undercarriage leg joins the airframe; any wrinkled or deformed skin could indicate a previous heavy landing. Likewise, the connection of the nosewheel to the engine frame may be visible to inspect for damage. Unfortunately it is not unknown for pilots to be reluctant to report a heavy landing – a matter of misplaced pride, perhaps – leaving the next pilot to face the consequences. Make a careful check of the undercarriage to avoid being caught out, and if you do have a heavy landing (which happens to everyone once in a while) be honest and report it. Now is a good place to stress that whilst an undercarriage may be designed to cope with considerable *vertical* loads, its tolerance to *sideways* loads is far less. This is one reason why fast taxying (which can cause considerable side loads when turning a corner) and tight turns around a locked tyre are bad for the undercarriage. Likewise, landing (for example in a crosswind) with significant sideways drift also risks excessive side loads and consequent damage to the undercarriage.

A brake unit, disc and hydraulic pipe on the mainwheel of a Piper PA-38

If the undercarriage leg is an oleo type, the amount of shiny piston showing will give an idea of whether the oleo is properly filled with air and oil. The POH/FM and/or a pilot experienced on type should be able to give you a guideline as to the normal amount of extension. Look also for any sign of leaking oil from the seals or casing. The torque links should be secure, and it should be possible to check the nut and split pin holding the assembly together. If the nosewheel has a shimmy damper, that can also be checked for security and condition. Where the undercarriage is fitted with disc brakes, the brake disc itself. should be shiny and not pitted or corroded. Take care around the brake unit; if the brakes have recently been used in anger, they could still be hot enough to burn. The brake lining or pad should be at least 0·1in (2·5mm) thick.

Inspect the tyre for signs of correct inflation – a grossly under-inflated tyre will flatten out where it meets the ground. The POH/FM will state the correct tyre pressures, although tyre pressure varies with temperature, so the pressure can only be properly checked when at 'ambient' (e.g. surrounding) temperature. The tyre is likely to be hotter than this for anything up to an hour after landing. If the aircraft is flying to a place where the temperature is significantly different from that at the home airfield (±25°C) the tyre pressures may need changing – refer to the POH/FM or maintenance manual for the proper figure. At higher temperatures the tyre pressure will need to be reduced; for lower temperatures it must be increased. Check the overall tyre condition, looking particularly for bulges, cuts, embedded objects and flat spots caused by skidding or turning around a locked tyre. The tread pattern should have a minimum depth of 2mm over at least 75% of the tyre. Any cuts should be less than 50% of the tread depth and not cross more than 50% of a tread rib. If the cord ply of the tyre is visible at *any* place on the tyre, it is unserviceable and should be reported. A marked bulge in the sidewall of the tyre should also be drawn to the attention of an engineer.

Be wary of a tyre that has been standing in a pool of fuel, or has had fuel or oil dripping on to it: neither is good for the tyre rubber. There may be a *creep mark* painted on the sidewall of the tyre and across on to the wheel to indicate tyre creep. The markings should remain in alignment; if they are 'split' the tyre is slipping around the wheel and if the marks are more than half split, consult an engineer. As a double check for tyre creep, find the inflation valve and see if it can be freely moved from side to side. If it is unyielding or very reluctant to budge, this can be another sign of tyre creep.

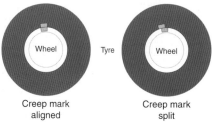

Tyre creep marks

Some aircraft have fairings or spats around the wheels and tyres, which can make proper inspection of the tyre or wheel more difficult. Be particularly vigilant for any mud, ice or debris trapped within the spat. An aviation safety publication reported removing over 40lb (19kg) of frozen mud from the mainwheel spats of a light aircraft which had been operating from a grass runway in winter!

The aircraft may have a hydraulic fluid reservoir in which the fluid level can be checked for quantity before flight. If the level can be checked, it should be. The hydraulic pipes around the undercarriage can be inspected for any leaks, bearing in mind that hydraulic fluid is usually coloured red.

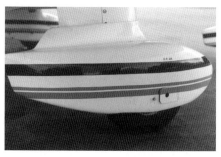

Finally, do remember to remove any chocks in front of or behind the wheels. This might sound too obvious to mention, until the day comes when even full power won't get the aircraft moving from the parking spot. Also on the 'apparently obvious' list is the removal of any towbar attached

Wheel 'spats' reduce drag, but can make the wheel and tyre more difficult to inspect, and can accumulate mud if operating on a soft surface

to the nosewheel assembly. Starting the engine with this attached can have noisy and expensive consequences.

Once ready to taxy, the brakes are normally checked within the first few feet of taxying. Once clear of other aircraft, differential braking can be checked too. When running up the engine during the power checks, look outside just to confirm that the parking brake really is holding the aircraft stationary. When lining-up for take-off, confirm that feet are clear of the brakes and that any brake handle is fully off. More than one pilot has tried to take-off with just a fraction of brake unintentionally applied, which is enough to lengthen the take-off run considerably. By the same token, always check carefully before landing that the parking brake is off and that the feet are not unintentionally applying pressure on the brake pedals. Touching down with the brakes on is the most common cause of ruined tyres on light aircraft.

The correct use of the brakes to bring the aircraft to a halt as quickly as possible – either on landing or after an abandoned take-off – demands a certain amount of skill on the part of the pilot, although 'maximum-effect' braking tends to be practised little in the standard PPL syllabus. Light aircraft do not have anti-skid systems to detect whether a wheel is about to lock, so the pilot must be alert for a skidding wheel and be prepared to reduce brake pressure accordingly. Be wary of applying very harsh braking immediately after touchdown; at this relatively high airspeed, the wings are still supporting some of the weight of the aircraft and it is easier to lock a wheel than at slower speed. Likewise, if the aircraft becomes airborne again (for example on passing over a bump on a grass runway) the wheel may stop spinning, and the next touchdown will be on a locked tyre. The correct technique is to apply braking pressure progressively, reaching the maximum as the aircraft slows down enough for the full weight to be on the wheels. The use of brakes as part of landing technique is described in the 'Flight Performance and Planning' chapter, but appreciate that an aircraft skidding with locked wheels will take further to stop than one under proper maximum braking. And certain surfaces reduce braking effectiveness considerably; long wet grass is an obvious example.

If very heavy braking has been used for any reason, that the brake assemblies will be very hot. In these circumstances it is best not to set the parking brake until the brakes have had a chance to cool off, instead use chocks to stop the aircraft rolling away.

When moving the aircraft by hand or with a tow vehicle, always try to use a proper towbar designed to fit on to the type of aircraft being moving. These towbars tend to have pins which fit into a bracket on the nosewheel assembly or a clamp fitting over the nosewheel hub. In either case, take care to not exceed the steering limits of the nosewheel whilst manoeuvring the aircraft, and remember that as a general rule the nosewheel assembly is not as robust as the main undercarriage. Make it a principle to keep the towbar in hand at all times when moving an aircraft. This should avoid forgetting about it and unintentionally starting the engine with the towbar still attached.

Wherever possible always use a towbar to manoeuvre an aircraft. Certain practices for manoeuvring an aircraft without the use of a towbar – such as sitting on the tailplane – may cause serious damage to the aircraft structure

▶ Revision

58   In the diagram below, name the parts labelled A, B and C

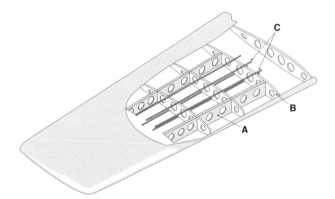

59   What is the definition of a monocoque structure?

60   Aircraft A has a wing span of 10m and a wing chord of 1m, aircraft B has a wing span of 15m and a chord of 2m. Which has the greater aspect ratio?

61   What is 'washout'?

62   Which type of boundary layer flow causes the most drag?

63   Name the parts of this fuselage construction labelled A and B

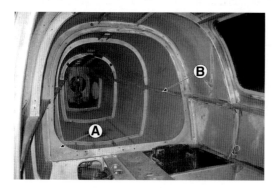

64   What is the common name given to a design arrangement whereby the tailplane (horizontal tail) is placed at the top of the fin (vertical tail)?

65   Should a pilot be concerned by slight wrinkling in the metal or fabric skin seen during a pre-flight inspection?

66   What is the name given to a tab fitted to the trailing edge of a stabilator, which moves in the same direction as the stabilator to increase control force?

67   What is the design purpose of the dorsal fin?

68   What is the name given to the limiting speed for extending flaps or flying with flap extended?

69   What is the primary purpose of a control lock?

70   To which sort of ground load is the undercarriage most vulnerable?

71   If the nosewheel is directly steered from the rudder pedals, how are the two normally connected?

72   During a pre-flight inspection a pilot finds oil leaking from the piston/cylinder seal of an oleo undercarriage leg. Is this acceptable?

73   What is the minimum tread depth acceptable over at least 75% of an aircraft tyre?

74   During a pre-flight inspection a pilot finds that in one spot the tyre has worn through to the cord ply. Is this acceptable?

75   What is the acceptable limit of tyre 'creep' as shown by the painted creep marks on the tyre sidewall and wheel?

      Answers at page fpp69-70

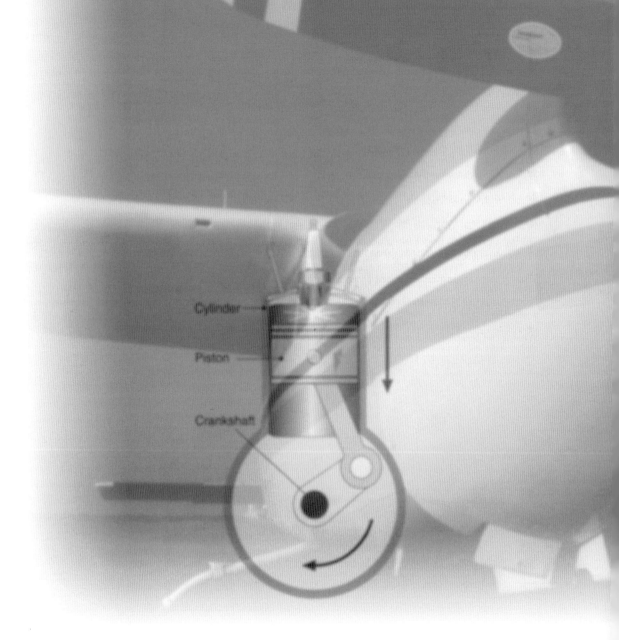

Aircraft General Knowledge
Aero Engines

Aircraft General Knowledge
Aero Engines

- ▶ Principles of Piston Engines
- ▶ The Four Stroke Cycle
- ▶ Basic Engine Design
- ▶ Two-Stroke Engines
- ▶ Rotating Combustion (Wankel) Engines
- ▶ Supercharging and Turbocharging
- ▶ Engine Designators
- ▶ Revision

▶ Principles of Piston Engines

The principle of the *reciprocating* piston engine, as found in virtually all cars and light aircraft, is very simple. The engine is fed with some flammable liquid (for example petrol) and mixed with air, without which combustion is not possible. This highly flammable fuel-air mixture is then ignited; as it burns it expands, and this expansion is harnessed to do the work the engine is designed for. This process creates noise, vibration, noxious exhaust gases and large amounts of heat – and some power too.

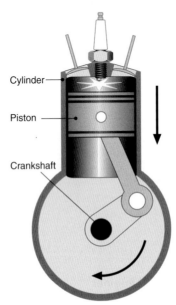

Cylinder

Piston

Crankshaft

The principle of an internal-combustion reciprocating engine. Fuel in the cylinder is ignited: as it burns, it expands and pushes on a piston. The vertical movement of the piston is converted into rotation of the crankshaft

The heart of this action takes place within a *cylinder*. This is where the fuel-air mixture is ignited, and its expansion as it burns pushes a *piston* down the cylinder. The piston is connected to a *crankshaft*, so that the reciprocating movement of the piston is converted into rotary movement needed to turn the crankshaft. If the piston engine is in a car, the crankshaft will transmit its motion via a gearbox to the wheels. An aircraft's piston engine will normally have a propeller bolted directly on to the front of the crankshaft.

▶ The Four Stroke Cycle

Most internal-combustion reciprocating engines – i.e. piston engines – used in light aircraft have a four-stroke cycle, also known as the *Otto* cycle. The Otto cycle takes place within the cylinder.

Firstly the fuel-air mixture must be introduced into the cylinder. This takes place as the piston moves down the cylinder, creating a suction. At the same time a valve (the *intake valve*) opens at the top of the cylinder, allowing the flammable fuel-air mixture to be drawn in. As the piston reaches the bottom of its travel, the intake valve closes. The piston now moves up the cylinder again, compressing the mixture.

As the piston approaches its uppermost position, a set of *spark plugs* at the top of the cylinder produce sparks. These sparks ignite the mixture, which burns rapidly and expands, pushing the piston back down the cylinder. The mixture does **not** explode; if it does, something is wrong.

When the piston reaches the bottom of its travel, a second valve (the *exhaust valve*) opens at the top of the cylinder. As the piston returns up the cylinder, it pushes the burnt remains of the fuel-air mixture out through this valve. At this point the exhaust valve closes, the intake valve re-opens, and as the piston descends it sucks in a fresh fuel-air mixture to repeat the cycle.

The four-stroke cycle is often described as *Induction*, *Compression*, *Expansion*, *Exhaust*;

the expansion part of the cycle is sometimes called the *power stroke*. The whole process can be colloquially summed up in the phrase "suck, squeeze, bang, blow".

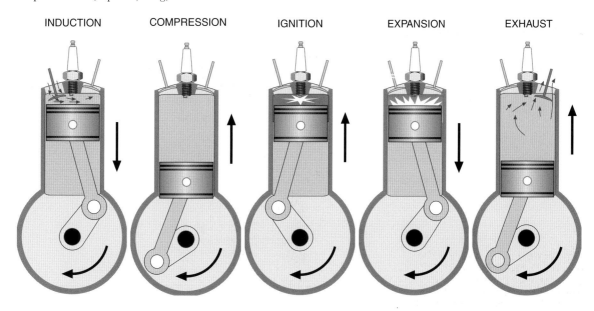

Aero-engines tend to operate at relatively low RPMs (compared to, say, car engines), and the cylinders tend to have a large volume. When the piston in a cylinder is at the bottom of its travel (known to engineers as Bottom Dead Centre – BDC), the volume in the cylinder above it is known as the *total cylinder volume*. When the piston is at the top of its travel (Top Dead Centre – TDC) the volume above it is the *clearance volume*. The ratio of total cylinder volume to clearance volume is called the compression ratio. As a general rule, the higher the compression ratio the more efficient the engine is in extracting the maximum power from the combustion of the fuel-air mixture in the cylinder. The practical limit of compression ratio is determined by the fuel used.

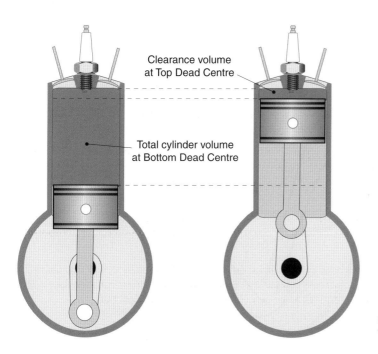

Compression ratio is the ratio of total cylinder volume to clearance volume

▶ Basic Engine Design

The cylinder (of which there is always more than one) is the heart of the engine, where the power comes from. The rest of the engine's systems are designed to get the fuel-air mixture to the cylinders and then ignite it, take away the burnt gases, translate the mechanical work of the pistons into useful power and keep the whole process turning smoothly.

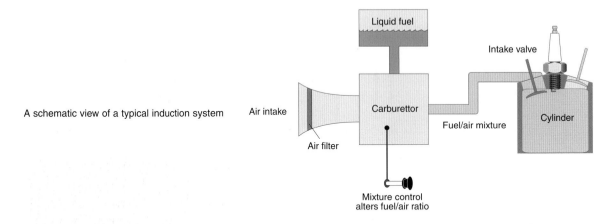

A schematic view of a typical induction system

The fuel to feed the engine will be kept in some sort of reservoir, from where it is taken to the *induction system*. The induction system takes in air from the atmosphere (normally through an air filter at the front of the engine) and adds liquid fuel from the fuel system to make a combustible fuel-air mixture. In most smaller aircraft engines this mixing is done in a *carburettor*. The pilot has a *throttle* to dictate the amount of fuel-air mixture entering the engine (which in simple terms determines the power produced by the engine) and a *mixture control* to vary the ratio of fuel to air. From the carburettor the fuel-air mixture travels along an induction tube to the cylinder, which it enters via the intake valve.

The the mixture inside the cylinder is ignited by the *ignition system*. This incorporates *magnetos* which produce a high-voltage electric current. This current moves along high-tension leads to the spark plug, at the end of which it jumps a small gap. The spark thus created ignites the flammable fuel-air mixture. It is important to appreciate that the fuel-air mixture should burn in a controlled way. If the mixture explodes in the cylinder instead of burning, the result is *detonation*. This will cause serious damage to the engine very quickly and must be avoided at all costs.

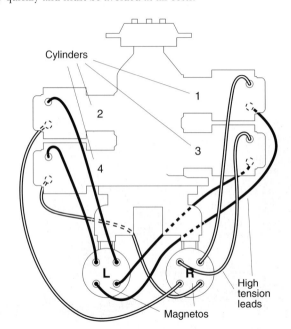

A schematic view of a typical two-magneto ignition system

To convert the reciprocating movement of the piston into a rotary motion, the piston is connected to the crankshaft by a *connecting rod* (often known as a *conrod*). The bearing between the conrod and the piston is known as the *small end*, and the larger bearing between the conrod and the crankshaft is called the *big end*. The opening of the intake and exhaust valves is controlled by a rotating *camshaft*, which is connected to the crankshaft but runs at half the engine speed because it only needs to activate the valves once for each two rotations of the crankshaft. Such a mechanical gearing to the piston travel ensures that the valves always open at the correct point in the Otto cycle.

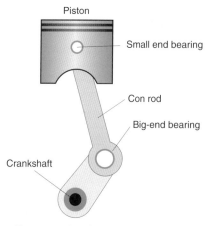

The connection of a piston to a crankshaft

The exhaust gases travel away from the cylinder to the exhaust system to be expelled through fairly short *exhaust tubes*. Surprisingly, at present few light aircraft are fitted with proper silencers although such devices were used on aircraft as long ago as the 1930s.

The burning of the fuel-air mixture in a piston engine produces a lot of heat – strictly speaking, reciprocating engines are more efficient at producing heat than power – so some form of cooling system is necessary. Most piston aero engines are *air-cooled*, whereby airflow is directed over the engine (especially the cylinders) to carry away heat. Less commonly, an aero engine may be *liquid-cooled*. In this case the cylinders are surrounded by a water-tight casing and the cooling liquid has to be cycled through a radiator to be cooled by the airflow.

Finally, the several thousand moving parts of the engine need lubrication, cleansing and sealing. This is done primarily by the *oil system*, which also aids cooling and helps prevent corrosion when the engine is not being used.

The four-stroke cycle only provides one power stroke in every four strokes. So an engine with a single cylinder would be unlikely to run very smoothly, even at the rotational speeds of most power units. Aero engines invariably have multiple cylinders, and usually an even number such as two, four, six, eight and so on. The arrangement of the cylinders has varied a great deal during the history of aeroplane design. Many early aircraft had *in-line* engines, with the cylinders spaced in a row along the crankshaft. The next development was the *rotary* engine, an unusual system whereby the entire engine (attached to the propeller) rotated around the crankshaft. A later variation on this theme is the *radial* engine, where the cylinders are arranged around the crankshaft but the engine is fixed and the crankshaft

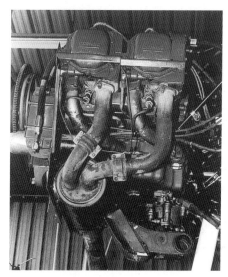

With the cowlings removed, the exhaust system of this four-cylinder Lycoming engine is quite visible

An in-line engine

A rotary engine

rotates. The cylinders can also be arranged in variants of a 'V' shape. However, most popular light-aircraft engines nowadays use the *horizontally opposed* layout. In this design the cylinders lie horizontally each side of the crankshaft.

Whatever its internal architecture, the engine sits in a tubular steel frame called the *engine mounting* and the front undercarriage of a nosewheel aircraft usually attaches to the underside of this structure. The engine mounting joins the fuselage at a bulkhead that acts as a *firewall*. The firewall is usually fabricated from a material such as stainless steel and protects the rest of the fuselage in the unlikely event of a fire in the engine compartment.

The radial engine of a Broussard

A 'V-type' engine

Firewall of a Piper PA-28, clearly visible with the engine removed

A Continental O-200 horizontally-opposed engine

▶Two-Stroke Engines

Perhaps because the vast majority of light aircraft (and virtually all training types) are powered by four-stroke engines, other types of reciprocating engines are over-looked by the official training syllabi. Nevertheless, there are several alternative powerplants for light aircraft, especially microlights, kitplanes and homebuilt designs. One engine option found in such aircraft (and a few production aircraft) is the *two-stroke* engine.

In a classic two-stroke engine, the fuel-air mixture is drawn into the crankcase as the piston is moving upward (assuming that the cylinder already contains a mixture ready for ignition). As the piston starts its downward stroke, the mixture in the crankcase is compressed and as the piston reaches the bottom of its travel, it uncovers the intake port so that the compressed fuel-air mixture enters the cylinder from the crankcase. Now the piston moves up the cylinder, and the mixture is ignited by the spark plugs. As the piston is pushed down the cylinder it uncovers first the exhaust port – to expel the spent exhaust gases – and then the intake port, allowing a fresh fuel-air mixture to enter the cylinder.

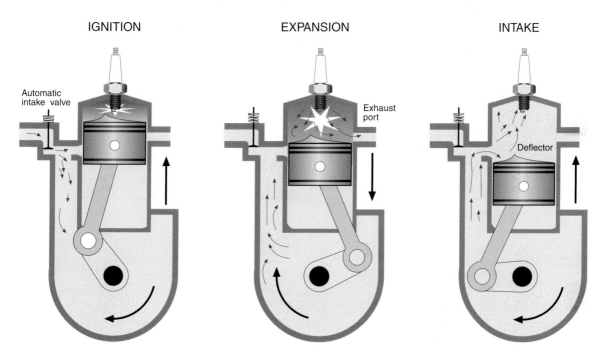

The operation of a two-stroke engine

This very simple and lightweight arrangement has two principal disadvantages. Engine cooling is often a problem, since every other stroke in the cycle is a power stroke; and the engine has to be lubricated by adding oil to the fuel (this pre-mixing has to be done and checked on each re-fuelling). This is a fiddly and messy process for the pilot, and the oily fuel also has a habit of leaving messy deposits on the spark plug leading to spark-plug 'fouling' problems.

An alternative two-stroke engine design utilises a *supercharger* (described shortly) to compress the fuel-air mixture before it reaches the intake port, dispensing with the need for the mixture to be compressed in the crankcase. An advantage of this design is that oil no longer needs to be mixed with the fuel, although the engine cooling considerations remain.

▶ Rotating Combustion (Wankel) Engines

The *Rotating Combustion* (RC) engine, commonly known as the *Wankel* engine after the inventor of the concept, has been available in cars for many years. It is now finding its way into aircraft too, thanks to developments of the original idea. Instead of the piston and hundreds of associated moving parts of a conventional reciprocating power-plant, the Wankel engine has only three major components – the *casing*, the *rotor* and the *central shaft*. The rotor has a quasi-triangular outline (for the pedantic, the correct name for its shape is an *epitrochoid*) and it rotates within an oval chamber inside the casing. The tips of the rotor have seals, so that three gas-tight chambers are formed as it rotates.

Despite its unconventional construction, the principle of the Wankel engine is very familiar. As the rotor rotates, a chamber collects a fuel-air mixture from the inlet port and carries it round the casing, thereby compressing it. As the chamber passes the spark plugs, the fuel-air mixture is ignited to provide the power and further rotation of the rotor allows the chamber to expel the exhaust gases through the exhaust port. The chamber then collects a fresh charge of fuel-air mixture. On the inside of the rotor, teeth intermesh with the central shaft to turn it and hence to drive the propeller, normally via a gearbox.

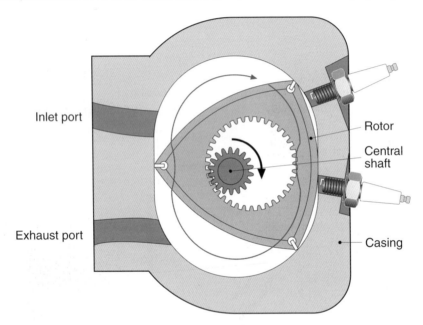

The operation of the Wankel Rotating Combustion engine

The Wankel concept promises lighter, smaller and quieter engines than traditional four-stroke designs, and also the possibility of using many different types of fuel. Whether the Wankel design – and the much-heralded turbocharged diesel engines – leads to a new era of cheaper, more efficient aircraft engines remains to be seen. They certainly should; piston aero-engines don't seem to have developed with the times in anything like the same way as their automotive counterparts.

▶ Supercharging and Turbocharging

Manifold pressure

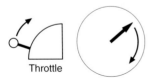

Throttle

Manifold pressure is determined by throttle position and air density

In a 'normally aspirated' piston engine, the pressure of the air entering the engine is simply dictated by the outside air pressure and the position of the throttle. The pressure measured in the induction manifold is known as the *manifold pressure*. With the throttle fully open, the engine of an average training aircraft might have a manifold pressure of around 26 inches of mercury (in.Hg) at sea level. As the aircraft climbs, even with the throttle still fully open, the manifold pressure will begin to fall due to the reducing air density. As the manifold pressure falls, so the engines power output decreases. As an average, the manifold pressure may fall by as much as 1 in. Hg. per 1000ft. So by 10,000 the 'full throttle' manifold pressure could be down to 16in Hg or thereabouts and not surprisingly, the engine power will be reduced accordingly. Even at full throttle, an average piston engine will only develop 75% of its maximum sea level power at 8000ft. It is an inherent feature of a normally aspirated engine that power available reduces quickly with increasing altitude. This is clearly a problem for an aircraft designed to fly high.

The first proper cure for this difficulty was the *supercharger*. The supercharger is a compressor in the intake manifold, driven by a mechanical linkage from the crankshaft. The compressor increases the manifold pressure at all altitudes and thereby increases the engine power, although care must be taken not to 'overboost' the engine at low altitudes. A development of the supercharger is the turbo-supercharger, more often known simply as the *turbocharger*. The turbocharger also has a compressor in the intake manifold, but this is driven by a turbine which receives its rotational energy from exhaust gas pressure. In practical operation, the turbocharger will provide a set maximum manifold pressure up to a certain density altitude (called the *critical altitude*), above which the manifold pressure will start to decline in line with the reducing air density. A modern turbocharger normally has some form of pressure relief valve called a *wastegate,* which prevents excessive manifold pressure from being generated especially on take-off and at lower altitudes at full throttle.

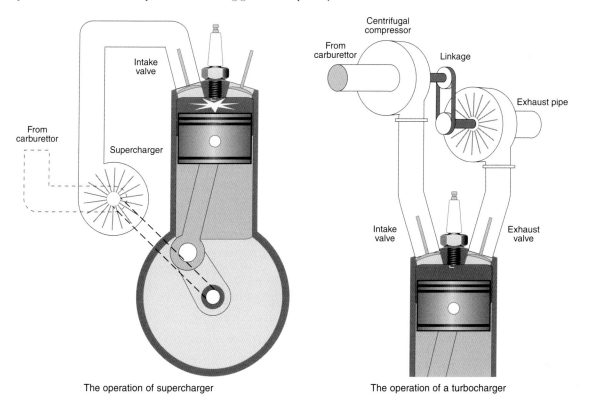

The operation of supercharger   The operation of a turbocharger

The turbocharger is commonly used on modern aero-engines to increase altitude capability. Typically it will allow a high-performance touring aircraft to operate at up to 25,000ft, although it does increase the power produced at low level too compared to a non-turbocharged engine.

The critical altitude for a turbocharged engine

▶ Engine Designators

The majority of modern production piston-engine training and touring aircraft are powered by American engines built by Lycoming or Continental, who both use similar engine designators. Purely for interest (this is not examined), the more common designators are as follows.

The first letter(s) of the designation can be decoded as follows:

G	=	Geared
O	=	Opposed (horizontally)
I	=	Fuel Injected
S	=	Supercharged
T	=	Turbocharged
A/AE	=	Aerobatic Engine
H	=	Helicopter use
V	=	Vertically mounted (for helicopters).

The numbers that follow are the engine capacity in cubic inches. This can be converted into litres by multiplying by 0·01639. The last group of letters/numbers usually refer to accessories, such as the type of magneto.

So the Continental IO-550B engine is a fuel-injected, horizontally opposed engine with a capacity of 550 cubic inches (or 9000cc) and B-type magnetos.

▶ Revision

76   What are the four stages of the 'Otto' cycle?

77   Which piston engine component converts the reciprocating movement of the pistons into the rotary movement of the propeller?

78   How many times does the intake valve open during one complete four-stroke cycle?

79   What is the name given to the volume in the cylinder above the piston when it is at bottom dead centre (BDC)?

80   What is the name given to the ratio of total cylinder volume to clearance volume?

81   What component, rotating at half the speed of the crankshaft, controls the opening of the intake and exhaust valves?

Answers at page fpp70

Aircraft General Knowledge
The Fuel System

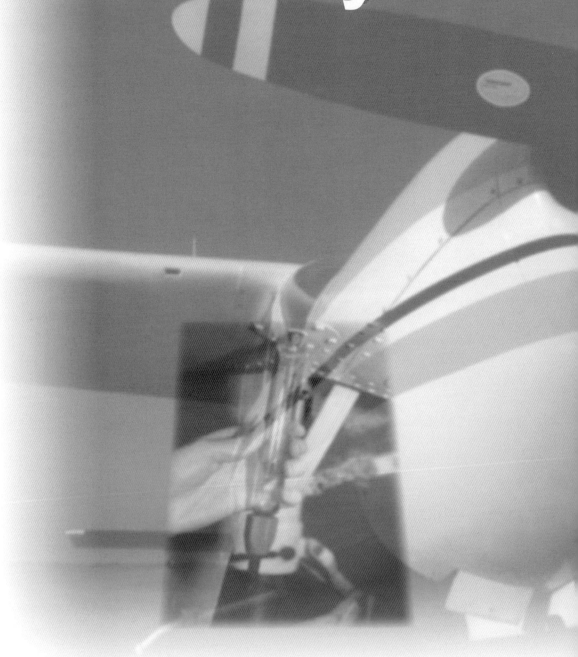

Aircraft General Knowledge
The Fuel System

Aircraft
General
Knowledge

▶ The Fuel System

▶ Fuel Grades

▶ Fuel System Serviceability Checks and Handling

▶ Revision

The Fuel System

▶The Fuel System

Of all the engine systems, the pilot has the greatest control over the *fuel system* and the *induction system*. So it is no coincidence that mis-management of these two systems causes the vast majority of engine failures in piston-engine aircraft.

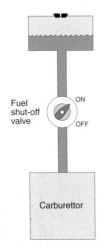

Fuel shut-off valve ON OFF

A simple gravity-feed fuel system

Carburettor

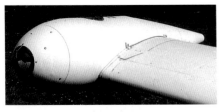

An external 'tip' tank on the wing tip of a Navion

A fuel-tank vent pipe under a wing

A 'bayonet-type' fuel drainer

At its simplest, the fuel system consists of a fuel tank located some vertical distance above the engine and a fuel line down which fuel flows by gravity to an on/off valve controlled by the pilot, through a filter and into the carburettor. This forms a so-called *gravity feed* system. At its most complex, a fuel system may consist of several tanks in different parts of the aircraft – some of which can be cross-connected as required – together with multiple fuel pumps, a priming system to deliver neat fuel to the cylinders for starting, sundry valves and controls and an assortment of contents gauges and flowmeters to monitor the system.

The fuel tanks are often located in the wings (hence references to left and right tanks) although many aircraft have them in the fuselage. The simplest tanks consist of little more than aluminium shells bolted into the aircraft structure, although more sophisticated aircraft may have fuel tanks formed as integral parts of the structure which are sealed off. Such integral tanks in the wings lead to the expression *wet wings*. Another option is the fuel *bladder*, essentially a rubberised bag also known as a *fuel cell* and often used as an option to increase an aircraft's fuel capacity. As well as those within the aircraft structure, external fuel tanks at the wing tips – *tip tanks* – or even tanks under the fuselage are used in some aircraft.

The fuel tank will have a filler port, closed with a fuel filler cap; a drain, so that fuel samples can be taken; an outlet to the fuel pipe leading to the carburettor; and some sort of venting to the atmosphere. Proper venting of the fuel system is of vital importance, especially in a gravity-feed fuel system, but is an aspect of aeroplane fuel systems which tends to be much overlooked by pilots. Imagine a 'TetraPak' container full of liquid, such as fruit juice. If the top of the packet is sealed and a small hole is made in the bottom, the liquid will begin to flow out. After a short time the flow will gradually decrease, because the departing liquid is leaving behind an area of very low pressure above it. In certain cases the sides of the pack will be pulled in; this phenomenon is called *oil-canning*. Eventually, despite the fact that there is still plenty of liquid in the container, the flow will stop altogether as the mass of liquid left is restrained by the suction in the container above it. But if another hole is made in the container above the liquid, the container is 'vented' to the atmosphere, the suction stops and the liquid will flow freely again.

If a fuel tank is not vented properly, the inevitable result will be that fuel stops flowing to the engine. This is not desirable. So the fuel tank is vented to the outside atmosphere, often by a tube from the top of the tank to the outside or a vent in the fuel cap itself. Blockage of a vent

A fuel drainer is normally fitted at the lowest point in the fuel tank and/or fuel system

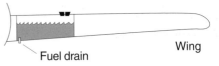

Fuel drain   Wing

pipe, or possibly the fitting of a non-vented fuel cap, can cause fuel stoppage. Hence the importance of checking that the fuel vent is clear and unobstructed.

A drain will be fitted to a fuel tank to allow a fuel sample to be drawn-off for checking. The most common type of fuel contamination comes from water. Water can get into the fuel because of condensation within a part-empty fuel tank; through a poorly-fitting fuel filler cap in heavy rain; or by contamination of an airfield's fuel supply. Because water is heavier than fuel, it tends to collect at the bottom of the fuel tank. For this reason the fuel drain will be fitted at the lowest point in the tank, although if the aircraft is not sitting level, the lowest point of the fuel tank might not be over the drain. Water in the tank could therefore be missed. Equally, rubber fuel cells have been known to collect water in the wrinkles and folds of the cell, again preventing it from reaching the fuel drain. Reciprocating engines do not run on water, indeed water-contaminated fuel can lead to a near-total loss of engine power, maybe just after take-off.

The pilot controls the fuel flow to the engine using the fuel selector in the cockpit. This may consist of a simple on/off valve or a set of selectors with several different options. The layout of fuel selectors, their method of operation and their markings, vary significantly between types – a far from ideal situation. Moreover, some are located outside the direct sight of the pilot, or may be operated only from one seat. A large number of engine failures are caused by simple mis-use of the fuel selector or *fuel starvation* (i.e. there was fuel on board but it wasn't reaching the engine). This can happen if a tank is run dry or if an empty tank is selected (it can also happen if the tank is incorrectly vented or if a fuel strainer has stuck open). Mis-selection of fuel is most common when a pilot is relatively new to the aircraft type, and is considered one of the least forgivable pilot errors. A pilot **must** fully understand the fuel system layout and operation of the fuel selector of **any** aircraft **before** getting airborne in it. 500ft AGL with a quiet engine is not a good place to start learning about the aircraft's fuel system.

The pilot must fully understand the operation of the aircrafts fuel system – is this fuel selector set to off or both?

With the exception of aircraft with purely gravity-fed fuel supplies, the fuel system will have at least one fuel pump. On light aircraft where the location of the fuel tank(s) means that fuel cannot flow to the engine by gravity there are usually two pumps – one engine-driven and one electrical. The engine-driven pump operates whenever the engine is running, and is responsible for drawing fuel from the tanks in normal circumstances. The electric fuel pump is operated from a switch in the cockpit and is used for starting, when changing fuel tanks and in the event of the failure of the engine-driven pump. For this latter reason, the electrical fuel pump is turned on during take-off and landing, as a back-up in case the engine-driven pump fails. It's also usual to turn the electric pump on when performing manoeuvres such as stalling or aerobatics.

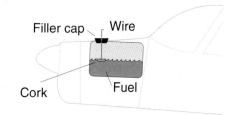

One of the simplest and most reliable fuel gauges – a cork on a piece of wire

All aircraft have some sort of fuel contents gauge. The simplest consists of a wire through the filler cap, attached to a cork which floats on the fuel in the tank. As the fuel level lowers, so less of the wire is visible above the filler cap. The wire can be graduated with marks for full, half-full, etc. Many pilots regard this arrangement as being no more or less accurate than any 'modern' fuel gauge, and indeed the contents gauges of most light aircraft use systems only marginally more sophisticated than the 'cork and wire' principle. In a 'modern' system a float sits on the surface of the fuel and is linked by an arm to an electrical sender unit. The movement of the arm alters the voltage leaving the unit, and this is applied to the fuel gauges in the cockpit. Alternatively, the float in the fuel tank may be mechanically linked to a fuel gauge on top of the tank. Another method of reading fuel contents is the *sight glass* – a glass tube linked to the fuel tank in which the fuel level is directly visible.

Whichever of these systems is in use, light-aircraft fuel gauges do **not** have a high reputation for accuracy. Accident and incident-report bulletins regularly carry stories of pilots who ran out of fuel despite the fact that the gauges allegedly said that there was still some left fuel in the tanks. And even if a perfect fuel gauge could be made, it might still be fooled by fuel sloshing around the tanks (for example during uncoordinated manoeuvres). Even on the ground, if the aircraft is sitting on a slope it can appear to have more fuel in its tanks than is actually the case. Tailwheel aircraft – which have a different attitude when sitting on the ground than when cruising in the air – will usually have gauges with two sets of markings, one for use on *terra firma* and the other for aloft.

The only sure way of checking fuel contents

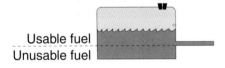

Usable and unusable fuel capacity

So if the fuel gauges cannot be trusted, what can? The answer is, the evidence of the pilot's own eyes. ***Always* visually check the fuel contents before flight**, even if this means a bit of clambering about on a high-wing aircraft. Many operators provide dipsticks to check the fuel level if it cannot be seen clearly through the filler pipe. Equally, some aircraft have a 'step' in the fuel tank – a strip of metal visible from the filler pipe – and the POH/FM may state the fuel level when the bottom of this step is reached, or it may be graduated. Given the amount of fuel actually on board the aircraft before departure, and a fuel plan of expected consumption during the flight, the pilot is much better equipped to make decisions concerning fuel state. The pilot can also check the aircraft's records (such as the technical log) to see when it was last refuelled, how much flying it has done since, and therefore how much fuel should be onboard.

Having checked the fuel before flight, there is the matter of monitoring the fuel contents in-flight. It has been said that the best fuel gauge ever made is the pilot's watch. If at take-off there was enough fuel on board for four hours of flight, a reliable timepiece should be giving a "When are you planning to land?" feeling after around three hours airborne. Monitoring the fuel gauges throughout the flight will show whether they agree with the in-flight observations and flight planning calculations (and the watch). If for any reason the fuel gauges head towards a dangerously low state, even though there should theoretically be plenty of fuel aboard, take the safest option – find somewhere to land and investigate. Maybe there is a fuel leak somewhere, or maybe the fuel consumption is unexpectedly high. Either way, landing early to investigate can prevent a minor problem becoming a major incident.

The POH/FM will probably divide the fuel capacity into *usable* and *unusable* fuel. Usable fuel is the fuel which can be drawn from the fuel tank. What remains in the tank – caught behind baffles, trapped in sumps and so on, is the unusable fuel – the last few dregs of AVGAS which cannot be persuaded to leave the tank. This can be as much as several gallons/litres. This inaccessible fuel is useless as far as the engine is concerned, although the fuel tank capacity quoted in the POH/FM will usually be the total of the usable and unusable fuel.

Aircraft which do not rely on a gravity-feed fuel supply normally have a fuel pressure gauge, indicating the pressure of the fuel flowing to the induction system. Fluctuating or low fuel pressure might indicate a blockage, or that the fuel supply is drying-up. Some aircraft may be fitted with a fuel flow gauge indicating fuel flow in terms of units per hour. This gauge may even be linked to a fuel flow computer. Like the 'trip computer' on many modern cars, this can calculate not just present fuel flow but also fuel remaining and endurance. It can even display range and anticipated fuel remaining at destination if it is linked to the navigation system. The apparent sophistication of such instruments, reading down to units such as tenths of a litre, should not obscure the fact that they are not necessarily any more accurate than a 'cork and wire' fuel gauge. Fuel computers require careful calibration after fitting, and errors in excess of 10% are quite common. Hence, again, the necessity of allowing reasonable reserves when fuel planning.

Whatever gauges are fitted, they should be monitored as part of the routine checks, and fuel pressure gauges should be watched especially closely when changing tanks.

▶ Fuel Grades

The aircraft's POH/FM and engine handbook will state the fuel grades approved for use. A piston-engine aero engine normally uses AVGAS (AViation GASoline) which is not at all the same as the petrol used in a car. AVGAS is graded according to its *octane* rating – the higher the grade, the higher the octane rating. The octane rating is a measure of the anti-detonation characteristics of the fuel, higher octane ratings have better anti-detonation characteristics. To reduce the risk of detonation, a very small amount of tetraethyl lead (TEL) is added to AVGAS.

The common AVGAS ratings listed in a POH/FM or engine handbook are:

GRADE	RATING	COLOUR	NOTES
80	80/87	Red	Being phased-out
100LL	100 Low Lead	Blue	Commonly available
100	100/130	Green	Rarely available
115/145	–	Purple	No longer available

As the table above shows, only 100LL AVGAS is commonly available nowadays. The basic rule-of-thumb is not to use a fuel with an octane rating **lower** than that approved because of the risk of detonation (described later). If a fuel with a higher octane rating is used, the extra tetraethyl lead (TEL) can cause lead deposits on the spark plugs.

The phasing-out of alternative AVGAS grades is not too serious since the vast majority of modern piston engines in aircraft are approved to use 100LL. Although engines approved to run on 80/87 fuel have experienced spark-plug fouling due to the extra lead in 100LL, this is mostly an inconvenience rather than a serious problem. There has been a move to approve the use of ordinary car petrol, called MOGAS (MOtor GASoline) for use in aircraft engines; leaded 'four-star' vehicle fuel usually has an octane rating of about 97 in the UK. Most airworthiness authorities (the CAA in the case of the UK) have published a list of types approved to use MOGAS and the applicable special operating procedures, including a maximum fuel-tank temperature limitation. There is some anecdotal evidence to suggest that MOGAS is not stored to the same standards as AVGAS and that it may be more prone to cause carburettor icing and vapour locking than AVGAS. There are also certain legal implications surrounding the transportation and storage of petrol between a filling station and the aircraft, if the airfield itself does not have a MOGAS supply. This said, a growing number of aircraft operate quite happily on MOGAS, particularly microlight, home-built and kitplane types. In the UK, a listing of types approved to use MOGAS and the relevant operating procedures is given in an *Airworthiness Notice*.

Assuming that the correct grade of fuel is going into the aircraft, it must be of a reasonable quality, i.e. free from contamination. If there is any reason to doubt the quality of the fuel about to go into an aircraft, filter it with a piece of leather chamois cloth. Better still, get it checked by an expert or don't use it at all.

▶ Fuel System Serviceability Checks and Handling

The first check of the fuel system is a careful calculation of the fuel quantity available before and during flight. The need for this has already been covered in some detail and will be referred to again, because having enough fuel is fundamental to the safe operation of the aeroplane. Even if a pilot 'knows' the tanks are full – perhaps because the technical log says so, or because he filled them himself the previous day – they *must* still be re-checked before flight. Clerical errors are quite possible, and instances of the theft of fuel from aircraft are not unknown. The old adage applies: **Never assume – check**.

A sample of the fuel should be taken as part of the pre-flight check, if the aircraft has been refuelled since its last flight, and also before the first flight of the day. Each tank will have a drain and it a fuel tester is used to draw off a sample of the fuel via the fuel drain or fuel strainer. When enough fuel has been drawn off, the tester is released from the drain – be sure to check that the fuel stops flowing. With the bayonet-type fuel drain in particular, the valve may stick open and allow the fuel to continue draining out and if this is allowed to continue the engine may ultimately suffer a failure due to lack of fuel.

The fuel sample is checked for colour and smell (to see if it is of the correct type) and also for contamination. The most usual contaminant is water, which will show as a clear bubble or bubbles underneath the fuel. If in any doubt, take another fuel sample and continue doing so until absolutely certain that what is seen is uncontaminated fuel of the correct type and grade. There may be a fuel drain close to the engine, for checking the fuel 'downstream' of the fuel tanks. Fuel can normally only be drawn from this drain if the fuel valve has been turned on in the cockpit, and some types require you a handle to be pulled (usually on top of the engine) to activate the fuel drain or strainer. To pull this handle whilst positioning the fuel tester to catch the fuel from the drain below can require a certain amount of manual dexterity. Nevertheless, just

Using a fuel tester to take a fuel sample for checking

letting the fuel run on to the ground proves nothing – it could be clear water running out. If the fuel sample is satisfactory, some pilots return it to the tank and others just throw it on to any nearby grass. Some airfields and refuelling facilities have a repository for waste fuel. Pouring fuel down the nearest drain is **not** recommended – drains full of flammable liquid are the last thing an airport needs!

The fuel vents should be checked for any blockages and be suspicious if there is a sudden sucking-in of air when removing the filler cap – this may indicate a venting problem. Take care when replacing the cap. If it is 'cross threaded' or misaligned, it may not close properly and fuel could be siphoned-out by the airflow during flight.

Procedures for the selection of fuel tanks are usually detailed in the aircraft's POH/FM and checklist. What follows is a description of the management of two common fuel system layouts; it does not overrule the aircraft checklist or POH/FM:

1. A fuel system with two fuel tanks and a three-position selector – LEFT, RIGHT, OFF.

The engine is started on the tank containing least fuel, if there is a differential, and the aircraft is taxyed using this tank, but the other (fuller) tank is selected for the power checks and take-off. If the aircraft has an electric fuel pump, this is turned on for take-off and left on until above 1000ft AGL. In the air the fuel quantities are checked on the fuel gauges, backed-up with the fuel plan, and the tanks are changed every 30-45 minutes to maintain them at about a similar level. Beware of a gross level difference between left and right tanks, since such an imbalance could cause control difficulties. Before changing tanks the electric fuel pump is turned on, and the fuel pressure is monitored until about 20 seconds after the changeover. If all is well, the fuel pump is turned off again whilst monitoring the fuel pressure for a further few seconds. Before landing, the tank with greatest contents is selected and the fuel pump is turned on as part of the pre-landing checks.

2. A fuel system with two fuel tanks and a four-position selector – LEFT, RIGHT, BOTH, OFF. It is assumed that the BOTH position is approved for take-off and landing.

The engine is started on the tank containing least fuel, if there is a differential. Before the aircraft is taxyed, the other tank is selected. For the power checks and take-off, BOTH tanks are selected. If the aircraft has an electric fuel pump, this is turned on for take-off and left on until above 1000ft AGL. In the air the fuel quantities are checked on the fuel gauges, backed-up with the fuel plan. The tanks are only selected differentially if an imbalance appears. Before changing tanks the electric fuel pump is turned on, and the fuel pressure is monitored until about 20 seconds after the changeover. If all is well, the fuel pump is turned off again whilst monitoring the fuel pressure for a further few seconds. Before landing, BOTH tanks are selected and the fuel pump is turned on as part of the pre-landing checks.

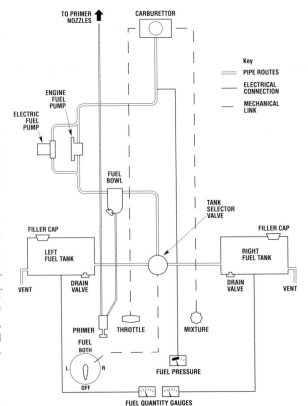

A two-tank pump-fed fuel system

Whatever the fuel-system layout, the underlying principle is that each fuel-selector position is tested whilst the aircraft is still on the ground and the fuel tank to be used for take-off is the one already verified during the power checks. Avoid changing fuel tanks just before take-off, and also avoid extreme 'running' take-offs (i.e. turning sharply on to the runway at speed). This may uncover the fuel pipe in the tank and interrupt the fuel supply to the engine.

After shutdown, the fuel selector is normally turned off. Some aircraft have a balance pipe between wing fuel tanks meaning that fuel may flow from a higher to lower tank if the fuel selector is left in the BOTH position, and may be lost through the fuel vent or overflow pipe if the tank fills up. On certain aircraft, it is necessary to select the LEFT or RIGHT position to avoid this occurrence. Check the POH/FM or ask an instructor experienced on type to find the recommended setting for the aircraft being flown.

▶ Revision

82   What is the serious potential problem caused by insufficient fuel tank venting in a gravity-feed fuel system?

83   What is the colour of 100LL AVGAS fuel?

84   What is the possible consequence of using a AVGAS grade of a lower octane than that recommended by the engine/aircraft manufacturer?

85   Where would a pilot find information regarding the use of MOGAS in a UK-registered aircraft?

Answers at page fpp70

Aircraft General Knowledge

The Induction System

ENGINE

CARBURETTOR

AIR FILTER   AIR INTAKE

Aircraft General Knowledge
The Induction System

▶ The Induction System

▶ Carburettor Icing

▶ Fuel Injection

▶ Serviceability Checks and Handling

▶ Revision

The Induction System

▶The Induction System

The induction system brings together the air and fuel; mixes them in the correct proportions; allows the pilot to select the amount of fuel-air mixture entering the engine and so set the engine's power output; and delivers the mixture to the cylinders.

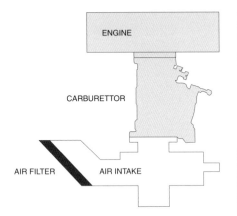

Most aero-engines have the air intake below an 'up-draft' carburettor, which increases the risk of an intake fire caused by over-priming

The intake of an aero-engine and, above and behind it, the carburettor

Air enters the induction system via an air filter, usually at the front of the engine. The filter removes particles of dust, sand and other unwanted debris that are found in the air, especially near the ground. The filtered air then travels along a pipe to a venturi. The venturi has the effect of increasing airflow speed and reducing air pressure; the higher the airflow speed, the lower the air pressure (that Bernoulli theorem again). The low pressure in the venturi draws fuel from the *float chamber* of the carburettor, where the fuel resides after entering from the fuel system. The float chamber has atmospheric pressure above the fuel and so the air pressure differential (higher in the float chamber than in the venturi) aids the flow of fuel into the venturi. The flow of air through the venturi is controlled by a *butterfly valve*, which is connected to the throttle. Moving the throttle forward opens the butterfly, drawing more fuel-air mixture into the engine and increasing engine power. Bringing the throttle back closes the butterfly, reducing the flow of fuel-air mixture into the engine and so reducing power. This is why pilots often refer to 'opening' and 'closing' the throttle.

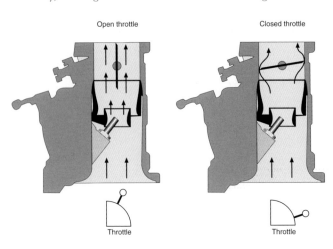

Open throttle   Closed throttle

Throttle   Throttle

The opening and closing of the butterfly valve (controlled by the throttle) sets the amount of air (and so fuel/air mixture) entering the engine

The carburettor allows the fuel flow to be adjusted in various ways and one such adjustment is the *accelerator pump*. This may be required because when the throttle is rapidly moved from idle to full power, or nearly so, there is a 'lag' between the butterfly opening and sufficient fuel entering the venturi to maintain the correct fuel-air mixture. This delay can cause the engine to falter and hesitate before delivering full power. To solve the problem, an accelerator pump can be connected to the throttle linkage which injects a shot of fuel into the venturi if the throttle is opened rapidly, thus avoiding the delay in obtaining full power. At the other end of the power scale, when the throttle is at idle with the butterfly valve nearly closed, there may be insufficient velocity of air through the venturi to draw fuel into the induction system. For this reason there will be an 'idling' or 'slow running' fuel jet which sprays fuel into the venturi when the throttle (and therefore the butterfly valve) is nearly closed. The engine will have a recommended RPM with the throttle closed; 500-700 RPM is a typical figure. An engineer can adjust the slow running jet to make sure this figure is obtained. If the engine idles at too high an RPM, the aircraft will tend to need constant braking during taxying, and landing distances may become excessive. If the idling RPM is too low, the engine may run unevenly or even stop when the throttle is closed.

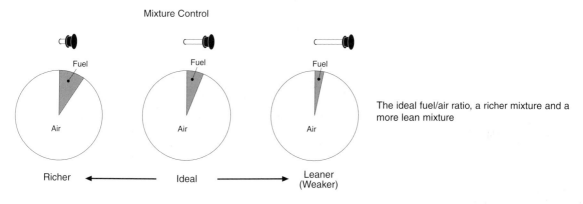

The ideal fuel/air ratio, a richer mixture and a more lean mixture

The carburettor supplies fuel to the induction system to maintain the required fuel-air mix, known as the *mixture*. Theoretically the ideal fuel-air mixture has a ratio of around 1 part fuel to somewhere between 12 and 15 parts air – the exact figure depends on the precise chemical composition of the fuel. This idealised ratio is sometimes referred to as the *stoichiometric* mixture, at which proportion all the fuel and all the oxygen in the mixture will be burnt in the cylinder. If the mixture is changed so that there is a surplus of air (say a ratio of one part fuel to 20 parts air – 1:20), it is becoming *leaner* (or *weaker*) than ideal. If the mixture is changed so that there is a surplus of fuel (say a ratio of 1:7), it is becoming *richer* than ideal. The mixture is varied using the mixture control in the cockpit. This adjusts the flow of fuel from the float chamber of the carburettor to vary the amount of fuel being drawn into the venturi.

Typically, a carburettor will be adjusted by an engineer so that when the cockpit mixture control is set to fully rich, the fuel-air ratio of the mixture at sea level is in fact slightly richer than the stoichiometric ratio. With this slightly 'over-rich' mixture, the excess of fuel aids engine cooling; the induction system is, in effect, spraying unburnt AVGAS into the cylinder and on to the valves and piston. As altitude increases, the air becomes gradually 'thinner' or less dense. If the same amount of fuel is entering the venturi, the air/fuel mixture will become increasingly rich in the less dense air, and eventually the engine will begin to lose power. To prevent this happening, the pilot can reduce the amount of fuel entering the venturi using the mixture control, to maintain the same fuel-air ratio. The operation of the mixture control is described more fully later.

The simple carburettor described above is of the *float* type. Another type of carburettor – the *pressure carburettor* – dispenses with the float chamber, replacing it with a series of diaphragms and linkages. There is no practical difference in operation as far as the pilot is concerned.

▶Carburettor Icing

The carburettor has been described as an instrument scientifically designed to deliver an incorrect mixture to an engine under all possible conditions of operation! Certainly it possesses several drawbacks. One major disadvantage of using a carburettor in an aircraft engine, and arguably the single most common cause of engine failures in piston-engine aircraft, is *carburettor icing*.

Carburettor icing can take one of two forms:

- *impact* icing of the air filter, caused by flight in known icing conditions;
- ice forming within the venturi itself, which can and does occur even if the aircraft is not flying in known icing conditions.

Impact icing occurs when ice, sleet or snow forms over the air intake and blocks the flow of air into the induction system. It can only occur if the aircraft is flown into 'known icing conditions', i.e. flight in cloud and/or precipitation when the air temperature is below freezing. Most light aircraft are not cleared for flight into known icing conditions, and impact icing should not occur if this restriction is adhered to.

Impact icing is relatively rare, not least because most pilots avoid known icing conditions in light aircraft. Therefore the most common cause of carburettor icing is the formation of ice within the venturi itself, (the venturi is the part of the carburettor where there is an increase in airflow speed and a reduction in air pressure), a decrease in air pressure implies a decrease in air temperature. In addition, the evaporation of fuel within the venturi further reduces the temperature. This latter effect is experienced when applying perfume or aftershave to the skin; the coldness is felt as the evaporation of the volatile solvent extracts heat from the skin. The combined effects of reduced pressure and fuel evaporation can cause the temperature inside the venturi to fall by as much as 30°C, and if the temperature of the air in the venturi falls below freezing (0°C), moisture within the air may form into ice on the sides of the venturi and on the throttle valve.

The temperature drop within the carburettor venturi

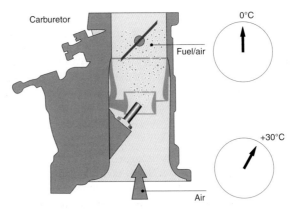

The conditions likely to cause carburettor icing

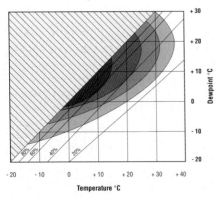

- ⬚ 100% Relative humidity
- ⬛ Serious icing – any power
- ⬛ Moderate icing – cruise power
  Serious icing – descent power
- ⬛ Serious icing – descent power
- ⬛ **Light icing – cruise or descent power**

Because of the large reduction in temperature within the venturi, carburettor icing can occur over a wide range of outside air temperatures (OATs). It typically occurs at OATs anywhere between -10°C and +30°C. Aside from temperature, the air's humidity is an important factor in carburettor icing; the greater the water content of the air at a given temperature, the greater the risk of carburettor icing. Having said this, visible water droplets (such as cloud, fog or precipitation) do not *have* to be present for carburettor icing to occur – although they do make it more likely. If all other conditions are equal, the lower the power setting the greater the risk of carburettor icing. For example, during a descent at low power the throttle valve may be almost closed, meaning that it takes less ice to block the venturi. Moreover, the reduced power meaning that there may be less residual heat in the engine, a situation which may be exacerbated if the airspeed is increased in the descent (thus increasing engine cooling).

Because carburettor icing can occur over such a wide range of temperature/humidity conditions, aircraft engines with a carburettor have a *carburettor heat* control. This operates a butterfly valve in the induction system, allowing hot air to enter the venturi; the average rise in air temperature is around 30°C if the engine is operating at cruise power. The hot air comes from an unfiltered air source routed around the exhaust pipes to warm the air. The fact that this air is unfiltered implies that sand, grit and other airborne debris may enter the engine, especially when on the ground. So it is advised not to use carburettor heat more than absolutely necessary when on the ground.

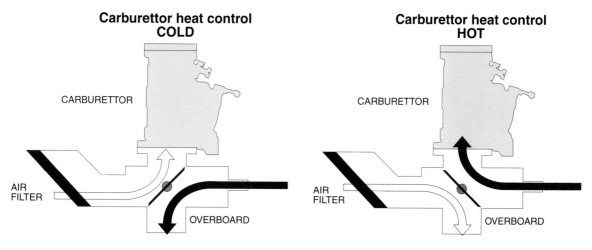

The carburettor heat system

There is normally a smooth reduction in RPM when carburettor heat is used, due to the less dense (hotter) air entering the engine. If carburettor ice is present, there may be temporary rough running as melted ice (i.e. water) passes through the engine. After using carburettor heat, the power (RPM) will revert to the same as before if no icing was present. If the RPM increases to a higher figure, this is an indication that carburettor icing was present. The use of the carburettor heat is described more fully later.

▶ Fuel Injection

More powerful (or higher-class) aero engines often have a *fuel injection* system instead of a carburettor. A fuel injection system meters the amount of fuel required by the engine and then injects it directly into the induction system at the intake valve of each individual cylinder. This increases the engine's efficiency and also gets rid of most of the defects of the carburettor. It is quite common in engines much bigger than those of the average training/touring aircraft, and virtually all modern aero engines of around 180 *horse power* (hp) or more have a fuel injection system.

The fuel distributor of a fuel injection system

The throttle and mixture controls of an injected engine work in the same way as on carburettor engines, but there is no carburettor heat control. Instead there is an *alternate induction air* control, to be used if the normal air inlet becomes blocked (e.g. in the event of impact icing). When alternate air is selected, air is fed into the induction system from a separate pipe within the engine cowling (where the air is warmer and cannot be blocked by external icing).

▶ Serviceability Checks and Handling

During the pre-flight inspection, the external air filter can be checked for blockages and security, and on some aircraft types you may be able to access the engine compartment to check the hot air inlet. The operation of the carburettor heat control is verified during the power checks, as is the idling engine RPM. More detailed information on the handling of the induction system, including the use of the carburettor heat and mixture controls, is found in the 'Engine Handling' chapter.

▶Revision

86   What is the primary purpose of the cockpit 'mixture' control?

87   What is the primary purpose of the accelerator pump?

88   At what throttle position is there greatest risk of carburettor icing (all other conditions remaining unchanged?)

Answers at page fpp70

Aircraft General Knowledge
The Ignition System

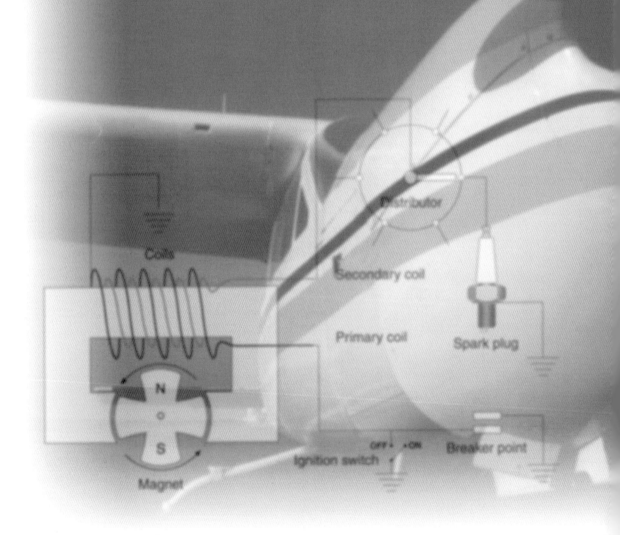

Coils

Secondary coil

Primary coil

Spark plug

Distributor

N
O
S

OFF ● ●ON

Ignition switch

Breaker point

Magnet

▶ The Ignition System

▶ Serviceability Checks and Handling

▶ Revision

▶The Ignition System

The ignition system provides the spark which ignites the fuel-air mixture within the cylinder.

The electric current required is generated by a *magneto*. A magneto contains a small magnet which rotates between two *coils,* essentially wire circuits wound around the frame of the magneto. One coil, the primary coil or primary circuit, is connected at one end to the ignition switch. The magnet within the magneto is rotated by a mechanical linkage to the engine crankshaft and as the magnet rotates, the fluxing magnetic field produces a flow of electrical current in the primary circuit. As the flow reaches its maximum, a set of breaker points open, causing the flow of current in the primary coil to stop (in essence the circuit is broken). When this happens the magnetic field surrounding the primary coil collapses, which induces a very high voltage in the secondary coil (or secondary circuit). This electric current travels to a distributor from where it is directed along leads – known as the *high tension leads* or the *ignition harness* – to each spark plug. At the end of the spark plug the current has to jump a gap, thus producing the spark which ignites the fuel-air mixture in the cylinder. The operation of the magneto is entirely a function of crankshaft rotation and it is completely independent of the aircraft's electrical system. In this respect the aero-engine is quite different from a car engine. Once an aircraft engine is running you can disconnect the battery and the electrical system and throw them away, but the magnetos will keep on working. An instructor may demonstrate this principle by turning off the master switch and hence closing down the electrical system. The engine keeps running regardless.

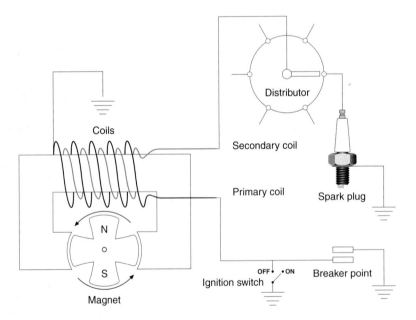

The requirement to adjust the timing of the spark so that it ignites the fuel-air mixture at precisely the right moment can keep an engineer occupied for hours. The timing of the spark is measured in terms of degrees of crankshaft rotation – after all, the travel of the piston is dictated by the rotation of the crankshaft. Typically, the spark should appear just before the piston reaches its highest point in the cylinder, a position known as 'Top Dead Centre' or TDC. In general terms the spark should occur when the crankshaft rotation is about 30° short of the piston reaching TDC. A spark occurring earlier is said to be *advanced*, a spark occurring later is said to be *retarded*. When engineers talking of "advancing" or "retarding" the timing, this is what it's all about. If the spark occurs too late in the Otto cycle, this can lead to gases being ejected from the cylinder whilst they are still burning (rather than when they have burnt-out). This may cause localised over-heating of parts of the cylinder – in particular the exhaust valve, the result is that the incoming fuel-air mixture might be ignited before the spark next fires. This early burning of the incoming fuel-air mixture, caused by excess heat in the cylinder, is called *pre-ignition*.

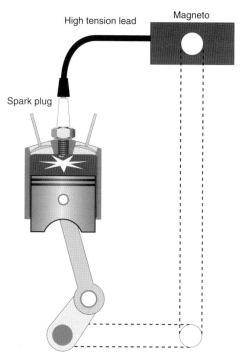

The spark within the cylinder is generated by a magneto, which is driven by crankshaft rotation

A magneto fitted to a Lycoming engine

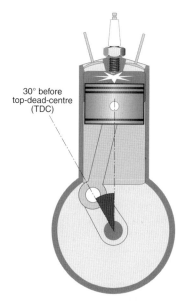

The typical timing of the ignition spark

Spark plugs and high-tension leads

The cylinder will have two spark plugs for efficiency and safety, and the ignition system will have two magnetos. Each magneto is connected to one of the spark plugs in each cylinder, so that should one magneto fail the engine will continue to run – albeit at a slightly reduced power – on the remaining one spark plug in each cylinder.

The ignition system is controlled by the magneto switches in the cockpit. When the magneto switches are set to 'Off', the switch in primary circuit (coil) is closed and the primary circuit is *earthed*. This means that even if the magnet in the magneto is rotated, it cannot induce a voltage in the secondary coil (circuit). Magneto switches often take the form of a key-operated control, with positions for 'Off'; 'R' (right magneto only); 'L' (left magneto only); Both (both magnetos – the normal key position) and 'Start', which engages the starter motor. Some aircraft have toggle switches for the magnetos, in which case the starter (if fitted) is operated by a separate button.

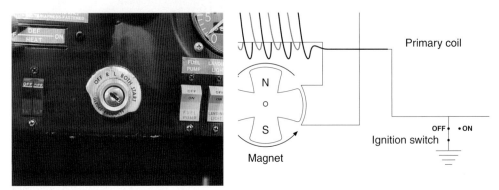

A typical 'key' magneto switch

To aid starting, a magneto may be fitted with an *impulse coupling*. When the engine is turning over slowly (such as when the starter is operated), a spring-loaded coupling in one magneto (usually the left) operates to provide a spark at the spark plugs which is more powerful than normal and also occurs later in the cycle (i.e. it is retarded). Once the engine is running, the impulse coupling automatically disengages so that the spark timing returns to normal. Out of interest, if the propeller of an engine with an impulse magneto is turned over slowly, an audible 'click' can be heard as the impulse coupling operates. Certain aero-engines have an *Induction Vibrator* or 'Shower of Sparks' system, again traditionally fitted to the left magneto. This system electronically achieves the same function as a mechanical impulse coupling, although in this case it operates until the magneto key is released from the 'Start' position. A few aircraft have a separate starting button, in which case the engine is started on the magneto fitted with an impulse coupling. Once the engine has started, the pilot selects both magnetos.

Spark plugs can be susceptible to 'fouling' if deposits of oil or lead build-up on the electrodes of the plug within the cylinder. Such fouling can occur in particular if the engine is allowed to 'idle' at a low RPM for a prolonged period. Fouling of the spark plugs will reduce engine power and lead to uneven 'lumpy' engine running.

▶Serviceability Checks and Handling

Depending on how accessible the engine compartment is, during the pre-flight inspection the pilot may be able to check that the high tension (HT) leads between the magnetos and the spark plugs can be checked for security and for signs of any 'fraying'. It is important to appreciate that when the magnetos are turned 'Off', it is the 'earthing' of the circuit that prevents a high voltage being produced by the magnet in the magneto and reaching the spark plugs. There is no practical way for a pilot to check this earthing during the pre-flight checks, but if it is faulty or if the magneto has become disconnected from the switch the engine is just as liable to fire as if that magneto is switched on. This is one very good reason for always treating the engine (and the propeller attached to it) as potentially 'live'. Also, in this condition selection of both magnetos to 'off' when the engine is running will fail to stop the engine.

During the power checks the engine is run up to near cruise power and the magnetos are individually selected to check that the resultant decrease in power is within defined limits. More detailed information on the handling and checking of the ignition system is found in the 'Engine Handling' chapter.

▶Revision

89 From where does a magneto derive the initial power to provide the ignition system with a spark?

90 A spark occurs later than a predetermined point in the Otto cycle, how can this situation be described?

91 If the primary circuit of a magneto becomes disconnected from the magneto switch, will selection of both magnetos to 'off' earth both of them?

92 If overhearing inside a cylinder causes the fuel/air mix to burn earlier than normal, what can this condition be called?

Answers at page fpp70

Aircraft General Knowledge
The Cooling System

Cowling

Baffle

Air inlet

Firewall

Air inlet

Adjustable exit
(cowl flap)

Aircraft General Knowledge
The Cooling System

▶ The Cooling System

▶ Serviceability Checks and Handling

▶ Revision

The Cooling System

▶The Cooling System

Piston engines are remarkably good at producing heat; in fact they produce far more heat than is good for them. An engine running too hot will suffer long-term engine damage and, eventually, failure of some major component such as an exhaust valve. Extreme overheating will lead to potential engine failure much faster, particularly if detonation occurs within the cylinders. Clearly, some form of engine cooling system is essential.

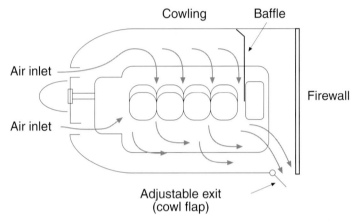

The flow of air over an air-cooled engine

An open cowl flap which increases airflow through the engine compartment

The vast majority of modern piston aero-engines are air-cooled, and the vast majority of aircraft have an engine which is covered by a *cowling*. The front of the cowling has inlets, and air entering these inlets is forced over the engine and directed by *baffles* (plates) and seals to flow evenly over all the hottest parts of the engine. The engine cylinders are covered in 'fins' which increase the surface area of the cylinder to allow the greatest possible heat dissipation. The air which has flowed over the engine exits the engine compartment through a gap in the cowling underneath the aircraft. A high-powered aircraft may have adjustable *cowl flaps* in the lower cowling. These are normally opened on the ground and during take-off and landing to increase the flow of air over the engine, but closed in cruising flight when there is plenty of cooling air and the engine is not working at full power. Cowl flaps are usually manually controlled from a control in the cockpit and allow the pilot to open the cowl flaps to increase engine cooling when required, but close the cowl flaps (and thereby reduce drag) at other times. In general terms, the quickest way to aid cooling of an engine is to reduce power and increase the amount of air flowing over the engine, either by increasing airspeed (in the air), or turning into the wind (on the ground). Engine temperature is also affected by changes in the fuel-air mixture ratio: a rich (excess fuel) mixture decreases engine temperature, a weak (excess air) mixture increases engine temperature to a certain point.

Axisymmetric air inlets on a new PA-28 Archer III

The need to direct air over the engine results in a drag penalty sometimes called *cooling drag*, which naturally the designer will seek to reduce. A recent development in this direction is the use of 'axisymmetric' inlets in the front cowling. One such design – in effect a new cowling arrangement for an out-of-production single-engine tourer – is claimed to increase cruise speed from 165kts to 180kts. Not surprisingly, this innovation is beginning to appear on many new aircraft.

A few aero-engines are liquid-cooled. On these engines a watertight 'jacket' surrounds the engine and liquid is circulated through some sort of radiator where it is cooled by the airflow. Although liquid-cooled aircraft engines are fairly rare now, the engines of many of the classic piston-engined fighters were cooled in this way – often needing massive radiators under the wings or fuselage as a consequence.

Air-cooled engines are particularly susceptible to 'shock cooling', which takes place when the temperature of an engine is reduced too rapidly. One of the quickest ways to shock cool an engine is to work an engine very hard, and then close the throttle and increase the airspeed. A fast, power-off descent at the end of a long cruise or just after a climb is ideal for shock cooling, which is very damaging to the engine.

A more powerful aero engine may be fitted with a Cylinder Head Temperature (CHT) gauge which measures the temperature within the cylinder head. The POH/FM will state a specific maximum temperature for the CHT and as well as monitoring this, the pilot can also ensure that the CHT is not cooled too quickly by shock cooling.

The under-wing radiator of a Spitfire

▶ Serviceability Checks and Handling

Once again, the access afforded to the engine compartment by the cowling design will dictate how far the pilot can check elements of the cooling system during the pre-flight inspection. The air inlets into the cowling should be unblocked – be on the alert for 'plugs' that are sometimes placed in these inlets to stop birds nesting in the engine compartment. If there is access to the engine compartment check that the baffles are in good condition, secure and unbroken. This is an often-overlooked aspect of the pre-flight check, but if the baffles are not doing their job properly, 'hot spots' can result around the engine leading to serious long-term damage.

▶ Revision

93   What is the main purpose of baffles within the engine compartment of an air-cooled engine?

94   What would be the normal position of adjustable cowl flaps during take-off and landing?

Answers at page fpp70

Aircraft General Knowledge
The Oil System

Piston rings

Oil scraper

Aircraft General Knowledge
The Oil System

▶ The Oil System

▶ Oil Grades

▶ Serviceability Checks and Handling

▶ Revision

▶The Oil System

Engineering textbooks state that oil provides lubrication, cooling, cleansing, sealing and protection from corrosion. Piloting textbooks may say less about the oil system, but what is certain is that any engine will run only for a very short time without an adequate supply of lubricant, so the oil system is worth looking after.

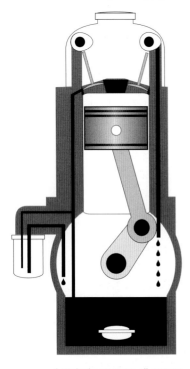

A typical wet-sump oil system

Relatively low-powered aero engines tend to hold their oil in a *sump* at the bottom of the crankcase and hence underneath the crankshaft. When the engine starts, an engine-driven oil pump draws oil up from the sump and circulates it around the engine, the crankcase and cylinder walls being arguably the areas where the oil's lubricating and cooling properties are needed the most. The gap between the piston and the cylinder wall is sealed with a number of *piston rings* fitted around the piston, which prevents gases escaping from the combustion process. Oil on the cylinder walls lubricates and seals the contact area between the cylinder and the piston rings, and the piston rings also maintain the necessary film of oil on the cylinder wall.

Within the oil system there will be an oil cooler which works in much the same way as the radiator in a liquid-cooled engine, oil is pumped through the cooler where cooling air flows over a series of small pipes, thus dissipating the heat from the hot oil. Should the oil cooler become blocked, a pressure-activated valve opens and allows oil to bypass the cooler. There will also be an additional oil pressure-relief valve which regulates the oil pressure, and prevents it from becoming too high. When the oil has circulated around the engine, it returns to the sump by gravity. In a *wet-sump* oil system, the sump also acts as the oil reservoir. In a *dry-sump* system, often found on larger aero engines and those installed in aerobatic aircraft, a *scavenge pump* takes the oil from the sump to a separate oil tank.

Early warning of impending mechanical problems in the engine can often be gleaned from the oil filter. During routine servicing the oil filter is either changed or cleaned out (depending on the type) when the oil is changed. The filter catches debris carried in suspension by the oil; shiny specks or shavings in the filter may be small pieces of metal which have been worn or abraded by excessive friction somewhere in the engine. A large amount of such particles will set an engineer looking for possible problems. Even more sophisticated techniques such as spectrographic oil analysis (SOAP) can detect engine wear or an abnormal event at a very early stage before significant damage occurs.

In the cockpit there are normally oil temperature and oil pressure gauges to monitor the oil system, and the POH/FM will state the permissible limits of temperature and pressure. Oil pressure is normally measured just after (downstream of) the oil pump. Oil temperature is also measured before the oil enters the 'hot sections' of the engine, often just after the oil has passed through the oil cooler. Low oil pressure and/or high oil temperature are signs of serious engine problems, and should be treated as an urgent reason for instituting a diversion to the nearest suitable airfield.

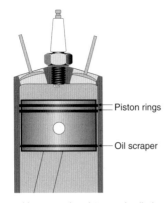

— Piston rings

— Oil scraper

Piston rings seal between the piston and cylinder and act as 'scrapers' to coat the cylinder wall with oil

▶ Oil Grades

Oil can be defined by its **type** and **grade**. There are two main **types** of oil available:

- ■ Straight Mineral Oil, normally called 'straight' oil; and
- ■ Ashless Dispersant (AD) Oil, sometimes called 'W' or 'D' oil because it may have that designator.

The engine handbook and POH/FM will usually have detailed advice about the correct oil type and grade to use under different circumstances. As a general rule, if any major work or maintenance has been carried out on the engine, it will be run on 'straight' oil for the first 50 hours or so and a note to this effect should be made in the aircraft's technical log. Straight oil is not as effective at lubricating as 'W' or 'D' oil, and the slightly reduced lubrication properties allow fresh components (such as new piston rings, which need to 'seat' properly) to wear a little and be 'broken in'. Apart from these short periods, the engine will probably be run on AD 'W' or 'D' oil. Most engineers prefer to drain the oil system and re-fill rather than mix 'W/D' or 'AD' oil with straight oil. Oil for automobile engines should *never* be used in an aero-engine, nor should oil for jet engines be used in a piston engine.

Within each oil type, the **grade** to use is determined by the average air temperature, which effects the viscosity (consistency) of the oil. The oil's viscosity is measured using the SAE system, but the commercial grade used by manufacturers is double the SAE number. The table below shows the average temperature bands for each oil grade:

Average Air Temperature	SAE number	Commercial Grade
Straight Oil		
Above 16°C (60°F)	SAE 50	100
-1°C to 32°C (30°F to 90°F)	SAE 40	SAE 80
-18°C to 21°C (0°F to 70°F)	SAE 30	65
Below -12°C (10°)	SAE 20	55
AD Oil		
Above 16°C (60°F)	SAE 50 or 40	W/D100 or W/D80
-1°C to 32°C (30°F to 90°F)	SAE 40	W/D80
-18°C to 21°C (0°F to 70°F)	SAE 30 or 40	W/D65 or W/D80
Below -12°C (10°)	SAE 30	W/D65

In addition to these 'monograde' oils there are also some 'multigrade' types, such as 15W/50, which can be used over a wider range of temperatures than a single 'monograde' oil. *This table is an approximate guide only, and does not overrule the instructions in the aircraft's POH/FM, engine handbook, and oil manufacturer's guidelines.*

There is no problem adding a different grade of oil to that already in the engine if the conditions dictate it, provided they are of the same type. However, in very cold conditions it is possible for oil with a high grade to become 'waxy' in a static engine, meaning that the engine has to be pre-heated before it can be started.

▶Serviceability Checks and Handling

During the pre-flight checks, the oil level is checked on a dipstick. For a wet-sump engine this can only be done properly if all the oil has returned to the sump, and it will be at least 10min after the engine has stopped before a proper oil quantity check can be made. To get an accurate reading, it helps to wipe the dipstick clean with a rag or piece of paper and then to re-insert it. The engine handbook and POH/FM will state the minimum acceptable oil quantity. It may also give an average oil consumption figure, so the pilot can assess whether the oil level will need topping-up. A marked increase in oil consumption without a good reason is a cause for concern and should be referred to an engineer.

An oil dipstick and filler pipe

It is not usually worth filling the oil to its maximum capacity because the system has a tendency to eject the 'top' litre or so of oil overboard through the *oil breather pipe* if filled to the maximum capacity. The oil breather pipe vents the sump to the atmosphere and usually exits underneath the engine. When replenishing the oil, be sure to double-check that the correct type and grade is being added – and if in doubt, ask someone. On re-securing the oil dipstick (most are of a 'screw' type) take care not to overtighten it. This serves no useful purpose and can even 'strip' (destroy) the thread of the oil cap, meaning that it is no longer secure. If a previous pilot has over-tightened the oil cap, it may be possible to open it using a couple of keys either side of the finger grip to increase leverage. After checking the oil level, and where possible, look over the engine with special attention to obvious oil leaks (which may tend to pool in the bottom of the cowling or leak on to the ground below). Any such leak clearly requires further investigation. Look also for oil leaks around the covers (rocker boxes) over the top of the cylinder heads, and from the valve pushrod tubes that run from these back to the crankcase.

▶ Revision

95   In a 'wet-sump' aero-engine, where is the oil reservoir?

96   At what point is the temperature of engine oil measured?

97   At what point is the pressure of engine oil measured?

98   Immediately after major engine maintenance work, what type of oil would a pilot *expect* to be in use?

99   Why can the oil level of a 'wet-sump' system not be checked immediately after the engine has stopped?

Answers page fpp71

Aircraft General Knowledge
The Propeller

Aircraft General Knowledge
The Propeller

▶ Principles of Propellers

▶ The Fixed-Pitch Propeller

▶ The Variable Pitch Propeller

▶ Propeller Handling and Serviceability Checks

▶ Revision

The Propeller

▶ Principles of Propellers

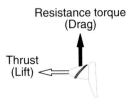

The forces acting on a rotating propeller

Blade angle, or pitch angle, of a propeller blade

The propeller is merely a type of aerofoil – i.e. a wing. Rotated by the engine, it creates lift along the horizontal axis of the aircraft (referred to as thrust in this instance) and also a resistance or drag, sometimes called *resistance torque*. It is thrust that provides the motion to move the aircraft forward. Just as the lift produced by a wing is largely a function of the angle and speed at which it is moving through the air; so the amount of thrust produced by the propeller is largely dictated by the angle of attack of the propeller blade and the speed (RPM) of the propeller and the engine horsepower (hp) used to drive it.

The angle of the propeller blade to its plane of rotation is called, simply enough, the *blade angle*, or *pitch angle*. A large pitch angle is a *coarse pitch*, a small pitch angle is a *fine pitch*.

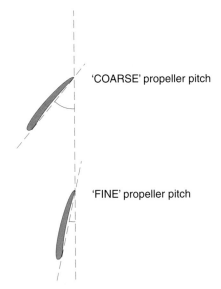

'COARSE' propeller pitch

'FINE' propeller pitch

A coarse blade angle and a fine blade angle

The 'twist' of the propeller blade angle

When the propeller is turning, the outer sections of the blades travel further in each rotation than the inner and because the entire blade completes a rotation at the same time, it follows that the outer part of the blade must be travelling faster than the inner. Because the outer part of the blade is moving faster than the inner, the blade or pitch angle is reduced towards the tip of the blade so that the propeller will have approximately the same angle of attack along its entire length. The resulting 'twist' in the blade is quite noticeable if viewed side-on. So the inner section of the propeller has a much greater **pitch angle** than the outer, but the **angle of attack** should be broadly similar along all parts of the blade once it is rotating.

While an aircraft is stationary, its propeller meets the air in its plane of rotation. However, as soon as the aircraft begins to move, the forward motion has an effect too. As the forward speed increases, the effective angle of attack of the propeller reduces (remembering that the angle of attack is the angle at which the aerofoil is meeting the airflow). Of course, as an aerofoil, a propeller blade has a particular angle of attack at which it is producing the maximum lift (thrust) for the minimum resistance/drag (torque). At any other angle of attack – altered by RPM and airspeed – the propeller is not at its most efficient.

So far we have considered the propulsion force of the aircraft in terms of thrust only. In fact, many important performance criteria rely on measurement of *power*. Thrust can be thought of as the propulsive force produced by the propeller. To take account of the forward motion of the aircraft, thrust is multiplied by airspeed to give power. Thus a propeller moving at 2400RPM on an aircraft flying at 100kts produces more power than one moving at 2400RPM if the aircraft is flying at 50kts.

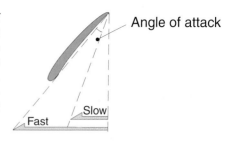

How airspeed changes the propeller's angle of attack

▶ The Fixed-Pitch Propeller

Most training aircraft have a *fixed-pitch* propeller whose pitch angle is fixed and cannot be altered. Such a propeller is most often fixed directly onto the engine's crankshaft and its construction is very simple with the blades and the hub often forming a single solid unit. Most modern aircraft have metal propellers, although wooden propellers can still be found especially on smaller aircraft. The propeller hub may be covered by a *spinner*, which helps to protect the hub from the elements and reduce aerodynamic drag.

A rotating propeller is subject to a multitude of forces; *centrifugal* force tries to throw the propeller blades out from the hub, and at the propeller tips there is a *thrust bending force* which tries to pull that part of the blade ahead of the rest. There is also a *centrifugal twisting force* which, if the propeller blade was free to twist relative to the hub, would cause the blade angle to reduce (a finer pitch) with increasing RPM. The slipstream effect of the propeller has already been described. Two other less significant yawing moments produced by the propeller in a climb are *asymmetric blade effect* and *torque*.

A typical fixed-pitch propeller

Asymmetric blade effect in a climb

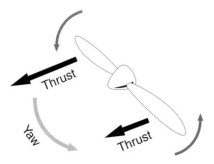

The up-going propeller blade has a smaller angle of attack than the down-going blade, producing less lift.

Asymmetric blade effect is caused by the different angles of attack experienced by the up-going and down-going propeller blades when the rotating propeller meets the airflow at an angle to the horizontal. During a climb, the down-going propeller blade has a higher angle of attack than the up-going, so that it is producing more lift – or in this case, thrust. The net result is a yawing force to the left where the propeller turns clockwise as seen from the cockpit (and vice versa).

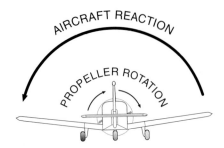

Torque effect - the aircraft wanting to rotate in the opposite direction to the propeller

Torque is the tendency of the aircraft to want to roll in the opposite direction to that in which the propeller is rotating. If the propeller rotates clockwise as seen from the cockpit (to the right) the aircraft will try to roll anti-clockwise (to the left). Rather like asymmetric blade effect, torque is not a major factor in relatively low-powered aircraft compared to the slipstream effect already described. The collective effects of power are sometimes known (particularly in the USA) as *p-effect*.

A fixed-pitch propeller can be likened to a car with one gear. The speed of the engine/propeller is measured with a *tachometer*, and rather like a car stuck in one gear, as a aircraft with a fixed-pitch propeller increases its speed, so engine/propeller RPM will increase, even though the throttle position is unchanged. If the aircraft slows down, engine/propeller RPM will decrease with a fixed throttle position. A fixed-pitch propeller can only be at its most efficient at one combination of RPM and airspeed, and so the designer has to choose a situation for the propeller to do its best work. If the chosen optimum point is cruising flight the propeller will obviously lose efficiency in any other flight situation. One way to combat this problem would be to have a choice of propellers available, each optimised for a different task. A coarser-pitch propeller may offer better cruise performance (the faster the cruise, the coarser the pitch), at the penalty of a longer take-off distance. A finer-pitch propeller may give better take-off and climb performance but a slower and less efficient cruise. Evidently the standard propeller fitted by the manufacturer will be a compromise and fitting a different propeller is only really practical if the aircraft is being used for one specific task, such as glider towing where the primary task is to climb efficiently. In this case, using a fine-pitch propeller gives good take-off and climb performance, which is more important than cruising efficiency. If a 'non-standard' propeller is fitted to an aircraft, there may be amended performance figures in the POH/FM.

▶The Variable Pitch Propeller

The simplicity of the fixed pitch propeller makes it the logical choice for an aircraft with a relatively low power engine cruising at slowish airspeed, but more powerful engines and faster cruise speeds require better efficiency from the propeller/engine combination.

An alteration in airspeed will alter the effective angle of attack of the propeller blade, and the propeller blade will do its most efficient work at a particular angle of attack. It follows that if the pilot can alter the propeller blade (pitch) angle in flight, it can maintain that efficient angle of attack over a wide range airspeeds. This can be done using the *variable pitch* propeller, in which the propeller blade is attached to the hub via a mounting or clamp that can be rotated, in effect altering the propeller blade angle. Now, using a pitch control lever in the cockpit, the pilot can change the propeller blade angle for different flight conditions, for example selecting a finer pitch (smaller blade angle) for the relatively slow speeds of take-off and climb, but a coarser pitch (larger pitch angle) for the faster cruise airspeed. Early variable pitch propellers did indeed operate as such simple devices, with a take-off/climb setting and a cruise setting. However, the modern-day variable-pitch propeller incorporates a *Constant Speed Unit* (CSU).

The simplest design of Constant Speed Unit (CSU), as found on single engine aircraft, is a mechanical device connected to a pitch-change mechanism on the propeller hub and the propeller blade mountings. When the propeller is rotating, the centrifugal twisting force tries to twist each propeller blade to a fine pitch. This force is opposed by a piston/cylinder assembly connected to each propeller blade which tries to move the blades to a coarse pitch and is powered hydraulically by oil from the engine's oil system. The balance between these forces is controlled by the CSU itself – a spring-loaded flyweight assembly which controls the oil pressure in the piston/cylinder assembly: pumping oil in increases the propeller blade angle (coarser pitch, lower RPM), allowing oil to flow out decreases the propeller blade angle (finer pitch, higher RPM). The CSU is controlled by the pitch lever in the cockpit which sets the spring/flyweight assembly at a particular RPM. If the RPM then tries to rise (for example, as the aircraft flies faster or if the throttle is opened), the flyweights spin faster and open a valve which pumps oil into the piston/cylinder to increase the blade angle and therefore maintain the pre-set RPM. If the aircraft slows or if the throttle is closed, the flyweights spin more slowly and the valve allows oil out of the piston/cylinder, so that centrifugal twisting force reduces the blade angle and so maintains the pre-set RPM. In summary, the pilot selects the required RPM using the pitch lever, and the CSU will then maintain this RPM over a wide range of throttle settings/airspeeds. Moreover, the pilot can select the most efficient RPM for each stage of flight, for example the pilot can set a fine propeller pitch (high RPM) for maximum take-off and climb performance but a more coarse pitch (slower RPM) to obtain the best cruise performance.

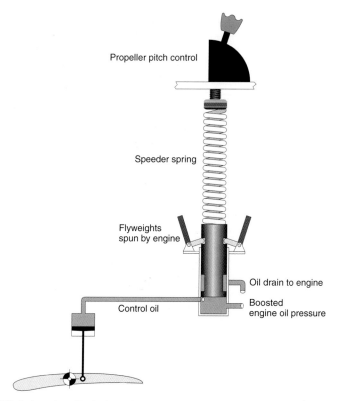

The fairly simple CSU design described above is not common to all variable pitch propellers. Certain aircraft have an electrically controlled pitch change mechanism, some have more complex CSUs and large counter-weights attached to the propeller blade mountings. However, in all instances the principle is the same, the pitch control is used to set the required RPM. The throttle, meanwhile, controls the amount of fuel/air mixture flowing into the engine and this is measured in terms of *manifold pressure*. Open the throttle (push it forward) and manifold pressure is increased, close the throttle (pull it back) and manifold pressure is decreased.

The POH/FM of an aircraft with a variable-pitch propeller will state engine power settings in terms of both manifold pressure (controlled by the throttle) and RPM (set with the pitch control). Commonly the propeller RPM is set to fully fine (highest RPM) for take-off and initial climb, and just before landing. In this way the maximum thrust is always available to the pilot at these critical stages of flight. Fine pitch/high RPM is similar to first gear in a car – to accelerate suddenly from low speed, first gear is better than fifth! When altering power settings, the golden rule is to increase RPM (pitch) before moving the throttle if **increasing** power, and decrease manifold pressure (throttle) before altering the pitch if **decreasing** power. This rule can be remembered as:

A variable pitch propeller with counter-weights attached to the blades and the pitch-change cylinder on the propeller hub

Rev up

Throttle down

Adherence to this rule and use of the RPM/manifold pressure setting stated in the POH/FM will avoid overstressing the engine by exceeding the maximum permitted RPM or applying too much manifold pressure at too low an RPM. One time when it is very easy to over-rev the engine is when selecting fully fine pitch (maximum RPM) during the pre-landing checks. The common mistake is to slam the pitch control lever to fully fine while airspeed is still relatively high. The result is not unlike what would be expected if a car was forced into first gear at 60mph – a sudden increase to the maximum permitted RPM (or beyond) accompanied by a howl from both the engine and propeller. There is a better way. As the aircraft slows, the CSU will try to maintain the set RPM by gradually reducing the propeller blade angle (moving towards

A pitch lever (centre) between the throttle (left) and mixture control (right)

a finer pitch). Eventually, the propeller blade will reach a 'fine pitch stop', and the blade angle cannot reduce any further. As airspeed continues to slow, so the RPM will start to fall below its pre-set figure even though the pitch lever has not been moved. Once this point occurs the pilot knows that fully fine RPM can be selected without over-revving the engine. Once fully fine pitch is set, the engine/propeller combination works just like a fixed-pitch propeller, with the RPM being susceptible to changes in both throttle setting and airspeed.

The VP propellers used on Multi Engine (ME) aircraft usually have one significant difference to those found on Single Engine Piston (SEP) aircraft in that they are capable of being *feathered*. A 'feathered' propeller is one where the blades are at a blade angle (around 90°) that is essentially 'edge on' to the airflow. This might be done in the event of an engine failure: the propeller is feathered so that it will stop rotating and with the minimum area presented to the airflow, it will create the minimum possible drag. Conversely, 'windmilling' propeller, one that is being rotated by the airflow rather than the engine, can create a huge amount of drag and no appreciable thrust. On a multi-engine aircraft the difference in drag between a feathered propeller and a windmilling one will almost certainly make the difference between being able to climb or maintain altitude on one engine, or being forced to descend.

This brief technical description should have given a good grounding in the theory and practice of variable-pitch (VP) propellers. However, quite apart from any licensing/rating requirements, if converting on to an aircraft with a VP or 'constant speed' propeller, the guidance of an instructor familiar with its operation should be sought and some time spent with the appropriate section of the aircraft's POH/FM.

▶ Propeller Handling and Serviceability Checks

The first rule of checking the propeller during the pre-flight checks is to always regard it as 'live', and treat it with due respect. To inspect the propeller blades, run a finger along the blade edges without moving the propeller to feel for cracks and 'nicks' or stone chips, particularly along the leading edge of the blade. Such damage, usually caused by stones or gravel, is especially dangerous in the area 6-12in (15-30cm) from the propeller tip. The propeller undergoes huge strains and stresses in flight; centrifugal force alone can easily amount to more than 40 tonnes, and a small nick can act as a fatigue point from which a crack can quickly develop. Ultimately, part of the blade may depart the aeroplane. Should this occur, the resulting severe vibration requires that the engine be shut down immediately. On the propeller blade there may be a smooth depression, where a nick has been filed down by an engineer; the allowable limits of this type of repair are quite strict, so seek advice if in doubt. Take time also to look around the ground below and ahead of the aircraft for stones, gravel or other debris and obstructions which might damage the propeller after starting. If a spinner is fitted, little of the propeller hub may be visible. However, the spinner itself can be checked for security (are all the retaining screws present?) and general condition. In very cold conditions, there is the possibility of water collecting within the hub, and then freezing into ice.

Propellers are designated by diameter and pitch. The propeller diameter is the distance across the propeller disk. This should allow adequate clearance between the propeller tips and the ground. A 'low' noseleg, combined with rough ground or dips, may reduce this clearance to zero, leading to a 'prop strike' as the propeller contacts the ground. Be wary also of taxying through long grass, which may hide holes or obstructions.

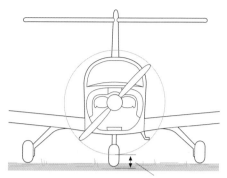

Propeller tip clearance

Propeller diameter and 'tip' or 'ground' clearance

An aircraft with a variable-pitch (VP) propeller is started and taxied in the 'fully fine' pitch setting, so there is no difference in handling at this stage between this and a fixed pitch propeller. During the power checks the operation of the CSU is checked by reducing the propeller RPM from a high power setting (typically 2000RPM) down to around 1500RPM and then returning it to fully fine. Aside from verifying the operation of the pitch-change mechanism, this action (usually repeated twice, especially for the first flight of the day) will circulate warm engine oil through the pitch change mechanism. The other aspect of propeller care common to both fixed pitch and VP propellers is to make all changes of throttle and pitch setting in a smooth and considered way. Slamming the throttle open and chopping it closed, or treating the pitch control in the same brutal manner, makes life very tough on a propeller whose centrifugal forces alone can be measured in tens of tonnes. Although in-flight failure of the propeller is rare, the long-term consequences of mistreating the engine/propeller combination are both risky and expensive.

A manifold pressure gauge (with fuel pressure in the lower half) and RPM gauge to the right. The engine/propeller is set at '25/25' – that is 25 inches of manifold pressure and 2500RPM

▶ Revision

100 Why does the propeller blade angle (pitch angle) vary along the propeller?

101 If an aircraft with a fixed pitch propeller accelerates without moving the throttle, what will be the effect (if any) on engine RPM?

102 If the propeller rotates clockwise as seen from the cockpit (to the right), how will torque effect act on the aircraft?

103 Should a pilot expect a propeller designed to maximise take-off and climb performance to be more 'fine' or 'coarse' in pitch than one designed to maximise cruise performance?

Answers see page fpp71

Aircraft General Knowledge
Engine Handling

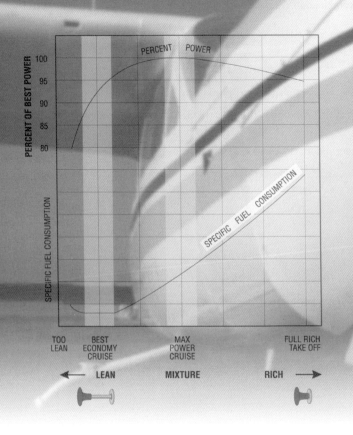

Aircraft General Knowledge
Engine Handling

The subject of engine handling is so important that it justifies a separate chapter. Looking after the engine and operating it properly not only enables the pilot to get the best performance from it but also has obvious safety benefits. The vast majority of engine failures in light aircraft are caused by some form of mis-handling – i.e. pilot error. It follows that such failures are altogether avoidable.

To look at the subject of engine handling we will follow the course of an imaginary cross-country flight, and discuss each aspect of engine handling as it presents itself. The following assumes a normally aspirated (i.e. non-turbocharged) engine fitted with a carburettor and a fixed pitch propeller.

▶ Starting Procedure

▶ Starting Problems

▶ Fire on Start

▶ Taxying, Power Checks, Take-Off

▶ Climbing

▶ In The Cruise

▶ Engine Problem Troubleshooting

▶ Descent

▶ After-landing and Shut Down

▶ Storage

▶ Revision

Engine Handling

▶ Starting Procedure

To prepare the engine for starting, follow the checklist or instructions in the aircraft's POH/FM. Different aircraft have different starting techniques; those for carburettor engines are different from those for fuel-injected engines, and different makes of fuel-injected engines may have different starting sequences. Using a checklist will avoid trying to start an engine with the mixture in the wrong position or some similar blunder.

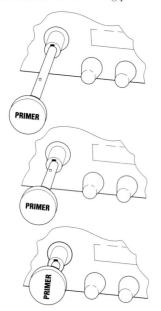

Operation of a manual fuel primer

A starter ring, visible under the cowling and behind the propeller, on to which the starter engages

Most carburettor engines are fitted with a *primer*, which in a typical training aircraft takes the form of a small plunger operated from the cockpit. The primer is unlocked by rotating the control until a small pin on the shaft is aligned with a cut-out in the collar. The primer is then pulled out to its full extent, at which point it will fill with fuel (this takes a few moments). The primer is then pushed fully in, and a resistance should be felt as the fuel is forced down the fuel lines. From there it is directed to the induction manifold and thence to the inlet valves. Bypassing the carburettor in this way ensures that there is plenty of fuel ready to go straight to the cylinders on starting.

The number of primes required is largely a function of the engine type and the length of time since it was last run. A typical four-cylinder engine may need three cycles of the primer when absolutely cold, or none at all if it has just been running. Different engines tend to have different techniques regarding priming, and an instructor or a pilot experienced on that engine type should be able to offer practical advice. Once priming is finished, care must be taken to lock the primer closed again. This is usually done by pushing the plunger all the way home so that the pin on the shaft passes through the slot in the collar, then rotating the plunger half a turn or so. Now try to pull the primer out: it should remain closed. If the primer is not locked properly it will allow extra fuel to flow to the cylinders once the engine has started. This will lead to rough running and possibly engine stoppage.

Once the engine is primed and the checklist has been completed as far as operation of the starter, it is good practice to look all around to see that the propeller area is clear and to shout out "Clear Prop!" This is a final warning to those outside the aircraft that the engine is about to start. The majority of training aircraft have a key-operated starter which is also the magneto switch. The key is turned to the position marked 'Start', and an electric starter at the front of the engine engages a large cog (known as the *starter ring*) behind the propeller. The starter turns the engine until it fires of its own accord. When this happens the key is released, and a spring will return the key to the 'Both' position.

A typical key-operated magneto switch and starter

Electric starter motors are now the norm for aircraft engines. Some older aircraft may have different systems such as the Coffmann cartridge starter, or indeed none at all. In the latter case, the pilot relies on someone hand-swinging the propeller. *Beware – do **not** try this until you have been fully briefed on how to do it.* Because "swinging the prop" has such potential for serious injury, and can only really be taught by 'hands-on' training, it will not be described in detail here. But hand-swinging must only be attempted by someone who has had proper, practical instruction from a competent person. The job involves not just the person at the propeller, but also a suitably qualified person in the cockpit: instructions and signals must be carefully agreed between these two people to avoid a very nasty accident.

Never hand-swing a propeller until you have had full, proper training

Even when qualified to hand-swing a propeller, avoid doing so with no one at the controls. Every year there are several starting accidents when a pilot 'elects' to try hand-swinging a propeller with nobody in the cockpit. Every so often this results in the engine starting, going to a much higher RPM than expected, and then moving away under its own power with nobody ay the controls. Even if nobody is injured by the runaway aircraft, it is almost inevitable that the hapless pilot is left with an exceedingly large bill – insurance companies tend to be unsympathetic in these cases – and an awful lot of explaining to do. In fairness, whilst the type of accident described above is depressingly common, actual injury to a person handswing-swinging a propeller is very rare. Maybe this is because those who swing propellers have been properly trained and are well aware of the potential dangers.

Once the engine does start, the first task is to set the proper RPM as stated in the checklist or POH/FM, typically 1000-1200RPM. It is important *not* to allow the engine to go to a much higher RPM or deliberately advance the throttle immediately to a high power setting. The engine needs a little time to warm up and for its systems – particularly the oil system – to come into operation. Taking a cold engine straight to high RPM is one way to cause long term engine damage.

After starting keep the engine to the recommended RPM (commonly 1000-1200) while it warms up

With the proper RPM set, the starter warning light (if fitted) should be checked. This indicates that the starter motor is engaged, and should light up when the starter is being operated but go out when the starter switch is released. If it remains lit, the starter motor is still engaged and is now being turned by the engine. Serious damage to the electrical system is the likely result of this situation, so the engine should be shut down immediately. Shortly after start, the oil pressure gauge is also checked; engines run very badly without sufficient oil pressure. If no oil pressure indication is seen within 30 seconds of starting, the engine should be shut down *at once*.

A starter warning light

▶ Starting Problems

If the engine does not start straight away, there are some basic trouble-shooting steps to take before calling for an engineer. A piston aero-engine needs fuel, air and a source of ignition to operate. Run through the starting checks again to make sure that nothing major has been missed. Assuming that there is no obvious problem, such as the starter motor failing to operate, the most likely scenario is that there is either too much or too little fuel in the induction system – i.e. the engine is over or under-primed. An under-primed engine will not fire at all. An over-primed (or *flooded*) engine may fire intermittently but fail to catch properly while emitting copious quantities of smoke from the exhaust. In either case, if the engine does not start readily do not operate the starter motor for more than about 20 seconds at a time and allow it at least a minute to cool after a long starting attempt.

To assess the likely problem, take into account the overall situation: a hot engine on a hot day will need less priming than a cold engine on a cold day. Based on this and the usual behaviour of the engine, decide whether it is under-primed and requires more fuel or is over-primed (flooded). If it is flooded, the excess can be cleared by moving the mixture to the fully lean position (usually marked as ICO or 'Idle Cut Off '). This cuts off the fuel supply. Then throttle is then set to about half-way open. Operate the starter and if the engine does start, quickly move the mixture to rich and retard the throttle to establish the normal after-start RPM.

▶ Fire on Start

Although a rare occurrence, it is possible for an engine to catch fire during starting if it has been over-primed. Most carburetted aircraft engines have the carburettor located underneath the engine, a so-called *up-draft* carburettor. This means that if the engine is flooded, fuel may flow back down the induction system and pool near the carburettor. If this fuel is ignited (perhaps by an engine backfire) the result is a fire in the induction system.

Fuel dripping from a carburettor that has been over-primed by 'pumping' the throttle

Such over-priming (flooding) is best avoided. Priming should be done strictly in accordance with the engine manual, the aircraft's POH/FM and the checklist. The most likely cause of flooding is the bad habit of 'pumping' the throttle of an engine with an accelerator pump in the carburettor. This forces neat fuel into the induction system and greatly increases the risk of a fire there.

If an engine fire does occur during starting, the best action is to keep turning the engine over if it is not yet running. Should the engine start, the fire may well be drawn out of the induction system. Run the engine normally for a minute or so. Then if there is no further sign of fire, shut down and have everything checked out. If the engine does not start, continue operating the starter for as long as possible to try to draw the fire into the engine. If the fire continues, shut down the engine – taking particular care to turn off the fuel – and exit the aircraft, carrying the fire extinguisher. To tackle the fire, the extinguisher can be operated directly into the air filter or underneath of the cowling. However, if in any doubt stand well back and leave the fire fighting to the professionals.

An engine fire on starting may well be out of sight of the pilot, so it is important to be alert for bystanders trying to attract attention during and after start. They may be trying to say something important.

▶Taxying, Power Checks, Take-Off

When taxying, take particular care to avoid hitting anything with the propeller. On a nosewheel aircraft there is normally adequate clearance between the tips and the ground, but an undulation or hole could compress the nose oleo far enough for the propeller to strike the ground. Long grass can hide ditches, holes or obstructions and if crossing from one surface type to another (for example from grass to tarmac) there may be a 'lip', depression or step where the two surfaces meet. The usual advice is to aim to cross slowly at an angle of 45° to the dividing line, with the minimum power necessary. If the aircraft is heading approximately into wind, hold the control column well back. These measures will reduce the risk of the propeller striking the ground or the nosewheel getting stuck in a 'dip' between surfaces. During normal taxying aircraft's speed is regulated with the throttle. To slow down, *always close the throttle before applying the brakes*; it is poor airmanship to use brakes against engine power. Whenever the aircraft is parked, set the recommended RPM which is usually 1000-1200. Do not allow the engine to idle (i.e. to run with the throttle fully closed) for any length of time. Doing so may allow oil or lead deposits to form on the spark plugs, which will have to be cleared if the engine is to develop full power.

GRASS

HARD SURFACE

Actions to take when crossing from a hard surface to a soft or vice-versa

Increase power gradually until the aircraft moves forward.

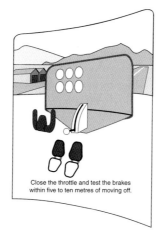

Close the throttle and test the brakes within five to ten metres of moving off.

When taxying, slow the aircraft by closing the throttle first, then using the brakes

The aircraft's checklist and POH/FM will give the sequence of the power checks. Before increasing the engine power, check that the oil temperature has begun to register and when increasing the power setting, look for a corresponding increase in oil pressure. If the engine falters as the throttle is opened, it is probably not yet warm enough for the power checks. As always, the throttle should always be advanced smoothly and steadily – avoid 'slamming' it open.

The checklist should be referred to for the power checks

Advancing the throttle steadily is done for three specific reasons:

- if an accelerator pump is fitted, a sudden throttle movement can cause an over-rich mixture. This can cause the engine to falter or even stop (in what is known as a *rich cut*).
- the engine crankshaft is fitted with counterweights to reduce vibration and damp out potentially damaging resonant frequencies. Sudden throttle movements can cause just the sort of vibration the counterweights are designed to avoid;
- sudden throttle movements may make it difficult for the carburettor to supply the correct fuel-air mixture throughout the RPM range, possibly resulting in a *'flat spot'* where the throttle movement causes the engine to falter.

At the selected power-check setting (commonly 1700-2000RPM) the carburettor heat control is operated. There should be a smooth drop in RPM, the usual reduction being around 100-150RPM (refer to the aircraft's checklist or POH/FM for exact figures). When the control is returned to the cold position, the RPM should return to the original setting. No change in RPM when the carburettor heat control is operated, or an excessive RPM drop with rough running which does not clear after a few seconds, are both signs of a problem requiring the attention of an engineer.

After the carburettor heat check, the magnetos are checked. The normal sequence for a key-type magneto switch is as follows. From the Both position, move the key one 'click' to the left. It should now be at the Left position, meaning that the only the Left magneto is operating and only one of the two spark plugs in each cylinder is producing a spark. The result should be a smooth RPM drop of around 100-150 (again refer to the aircraft's checklist or POH/FM for exact figures). There should be no excessive RPM drop or rough running. After a couple of seconds, return the key to the Both position and the RPM should return to the original setting. Now move the key two clicks to the left so that it is in the Right position. Now only the Right magneto is operating and the 'other' spark plug in each cylinder is sparking. The RPM drop should again be smooth with no rough running, and the new and lower value should be no more than about 50RPM different from the figure when the Left magneto was being operated alone. The key is now returned to the Both position.

An excessive or sudden RPM drop, rough running or a major difference between the individual RPM reductions can all be signs of a problem. Such symptoms are often caused by spark-plug fouling (i.e. lead or oil deposits on the spark plug) especially if the engine has been allowed to idle for a prolonged period in cold weather conditions. The pilot can attempt to clear this problem by increasing the power to near-cruise power setting and then leaning the mixture until the RPM begins to fall. This will increase the temperature inside the cylinders and may 'burn off' any spark-plug deposits. Only do this under the supervision of a flying instructor, and avoid excessive power settings or excessively lean mixtures. After a short period, return the RPM to the power-check setting and the mixture to rich and re-check the magnetos. If the problem has not cleared, the flight should be abandoned. This is frustrating, but much better than getting airborne with a potential problem – there is no point in doing checks and then ignoring the results. The phrase "It should be all right" is high on the list of famous last words.

Be alert for no RPM drop at all when selecting the magnetos individually. This indicates that one or both of them is remaining on permanently and cannot be switched off – a so-called 'live' magneto. This is a potentially dangerous situation requiring immediate referral to an engineer.

After the carburettor heat and magneto checks, the engine gauges (cylinder-head temperature, oil temperature, oil pressure, fuel pressure etc.) are checked for normal readings within the limits specified in the checklist or POH/FM. The power is now *smoothly* reduced until the throttle control is fully back; in other words the throttle is closed as far as possible. The result should be smooth idling within the permitted idling RPM range. With this verified, the RPM is returned to the normal 'parked' power setting, and the remainder of the pre take-off checks can be completed. As part of these, the primer should be verified as being locked closed, and if appropriate the fuel pump should be turned on.

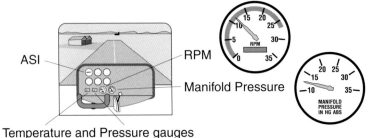

To monitor engine power on take-off, check the RPM (and manifold pressure gauge if fitted), temperature and pressure gauges, and air speed indicator (for normal acceleration)

ASI

RPM

Manifold Pressure

Temperature and Pressure gauges

Lining up on the runway is the time for a final look around the cockpit to see that the engine controls are properly set. The fuel selector, magneto switch and carburettor heat controls are the most likely items to be mis-set, so they are worth a final check before starting the take-off. If conditions are particularly favourable for carburettor icing – lots of moisture, maybe rain, drizzle or standing water – consider making a further carburettor heat check just before starting the take-off. Normally take-off is made with the mixture in the fully rich position. However, at a particularly high elevation airfield (above 3000ft AMSL, for example) it may be necessary to lean the mixture at the power check RPM to achieve the maximum power output, and to make the take-off with the mixture in this 'leaned' position.

During the take-off run itself the oil pressure and temperature gauges (usually referred to as the 'Ts and Ps') are checked to ensure that they are within limits. It's also sensible to check the RPM gauge to see if normal take-off power is being produced. When the aircraft is not moving, or is moving very slowly, the propeller cannot reach its maximum RPM. The best RPM the engine/propeller can produce when the aircraft is stationary is known as the 'static RPM' and may be a good 20% less than the maximum RPM attainable in flight. The other engine instruments can also be checked – but it is just as important to take in all the visual, auditory and motional cues and decide whether the take-off *feels* normal. Does the acceleration seem normal? Does the engine usually sound like that? Is there any abnormal vibration? These are the sort of clues that can signal a problem long before the gauges do.

▶ Climbing

The engine is working very hard during the climb to cruising level, but has relatively little cooling air passing over it because of the relatively slow airspeed in the climb. So watch the engine gauges closely for signs of overheating. If the oil temperature moves towards the yellow cautionary area of the gauge, increasing airspeed and reducing power are both effective cooling measures. In fact, once clear of obstacles, climbing at a faster airspeed than that for best climb rate helps keep the engine cool whilst increasing the groundspeed – at the cost of a reduced rate of climb, of course.

Rate of climb is a good indicator of engine performance, since climb performance is dictated by the excess of power available over power required. If the aircraft is consistently failing to climb as it should at best-rate-of-climb airspeed and there is no obvious cause such as poor technique, high temperatures or altitude, it is possible that the engine is not producing full power for one reason or another.

Whilst the engine is operating at more than 75% power – as it normally is at low altitude during the climb – carburettor heat is not used. Some aircraft POH/FMs recommend leaning the mixture above a certain altitude (commonly 3000ft) to maintain full power in the climb. It is also worth noting that the greatest engine power output is obtained at the highest RPM: with increasing altitude, engine power and engine RPM reduce.

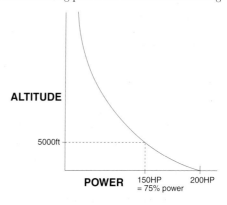

The reduction in 'percentage power' caused by altitude

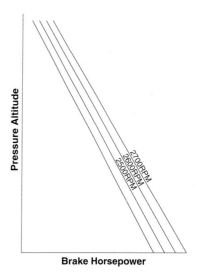

Variation of horsepower with altitude

▶ In The Cruise

Engine handling in the cruise focuses on getting the best performance from the engine whilst monitoring it regularly. Having set the cruise power and with the aircraft in the cruise configuration, a cruise check is the next obvious action. The actions of a cruise check (such as those conjured up by the FREDA or FEEL mnemonics) include checking the engine gauges, monitoring the fuel system and, in particular, checking for carburettor icing.

If an aircraft has a fixed-pitch propeller, the loss of power caused by carburettor icing is first evident as a decrease in RPM, although the pilot may first notice a loss of airspeed or altitude. On an aircraft with a variable-pitch propeller, manifold pressure will reduce rather than RPM, accompanied by a loss of airspeed or altitude. To check for carburettor icing, place the carburettor heat control in the fully hot position. There will be a drop in RPM, possibly accompanied by a little rough running if the hot air is melting ice in the carburettor and so causing water to pass through the engine. As the ice is cleared, the rough running should cease; when the carburettor heat is returned to cold, the RPM will probably return to a figure which is slightly higher than it was before the control was operated. However, if there was no carburettor icing the RPM will revert to the same value as before the check.

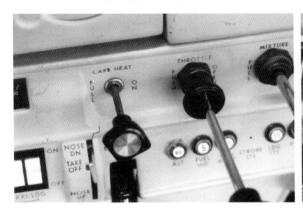

Two types of carburettor heat control

Visible moisture such as clouds and rain **does not** have to be present for carburettor icing to occur. Nor does the outside air temperature have to be below freezing (0°C). The drop in temperature in the carburettor venturi can be anything up to 30°C, which is why carburettor icing is considered possible anywhere in the air temperature range between -10 and +30°C. The deciding factor, however, is the humidity – the more humid the air, the greater the risk. In general, carburettor icing is considered unlikely at very low temperatures (below about -10°C) because any water content in the induction air will tend to exist as solid ice crystals. These will pass through the venturi without sticking to anything. Under such circumstances the use of carburettor heat can actually raise the temperature in the venturi to a level where ice is more likely to form.

Very occasionally (if flying through intense rain, for example) the pilot may consider leaving the carburettor heat in the hot position for as long as the conditions persist. If this is done, it is worth leaning the mixture to ensure the smooth the running of the engine; the less dense hot air leads to a richer mixture than normal. The prolonged use of the carburettor heating will inevitably increase fuel consumption.

Factors affecting carburettor icing and the use of the carburettor heat control have already been discussed in detail in PPL 1 – Flying Training (Exercise 8 supplement); PPL 3 – Navigation, Meteorology (the Icing chapter); and in this volume. It is good practice to revise these now.

Once settled in the cruise the question of leaning the mixture arises. The conventional wisdom is that the need to lean the mixture is dictated by altitude, and that once flying above a stated height – typically around 3000ft to 5000ft – it is necessary to adjust the fuel-air mixture to prevent the less dense air at altitude causing an over-rich mixture and consequent loss of power. Consequently, many pilots believe that they cannot lean the mixture below 3000ft (or 5000ft, or whatever). This is simply not true.

The pilot can, and arguably should, lean the mixture at any altitude – provided that the mixture is re-adjusted when next altering altitude or power. The only real limitation is set by power output. Leaning the mixture **not** advisable whenever the engine is operating at more than 75% power. This percentage power means the actual power output of the engine compared with its 'rated' horsepower (hp). If an engine has a 'rated' power of 100hp (i.e. its maximum possible power output at sea level), the mixture can be leaned any time the engine is producing 75hp or less. Incidentally, manufacturers rarely advise cruising with more than 75% power set. The power output of the engine is determined by the RPM, the throttle position, the altitude and the temperature. The POH/FM will have tables and graphs for cruise performance at various power settings, altitudes and temperatures, and should state the percentage power in each case. As a general rule, at full throttle most training aircraft with normally aspirated engines will reach 75% power at around 8000ft in the 'standard' atmosphere although the POH/FM will give the exact figures.

The following is a simple sequence for leaning an engine with a fixed-pitch propeller and with only an RPM gauge (tachometer) for guidance.

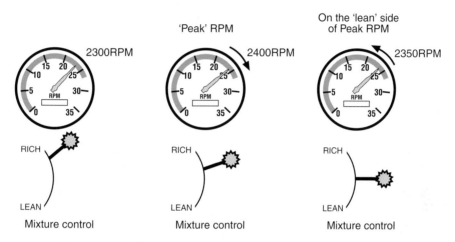

Movement of the RPM gauge of a fixed-pitch propeller as the mixture is leaned

With the RPM set at the recommended cruise power, the mixture control is slowly moved back to lean the mixture. The RPM will rise as the mixture approaches the ideal for efficient operation. As the mixture is leaned further the RPM will peak, and then start to fall. If the mixture is leaned even further, the engine will eventually begin to run roughly. This rough running marks the point beyond which the mixture cannot be leaned any further. The question now is just where to set the mixture control and if the aircraft's POH/FM has a recommended leaning procedure, this should be used. At the peak RPM the engine is leaned for maximum power but it is not returning the best fuel economy. Setting the mixture so that the RPM is 25-50 lower on the 'lean' side of the RPM peak will give something very close to best economy at the expense of slightly reduced power, usually resulting in a loss of no more than 2-3kts airspeed. In the absence of advice to the contrary, some pilots will just enrich the mixture from the rough-running point until the engine is running smoothly again, and leave it at that. Others will opt to richen the mixture until the RPM is about 50 below peak on the 'rich' side of the peak figure. The engine will run cooler with this slightly rich mixture, at the cost of slightly increased fuel consumption.

Use of the mixture control in cruising flight reduces fuel consumption significantly, especially at higher altitudes. The mixture should be leaned during cruising operation above 5000 ft. altitude and at pilot's discretion at lower altitudes when 75% power or less is being used. If any doubt exists as to the amount of power being used, the mixture should be in the full RICH position for all operations under 5000 feet.

To lean the mixture, disengage the lock and pull the mixture control back.

The airplane is equipped with a exhaust gas temperature (EGT) gauge, a more accurate means of leaning for the pilot. Best economy mixture is obtained by moving the mixture control aft until peak EGT is reached. Best power mixture is obtained by leaning to peak EGT and then enrichening until the EGT is 100F. rich of the peak value. Under some conditions of altitude and throttle position, the engine may exhibit roughness before peak EGT is reached. If this occurs, the EGT corresponding to the onset of engine roughness should be used as the peak reference value.

Whatever one's favoured technique, the range/endurance performance figures in the POH/FM will be based on a specified leaning procedure. Failure to lean the engine in the manner stated will mean that the fuel consumption claimed is unlikely to be matched. Aircraft have been known to run out of fuel simply because the pilot worked on the basis of the fuel consumption figures in the POH/FM without applying the necessary leaning procedure.

Leaning recommendations in a POH/FM. The quoted fuel-consumption figures will only be matched if this technique is used

Once the mixture has been set, a change in altitude or power setting (particularly an increase in power) will require a change in mixture setting to maintain proper operation and to keep the engine running smoothly. Correct leaning of the mixture results in increased power and reduced fuel consumption as well as smoother and more efficient engine operation.

Mixture setting has a bearing on engine cooling. At an over-rich mixture setting (such as when the mixture control is set to fully rich at altitude), the induction system is spraying unburned fuel through the cylinders and out of the exhaust pipe. As the mixture is leaned, there is less excess fuel in the fuel-air mixture and the temperature within the cylinder will rise. The temperature in the cylinder continues to rise as the peak RPM is passed, and only starts to fall as the mixture becomes excessively lean. This is about the point at which the engine begins to run roughly.

The main danger of using an excessively lean (i.e. too weak) mixture is *detonation* – especially at high power settings. Detonation is often likened to a hammer blow on the piston head, and amounts to a destructive explosion of the fuel-air mixture in the cylinder due to excessive pressure or temperature, rather than the controlled burning of normal combustion. Detonation in a car engine causes a distinctive 'pinking' noise but unfortunately this is not audible in the case of the aero-engine. However, the vibration and loss of power it produces should certainly be evident. Detonation is something to be avoided at all costs; it can burn a hole through a piston head in a matter of seconds, with destruction of the engine following shortly afterwards.

The relationship between engine power, fuel consumption and mixture

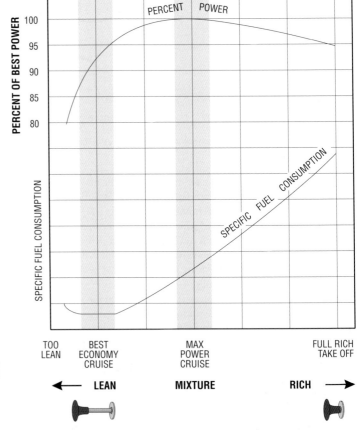

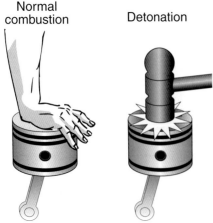

Normal combustion   Detonation

Detonation – an uncontrolled explosion within the cylinder, likely to cause serious engine damage in a short space of time

The classic time for detonation to occur is when an engine has been properly leaned in the cruise but the pilot then increases power – to climb for example – without first enriching the mixture. Turbocharged engines are especially sensitive in this respect. Detonation is most often caused by misuse of the *throttle* (too much power for too lean a mixture) rather than by consciously leaning the *mixture* too far at a cruise power setting. Once the mixture has been leaned, *a change in power setting (especially an increase) will first require a change in mixture setting.*

More powerful aircraft engines often have additional gauges to help the leaning process, commonly indicating cylinder-head temperature (CHT) and exhaust-gas temperature (EGT).

The POH/FM may state a specific limitation for the CHT and this should be observed at all times, remembering that richening the mixture is only one of the options for increasing cooling. Reducing power and increasing airspeed are also good for cooling the engine.

The EGT gauge is specifically designed to enable very precise leaning of the mixture to be made without the risk of damaging the engine. Procedures will be given in the POH/FM, but as a general rule maximum power is obtained with the EGT 90-150°F on the 'rich' side of the peak (hottest) EGT, and best economy mixture occurs with the EGT about 25°F on the 'lean' side of the peak EGT. The actual EGT figure is less important than the temperature trend, and the current EGT in relation to peak EGT.

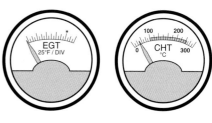

A CHT and EGT gauge

Apart from managing the fuel system to keep fuel flowing to the engine and the proper use of the mixture control and carburettor heat control, engine handling in the cruise is a matter of monitoring the engine instruments and being aware of any unexpected noises or vibrations – in short, displaying situational awareness. If it is necessary to keep increasing the throttle setting to maintain height or airspeed, something may well be amiss. If the fuel consumption seems unexpectedly high, or if the oil temperature is higher than normal, or if the oil pressure seems low, there is bound to be some reason. Such signs should not be ignored.

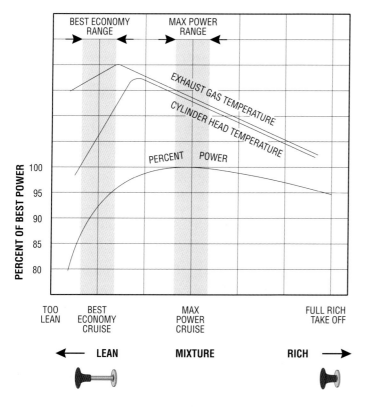

The relationship between mixture, engine power and engine temperatures

▶Engine Problem Troubleshooting

Although engine failures are not the most common cause of aircraft accidents, the possibility of engine failure often concerns pilots. Prevention is better than cure, and prevention starts with regular cruise checks.

Apart from management of the fuel system and regular operation of the carburettor heat control, the cruise check is an opportunity to review the health of the engine. Pay close attention to the oil pressure and oil temperature gauges. Rising oil temperature and falling oil pressure almost certainly indicate an impending mechanical problem of some kind. If unsure whether the needle is moving (light-aircraft gauges are not always especially legible or clear), make a mark with a chinagraph pencil or similar on the instrument face over the needle position. Next time the gauge is checked, any movement of the needle can be seen straight away. Regular monitoring of the gauges can prevent an incident turning into an accident, indeed there are plenty of recorded cases where an alert pilot spotted an impending problem and safely diverted to a nearby airfield before the situation became critical.

Oil pressure and temperature gauges, with fuel pressure and fuel contents gauges alongside

If the engine starts to show clear signs of distress, some intelligent troubleshooting may quickly isolate the root cause. Mechanical failure of the engine or propeller is normally marked by a good deal of mechanical noise, rough running and possibly severe vibration. The vibration itself can cause secondary damage and control problems, so getting it under control is a priority. Try reducing the power to find a smooth power setting. This may leave enough power to maintain level flight, or make a gradual descent whilst conserving as much height as possible. However, if severe vibration and power loss continues, shut down the engine without delay and go into the standard forced-landing procedure before things get even worse.

If the problem is more insidious, such as less severe rough-running or loss of power, the possible remedies can be roughly divided into three groups, in order of importance:

- ■ Carburettor Heat & Fuel. Carburettor icing and fuel starvation (fuel in the tanks but not reaching the engine) or fuel exhaustion (running out of fuel) are the most common causes of engine failures in light aircraft.

  Set the carb. heat to hot, change fuel tanks and turn on the fuel pump if applicable.

- ■ Throttle, Mixture, Magnetos, Primer. Any of these controls may have been accidentally knocked or mis-set.

  Has the throttle been accidentally closed? Check the mixture position, check that the magnetos are on both, check that the primer is locked. Try different mixture settings and throttle settings, select each individual magneto in turn.

- ■ Ancillaries

  Check the engine and fuel gauges for any abnormal indications. Are there any external signs of trouble? Check out other possible sources of the noise/vibration.

The last group is more important than might appear at first sight. The point of this systematic approach is to try to locate the actual or likely problem whilst avoiding making hasty or unsound decisions. The dangers of acting before thinking were illustrated by the pilot who experienced a vibration running through the aircraft just after take-off. Convinced that this was a mechanical engine failure, the pilot shut down the engine and made a forced landing off the airfield. The cause of the vibration turned-out to be a seat-belt stuck in the door, with the loose end being battered against the fuselage by the airflow. A few seconds of considered troubleshooting might have avoided such an incident.

One extremely serious (and extremely rare) emergency is that of an engine fire, which may be caused by a fuel or oil leak igniting. If an engine fire is suspected – and it is worth taking a few seconds to check for sure that there is not some alternative cause such as an electrical problem – the engine should be shut down *immediately* in accordance with the actions outlined in the aircraft's POH/FM. In the absence of specific actions in the POH/FM the usual recommendation for immediate action is to close the throttle, turn off the fuel and close the cabin heater controls, because the cockpit heater pipes normally run through the firewall between the engine compartment and the cockpit. Closing off the heater vents should seal the firewall and stop a fire in the engine compartment from reaching the cockpit. With the correct actions taken, the fire should go out and the forced-landing procedure can be followed – remembering *not* to attempt to restart the engine. If the fire does not go out, the absolute Number One priority is to get on to the ground before the fire gets out of control. Use any available combination of flaps, sideslipping and high airspeed to get down quickly, and aim for the best landing area available.

It is worth stressing the extreme rarity of an in-flight engine fire. Engine failures are rare, engine fires are extremely rare and an 'out-of-control' fire that does not extinguish once the correct actions are taken is virtually unheard-of. There was an incident when a pilot smelt burning, deduced an engine fire and shut down the engine without further investigation. The pilot walked away from the subsequent forced landing but it was subsequently discovered that the burning smell was actually smoke from some nearby industrial chimneys: there was nothing wrong with the aircraft. A few seconds of considered troubleshooting could have saved a lot of embarrassment.

▶ Descent

The descent is a time when engine cooling becomes a major issue, the common problem in a descent being that the engine becomes too cool rather than too hot. The danger is that a low-power, high-speed descent entered suddenly from the cruise can *shock-cool* the engine. Although sudden engine failure is unlikely, the long-term damage caused by shock-cooling the engine is definitely best avoided. It is much better to plan the descent well in advance, and make a more gentle descent at a higher power setting. This is much easier on the engine, and incidentally will be more appreciated by passengers too. If the mixture has been leaned, any change in power setting or altitude will require a change in the mixture setting. For a powered cruise descent, the mixture is gradually enriched in preparation for landing.

2500RPM   120 knots

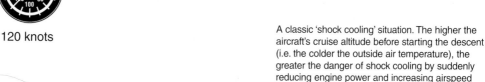

A classic 'shock cooling' situation. The higher the aircraft's cruise altitude before starting the descent (i.e. the colder the outside air temperature), the greater the danger of shock cooling by suddenly reducing engine power and increasing airspeed

1500RPM   150 knots

The reduced power setting normally associated with a descent also increases the risk of carburettor icing. Weather conditions are all-important here, and the humidity is the major factor to consider. If conditions are favourable for carburettor icing, or if it has been experience anywhere *en route*, consider setting the carb. heat to hot whilst the engine is still running at cruise power and leaving it there throughout the descent. Alternatively, make regular carb. heat checks. The basic rule is that the lower the power setting, the greater the risk of carburettor icing. As a matter of fact, the low power used in the descent may actually mask a loss of power caused by icing. So if the throttle is nearly closed, it may be worth opening it every 1000ft or so to confirm that power is still available. This action should also provide hot air for the carburettor heat system.

The use of carburettor heat through the approach and landing is subject to aircraft type and operator procedures. In some cases the carburettor heat is left hot throughout the approach and landing. In other cases the carburettor heat is set to cold shortly before landing. If a go-round is necessary, the carburettor heat must be set to cold in order to achieve full power. The mixture is usually set fully rich as part of the pre-landing checks unless the landing is taking place at a very high-altitude airfield

▶After-landing and Shut Down

Once clear of the runway after landing, the after-landing checks can be completed. These include checking that the carburettor heat is set to cold – this is important on the ground because the carburettor heat inlet is usually unfiltered and thus allows dust, sand, etc. straight into the engine, potentially increasing wear. Taxying to the parking spot normally allows the engine to continue to cool gradually. Do not allow the engine to idle for long periods, however, because this may lead to fouling of the spark plugs.

Some operators will run the engine at a slightly increased RPM (around 1500 or thereabouts) just before closing it down. This is usually done to guard against spark-plug fouling, especially if there has been a long taxy from the landing runway to the parking spot.

Once parked, the pre-shutdown checks usually include a check of the magnetos at the parked RPM. Here the pilot is looking for rough running, an excessive power loss or even no drop at all. As before, the latter is a possible sign of a 'live' magneto. The danger of a 'live' magneto is that even with the key out of the ignition switch and with the magnetos supposedly turned off, turning over the propeller will cause a spark at the spark plug and the engine might just fire up and run. Exactly the same thing might happen if somebody moved the propeller prior to manoeuvring the aircraft by hand. So if a magneto is believed to be 'live' the engine should be closed down, and nobody allowed near the propeller whilst calling in an engineer.

Assuming that the shutdown checks are all satisfactory, the engine is stopped by moving the mixture control to the ICO (Idle Cut Off) position, which cuts off the fuel supply at the carburettor. After a few seconds the RPM will probably increase momentarily and then the engine will run down and stop. Stopping the engine in this way should purge the engine of unburned fuel, thus reducing the chances of corrosion or of the engine accidentally starting. Before leaving the aircraft, make a final check to ensure that all the systems – including the magnetos – have been turned off. **Remember that if the magnetos are left on, the propeller is still potentially live and lethal.** In fact, it's sensible to treat the propeller in this way at all times in any case.

▶Storage

Like cars and other motorised vehicles, aircraft are not designed to be used infrequently. If the aircraft is not going to be used for some time, it will pay to take the advice of an engineer. The engine is particularly vulnerable to corrosion, and limited inhibiting of the engine and blocking of filters and inlets may be highly advisable. By the same token, if an aircraft has not been flown for some time, take particular care during the pre-flight inspection to look for damage, corrosion and even birds' nests. Each spring there are several reports of pilots finding nests under the cowlings of aircraft that have seen little activity in the winter months, so a close look around the engine is wise.

The traditional recommendation is that, when an aircraft is not being flown regularly, a periodic run of the engine and associated systems should help prevent problems. Unfortunately, recent evidence from sophisticated oil-analysis techniques suggests that this may not be the case, and that running the engine for a short period every now and then may actually be counter-productive. The best recommendation is to take advice from the engine manufacturer. If an engine has not been run for some time, there is a danger of *hydraulic lock*. This occurs when oil seeps past the piston rings and into the combustion section of the cylinder (i.e. the portion above the piston head). If a hydraulic lock forms, serious damage can be caused to the engine when it starts. Because of their design, engines with horizontally opposed cylinders are rarely affected by hydraulic locking. However, the lower cylinders of a radial engine – or the cylinders of an inverted engine – can be vulnerable to oil seeping in. Such engines are largely found on vintage aircraft, and experienced pilots of these types often hand-pull the propeller through a couple of revolutions if the engine has not run for a few days or more. If the propeller pulls through smoothly, hydraulic lock is not present. But **do not** try pulling a propeller by hand without the proper training.

An oil change is highly advisable for an engine that has not been run for some time. The aircraft and engine maintenance documents may give exact advice, but as a general rule engineers recommend changing the oil every 50 flying hours or four months, whichever occurs first.

▶ Revision

104 After engine start, for how long can the engine be left to run if the starter warning light remains lit?

105 What is the maximum time for the engine to run after starting while waiting for oil pressure to register?

106 If an aircraft is fitted with a fixed-pitch propeller, what is likely to be the first indication of carburettor icing?

107 As altitude increases, if the cockpit mixture control is not adjusted what will be the effect on the fuel-air mixture?

108 Assuming an engine with a fixed-pitch propeller, at what position would the pilot set the mixture control in relation to RPM in order to obtain the 'maximum power mixture'

109 What are the potential dangers of running an engine with an excessively lean (weak) mixture?

110 What are the major engine handling considerations during a descent?

Answers at page fpp71

Aircraft General Knowledge

Aircraft Systems

Aircraft General Knowledge
Aircraft Systems

▶ Principles of Electrical Circuits

▶ Aircraft Batteries

▶ Generators and Alternators

▶ Aircraft Electrical Systems

▶ The Master Switch

▶ Electrical Failure

▶ Bonding

▶ External Power

▶ Electrical System Serviceability Checks

▶ The Suction System

▶ Suction System Serviceability Checks

▶ The Pitot-Static System

▶ The Static Source

▶ The Pitot Source

▶ Position and Manoeuvre-Induced Errors

▶ Pitot-Static System Serviceability Checks

▶ Revision

Aircraft Systems

▶ Principles of Electrical Circuits

The electricity supply within an aircraft is perhaps the least well understood of all its systems, but a background knowledge of the basic principles can be very useful.

Imagine a typical small torch, powered by one or two AAA or AA batteries, taken apart to separate the bulb unit and the battery(ies). If the positive (+) terminal of the battery is connected to the bulb's centre contact, either directly or using something metallic that will conduct electricity, the result is – nothing. This is because the circuit has not been completed and no current is flowing. So now connect the negative (-) end of the battery to a metallic part of the bulb unit, using a metal wire or similar material that will conduct electricity. The bulb will light up because the circuit has been completed (*closed*).

A simple electrical circuit which has not been 'closed'

Electrical symbol for a battery

The electrical circuit closed, and current flowing

In many torches the negative end of the battery connects to the metal casing of the torch body, which in turn is attached to the bulb unit. So the negative side of the circuit is complete, leaving the circuit to be closed by the switch. In most aircraft constructed from metal the electrical circuit to a component is closed in much same way. Each electrical component is *grounded* (or *earthed*) to the metallic aircraft structure, which itself is connected to the negative terminal of the battery. If the aircraft is not of metal construction (e.g. a wooden or composite structure, which does not conduct electricity) metal strips will be incorporated into the structure to allow electrical circuits to be closed.

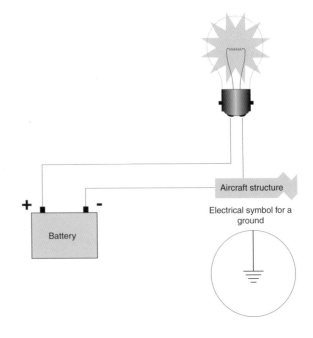

Aircraft structure

Electrical symbol for a ground

Battery

The earthing, or grounding, of an aircraft's electrical circuit

The basic electrical circuit works, however it is not very practical to manually connect bits of wire to various components to make them work. Instead a device is incorporated into the circuitry, by which the pilot can open or close a particular circuit at will: this device is a *switch*. As long as the switch is open, the circuit is not completed and no electrical current is flowing. When the switch is closed the current flows and the light, motor, radio, etc. can operate. Whenever manipulating an electrical circuit, always take care not to allow yourself to close a circuit inadvertently. (particularly by giving the circuit an earth or ground path). And also bear in mind that the prospective current from large lead-acid batteries such as those used in cars and aircraft can be high enough to cause an awful lot of heat to be generated in a short-circuit. A ring or watch bracelet can prove the point quite painfully.

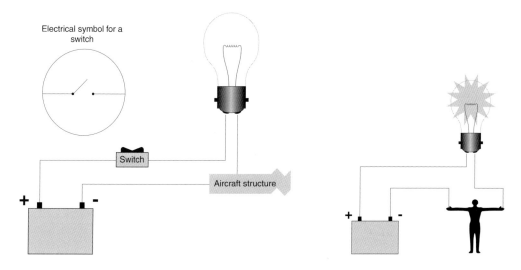

A switch used to control the opening and closing of an electrical circuit   How not to complete an electrical circuit

▶Aircraft Batteries

A *battery* is a device for storing electricity; it converts chemical energy into electrical energy. The majority of light aircraft have *lead-acid* batteries in which electricity is produced by the chemical action between pieces of lead (the *plates*) and sulphuric acid (the *electrolyte*). The battery is kept in a vented box, often located in the engine compartment. Because the sulphuric acid electrolyte within the battery is exceedingly corrosive stuff, quite capable of eating its way through clothing and skin, any spillage should be immediately doused in plenty of water and sodium bicarbonate (baking powder) if available.

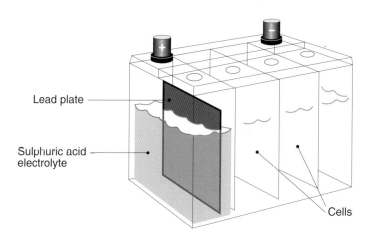

Lead plate

Sulphuric acid
electrolyte

Basic construction of a standard lead-acid battery

Cells

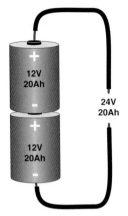

An electrical circuit connected in series

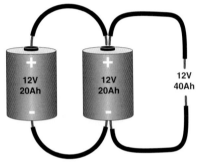

An electrical circuit connected in parallel

A battery is rated in the form of a *voltage* and number of *ampere-hours*: one ampere-hour (Ah) is the flow of one ampere for one hour. The ampere or amp is a measure of electrical current. A typical light-aircraft battery will have a rating of around 20-30Ah. The ampere-hours rating means in theory that when fully charged, a 30Ah battery can produce 30 amps for a period of one hour, or one amp for a period of 30 hours, or 10 amps for 3 hours, or indeed any combination adding up to 30. In practice, useful battery capacity is somewhat less than this theoretical rating, particularly when the battery is providing a lot of current. *Volts* (V) are a measure of the electrical 'pressure' pushing the current through the system. A typical light-aircraft battery will be of 12 or 24v.

If there is more than one battery in an electrical system, they can be connected in *series* or in *parallel*. If two 12V 20Ah batteries are connected in series, the resulting voltage will be the sum of the two but the capacity will be that of one battery. In other words, the combination adds up to a 24V 20Ah battery.

If two 12V 20Ah batteries are connected in parallel, the voltage will be as for one battery but the capacity is the sum of the ratings. So they act as a 12V 40Ah battery. Where an aircraft has more than one battery they are usually connected in parallel, not least because pumping excess voltage into the aircraft's electrical system (e.g. 24 volts when it is a 12 volt system) has serious and expensive consequences.

The battery is an important part of the electrical system, but using it as a sole source of electrical power is not a practical proposition for most powered aircraft. Flight duration would be limited by the finite battery capacity, or electrical services could only be used intermittently, and a lot of time would be needed to re-charge the battery between flights. What is needed is a means of creating electrical power.

▶Generators and Alternators

Formally speaking, the term *generator* applies to any device used to produce electrical current by creating an electromagnetic field between magnets. The rotation required to create the electromagnetic field is obtained by taking some type of drive from the engine, so that the generator will produce electricity whenever the engine is running. Unfortunately, the word has also acquired a secondary meaning. When a pilot or engineer refers to a "generator" in the context of an aircraft, the reference is usually to a particular type of machine which produces *Direct Current* (DC) electricity. It can be said that DC is electricity which always flows in the same direction. A DC generator is essentially self-contained and begins producing electricity as soon as the engine starts. However, generators have a number of disadvantages, including their size and weight and the fact that at relatively slow RPM (such as that of light aircraft piston engines) they are not very efficient at producing electricity.

A light-aircraft alternator

Although jet-engined aircraft mostly use generators, light aeroplanes tend to use *alternators*. An alternator is essentially a smaller and lighter form of generator, capable of producing useful current at much lower RPM than a traditional generator. These features make it ideally suited for use with a piston engine. The main drawback of the alternator is that it produces *Alternating Current* (AC) electricity. In an AC system such as the output of an alternator, the current periodically changes its direction of flow. Thus AC cannot be used directly in an electrical system designed for DC. Almost all light aircraft have DC electrical systems, and a battery produces DC electricity. So the AC electricity produced by an alternator has to be changed into DC, which is done by means of a *rectifier* mounted on the back of the alternator.

Unlike a generator, an alternator requires an external input of electricity to produce the magnetic field required for it to work, in other words the alternator is not self-contained in the same way as a generator. The initial electrical supply comes from the battery, which is said to be providing the current for *excitation* of the alternator.

▶ Aircraft Electrical Systems

A typical light-aircraft electrical system will incorporate a battery to store electricity, to provide power when the alternator is not operating (e.g. for engine starting) and supply current for the initial excitation of the alternator. The alternator uses the engine rotation to generate electricity to keep the battery charged and provide current to the various electrical components.

Electricity is distributed via one or more *busbars*. In its simplest form, a busbar is a copper strip or brass bar which connects the battery and alternator to the cables supplying the electrical and electronic items in the aeroplane. In some light aircraft the *avionics* (radio, transponder etc.) are supplied via a separate 'avionics' busbar. These items are particularly vulnerable to damage caused by sharp fluctuations in voltage and current, such as can occur during engine starting. By connecting these services to a separate busbar they can be isolated from the electrical system during engine start. If the avionics do not have a separate busbar (as is the case in most training aircraft) all radios and the like are turned off before starting the engine.

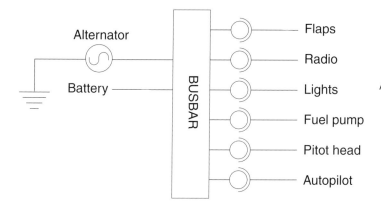

A busbar, which distributes current

Each electrical component has its own protection device to isolate it from the circuit in the event of excessive current. *Fuses* were the first items used for this requirement, and are still widely employed for circuit protection purposes. A fuse consists in essence of a glass or ceramic tube surrounding a wire, with metal caps at each end of the fuse which allow the current to flow through. The wire within the fuse will be rated so that it can carry a certain current. If this current is exceeded, the wire becomes very hot and melts, thus breaking (opening) the circuit. When this happens the fuse is said to have 'blown', and if the fuse is a glass-bodied type the pilot will be able to see that the wire within the fuse is broken.

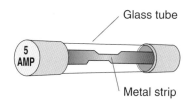

An electrical fuse, with its rating marked on the top

Fuses are normally located in a panel with just the fuse caps showing. If a pilot suspects that a fuse has blown (because a particular service is not working) it is necessary to remove the fuse and check it visually. Spare fuses are carried, and a blown fuse can be replaced with a fuse of the same rating – marked on the fuse and fuse holder. The fuse can only be replaced once; if it blows again, **do not** replace the fuse a second time. Additionally, a blown fuse must **never** be replaced with a fuse of a higher rating.

A fuse panel, each fuse holder marked with the service it protects

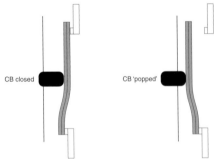

A circuit breaker

A panel of circuit breakers

A typical zero-centre ammeter. In the event of a failure of the alternator, the ammeter shows the flow of current out of the battery

Although fuses are still found in many aircraft, the modern trend is to protect electrical devices with a *Circuit Breaker* (CB). A CB performs the same function as a fuse insofar as it acts to isolate a component if a pre-determined current is exceeded. A CB makes use of a bi-metallic strip (two different metals held together). If excessive current flows through the CB, the heat produced distorts the strip. This causes it to 'unlatch' from a small catch and a spring pushes the strip outwards, breaking the contact (hence opening the circuit) and isolating the component. In this case the top cap of the CB can be seen sticking out of the panel, in which case the device is said to have 'popped' or 'tripped'. Once a CB has tripped, the bi-metallic strip will begin to cool and return to its original shape. After a couple of minutes it should be possible to re-set the CB by pushing it back in. This should only be done once – if the CB trips again, **do not** try to re-set it a second time. The end of a CB is marked with a rating (in amps).

To enable the pilot to monitor the health of the electrical system, the aircraft will have an *ammeter*. An ammeter measures the flow of current in the electrical system, although unfortunately the presentation of the instrument and exactly what it is measuring varies between different aircraft types. What follows is a general guide which should be checked against the POH/FM for the aircraft being flown.

The *zero-centre* ammeter is normally connected between the battery and the main busbar to show the charging rate of the battery. If the alternator is working properly and supplying power to the electrical system (and simultaneously charging the battery), the ammeter will show a positive (+) charge. At certain times – just after a prolonged engine start, for example, or when numerous electrical services are turned on – the reading may be quite high because a high 'charging current' is flowing from the alternator to recharge the battery. If the alternator is not working properly, or if it is *off-line* (isolated from the electrical system) and the battery is supplying all electrical power to the aeroplane, the ammeter will show a negative (-) charge, indicating the amount of current flowing out of the battery. The more electrical services that are operating, the greater the flow of current out of the battery (and the shorter its useful life).

A zero-centre ammeter, showing the charging rate of the battery

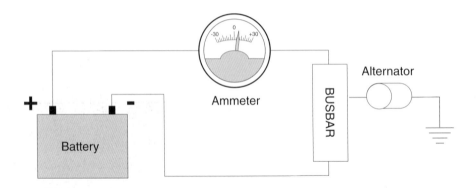

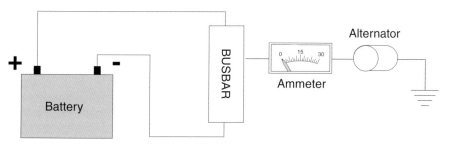

A left-centre ammeter showing the flow of current from the alternator to the electrical system

A *left-centre* ammeter (also known as a *loadmeter* or *load ammeter*) is installed between the alternator and the main busbar to show the flow of current from the alternator to the electrical system. The greater the load placed on the alternator (e.g. the greater the number of electrical items turned on) the higher the ammeter's indicated current. This will also see a high reading if the battery is drawing a lot of current to re-charge (just after engine starting, for example). This type of ammeter shows only positive current flow. If the alternator is faulty or off-line, the instrument indicates zero because under these conditions no current is flowing from the alternator to the system – the battery is supplying all electrical power. The difficulty with this method of presentation is that it can sometimes be difficult to distinguish between a very low current flow and a true zero indication.

Many aircraft are fitted with a Low Voltage (LV) warning light. This illuminates if the alternator fails or is off-line, indicating that the battery is supplying all electrical power. Some light aeroplanes also have *annunciator* panels, essentially a bank of warning lights. One marked ALT indicates that the alternator is off-line. A *voltmeter* may also be fitted which indicates the present voltage of the electrical system.

An annunciator panel with vacuum (suction), alternator and oil-pressure warning lights

▶The Master Switch

Most modern light aircraft enable the pilot to control the electrical system through a standard *Master Switch*. This has two halves, one labelled 'Bat' (battery) and the other 'Alt' (alternator). The Bat half of the switch can be operated independently, so that only the battery is supplying electricity to the system. However, turning on the Alt side of the switch automatically turns on the Bat side too; because the alternator needs initial current from the battery to operate. The significance of this is that if the battery is totally discharged, the alternator will not work because it is not properly excited, even if the engine is started in some other way such as hand-swinging. Thus no power can be supplied to the electrical system and the battery cannot be recharged.

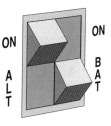

A standard master switch

As a general rule, both halves of the master switch are operated together. If there is some problem with the electrical system, such as the alternator going off-line, it can be re-set by turning the Master Switch off, waiting a few moments and then turning it back on again.

There may be a separate 'avionics' master switch controlling the radios, transponder and so on. This normally takes the form of a simple on/off switch, without the option to select the battery separately. If fitted, this switch should always be turned off before starting the engine.

A master switch with just the battery selected

In a conventional aero engine, the aircraft's electrical system **does not** provide the current to generate the spark at the spark plugs. Neither is it involved in any other basic engine function. For example, if the fuel needs to be pumped from the fuel tanks to the engine, there will be at least one engine-driven fuel pump in addition to an electrical item. Once the engine is running, the state of the battery or alternator will not directly affect the engine. Turn off the master switch and in most aircraft the engine will carry on running.

▶ Electrical Failure

If the alternator does fail – as indicated by the ammeter and also the Low Voltage and ALT light if fitted – the battery is supplying all electrical power. The generator/alternator can usually be reset by turning the master switch off for a few seconds and then turning it back on again. If this does not restore the alternator function, there is only the finite amount of battery charge left to run the electrical system.

The 'life' of the battery will depend on its state of charge and the load placed upon it. Consider a 25Ah battery as a 25gal water tank. In normal use the tank is topped up by a pump, just as the alternator recharges a battery as current flows out of it. If this topping-up process stops for some reason, there is now a limited amount of electricity (water) to use. There is no way of knowing exactly how much 'reserve' is left, because there is no easy way of finding out exactly how full the battery (or water tank) is.

If the alternator cannot be restored, the first priority is to get into VMC with good sight of the ground and inform ATC of what has happened. Now think carefully about how much power is going out of the battery. Each electrical component draws a set amount of current (expressed in amps) and every item can be thought of as a tap in a water system. The higher its current rating – shown on the associated fuse or CB – the faster it will empty the reserve of electricity. Leaving all the taps wide open will quickly empty any water tank not being topped-up. Likewise, using lots of current-hungry items of electrical equipment will quickly flatten a battery not receiving a charge. So reduce electrical services to the *absolute minimum* needed for safe flight. In a light aircraft there are few electrical items absolutely essential to daytime VFR flight. For example, use the radio sparingly, transmitting uses far more current than receiving. Think of the water system again: turn off all the taps not really needed, and be frugal with those left running. Aside from the radios and lights, other services often powered by electricity in a light aircraft include the turn co-ordinator, the fuel gauges (and possibly some of the engine instruments), the flaps on a high-wing aircraft, any secondary fuel pump and items such as the stall warner and pitot heater.

Even if all electrical power is lost – either gradually as the battery runs down, or suddenly if the whole system fails – a non-radio and possibly flapless landing does not usually present too many serious problems in a light aircraft. With the engine running the main concern should be navigating to an airfield where a non-radio approach and landing can be made.

▶ Bonding

To recap the basic electricity theory for a moment, the completion of electrical circuits within the aircraft requires that the negative terminals of all electrical items and the negative terminal of the battery are connected to the metallic (i.e. conductive) portions of the aircraft structure. The latter then becomes an 'earth' or 'ground'. There must be a continuous conducting path throughout the aircraft for this technique to work effectively. If the path is incomplete, a part of the aircraft may become electrically isolated. Apart from breaking the electrical circuit, any discontinuity could lead to differing levels of electric charge building up on different parts of the aircraft, possibly causing sparks to jump between them. At the very least this can be a nuisance and cause interference with the radios; at worst, sparks around the fuel system could have very serious consequences. To prevent this, small wires called *bonding* wires, can be used to ensure a path for the flow of electricity. These may be seen, for example, between the wing and the ailerons.

An aircraft may build up a strong *static* electrical charge in flight, especially if flying through heavy precipitation or near an active thunderstorm. Like sparks, static electricity can interfere with radio reception and sensitive electrical items. *Static wicks* are usually located at the trailing edge of the control surfaces which allow static electricity to dissipate into the atmosphere, remembering that the electrical bonding of the aircraft's structure will allow a clear path for current to flow to the wicks. To help the process, aircraft tyres are made of a special compound with good electrical conducting properties. When an aircraft lands, static electricity is earthed.

Static electricity discharges can be most dangerous during refuelling. Normally a bonding wire from the refuelling installation is attached to a metallic part of the aircraft to ensure that both the refuelling installation and the aircraft have the same electrical charge. Keeping the metal end of the refuelling hose in contact with the aircraft's metal filler pipe also helps to prevent sparks.

Static wicks to dissipate static electricity fitted to the trailing edge of an aileron

▶ External Power

Many aircraft have a socket which allows an external power source to be connected to the electrical system. External power can be used to operate the system for extended periods when the engine is not running (i.e. during maintenance) or to aid engine starting if the battery power is low. However, if the battery is completely discharged, starting the engine with external power will still not make the alternator work for the reasons already discussed. The aircraft's POH/FM will have specific instructions for the use of external power and these **must** be followed closely. It is imperative to use an external power source of the correct voltage. Connecting an external power source whose output voltage is higher than that of the aircraft's electrical system (the usual error being the application of a 24V or 110V source to a 12V aeroplane) will invariably inflict serious and expensive damage. The external power socket often has the correct voltage marked as a reminder. But don't assume, check.

An external power socket

▶ Electrical System Serviceability Checks

During the pre-flight checks the pilot can verify some elements of the aircraft's electrical system. The battery will be located within a vented box, often (but not always) located in the engine compartment. The condition of this and the vent pipe from the battery can be checked when examining the engine, looking particularly for corrosion which may be caused by spillage of the battery electrolyte. The alternator, often visible through a front air inlet in the cowling, is pretty much a sealed unit although the pilot may be able to check the tension on the drive belt between the engine and the alternator. The bonding wires and static wicks can also be scrutinised for security and any burn marks, the latter possibly indicating a poor connection. If the aircraft has fuses, spare items should be available in the cockpit.

Before engine starting, the master switch is used to connect the battery to the electrical system. The ammeter will show a zero or discharge (depending on type) and the Low Voltage light (if fitted) will illuminate to show that the alternator is not supplying any power. After start, the ammeter should show a positive charge; the Low Voltage light should go out and the circuit-breaker panel can be checked for any 'popped' CBs. The ammeter indication is normally verified during the power checks, and as a further check the ammeter can also be watched whilst a high-current item such as the pitot heat is momentarily switched on. The result should be a discernible movement of the ammeter needle.

The ammeter reading is noted during the cruise checks; a major change in reading can provide advance warning of a problem. Actions in the event of a blown fuse or popped circuit breaker have already been discussed, as has the possibility of a loss of electrical power. The only other – rare – occurrence is that of an electrical fire. This will normally be characterised by an extremely 'hot' and acrid smell, caused by electrical insulation melting. Smoke may also emerge from behind or around the instrument panel. Either or both are disconcerting, so first and foremost **fly the aeroplane**. If smoke and smells manifest themselves just after a particular electrical item has been turned on, the obvious action is to turn it off and see if the smoke stops. If not, the master switch can be turned off to see whether this clears the problem. If either action works the pilot should divert and land at the earliest opportunity, obviously without turning the master switch or individual item back on again. If neither action achieves the desired effect, the pilot will need to carry out the emergency check-list actions for an electrical fire.

▶ The Suction System

The *suction* system (sometimes referred as the *vacuum* system) provides a suction to drive non-electrical gyro-based flight instruments such as the Heading Indicator and Attitude Indicator. An engine-driven vacuum pump creates a low-pressure at one end of the pipe-work which draws air through the system; within each instrument the resulting blast of air flows through a small nozzle. This jet of air is directed on to the wheel (rotor) of a gyroscope into which small notches or buckets have been cut. The result of the force of this jet of air acting against the notches in the gyro rotor is that it spins at very high speed.

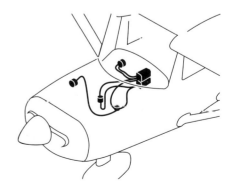

Layout of a typical suction system

A vacuum pump with the plastic coupling at the front

A venturi driving the suction system. This is only effective once the aircraft is airborne

In a typical light aircraft installation, an engine-driven vacuum pump draws air through an inlet (usually behind the instrument panel) which is filtered. Beyond the filter the air is then drawn through the gyro instruments (which, again, often have filters at their inlet) and so to the vacuum pump, from where it is dumped 'overboard' through a small pipe. There is an adjustable regulator fitted, usually somewhere between the instruments and the pump, to ensure that the correct level of suction is coursing through the system. Should the main filter become blocked (a relatively rare occurrence), air is drawn in through the regulator, in effect bypassing the gyro instruments. The operation of the suction system is to all intents and purposes automatic – the vacuum pump is driven by the engine, so once the engine is running the suction system is operating. Modern vacuum pumps have a plastic coupling to the engine, so that if the pump seizes, the coupling will shear rather than transmit excessive forces back to the engine. One feature of such vacuum pumps, which usually have a useful life of around 1000 flying hours, is that if they do fail they tend to do so totally and without warning. Some single-engine touring aircraft, and most multi-engine aircraft, have dual vacuum pumps with valves so that if one fails, it is isolated and the system powered by the remaining good pump.

Some aircraft do not use a vacuum pump but instead have a venturi attached to the outside of the aircraft. This venturi creates a suction once the aircraft is airborne, so the gyro instruments cannot give reliable readings until a few minutes after take-off. The venturi is also susceptible to icing. Both issues make reliable usage in IMC unlikely.

▶ Suction System Serviceability Checks

A suction gauge

The strength of the suction created within the suction system is measured and displayed to the pilot on a suction gauge. This is the best indicator of the serviceability of the suction system, although unfortunately suction gauge readings are considered to be far from reliable. The suction gauge should be checked before take-off (if an engine-driven vacuum pump is fitted) and also as part of the cruise checks in-flight. The POH/FM will give the acceptable suction readings, but some five inches of mercury (5in.Hg) is a common value at cruise power settings.

▶ The Pitot-Static System

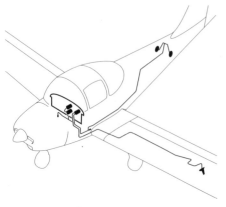

The layout of a standard pitot-static system

The *pitot-static* system supplies air pressure to the pressure measuring instruments. Static pressure is fed to the altimeter and the vertical speed indicator (VSI); pitot *and* static pressure is fed to the airspeed indicator (ASI). The correct operation and checking of this system is vital if accurate vertical position and airspeed information is to be available to the pilot.

▶The Static Source

Static pressure is the 'ambient' pressure of the surrounding air – the pressure we are all surrounded by every day. Certain pressure-sensing instruments – the Vertical Speed Indicator (VSI), the altimeter and the Airspeed Indicator (ASI) rely on static pressure to give accurate readings to the pilot. Static pressure is sensed from a *static port*, often located on the side of the fuselage, or possibly from a vent on the *pitot-static head* (described shortly). A static port on the fuselage often takes the form of a metal disc with a number of holes. Some aircraft have a single static port, usually on one side of the fuselage; others have two, generally mounted on opposite sides of the fuselage. Using two ports helps to minimise errors caused by out-of-balance manoeuvres (such as sideslipping) which might otherwise affect the pressure being sensed. If the static source is on the pitot-static head, it will consist of a small opening on the side of the head. Flexible plastic tubing allows static pressure from the static port to reach the pressure-sensing instruments.

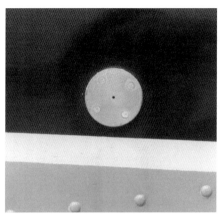

A static port

The static system is quite simple, and about the only things that can go wrong are either a leak or a blockage of the static port or tubing e.g. by ice. Some aircraft have a drain in the pitot-static system, to allow any accumulated water to be drawn off rather than block the lines. Some aircraft also have an 'alternate static source'. This is a valve which, when opened, allows air from within the cockpit to enter the static system. Although the static air pressure in the cockpit is usually a little less than that outside the aircraft, a static-pressure source with a relatively small error is a great deal better than no static pressure sensing at all. In fact, the POH may have correction table to be referred to when using the alternate static source.

If there is an evident problem but no alternate static source is fitted, smashing the glass of one of the pressure instruments (the Vertical Speed Indicator is the best candidate) will allow static air into the system. Such drastic action will probably require considerable force – the blunt end of a fire extinguisher may do it – and so should be considered as a last resort.

▶The Pitot Source

The pitot source is an opening facing into the airflow which measures the pressure of moving air bought to a rest in the tube (often called pitot pressure). The pitot source is usually placed in a *pitot tube* or pitot-static head (sometimes known as a pressure head) located where it can sense a relatively undisturbed airflow – commonly under one wing or at the top of the fin. As with the static source, flexible tubing transmits the pitot pressure to the relevant pressure instrument – in this case the Airspeed Indicator (ASI). The most likely cause of an in-flight blockage of the pitot source is icing. For this reason the pitot may well be fitted with an electrically-powered heating element labelled in the cockpit as 'Pitot Heat'.

A pitot tube

A pitot-static head

▶ Position and Manoeuvre-Induced Errors

Because the pitot-static system senses pressure around the aircraft, anything that alters the pressure locally at one of the sensing points can lead to errors in the reading of the pressure-sensing instruments.

Position error is caused by any local disturbance in the airflow around a sensing port. The designer will seek to minimise any such effect by putting the sensing ports where the airflow is as undisturbed as possible – on a mast under the wing for example. Nevertheless, the pitot pressure in particular can effected by position error – especially when flying at a high angle of attack, when the air is not entering the pitot tube directly but possibly at an indirect angle. This can lead to significant errors (5-10kts) in indicated airspeed and there may be a corrective table or graph in the POH/FM.

Manoeuvre-induced error can be caused by a sudden manoeuvre, and in particular by an out-of-balance manoeuvre (such as sideslipping) which again causes localised airflow disturbances or can alter the angle of the airflow into the sensing ports. In aircraft which only have a single static pressure sensing port on one side of the fuselage, there can be a significant difference in airspeed readings depending in which direction the aircraft is slipping. Changes in aircraft configuration (such as raising and lowering flaps or undercarriage) can also lead to errors in the readings of the pressure-sensing instruments.

▶ Pitot-Static System Serviceability Checks

During the pre-flight inspection, the pitot and static sources are checked to ensure they are clear and unblocked. It is quite common to have a cover protecting the pitot tube – usually marked with a distinctive warning flag. Obviously it is essential to remove any cover before flight. Less commonly, the static source may also have a cover which must be removed. It is common practice for a pitot or static cover to have a red warning flag or tape to make it more visible. Check also for a taped-over port; the static vent may have been covered during maintenance or painting. Missing this point has caused at least one fatal airliner accident. Some aircraft have a built-in pitot cover consisting of a metal plate covering the pitot when the aircraft is at rest. When the aircraft starts to move, the airflow pushes on a flat plate and the cover hinges up, uncovering the pitot head. Make sure that this moves freely when pressure is applied to the flat plate. **Never** blow into either the pitot or static source, this can seriously damage the pressure instruments.

The possibility of a blocked pitot or static source is greatly increased in certain hotter parts of the world (and even during in a north European summer) where insects may use the openings as nests.

If the pitot has a heating element, this can be checked by turning the pitot heat on and then feeling the side of the pitot with your fingers. Do not grip the pitot tightly whilst doing this check because it can get very warm quite quickly and the unwary may leave burnt skin on the pitot! Having established that the pitot heat is working turn it off straight away. Pitot heat places a heavy load on the battery, and without cooling airflow the pitot heater itself can overheat quickly.

Any covers on the pitot head or static ports must be removed before flight. These covers usually have a red streamer or flag to make them more visible

▶ Revision

111 If two 12 volt, 20 amp batteries are connected in parallel, what will be the resulting voltage and capacity?

112 If two 12 volt, 20 amp batteries are connected in series, what will be the resulting voltage and capacity?

113 In a modern light aircraft, what is the most common primary means of generating electricity?

114 What type of current normally flows in a light aircraft's electrical system?

115 If a fuse rated at 10 amps 'blows', what is the maximum rating of replacement that can be fitted?

116 If a Circuit Breaker (CB) 'pops' or 'trips', how many times can it be re-set?

117 In the diagram below, what is indicated by the *zero-centre* ammeter?

118 In the diagram below, what is indicated by the *left-centre* ammeter?

119 A standard 'split' Master Switch has two halves, one for the alternator (ALT), one for the battery (BAT). The battery can be selected without the alternator, but not vice versa. Why?

120 If the filter of a suction system becomes blocked, will the instruments connected to the suction system continue to operate?

121 What instruments are typically driven by the suction system of an average light aircraft?

122 Is static pressure within the cockpit of an unpressurised light aircraft usually exactly the same as the external static pressure?

123 In what flight situation is position error of pitot pressure most likely to occur?

Answers at page fpp71

Aircraft General Knowledge
Instruments

Aircraft General Knowledge
Instruments

▶ The Altimeter

▶ Altimeter Errors

▶ Altimeter Serviceability Checks

▶ The Vertical Speed Indicator (VSI)

▶ VSI Serviceability Checks

▶ The Airspeed Indicator (ASI)

▶ Airspeed Indicator Errors

▶ Airspeed Indicator Serviceability Checks

▶ Principles of Gyroscopes

▶ The Turn Indicator

▶ The Turn Co-ordinator

▶ Turn Co-ordinator Serviceability Checks

▶ The Attitude Indicator (AI)

▶ Attitude Indicator Serviceability Checks

▶ The Heading Indicator

▶ Heading Indicator Serviceability Checks

▶ The Magnetic Compass

▶ Compass Serviceability Checks

▶ Revision

►The Altimeter

The altimeter is the simplest of the pressure-measuring instruments. It is, in essence, an aneroid barometer and measures the action of static air pressure from the static source on a sealed capsule. The expansion or contraction of the capsule is transmitted via linkages to the instrument face, where the measured pressure is displayed in the form of a vertical distance above (or occasionally below) a datum selected by the pilot. The pilot selects the datum in the altimeter subscale window, sometimes called the *barometric scale*, in the form of a pressure setting. The three common datums are:

The principle of a simple altimeter

- **QFE** When QFE is set on the altimeter, it will read *height* above or below a specific point on the ground, normally an airfield or runway threshold
- **QNH** When QNH is set on the altimeter, it will read *altitude* above or below mean sea level
- **Standard Setting** When the standard setting (1013mb/hPa, 29·92in.Hg) is set on the altimeter it will read *Flight Level* above or below this pressure level.

The most common altimeter pressure settings

Altimeter Settings

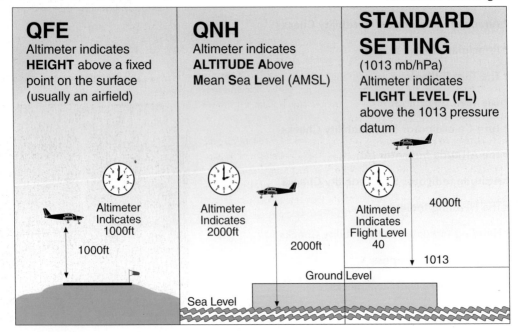

QFE
Altimeter indicates
HEIGHT above a fixed
point on the surface
(usually an airfield)

Altimeter Indicates 1000ft

1000ft

QNH
Altimeter indicates
ALTITUDE Above
Mean **S**ea **L**evel (AMSL)

Altimeter Indicates 2000ft

2000ft

STANDARD SETTING
(1013 mb/hPa)
Altimeter indicates
FLIGHT LEVEL (FL)
above the 1013 pressure datum

Altimeter Indicates Flight Level 40

4000ft

1013

Ground Level

Sea Level

The altimeter works on the principle that pressure *decreases* as altitude *increases*. In the International Standard Atmosphere (ISA) the rate of change is approximately thirty feet per millibar/hectopascal. In other words, for every 30ft increase in altitude the pressure drops by 1mb/hPa. Because the use of the altimeter has already been described in some detail in each of the preceding three books of this series, the following assumes some pre-knowledge of altimeter setting procedures and the International Standard Atmosphere. Now is a good time to revise those sections if in any doubt about them, however, in summary, there are two particular definitions when discussing the altimeter:

Pressure Altitude The altimeter reading when the standard setting (1013mb/hPa, 29·92in.Hg) is set on the altimeter. Pressure altitude is a Flight Level, and is often used in performance calculations.

True Altitude The exact height of the aircraft Above Mean Sea Level. It can be found by correcting the altimeter reading for temperature error (the difference between the ISA temperature at a particular pressure altitude and the actual temperature there). This can only be done with a flight computer, and so even with the correct QNH set, the altitude shown can be in error by several hundred feet even at lower levels.

There are two main instrument presentations used for altimeters. The most common in light aircraft is the *three-pointer* dial. In this presentation the long pointer shows hundreds of feet, the shorter pointer shows thousands of feet and the third pointer (with a triangle at its periphery) indicates tens of thousands of feet. On most altimeters found in light aircraft this third pointer is actually part of an inner disk which rotates to uncover a striped area on the instrument face. Below 10,000ft the entire striped area is visible. Above 10,000ft the rotation of the disk begins to cover this area, and by about 15,000ft the striped area is completely covered. The warning stripes were introduced as aircraft began to fly higher on a regular basis, to warn the pilot that the aircraft was around 10,000ft or below. The pilot should pay particular attention to the altimeter reading if operating at high altitudes with a three-pointer altimeter presentation.

For aircraft regularly operating above 10,000ft, a more popular altimeter presentation is the *digital* or *drum-pointer* type. The digital presentation has a single needle indicating hundreds of feet and on the inner face of the dial, a digital display shows tens of thousands, thousands and hundreds. The drum-pointer display also has a needle showing hundreds of feet, but the drum shows only thousands and tens of thousands. Either of these display types gives a much clear indication of altitude and are common in larger aircraft.

Before leaving the subject of altimeter presentation, a number of aircraft have altimeters calibrated in metres rather than feet and use non-standard units of pressure measurement – millimetres of mercury, for example. This applies especially to aeroplanes originating in eastern Europe. The potential for confusion is obvious and aircraft with such instruments are often only cleared for VFR flight in the UK.

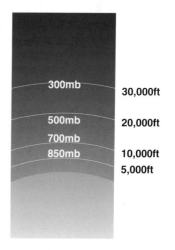

The reduction in pressure in the International Standard Atmosphere (ISA)

The 'three-pointer' altimeter presentation used in most GA aircraft. The striped area is visible when the aircraft is below 10,000ft or so

The more advanced 'drum and pointer' altimeter display

▶Altimeter Errors

The altimeter can be subject to several errors. These are summarised below:

Instrument Error Despite the best efforts of the manufacturer, certain small imperfections are bound to affect the accuracy of the altimeter. By itself, however, instrument error is unlikely to have a significant effect on the altimeter reading.

Time Lag It takes a finite time for a pressure change at the static source to be transmitted along the static pipes, measured in the instrument and the resulting movements of the capsule converted into an altimeter reading via a series of mechanical linkages. This time lag is at its worst during a particularly steep climb or descent, but even so is unlikely to amount to a delay of more than a second or so.

Position Error Disturbance of the airflow over a single static source will cause pressure fluctuations which will affect the altimeter reading. Having two static sources should remove nearly all position error. If the aircraft has an alternate static source, the altimeter reading may change suddenly (by anything up to 100ft) if alternate static is selected in flight because the static pressure inside the cockpit will not be exactly the same as that outside.

Manoeuvre-Induced Error A sudden change in attitude – or sideslipping, lowering flaps and so on – can all affect the static pressure being sensed at the static source. Again, having more than one static source removes much of this error.

Temperature Error The altimeter is constructed and calibrated on the basis of the International Standard Atmosphere (ISA). If the temperature at any level deviates from ISA, the altimeter reading will be in error. The use of the flight computer to calculate true altitude, given a pressure altitude and actual temperature, is described in the 'Navigation' section of PPL 3.

Barometric Error This means simply having the wrong pressure set on the altimeter subscale. It may be caused by a misheard radio message, mis-setting the altimeter or failure to update the pressure setting over a period of time. However, arguably the most common cause of barometric error is failure by the pilot to appreciate which altimeter setting is being used. Imagine a pilot approaching an airfield whose elevation (its altitude above sea level) is 750ft. The QNH is 1020mb, the QFE 995mb. The pilot is in IMC and begins the descent without changing from QNH to QFE. With QNH set, the altimeter is reading altitude above sea level – but if the pilot thinks that it is reading height above the airfield (the reading with QFE set) he has a major probem. A descent to 1000ft indicated with the QNH set on the subscale means that the aircraft is only 250ft above the airfield. A descent to 500ft means that the flight may terminate short of the airfield, even though the altimeter still reads 750ft at the moment of impact.

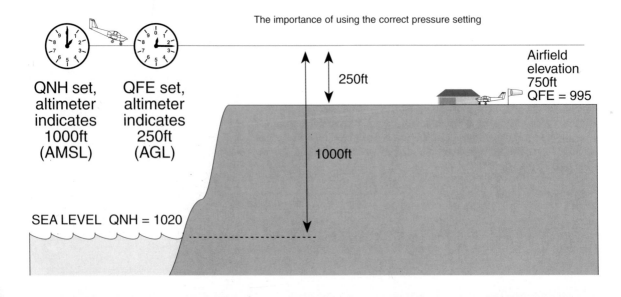

The importance of using the correct pressure setting

QNH set, altimeter indicates 1000ft (AMSL)

QFE set, altimeter indicates 250ft (AGL)

250ft

1000ft

Airfield elevation 750ft QFE = 995

SEA LEVEL QNH = 1020

Detailed altimeter-setting procedures are covered in PPL 2 and PPL3. A pressure altimeter is *not* a magic device measuring and displaying distance to the surface. It is merely a barometer which measures the pressure and displays it as a vertical distance above or below the datum set by the pilot. Think of the altimeter in this way and always treat it with due respect, *especially* if flying in IMC.

Apart from the errors described above, the altimeter will also give an inaccurate reading if the static source becomes blocked. With a blocked static source the altimeter will continue to measure the static pressure trapped in the system and so will read the altitude/height/flight level at which the blockage occurred – regardless of any climb or descent.

▶Altimeter Serviceability Checks

The correct place to check the altimeter is on the apron prior to taxying for departure. At large airfields the apron elevation is published in the AIP and (theoretically) displayed in the flight briefing office. So the pilot can simply set the QNH as passed by ATC and check the reading on the altimeter; it should be within 50ft of the stated apron elevation. In the absence of the apron elevation figure, the airfield elevation as marked on maps and flight guides can be used to check the altimeter reading when QNH is set. With QFE set, the altimeter should read zero on the ground. Again a tolerance of ±50ft is generally acceptable.

If the QNH/QFE figures at the airfield of departure are not available, obtaining the regional QNH from a met. office or the QNH of a nearby airfield is recommended. As a last resort the pilot can set the known airfield elevation on the altimeter and read off the QNH, but this does not allow a check of the accuracy of the instrument reading.

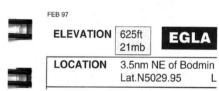

FEB 97

	ELEVATION	625ft	**EGLA**
		21mb	
	LOCATION	3.5nm NE of Bodmin	
		Lat.N5029.95	L

Checking the altimeter with QNH against a known airfield elevation

▶The Vertical Speed Indicator (VSI)

The vertical speed indicator is an instrument which measures the *rate of change* of the static pressure. Inside the instrument is a capsule into which static pressure is fed. Static pressure also enters the instrument casing so that it surrounds the capsule, but it is routed via a restriction so that it is delayed slightly before it enters the instrument casing. When the aircraft is flying level, the static pressure remains constant over an extended period of time and pressure inside and outside the capsule equalises. Hence there is no pressure differential between the inside of the capsule and the static air surrounding it, and therefore no expansion or contraction of the capsule takes place. In these circumstances the VSI reads zero. If the aircraft starts to climb, the static pressure inside the capsule will start to fall but the surrounding static pressure is still that of the aircraft's level a few moments ago. As a result the capsule contracts slightly; its movement is transmitted via linkages to the instrument needle and a rate of climb is shown. The greater the rate of pressure change, the greater the movement of the capsule and the greater the rate of climb shown on the VSI dial. In a descent, the pressure differential is reversed. Now the movement of the capsule expanding is translated into a rate of descent on the VSI dial.

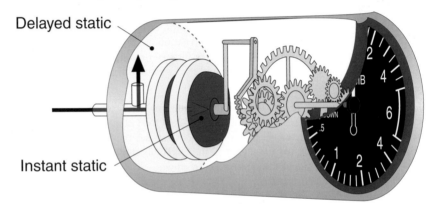

Delayed static

Instant static

The principle of operation of a
vertical speed indicator (VSI)

A VSI showing a 500ft/min rate of climb

Without stops fitted, a VSI may give a reverse indication in the event of a high
rate of climb/descent

The presentation of the VSI dial is mostly standardised, with just one possible pitfall. Not all VSI dials are fitted with 'stops' at the maximum indicated rate of climb or descent. So an extreme rate of climb or descent may be indicated in the opposite sense.

The VSI suffers from many of the same errors as the altimeter, namely *instrument error, time lag, position error* and *manoeuvre-induced error*. The VSI is particularly susceptible to the two latter errors, especially if they result from large and rapid movements in pitch (for example, recovery from a dive) and the VSI reading may lag several seconds behind the aircraft. To counter this problem, more sophisticated aircraft may be fitted with an *Instantaneous VSI* (IVSI). This is essentially a VSI with an accelerometer unit incorporated into the linkages to sense vertical acceleration. As soon as there is some vertical movement, inertia causes this motion to be measured by the accelerometer and transmitted to the needle reading, giving a near-instant indication of a climb or descent. After a few moments the accelerometer response dies down, but by this time the change in static pressure is being indicated on the IVSI dial. Other than this description, all references to VSI in this chapter refer to a 'standard' (i.e. non-instantaneous) VSI.

If the static source becomes blocked, the static pressure inside a standard VSI will quickly equalise and it will merely indicate zero (i.e. level flight) regardless of the actual rate of climb/descent.

▶ VSI Serviceability Checks

On the ground the VSI should simply read zero, but because it is not a vital instrument for VFR flight, a reading on the ground of within ±200ft/min of zero is normally considered acceptable. In flight it is possible to check VSI accuracy against the altimeter in level flight (it should read zero of course), and against an altimeter and a stopwatch in a steady climb or descent to verify Rate Of Climb (ROC) or Rate Of Descent (ROD) readings.

▶ The Airspeed Indicator (ASI)

The ASI measures airspeed based on the pressure exerted by the airflow being brought to rest inside the pitot tube. This pressure is known as *stagnation pressure* (because the air is stagnating or stopping in the pitot tube) and sometimes as *pitot pressure*.

Stagnation pressure has two elements:

- static pressure, as would be experienced even when there is no moving airflow into the pitot
- dynamic pressure, the additional pressure caused by the velocity and density of the air

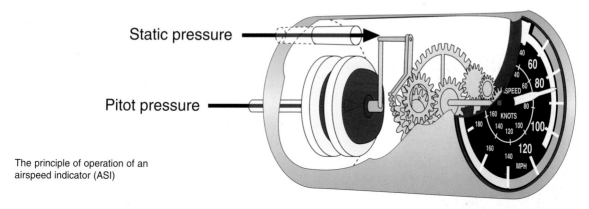

The principle of operation of an airspeed indicator (ASI)

For airspeed purposes it is dynamic pressure that needs to be measured, so a way has to be found to cancel-out the static pressure from the measuring process. This is done by supplying the total pressure from the pitot source to a capsule within the ASI and feeding static pressure from the static source(s) into the instrument casing surrounding the capsule. In this way, a change in static pressure alone will not cause the capsule to expand or contract – only a change in dynamic pressure will effect the capsule. An increase in dynamic pressure causes the capsule to expand, and this expansion is transmitted to the needle of the ASI by a mechanical linkage to show increased airspeed. A reduction in dynamic pressure causes the capsule to contract, which is converted and presented as reduced airspeed.

So the ASI measures dynamic pressure and displays this on the instrument dial in the form of airspeed. Dynamic pressure is an important element of the aerodynamic forces of lift and drag, and affects the handling and performance of the aircraft. Most of the important limitations (speed at which the stalling angle of attack will occur; never-exceed speed; maximum speed for lowering flaps and the like) and performance criteria (take-off speed; climb speed; landing speed, etc.) are defined by dynamic pressure. Since this is displayed to the pilot as indicated airspeed, it becomes possible to take quick decisions and actions based directly on varying dynamic pressures. It is worth noting that, for practical purposes, the aircraft will stall at the same *Indicated Air Speed* (IAS) irrespective of altitude, temperature and so on. Likewise, airspeeds which are set by reference to the stall speed – such as approach and landing speeds – are not affected by altitude and temperature variations.

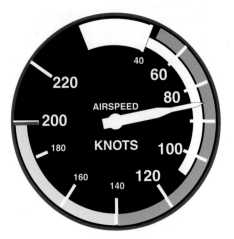

An ASI with statue miles per hour (MPH) on the
outer scale, and nautical miles per hour (Knots)
on the inner scale

A colour-coded ASI

The presentation of airspeed information should be pretty straightforward, the mechanical dial-and-pointer display is just about universal in light aircraft (although a speed 'ribbon' is common in electronic displays). The main pitfall is the unit of speed used on the dial. Airspeed can be measured in knots, miles per hour or kilometres per hour and differing examples of the same aircraft types may have ASIs reading in different units. Alternatively, the ASI dial may have inner and outer scales with differing units. It follows that if flying an aircraft for the first time, check carefully which units used – and which are shown where on the ASI – *before* starting the take-off, because climbing at 85mph instead of 85kts is not good practice.

Key indicated airspeed (IAS) limitations and ranges are usually presented to the pilot on the airspeed indicator. This is most commonly done using a system of colour coding. The following applies to a single-engine light aircraft:

White Arc	Extends from Vso to the flap limiting speed (VFE)
Green Arc	Extends from Vs1 to VNO
Yellow Arc	The 'caution' airspeed range, flight in smooth conditions only
Red Line	The VNE speed

Thus the white arc reflects the speed range for flight with the flaps lowered (the flap operating range); the green arc represents the normal operating range; the yellow arc represents the caution range and the red line represents the never exceed speed.

For reference, the main 'V' speed definitions are:

Vs0 stalling speed in the landing configuration. In a light aircraft this is usually taken as maximum weight, most forward CG, landing gear down, flaps fully down and power off.

Vs1 the stalling speed in a specified configuration. In a light aircraft this is usually taken as maximum weight, most forward CG, landing gear up (if retractable), flaps up and power off.

VFE the maximum speed for flight with flaps extended.

VA the design manoeuvring speed. The maximum speed at which full and sudden flight control movements can be made without the danger of over-stressing the structure.

VNO the maximum Normal Operating or structural cruising speed, only to be exceeded with caution and in smooth conditions.

VNE the Never Exceed speed, not to be exceeded in any circumstances.

►Airspeed Indicator Errors

The ASI suffers from many of the same errors as the other pressure instruments, namely *instrument error*, *time lag*, *position error*, and *manoeuvre-induced error*. Of these, the ASI is particularly susceptible to position error, which is usually most marked at slow airspeeds – errors of up to 10kts are not unknown. To compensate specifically for instrument and position error, the aircraft's POH/FM will have a table or graph showing the magnitude of the error over a range of airspeeds.

The reading taken directly from the ASI dial is called *Indicated Airspeed* or IAS. If IAS is corrected for instrument and position error, the resulting airspeed is known as *Calibrated Airspeed (CAS)* or *Rectified Airspeed (RAS)*.

At cruising airspeeds and altitudes, the airspeed indicator is perhaps most affected by *density error*. Airspeed is related to dynamic pressure, and dynamic pressure is found by the following formula:

Dynamic Pressure = half air density x velocity squared,

or, to use the proper symbols:

$q = \frac{1}{2}\rho V^2$

kts	
IAS	CAS
40	49
50	55
60	62
70	70
80	80
90	89
100	99
110	108
120	118
130	128
140	138

A POH/FM table showing the relationship of calibrated airspeed to indicated airspeed over a range of airspeeds. Note that the difference is greatest at low airspeeds

Therefore a change in velocity means a change in dynamic pressure, and the ASI needle moves accordingly. But a change in air density will **also** change the dynamic pressure and thus the indicated airspeed, even if the velocity remains unchanged. Like the other pressure instruments, the ASI is calibrated to International Standard Atmosphere conditions, these including a sea-level density of 1·225kg/m3. So at sea level in ISA conditions, there is no density error. However, as the aircraft climbs the air density quickly moves away from the ISA sea-level density and so an error is introduced. As a general rule, the lower the pressure and the higher the temperature, the greater the density error. Density error causes the ASI to under-read, so the indicated airspeed (and the calibrated airspeed, CAS) is less than the aircraft's actual speed through the air. As a very approximate rule of thumb, the difference is about 2% per 1000ft altitude up to about 10,000ft, so a CAS of 150kts equates an actual airspeed or *True Airspeed (TAS)* at 10,000ft of around 180kts.

As a general rule, the reduction in density means that the higher the altitude, the greater the difference between indicated and true airspeed. Apart from exceptional conditions, TAS is always more than IAS

TAS	IAS 150 knots	Pressure Altitude
205		20,000ft
183		15,000ft
174		10,000ft
162		5,000ft

Although indicated airspeed (IAS) or calibrated airspeed (CAS) are crucial factors in controlling the aircraft, the true airspeed (TAS) must be known to make time/speed/distance calculations. The formula for calculating density error and so finding TAS is not too complex, and in the past tables and graphs were used to do this. However, a more practical way to find TAS is by using the flight computer. This calculation has already been described in the Navigation section of PPL 3, but a short refresher follows.

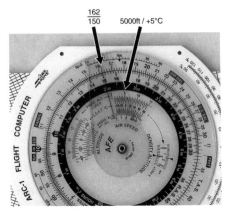

162
150   5000ft / +5°C

Use of a flight computer to calculate TAS

In the Air Speed window of the flight calculator, the flight level (i.e. the altitude with 1013mb/hPa set on the altimeter sub-scale) is set against the Outside Air Temperature (OAT). With this done, the CAS or RAS is located on the inner scale and the TAS is read off above it on the outer scale.

For example, at a pressure altitude (Flight Level) of 5000ft and an OAT of +5°C, a CAS of 150kts gives a TAS of 162kts.

Some Airspeed Indicators have a small window on the periphery of the indicated airspeed markings. When the setting control is used so that pressure altitude and temperature are set in a smaller window, the outer end of the airspeed needle will rest over the approximate TAS.

So:

the reading on the airspeed indicator is IAS – Indicated Airspeed.

IAS corrected for instrument and position error gives CAS – Calibrated Airspeed.

CAS corrected for density error gives TAS – True Air Speed.

For high-speed aircraft (e.g. those operating at speeds in excess of about 300kts TAS) a further correction is made for *Compressibility Error*, which occurs as the air compresses when it is brought to rest in the pitot tube. This error can be calculated on an advanced flight computer as used by aspiring professional pilots, but is insignificant below 300kts or so. The only other airspeed-related term sometimes used is *Equivalent Air Speed* – EAS. This is CAS corrected for compressibility error *but not* density error. EAS is often used when discussing the aerodynamics of high-speed aircraft.

The ASI reading can be affected by a blockage of the pitot or static sources, and the result is best described by example. Imagine an aircraft taking-off on a sunny summer day; all is normal until a large wasp becomes stuck in the pitot tube just as the aircraft gets airborne, trapping the pitot pressure in the system. As the aircraft climbs the static pressure reduces, which allows the capsule within the ASI to expand, purely because the static pressure surrounding it is less. Thus the instrument will tend to overread, indicating that the IAS is higher than it actually is. The higher the aircraft climbs, the greater the error. If the pilot believes the erroneous airspeed indication and disregards other clues such as an unusually high nose-attitude, the aircraft will eventually run out of airspeed and stall. Such a combination of a blocked pitot tube and lack of awareness on the part of the crew has caused a fatal airliner accident.

The effect of blockage of the pitot tube during a climb. By sketching a diagram, it should be possible to answer an examination question regarding blockage of the pitot or static source and the effect on indicated airspeed

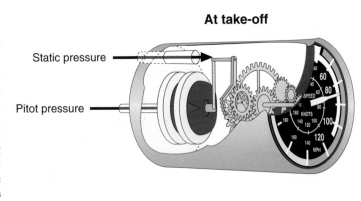

At take-off

Static pressure

Pitot pressure

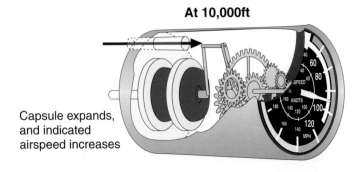

At 10,000ft

Capsule expands, and indicated airspeed increases

As far as examination questions about the ASI are concerned, those about blockage of the pitot or static source can be tackled by knowing the working principle of the ASI as already outlined. It should then be possible to deduce the result of any combination of pitot or static blockage in a climb, descent or level flight. Sketching out the pitot/static connections and the ASI capsule may be helpful. In real life, if a pilot suspects a pitot or static blockage, using pitot heat and/or the alternate static source may help. If there is no back-up ASI (or an electronically derived groundspeed read-out such as that available from DME or GPS, which can help verify a gross error) the best practical advice is to use the normal attitudes and power settings to fly by. It is a worthwhile exercise to try some manoeuvres at a safe altitude, including a simulated approach, whilst an instructor covers the ASI. The use of sensible attitudes and power settings should give airspeeds very close to the normal target speeds.

▶ Airspeed Indicator Serviceability Checks

The importance of checking that the pitot tube (or pitot head) openings are unblocked and uncovered has already been described in 'Pitot-Static System Serviceability Checks'. During taxying and pre-take-off checks the ASI should read zero (most give no indication below 20-30kts) unless taxying *very* fast or in very windy conditions. Usually the first opportunity to check the ASI is during the take-off run, when it should show an increasing airspeed. Once airborne there is not often an opportunity to verify the ASI reading, except that is should be in-line with the power and attitude set. If the ASI reading does become suspect, use of the alternate static source and/or pitot heat should be considered.

▶ Principles of Gyroscopes

A gyroscope is a rapidly spinning wheel rotating around an axis, usually mounted in a series of rings (*gimbals*) to stop it rolling away. Once spinning at a sufficient rate, a gyroscope will maintain its spin axis and this makes it useful for instruments designed to give an indication relative to a fixed position while the aircraft moves around.

A gyroscope has two principle properties, *rigidity* and *precession*.

Rigidity is the inertia of the gyroscope that means it will continue spinning in the same plane unless it is acted upon by an external force. In the absence of any such force, the spin axis of the gyro will continue to point to the same place in space that it was set to. The greater the rigidity of the gyro, the less it will be influenced by an external force, and so a certain degree of rigidity is required in a gyro. There are three main ways to increase the rigidity of a gyroscope:

- Increase the spin speed of the gyro
- Increase the mass of the gyro
- Increase the effective radius of the gyro

The faster a gyro spins, the longer it will stay upright until it slows down enough for gravity to wobble it off its axis. Likewise a larger or heavier gyro resists a greater external force than a smaller or lighter one.

Although the property of rigidity is relatively straightforward to understand, the property of precession is less obvious. If sufficient external force is applied to a gyroscope to deflect it from its spin axis, the force does not act directly as applied. Instead it acts through 90° in the direction of the rotation of the gyro. In other words, if a gyro is spinning anti-clockwise, and a force is applied at the front edge of the gyro, the gyro will actually twist as if the force had been applied at the bottom. This particular property of a gyro can manifest itself in unexpected ways. For example, a propeller – spinning rapidly – acts as a gyroscope. This means that when the tail of a tailwheel aircraft is raised during take-off, this change in pitch is translated into yaw, causing the aircraft to swerve to the left or right (depending on the direction of rotation of the propeller).

A suction-driven gyro, the jet directs airflow onto buckets cut into the gyro rotor

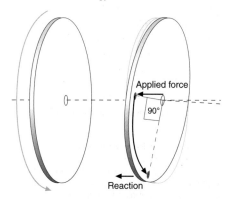

▶ The Turn Indicator

The turn indicator is an instrument which uses a *rate gyro* to measure rate of turn. The axis of the gyro is horizontal and a spring is attached to the axis. When the aircraft starts to turn, the yawing force is precessed causing a pitching force which makes the gyro 'tilt' and a needle attached to the gyro gimbal measures this 'tilt' in terms of a rate of turn. The greater the rate of turn, the greater the gyro tilt.

A turn and slip indicator. The bottom needle indicates rate of turn, the top needle shows balance (slip or skid)

A 'needle and ball' display; the needle showing rate of turn, the ball showing balance

There are two types of instrument for showing rate of turn information. The original instrument – which is correctly known as the *turn indicator* or sometimes the *turn and slip* – most often has a 'needle and ball' presentation. The "rate" of any turn is shown by the needle pointing in the relevant direction to a mark on the instrument face. The key rate of turn is 'Rate One', at which the aircraft is altering heading at the rate of three degrees per second. At this rate of turn the aircraft will reverse direction (i.e. make a 180° turn) in 60 seconds and fly a complete circle (360°) in two minutes.

As an aircraft flies faster, so greater force is required to make it turn. It follows that in a properly balanced turn, the angle of bank necessary to achieve a set rate of turn increases as airspeed increases. As a rule of thumb, to find the angle of bank necessary to achieve Rate One in a properly balanced turn, divide the true airspeed (TAS) by 10 and add 7. Therefore a Rate One turn at 100kts TAS requires 17° of bank, whereas achieving the same rate of turn at 400kts requires no less than 47° of bank. The pure turn indicator knows nothing about the angle of bank, it only measures the rate of change of direction. A pilot is interested in the rate of turn, but will also want to know that the aircraft is being flown in balance and so the turn indicator also incorporates some form of indicator to show if the aircraft is slipping or skidding.

The modern slip or balance indicator is nothing more sophisticated than a ball in a curved spirit-level. If the aircraft is in balance, the ball will be central. If the aircraft is out of balance (i.e. skidding or slipping) the ball will displace to one side or the other. To correct this situation, use rudder on the side indicated until the ball centralises. So if the ball is out to the right, apply right rudder until it centralises. Interpretation of the slip or balance ball can be crudely summarised as "tread on the ball".

▶ The Turn Co-ordinator

One disadvantage of the pure turn indicator is that it gives no indication of roll or bank angle; it only shows the *rate* of turn. To counter this problem, the gimbal of the gyro can be angled (usually at about 30° to the horizontal) so that the gyro will now sense and indicate roll as well as yaw. This is commonly done in a modern *turn co-ordinator*. When the

A modern 'turn co-ordinator'. The aircraft symbol indicates rate of turn and angle of bank (but not pitch), the ball shows balance

wings are banked to start a turn, the turn co-ordinator will show this before a significant rate of turn develops thus giving an indication of bank. As the turn develops, so the rate of turn is indicated. This gives the turn co-ordinator a dual function in indicating both roll and rate of turn. However – despite the presentation in the form of a small model aircraft – it does not give any pitch information and the instrument often has a placard to that effect.

One drawback of the turn co-ordinator is that the instrument face is normally vague about what indication represents a Rate One turn, unfortunately it is almost certainly *not* when the model aircraft's wing is on the left or right mark. Therefore, before using a turn co-ordinator in real IMC conditions, it may be worth calibrating it whilst doing some turns timed against a stopwatch to measure the true rate of change of direction.

▶Turn Co-ordinator Serviceability Checks

Traditionally, the turn co-ordinator uses a different power source to that used by the other two gyro flight instruments – the Attitude Indicator (AI) and the Heading Indicator (HI) – in order to provide a back-up should their power source fail. As most light aircraft use the suction system to drive the AI and HI, this means that the turn co-ordinator is usually electrically powered. The turn co-ordinator will often have a small warning 'flag' (usually red) which comes into view if the instrument is not receiving electrical power. If the RPM of the gyro in a turn co-ordinator drops below its normal range, the rate of turn will under-read, in effect showing less than the actual rate of turn.

The turn co-ordinator or turn indicator can be checked in the turns whilst taxying. The aircraft symbol or needle should show a turn in the correct direction, and the ball will show a yaw or skid in the opposite direction because the turn is flat rather than banked and balanced.

▶The Attitude Indicator (AI)

The *Attitude Indicator* or AI is sometimes known by its former title of *Artificial Horizon*, or even *Gyro Horizon*, and it utilises an earth gyro that has freedom of movement in all three planes and indicates the aircraft's attitude via a model horizon attached to the gimbals. The gyro spins in a horizontal plane and if the gyro is driven by suction (most in light aircraft are), the air escapes past four vanes located on each side of the square pendulous unit underneath the sealed gyro housing. When the gyro is spinning and the gyro axis is upright, the air escapes from these ports in equal measure. Should the axis move away from the vertical, the vanes partly covering the ports will move so that more air escapes from the port which (via precession) will apply a force to right the gyro axis.

The display of a modern AI consists of a model horizon, with blue (for the sky) above the horizon line and brown (for the ground) below the horizon line. Markings above and below the horizon are usually at every five degrees of pitch angle and around the edge of the display, lines indicate angle of bank with points at 10°, 20°, 30°, 45° and 60°. In front of this display is a model aircraft whose position may be adjustable by the pilot (this is normally only done on the ground). The position of the model aircraft in relation to the AI horizon represents the pitch and roll angle of the real aircraft. In flight, it appears to the pilot that the model aircraft is banking or pitching. In reality the model aircraft is fixed and it is the gyro, maintaining the proper alignment of the AI horizon relative to the aircraft, that creates the illusion of the model aircraft pitching and rolling.

In interpreting the AI display, it must be remembered that a very small movement on the AI can represent a big change in attitude. This is

A general 'cutaway' view of an Attitude Indicator, with a horizontally-mounted earth gyro

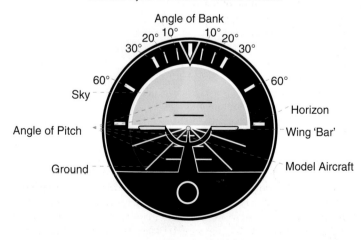

Standard layout of a modern attitude indicator

Straight and level flight

especially true in pitch, when at first it is easy to underestimate the true pitch angle based on the AI display. This point is covered in Exercise 19 (Instrument Flying) of PPL 1. Some (but not all) AIs used in light aircraft have roll limits beyond which the gyroscope will 'topple', typical limits for a suction-powered AI being 60° in roll. The AI may have a *caging* control, which locks the gimbals in place and thus prevents wear and tear on the gyro if it is known that the AI limits are going to be exceeded (e.g. during aerobatics), however many modern AIs do not have this caging facility as they are not restricted by roll limitations.

▶Attitude Indicator Serviceability Checks

In the case of an AI powered by an engine-driven vacuum pump (which is the norm for training aircraft), some seven minutes is normally required for the gyro to reach full operating speed after the engine has been started; until then the AI will give unreliable indications. When taxying, the AI should give a 'sensible' pitch and bank indication and should not show a false angle of bank when turning on the ground. There is rarely a separate warning indication to indicate a problem

with a suction-driven AI, and the suction gauge is the main indicator to monitor. If the suction system does fail, the gyro will take several minutes to slow down and errors in the AI display will only occur gradually. Insidious errors can be difficult to spot on their own so if the AI starts to disagree with other instruments, some concentration is required to establish which instrument is in error if flying in IMC. Pitch indications can be checked against the ASI, altimeter and VSI; roll indications can be checked against the Heading Indicator and turn co-ordinator.

Electrically-driven AIs are found in some light aircraft and gliders. Although the principle of operation is the same as for a suction-driven instrument, electrically-driven AIs tend to have a red warning flag that appears if the unit loses electrical power. This gives a much clear warning of a failure compared to a suction-driven unit.

An electrically-driven AI, note the caging control and the red-warning flag to show that the unit is not receiving electrical power

A vacuum pump failure that occurred, ironically enough, whilst the author was editing the second edition of this book. The suction gauge reading (left-hand side of instrument panel) has fallen to zero, whilst the AI and HI have run down. Despite this they give indications that are surprisingly stable – except that the actual heading when this photo was taken was 330, and not 070 as shown on the HI

▶ The Heading Indicator

The *Heading Indicator* or HI, is also known as the *Direction Indicator* (DI) or even the *Directional Gyro Indicator* uses a directional gyroscope to indicate direction. The gyroscope is mounted vertically with a gimbal that acts on a series of gears to move the heading display.

The heading indicator was the first gyroscopic instrument to be used in aircraft. Early HI designs displayed direction on a moving ribbon but most modern HIs have a vertical card face which is much easier to interpret. The HI is much easier to interpret than a compass, and unlike a compass it is not subject to turning and acceleration errors.

A general 'cutaway' view of an Heading Indicator, with vertically mounted directional gyroscope

Display of an original 'ribbon' style heading indicator

The more user-friendly display of a vertical card heading indicator

The HI is set by reference to the compass and its reading should be checked against the compass regularly. Checking the HI reading against the compass, and any subsequent adjustment of the HI, should only be done when the aircraft is in steady, wings-level flight at a constant airspeed. The HI is adjusted using a knob to 'cage' the gyro and rotate the display to select the correct direction. On some HIs the gyro can be fully caged; on others, the knob is spring-loaded to uncage the gyro once released. To avoid inadvertently leaving the gyro caged (and hence locking the HI on to one direction), many pilots try to get into the habit of turning the setting knob after re-setting the instrument. The knob should turn freely without affecting the display.

The HI has limits of aircraft movement beyond which it will 'topple'. The average limit is around 60° of bank. It has two main errors: *real wander* and *apparent wander,* also known as *real drift* and *apparent drift.*

Real wander is caused by worn bearings, wear and tear, friction, an out-of-balance gyro, a gyro turning at the wrong speed or anything else which causes the gyro to not maintain proper rigidity. The indicated heading will slowly wander away from the actual as the error feeds through to the HI display.

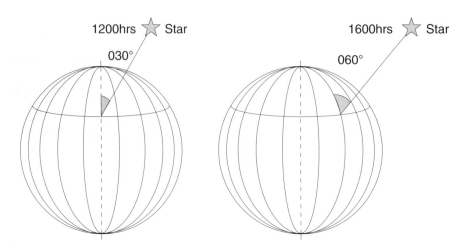

The effect of apparent wander – as the earth rotates the gyro maintains its axis relative to a fixed point in space, not to a point on the earth

Apparent wander is caused by the earth's rotation, and the motion of the gyro across the earth. A gyroscope's rigidity causes its axis to remain aligned with reference to a fixed point in space, **not** a point on the surface of the earth. So as the earth rotates, the gyro continues to align itself with what used to be called the "fixed stars". As far as the pilot is concerned, the gyro is apparently moving its axis (seen on the HI as a change of heading) even though a constant direction is being maintained. The effect can be seen over a period of time even if the aircraft is on the ground and not moved at all. The amount of apparent wander depends on the latitude of the gyro. To an idea of the magnitude of error, an uncorrected HI in northern Europe will experience a heading change of about eight degrees an hour.

Because the magnitude of apparent wander is a known factor, a compensating device (known as the *latitude nut*) is fitted inside the HI and is set according to the average latitude in which the aircraft is expected to operate. One consequence is that if the instrument's location is changed significantly (by more than about 10° of latitude) on a long-term basis, the device may need adjustment.

If the gyro is moved across the face of the earth, a further complication (sometimes called *transport wander*) is introduced. Aspiring professional pilots can look forward to a detailed investigation into phenomena such as apparent wander and transport wander; at this stage it is enough to appreciate that the HI must be regularly checked against the compass for accuracy.

One expression the pilot may come across in relation to more sophisticated aircraft is a *slaved* HI. This is a system whereby the HI is automatically adjusted from a remote compass (often in the wing tip) although the pilot still has a compass in the cockpit for cross-checking and back-up.

▶ Heading Indicator Serviceability Checks

Once the suction system is operating, the suction-driven HI can be set by reference to the compass. It can then be checked by making turns whilst taxiing. In a right-hand turn the reading should increase; in a left-hand turn readings should decrease. The reading is verified during the pre take-off checks, and can be cross-checked against the known runway QDM once lined-up for take-off.

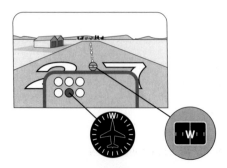

In flight the HI is regularly checked against the compass. This must be done when the compass is not experiencing an error, such as during turning or speed changes. Once again, some aircraft have an electrically-driven HI, which may display a prominent warning flag if electrical power is not reaching the unit.

Checking the HI and compass against a known direction (in this case the runway QDM)

▶The Magnetic Compass

The principle of a magnetic needle which aligns itself with the earth's magnetic field and thereby indicates direction has been used in navigation for thousands of years. Today, even the most sophisticated aircraft still has a compass somewhere in the cockpit, if only for use as a last-resort back-up.

The typical direct-reading 'E'-type compass found in a light aircraft consists of a series of magnets suspended in a fluid – this fluid damps movement of the magnets, reduces friction and supports the magnet assembly which rests on a pivot. A compass-rose card is attached to the magnet assembly and direction is read from a 'lubber' line on the window in the compass housing.

An 'E' type compass

The compass is subject to three principal errors which a pilot needs to know about. *Variation* and *deviation* have already been discussed in some detail in the Navigation section of PPL 3, although a brief refresher follows. The other error to consider is *dip*.

Variation is caused by the fact that the magnetic poles are not in the same place as the actual (or true) geographic poles. The magnetic compass aligns to the magnetic poles and so a magnetic direction referenced to *magnetic north* is different from a true direction derived from true north. On an aeronautical map, *isogonals* (lines passing through points of equal magnetic variation) allow the pilot determine the difference between a magnetic direction and a true direction at any particular location.

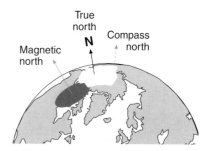

The effect of variation and deviation

Deviation is caused by the effect of the aircraft's own magnetic field upon the compass. The compass can be adjusted by an engineer to minimise these errors, and any residual error is recorded on a compass correction card which shows the difference (deviation) between the indicated compass heading and the actual magnetic heading. The pilot should beware of placing magnetic and metallic materials (for example, a headset, GPS, or clip of a kneeboard) near the compass as the magnetic properties of such items can significantly affect the compass reading, errors of up to 30° have be demonstrated. Larger items, even if carried some distance from the compass, may also effect its reading. Almost any metallic object could be magnetised strongly enough to add an extra and unpredictable deviation to the compass – the classic example is a set of golf clubs.

For	N	30	60	E	120	150
Steer	359	032	061	090	119	151
For	S	210	240	W	300	330
Steer	184	213	241	269	299	332
DATE						AIRPATH

A compass deviation card

Dip occurs as the magnets of the compass try to align with the earth's magnetic field, which exists in three dimensions. Whilst the earth's magnetic field is almost parallel to the surface at the equator, it is close to vertical at the poles. As a result, the magnets of the compass tend to pull downwards towards the magnetic pole; the nearer the aircraft is to the pole, the greater the angle of dip. In an E-type compass the magnets are suspended on a pivot, and even after correction by an engineer a residual dip angle is left. One effect of dip is that the centre of gravity (CG) of the magnet assembly does not pass exactly through the pivot. This effect of inertia upon the CG means that when a force is applied to the compass assembly – such as turning or accelerating or decelerating, the CG moves relative to the pivot point causing the compass to turn away from the proper magnetic heading.

The effect of magnetic 'dip' is most marked above 70°N

In the turn, the turning error caused by dip is greatest on northerly and southerly headings and zero on easterly and westerly headings. In the northern hemisphere when turning northwards, the compass tends to be **sluggish** – that is, it reads less than the actual heading, the amount of error being about 30° on turning through a northerly heading. Thus a northerly turn should be stopped short of the desired heading; the pilot should **undershoot** the heading required. Knowing that turning error is zero on an easterly or westerly heading and 30° on a northerly heading, the error on intermediate headings can be estimated (e.g. stop the turn 15° early when turning on to north-west). When turning to the south, the compass is **lively** and reads more than the actual heading. So the pilot should continue a southerly turn past the desired heading (**overshoot** the heading) with the error on south again being about 30°. So in the northern hemisphere, the compass turning error can be summarised as **UNOS – Undershoot North, Overshoot South**.

The practical application of UNOS in the northern hemisphere

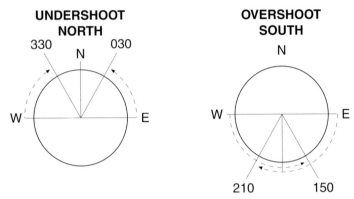

A couple of examples will illustrate the practical application of this rule. Turning the shortest way from east on to north, the pilot would undershoot by 30° – stopping the turn when the compass reads 030°. Turning the shortest way from west on to south-east, the pilot would overshoot by 15°, i.e. stop the turn when the compass is reads 120°.

A more basic turning error is that of simply commencing the turn in the opposite direction to that required. Because of the presentation of the E-type direct reading compass, it is easy to turn the wrong way so mentally review which way to turn *before* starting the turn if using the compass for heading reference. If there is a HI or VOR with a vertical card on the panel, this can help confirm whether a left or right turn is required. Some aircraft are fitted with a vertical card-type compass which minimises the chance of turning the wrong way, although these are far less common than the E-type.

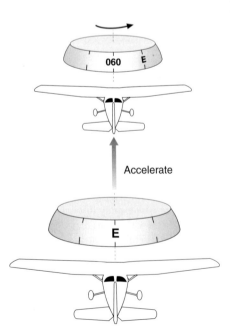

Acceleration and deceleration errors are at their greatest on easterly and westerly headings, and least on northerly and southerly headings. An acceleration causes an apparent turn to north and a deceleration causes an apparent turn to south, even if the heading is actually constant. These errors, as with the turning errors, are reversed in the southern hemisphere.

Acceleration error on an easterly heading in the northern hemisphere

Accelerate north, decelerate south – ANDS

▶Compass Serviceability Checks

Before starting the compass can be checked for any crack in the instrument glass or obvious discoloration of the suspension fluid. There should be no bubbles in the fluid, and a gentle application of finger pressure to the unit will reveal whether the magnet assembly is free to move. The compass reading can also be checked for any gross error at this stage and it's good airmanship to ensure that the appropriate deviation card is in the aircraft as well. During taxying, the compass reading should decrease when turning left and increase when turning right. When lining up on the runway, the reading can be checked against the known runway QDM.

In flight, the only real check that can be made of the compass is that it seems to be giving a generally sensible indication. Dip will make the ordinary direct-reading compass unreliable at extreme latitudes, beyond about 70N or S. Apart from this problem, and the possibility of magnetic materials in the aircraft causing excessive deviation, an in-flight failure of the compass itself is virtually unknown.

The accuracy of a compass can be checked on the ground by an engineer, who will undertake a procedure known as 'swinging the compass'. A compass swing must be carried out at fixed intervals stated in the aircraft's maintenance schedule, and also after any of the following events:

- a hard landing,
- a lightning strike,
- replacement of major components, including electrical and radio equipment,
- if the aircraft has been standing on one heading for more than a month.

▶ Revision

124 Which aircraft instrument(s) measure static pressure only?

125 Which aircraft instrument(s) measure both pitot and static pressure?

126 During a climb at 500fpm, the static source becomes blocked at 4000ft altitude. After a further 2 minutes of climb at the same rate, what will the altimeter and vertical speed indicator read?

127 An airfield has an elevation of 210ft amsl. The airfield QNH is 1002mb/hPa, airfield QFE is 995mb/hPa. If QNH is set on the altimeter on the airfield apron, what is the range of altimeter reading for a serviceable altimeter?

128 An aircraft has a recommended short-field approach speed of 59 knots indicated airspeed (IAS). What short-field approach speed should a pilot use in sea-level ISA conditions, and which if landing at a 5000ft elevation airfield when the temperature is +25°C and the QNH is 1001mb/hPa?

129 What pressure(s) is/are sampled by the Airspeed Indicator (ASI)?

130 What is the significance of the yellow arc on an airspeed indicator?

131 What is meant by 'Va' airspeed, and what is its significance?

132 What airspeed limitation is represented by the upper (faster) limit of the green arc on an airspeed indicator?

133 What error(s) are taken into account when converting indicated airspeed (IAS) into calibrated airspeed (CAS)?

134 An aircraft at 10,000ft has an indicated airspeed (IAS) of 100 knots. The QNH is 1001mb/hPa, the Outside Air Temperature (OAT) is +5°C at 10,000ft. Without using a flight computer, true airspeed (TAS) be expected to be less than, equal to, or more than IAS?

135 During a climb the pitot source becomes blocked. As the climb continues how will the ASI reading be effected?

136 What are the two principle properties of a gyroscope?

137 Name two ways of increasing gyro rigidity.

138 Which gyro instrument utilises a rate gyro?

139 Whilst taxying before take-off, the aircraft is turned to the left on a level piece of taxyway. What indication would the pilot expect from a properly functioning turn co-ordinator?

140 Which of the following do **not** contain a gyro?

Turn Co-ordinator, Airspeed Indicator, Heading Indicator, Compass, Attitude Indicator, Altimeter

141 What is apparent wander (apparent drift) and what instrument(s) does it effect?

142 Excluding the external casing and window, what are the principal components of an aircraft direct-reading compass?

143 A compass deviation card corrects _____ heading for _____ resulting in a _____ heading (fill in the blanks)

144 An aircraft is turning the shortest way from west (270°) onto north (000°) in the northern hemisphere. As the aircraft actually passes through magnetic north, what reading would be expected on a properly set HI and compass respectively?

145 In the northern hemisphere, an aircraft accelerates whilst maintain a constant westerly direction on the HI. How will the compass reading be affected?

Answers at page fpp72

Aircraft General Knowledge
Airworthiness

Aircraft General Knowledge
Airworthiness

► Aircraft Documents

► Aircraft Maintenance

► Pilot Maintenance

► Modifications

► Revision

Airworthiness

▶ Aircraft Documents

The aircraft's **Pilot's Operating Handbook/Flight Manual** (POH/FM) is in essence an owner's handbook. It has been referred to many times in this volume because the POH/FM contains information vital to the safe operation of the aircraft, and every pilot should be thoroughly familiar with the information in the POH/FM for any aircraft they fly. Procedures, techniques, limitations and performance standards are all found in the POH/FM, and ignoring this information has major legal and safety implications. The Certificate of Airworthiness (C of A – described shortly) is only valid as long as the aircraft is operated within the limitations contained in the POH/FM. Operating outside these limits automatically invalidates the C of A.

The airworthiness authority that certifies an aircraft for its area of responsibility (the CAA in the case of the UK) may choose to amend the POH/FM or add supplemental information, for example if they do not agree with a particular technique or if they find the performance figures over-optimistic. A CAA supplement over-rules the original POH/FM material.

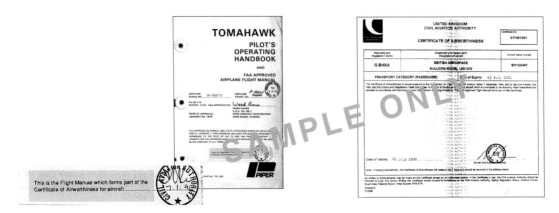

The POH/FM forms part of the Certificate of Airworthiness

A Certificate of Airworthiness, valid for the period stated on the certificate

A **Certificate of Airworthiness** (C of A) confirms that an aircraft is certified to an internationally acceptable standard in terms of design, construction, performance, etc. and may be issued in a certain category, which indicates the purpose for which the aircraft can be used.

With only a very few exceptions, no aircraft can fly without a valid C of A.

The C of A will state any particular restrictions or conditions of issue, will display its period of validity and may state that the POH/FM forms part of the C of A. Ignoring these conditions of use, exceeding the period of validity or operating outside the limitations and procedures outlined in the POH/FM are all good ways to invalidate the C of A, leaving the pilot in command open to far-reaching and expensive penalties. The C of A also becomes invalid if the aircraft or its equipment is repaired, modified or maintained in a manner not approved by the CAA, or if a mandatory inspection or modification is not carried out. The clause regarding modification means that a C of A may also be invalidated if some part of the aircraft structure or equipment is removed, so check carefully before stripping the aircraft of a part (such as a fairing) even if you consider it to be a minor item.

At the time of writing there is a transition in the UK to C of A's issued by the European Aviation Safety Agency (EASA). Periods of validity will vary until a date, expected to be in 2007, when non-expiring C of As will be issued, which will be validated by an Airworthiness Review Certificate (ARC).

As an alternative to a C of A, an aircraft may be granted a Permit to Fly. A Permit to Fly generally applies to homebuilt, kitplane, experimental or microlight aircraft or an aircraft which is otherwise not suitable for a C of A (e.g. vintage and ex-military aircraft). In the UK the inspection and maintenance requirements of 'permit' aircraft are mostly managed by the Popular Flying Association (PFA), and the British Microlight Aircraft Association (BMAA) for many microlight aircraft. Many other countries have broadly similar arrangements, in the USA there is an 'experimental' category of aircraft.

A Permit to Fly

A Permit to Fly usually contains specific conditions regarding the operation of the aircraft, more restrictive than those of an aircraft with a C of A. Common restrictions for a 'permit' aircraft are:

- Flights will be restricted to day Visual Flight Rules (VFR) only.

- The aircraft will not be permitted to fly over congested areas.

- The aircraft will normally be restricted to flight within the airspace of the issuing state, except with the prior agreement of the country in which the flights are to be made.

- Limitations may be placed upon the numbers of persons to be carried in the aircraft, either in general, or in specific circumstances.

- The aircraft must have placards showing operating limitations and conditions.

A Certificate of Maintenance Review

If an aircraft has a Transport or Aerial Work Category C of A, it must be maintained in accordance with an approved maintenance schedule or the Light Aircraft Maintenance Scheme (LAMS – described shortly) if the aircraft does not exceed 2730kg Maximum Take-off Weight Authorised (MTWA). An aircraft with a Private Category C of A *must* be maintained to the LAMS if it does not exceed 2730kg MTWA. Maintenance schedules are described more fully later, but an aircraft with a Transport or Aerial Work Category C of A must have a valid **Certificate of Maintenance Review** in force to show that the aircraft has been maintained to an approved schedule. The C of MR will show the date of issue, the date or flying hours at which the next review must take place, and the signature of the issuing licensed aircraft maintenance engineer.

A Certificate of Release to Service

When maintenance is carried out on an aircraft that has a Certificate of Airworthiness, a **Certificate of Release to Service** will be raised. This certifies that work carried out on the aircraft has been done in accordance with CAA and company procedures and approvals. Work carried out by a pilot/owner (in accordance with permitted repairs and replacements, described shortly) does not require a Certificate of Release to Service.

To enable the pilot to make accurate weight and centre-of-gravity calculations, the aircraft is weighed when manufactured or first registered and the resulting information is available in the **Weight and Centre of Gravity Schedule** (commonly known as the 'weight schedule'). The aircraft is re-weighed periodically to check the figures in the weight schedule, and is also re-weighed after any major repair or modification.

A Weight and Centre of Gravity Schedule

A Transport-category Certificate of Approval of Aircraft Radio Installation

The aircraft's radio equipment and its installation must be approved by a **Certificate of Approval of Aircraft Radio Installation**. Any change of radio equipment means that a new certificate must be obtained. Items that are not part of the aircraft's radio equipment, such as headsets, do not have to be covered by this certificate. However, in the case of an item such as a 'portable' GPS receiver, fixed to the aircraft and 'hard wired' to the aircraft's own electricity supply (i.e. via a cigarette lighter socket), the situation is less clear-cut and appropriate advice must be sought.

An aircraft with a Transport or Aerial Work category C of A must have a **Technical Log**. The technical log contains details of each flight and must be signed by the commander of the aircraft at the end of each flight. In particular, the Technical Log contains details of any defects in the aircraft or its equipment, and subsequent rectification action.

A Technical Log

A 'defect sheet' from a technical log

All aircraft must have individual **logbooks** for the airframe and engine(s) and, in the case of a variable-pitch propeller, for the propeller(s) too. Details of each flight are recorded in these logbooks together with particulars of maintenance, modifications, repairs, overhauls, etc.

▶Aircraft Maintenance

A state will specify scheduled maintenance inspections for all aircraft, to be carried out at set intervals. Within the UK, for a light aircraft of less than 2730kg MTWA with a C of A (as opposed to a Permit to Fly) the **Light Aircraft Maintenance Scheme** (LAMS) applies. In general terms, the following checks apply under the LAMS:

Check A (also known as the *DI* or *Daily Inspection*). In practical terms this is a thorough pre-flight inspection of the aircraft and its documents carried-out before the first flight of the day. Items checked on the Check A that are not necessarily carried out on every pre-flight inspection include an inspection of all aircraft documents, the draining and checking of fuel samples, manual override and disengagement checks on the autopilot, avionic equipment checks, inspection of seats, belts and harnesses for satisfactory condition, locking and release and a check of emergency equipment including the validity of inspection dates.

50 Hour Check. A detailed inspection of the aircraft, usually including an oil change.

150 Hour Check. More detailed than the 50-hour check, and includes checking/changing spark plugs, checking magneto timing, inspecting the engine and attached components, the electrical system, flying controls, undercarriage, steering and braking systems, major structural components etc.

Annual Check. A major inspection of the airframe, engine and all systems and components.

An identification plate, showing the exact make and model of the aircraft, and its serial number

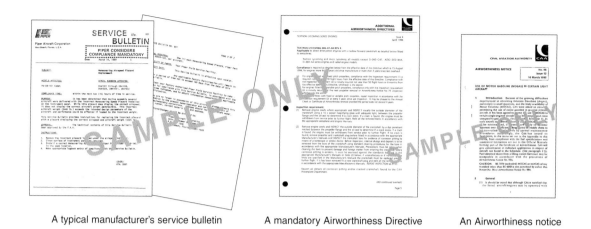

A typical manufacturer's service bulletin   A mandatory Airworthiness Directive   An Airworthiness notice

STAR Annual Check. In the case of Transport, Aerial Work and Private Category C of A aircraft of less than 2730kg, the renewal of the C of A (usually every three years) is marked by an expanded Annual Check known as the STAR Annual Check, or more commonly "the C of A". When this check is complete the aircraft is test-flown to ensure that it is functioning correctly and performing to the standards set out in the aircraft's POH/FM.

The checks above are carried-out to the following schedule:

Transport & Aerial Work Category C of A	**Private Category C of A**
Check A – Before first flight of the day	Check A – Before first flight of the day
50 Hour Check – not exceeding 50 flying hours	50 Hour Check – not exceeding 50 flying hours or six months, whichever is sooner
150 Hour Check – not exceeding 150 flying hours	150 Hour Check – not exceeding 150 flying hours
Annual Check – not exceeding 12 months	Annual Check – not exceeding 12 months

Work carried out during scheduled inspections is done to the CAA-approved schedule and in accordance with the manufacturer's recommendations. Often individual components have a 'service life' based on flying hours, after which they must be inspected or replaced. The manufacturer may also issue **service bulletins**, which publicise a recommended service procedure to make the aircraft, engine or component safer or prolong service life.

If an airworthiness authority becomes aware of a factor that could affect the safety of a particular aircraft type, it can issue an **Airworthiness Directive** (**AD**) notifying a mandatory inspection or modification. Often an AD is used to make a manufacturer's service bulletin recommendations compulsory and when an AD is issued, it may well state that the required inspection or modification has to be done within a certain number of days or flying hours. Very occasionally, if the problem the AD is addressing is particularly serious, the aircraft type may be grounded pending completion of the AD. As part of a scheduled inspection, the aircraft documentation is checked to ensure that any relevant ADs have been complied with.

The CAA also publish **Airworthiness Notices**, these circulate general information regarding aircraft airworthiness to engineering organisations and aircraft owners.

If an aircraft has a Permit to Fly, scheduled inspections are normally agreed between the operator and the CAA, the Popular Flying Association (PFA) or the British Microlight Aircraft Association (BMAA) – depending on which organisation is responsible for administrating the Permit to Fly.

▶Pilot Maintenance

In general, all maintenance on an aircraft with a C of A must be carried out and inspected by a licensed aircraft engineer. However, in the UK the CAA has made provision for certain items to be performed by a pilot who is not a licensed aircraft engineer if the aircraft is less than 2730kg and has a Private or Special category C of A. The exact details are given in the Air Navigation (General) Regulations, but in principle the following are permitted:

- Replacement of undercarriage tyres, landing skids or skid shoes.
- Replacement of elastic shock absorbers on the undercarriage.
- Replacement of defective safety wiring or split pins, **except** those in engine, transmission, rotor or flight control systems.
- Patch repairs to fabric covering not needing rib stitching and not involving the removal of control surfaces or structural parts.
- Repairs to the interior upholstery and furnishing of an aircraft not involving the operation of any system nor the structure of the aircraft.
- Repairs (other than welding) to non-structural fairings, covers and cowlings.
- Replacement of side windows.
- Replacement of belts and harnesses.
- Replacement of seats and seat parts.
- Replacement of bulbs, reflectors, lenses or lights.
- Replacement of a cowling which does not involve the removal of propellers/rotors or the disconnecting of engine or flight controls.
- Replacement of unserviceable spark plugs.
- Replacement of batteries.
- Replacement of wings, tail surfaces or controls designed to be attached immediately before flight and removed after flight.
- Replacement of main rotor blades designed to be removed and not requiring special tools.
- Replacement of generator and fan belts designed to be removed and not requiring special tools.
- Replacement of a VHF communication radio which is not combined with a navigation radio.

In addition to these repairs and replacements, and in accordance with the same restrictions, a pilot can carry out a 50-hour check on an aeroplane but *not* a rotorcraft (e.g. helicopter).

Of course, being *legally* entitled to change a spark plug – for example – does not mean that the pilot is automatically capable of doing the job *properly* and has the necessary equipment and information. Even if the pilot is happy with his own engineering expertise, the CAA advises that pilots who carry out their own maintenance should consider co-operating with an approved maintenance organisation. This is common-sense advice that can avoid expensive and potentially dangerous mistakes.

Details of any maintenance work carried out by a pilot who is the owner or operator of an aircraft must be entered into the aircraft's logbook(s), and this entry must be dated and signed by the person who carried out the work. In common with other maintenance work, all equipment and parts used on an aircraft with a C of A must be of a type approved by the CAA.

A pilot may also occasionally be called upon to make a 'duplicate control system inspection'. If one of the aircraft's control systems has undergone any type of maintenance or adjustment, it must be inspected by two people to confirm that the work has been properly carried out and that it is functioning properly. The initial inspection is done by a licensed engineer, and the second part of the inspection is normally done by another engineer. However, if the aircraft is away from base, the second part of the inspection can be carried out by a pilot qualified on type.

▶ Modifications

There is a thriving industry, based mostly in the USA, which offers modifications to existing aircraft types – often in the form of 'kits' replacing certain aircraft components. Common modifications are new wing tips and wing vortex generators to give allegedly better short field performance or 'gap sealers' for flaps or ailerons and re-shaped cowlings to improve cruising speed. Companies marketing such modifications often refer to their products as having a *Supplemental Type Certificate* or *STC*. This means that the modification has been approved by the Federal Aviation Authority (FAA), the US equivalent of the UK CAA. An STC has no legal basis in the UK. **Any** replacement or modification to an aircraft with a UK C of A **must** be approved by the CAA or the European Aviation Safety Agency (EASA), which is taking on responsibility for European airworthiness issues.

Where such a modification is approved by the CAA, the POH/FM performance and limitation figures may well change. So if flying such an aircraft, a detailed look in the POH/FM before flight is prudent.

▶ Revision

146   For a UK-registered aircraft, the POH/FM states a short-field take-off technique, a CAA supplement gives a different technique. Which should the pilot follow?

147   For what period is a Certificate of Airworthiness normally valid?

148   Under the provisions of the Air Navigation Order, a pilot who is the owner or operator of an aircraft carries-out some minor maintenance work. How should this work be recorded?

149   An aircraft control system has undergone minor adjustment at an airfield which is not the aircraft's home base. Who may carry-out the second part of the duplicate inspection?

Answers at page fpp72

Aircraft General Knowledge

Aeroplane Flight Safety

Exhaust pipes from engine cylinders

Air

Exhaust exit

Heater valve
set to HOT

Heated air to cabin

Cabin heat box

Heater valve
set to COLD

Heated air sent overboard

Aircraft General Knowledge
Aeroplane Flight Safety

▶ Seat Belts and Harnesses and Seat Adjustment

▶ First Aid Kits

▶ Fire Extinguishers

▶ Survival Equipment

▶ De-Icing Systems

▶ Cabin Heating and Ventilation Systems

▶ Refuelling Precautions

▶ Dangerous Goods

▶ Revision

Aeroplane Flight Safety

▶ Seat Belts and Harnesses and Seat Adjustment

The seat belts or harnesses are an item of aircraft equipment that often receive no more than a passing glance from pilots as they check 'hatches and harnesses' before take-off and landing. Nevertheless, in the event of an accident, a properly secured seat belt or harness can be – quite literally – a life saver.

The most basic restraint is a simple safety belt 'lap strap', which secures just below the waist. The problem with this arrangement is that in the event of a strong deceleration, the upper body tends to 'jack-knife' forwards and down. This normally involves some part of the head, face or upper body coming into hard contact with whatever is immediately ahead, which in the case of front seat occupants normally means glass, dials, switches and levers. This, together with the associated 'whiplash' as the head recoils back, is clearly not good.

Seat belts in a PA-28 Cherokee

For this reason, the vast majority of front seats will have at the very least a safety belt plus a diagonal 'shoulder' strap. In the case of UK-registered aircraft with a Maximum Total Weight Authorised (MTWA) of 2730kg or less, a safety belt with diagonal shoulder strap is mandatory for the pilot and co-pilot seats unless the CAA is satisfied that it is impractical to fit a diagonal shoulder strap, such as might be the case in a vintage aircraft. In any case, if a diagonal shoulder strap is provided, it should always be used as it is well proven that 'upper torso restraint' is a major factor in reducing injuries in the event of an accident.

A full safety harness, which fits across the waist and over both shoulders, is mandatory on the front seats of UK-registered aircraft with a Maximum Total Weight Authorised exceeding 2730kg; although the CAA may permit a seat belt with diagonal shoulder strap instead if it is impractical to fit a safety harness. A full safety harness offers very good protection in the event of strong deceleration and a full safety harness is mandatory for aircraft and gliders carrying-out aerobatic manoeuvres, although an aircraft carrying out just 'erect' spins and no other aerobatic manoeuvres *may* be approved by the CAA to have just a safety belt and diagonal harness fitted to the front seats.

As part of the pre-flight checks it is worth looking over the seat belts and harnesses for the general condition and security of the belts themselves, the buckles and the attachment points. Particular danger signs are worn or frayed belts and excessive play in the buckle or adjustment system. If the shoulder belt features an 'inertia reel' restraint, giving a sharp tug (excessive force is *not* required) on the strap will test if the reel locks. Once the seat is in the desired position, the pilot should adjust the seat belt or harness so that it is snug rather than breath-takingly tight. The buckle locking and unlocking procedure should also be checked – they are not the same on all aircraft.

The adjustment available in the seats will vary considerably between aircraft types: some can be fully adjusted fore and aft, up and down and for tilt and lumbar support also. Others simply feature an extra cushion that can be placed underneath or behind the occupant. The security of the seat adjustment mechanism is all important, a seat back that collapses just after take-off, or a seat that slides to the back of its rails at a similar moment, is exceptionally dangerous. So, any time after adjusting the seat position on the ground, check that the seat is properly locked by trying to rock it fore and aft – the seat should stay firmly locked in position. This is also worth re-doing as part of the pre-take off checks. Experienced pilots of Cessna single engine aircraft in particular tend to have a close look at the seat rails and adjustment/locking mechanism as part of their pre-flight checks.

▶First Aid Kits

The first aid kit carried in an aircraft does not have to be of a type approved by the CAA, although the required contents are specified. As part of the pre-flight checks verify that the first aid kit is in place and properly secured. Periodically it is worth opening the box to check the contents and to see that any dated items (such as some burn creams etc.) are within their stated use-by date.

▶Fire Extinguishers

Any fire is clearly a major hazard either on the ground or in the air. On the ground, various types of extinguisher are normally situated in hangers, buildings and refuelling installations. The most common types, and their recommended uses, are shown below:

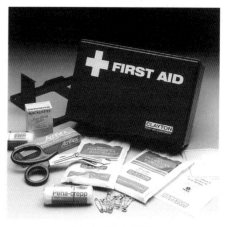

A typical first aid kit

- **Water extinguishers** are only really effective for use on fires involving wood, paper or cloth.

- **Foam extinguishers** can be used on fires involving wood, paper, cloth, and flammable liquids.

- **Carbon Dioxide extinguishers** can be used on fires involving flammable liquids and on electrical fires.

- **Dry Powder extinguishers** can be used on fires involving flammable liquids, gases and on electrical fires (they are also recommended for use on a wheel fire, which will probably involve the brakes).

- **BCF extinguishers** can be used for all types of fire.

The most common type of extinguisher carried on modern aircraft is the BCF extinguisher, containing an agent called Halon 1211. Before flight, the fire extinguisher should be in place and properly secured. The latter is particularly important as during flight in turbulence or in the middle of an aerobatic manoeuvre it can be very distracting to have a fire extinguisher loose in the cockpit! The extinguisher will probably have a gauge on the handle, whose needle should be in the green arc.

In the event of an engine fire on the ground, and in the absence of professional fire-fighters, the cockpit BCF extinguisher can be used to try to contain the fire, provided this does not put the user at any risk by doing so. It is wise to try to stay 'up wind' of any smoke or fumes and always leave an open escape route. The extinguisher is best discharged into an opening or intake somewhere close to the base of the fire. If an extinguisher is used in this way, even for a 'minor' fire, an aircraft engineer will need to inspect the aircraft before restarting the engine.

A Carbon Dioxide fire extinguisher

If it is necessary to use a BCF extinguisher in the cockpit, all vents and windows should be closed before using the extinguisher. Once the fire is out, the cockpit should be well ventilated to clear out the residual fumes.

▶Survival Equipment

The carriage of the equipment described in this chapter is detailed in a schedule of the Air Navigation Order, the legal instrument that gives these requirements the force of law. Surprisingly, within this schedule there is no legal requirement for a non-public transport flight to carry any sort of marine survival equipment when flying out of gliding distance of land. Nevertheless, it is well recognised that it would be extremely foolish to make an over-water flight without some sort of flotation aid for all on board.

The common protocol for a single-engine aircraft is that lifejackets should be worn (but *not* inflated) by all occupants when flying out of gliding range of dry land. There are three basic types of aviation lifejacket:

- **Valise**. These are packed into a rigid or flexible container, as found under the seat of an airliners. Until recently these were the most common type used in light aircraft. The problem is that these lifejackets are **not** normally designed to be regularly unpacked, worn, and then re-packed. They are, in essence, 'wear once' designs.

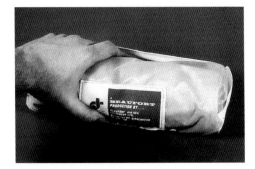

A 'Valise' type lifejacket

- **Constant Wear Pouch.** These lifejackets are packed within a pouch which is worn on a belt around the waist. The pouch remains closed unless the lifejacket is to used for real, in which case the pouch is opened and the lifejacket pulled over the head.

A 'Constant Wear Collar' type lifejacket

- **Constant Wear Collar**. These lifejackets are worn rather like a safety harness, and clip around the waist with webs passing over the shoulders. This type of lifejacket is increasingly popular, offering increased practicality, durability, reliability for General Aviation operations when compared to other designs.

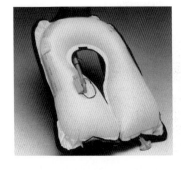

An inflated lifejacket

In service, a lifejacket should be put on and adjusted *before* flight – the confines of a light aircraft cockpit are no place to try putting on a lifejacket whilst also flying the aeroplane. In the event of a ditching, the lifejacket is **not** inflated until the occupant is **outside** the aircraft (otherwise, the bulk of the inflated lifejacket makes movement difficult, and also increases the risk of puncturing the inflation chambers). To inflate, the red toggle is pulled, which activates the Carbon Dioxide (CO_2) bottle which inflates the lifejacket. The lifejacket will have an air tube so that you can 'top-up' the inflation by mouth if need be. The lifejacket should have a light, and a whistle to attract attention. More advanced types also have a spray hood to protect the head from the elements and reduce heat loss.

Whilst a lifejacket will keep its wearer afloat in the water, on its own it is of limited use in cold seas (such as those around northern Europe) as survival time in the sea when it is at its coldest can be measured in minutes rather than hours. For this reason most sensible pilots also carry a liferaft when flying over water. A liferaft will keep its occupants reasonably dry and out of the elements. It is also a lot easier for the search and rescue services to spot a liferaft in many square miles of sea than just a lifejacket.

A standard aviation liferaft

To be any good, survival equipment has to operate properly when it is needed. Lifejackets and liferafts should be regularly serviced (once a year is the usual recommendation), and cared for carefully in service. A lifejacket in a crumpled heap, under a collection of heavy junk, at the bottom of a filing cabinet, is not being properly looked after and its chances of working at all are slim. A lifejacket and liferaft servicing organisation in the UK reports a 30% failure rate on the older and more mis-treated lifejackets it tests…

A liferaft should be carried within easy reach of the pilot or passengers. A liferaft out-of-reach in a baggage compartment is nothing better than useless weight. The liferaft is only inflated once clear of the aircraft, by pulling a toggle which activates the CO_2 inflation system.

The care and use of marine survival equipment is described in more detail in PPL5 – Human Factors and Flight Safety.

▶ De-Icing Systems

Although few basic training aircraft are cleared for flight into known icing conditions, most do carry equipment that can be used in the event of an accidental encounter with icing conditions, in the form of the pitot heater, the windscreen demister and possibly an alternate static source. However, none of these devices alters the vital importance of avoiding an icing environment unless the aircraft is specifically certified for flight into known icing conditions.

If an aircraft is cleared for flight into icing conditions, it will have specific de-icing equipment to help prevent or remove icing from the vulnerable areas of the aircraft, such as the windscreen, wind and tail leading edges and the propellers.

Phneumatic de-icing 'boots' on the leading edge of this Kingair's horizontal tailplane and fin

The airframe de-icing of a piston-engines aircraft is almost always of the 'pneumatic boot' type. This is essentially a set of rubber 'boots' located along the wing leading edge and possibly on the leading edge of the horizontal and vertical tail too. This boot is often connected to the same suction system that powers some of the gyro flight instruments. With the engine running, a slight suction pressure holds the boots in the deflated position. If the aircraft does encounter icing conditions, the pilot waits until a small accumulation of ice (say around 1·5cm or 1/2in) has formed. The boots are then activated and a positive air pressure inflates them, breaking away the ice as they expand.

It must be stressed here that the precise operation of **any** de-icing system should be fully detailed in the aircraft's POH/FM. It is essential that the pilot is fully familiar with these procedures as they can vary between difference aircraft types.

The propeller leading edges may be protected by a series of heating elements; some operate on an automatic cycle when activated, some need to be manually turned on and off. Alternatively there may be a set of pipes that, when activated, pump a de-icing fluid onto the propeller blade and centrifugal force spreads this fluid across the blade. This system is used more to prevent ice formation rather than removing ice once it has formed.

Aside from the windscreen demisting control, there may also be an electrical heating element either built into the windscreen, or placed within a section of transparent material fixed to the windscreen ahead of the pilot. Because of the heat generated by the element, it is often not approved for use on the ground, as the lack of cooling airflow may cause the windscreen itself to begin to melt and deform.

The general condition of any de-icing equipment can be checked before flight – and indeed the leading-edge boots may be covered in small patches just like those from a bicycle repair kit! The aircraft's POH/FM and checklist may also detail pre-take off checks of these items, such as activating the leading edge boots to see that they inflate properly.

▶ Cabin Heating and Ventilation Systems

Almost all enclosed cockpits have had some form of ventilation system, and possibly reasonable heating too.

The ventilation system in a light aircraft will normally be nothing more sophisticated than an inlet facing into the airflow and acting as a 'scoop' for fresh air. A pipe from this is connected to an outlet in the cockpit, where a control regulates the flow of fresh air into the cabin. One of the few things to watch for when using fresh air is not to allow vented air to blow directly on to the face. It is quite possible for an insect or other airborne object to make its way into the inlet and then be ejected from the vent with considerable force. Some aircraft also have a DV (*Direct Vision*) panel in the windscreen, side window or canopy. Opening this not only allows a clear view if vision is obstructed in some way (for example by ice), but also usually allows copious amounts of fresh air into the cabin if extra ventilation is needed. The force of air coming through the vents is normally provided by the propeller slipstream and airflow over the aircraft. The obvious implication is that the fresh air vents may be relatively ineffective on the ground; many light aircraft cockpits are rather uncomfortable on hot days until the engine is started.

Light-aircraft heating and demisting systems usually work by taking air from an external source and passing it into a jacket or shroud around an exhaust pipe in the engine compartment. Here it picks up waste heat from the exhaust pipe, and the resulting heated air passes into the cockpit via warm-air vents controlled by the pilot. It is a simple system, but there are some points of note.

The fresh-air vent of this Cessna 152 takes its air from an inlet in the wing leading edge. The dial is an Outside Air Temperature (OAT) gauge

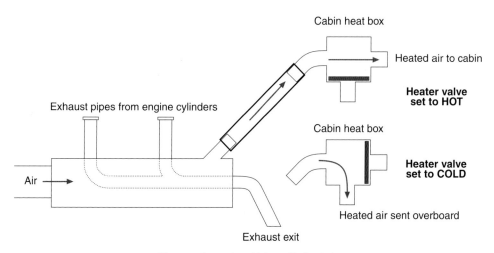

The use of an exhaust 'shroud' to heat air

■ The air will only pick up significant heat from the exhaust once the engine has warmed up. So the engine must run for a few minutes before the heater becomes effective. Furthermore, the airflow is usually 'ram air' – that is, the pressure in the system is driven by the airflow into the heating inlet. While the aircraft is on the ground, the flow of warm air may be quite weak and windscreen demisting in particular can take a little while to become effective.

■ The heater system opens a path through the firewall from the engine compartment to the cabin. For this reason the heater controls are usually closed before starting the engine, in case of an engine fire during the starting procedure. If an engine fire is suspected at any time, the heater controls should again be shut off to seal the firewall.

■ Finally, the method used for providing heated air opens up the possibility of *Carbon Monoxide* (CO) poisoning. Carbon monoxide is a colourless, odourless gas formed by incomplete combustion. It is virtually always present in exhaust gases, and it follows that a crack in the exhaust pipe leading through the heater shroud could allow CO gas into the cockpit via the heated air. **Carbon monoxide is a deadly poison**. Inhaling it leads to dizziness, headaches and blurred vision, a rapid impairment of normal mental functions and ultimately unconsciousness and death. Because CO poisoning effects the higher brain functions first, the victim may be completely unaware of any impairment, instead gradually falling into a dream-like 'dumb and happy' state. The subject of carbon monoxide poisoning is covered in more detail in the 'Human Factors' section of PPL5. Many aircraft are fitted with a CO detector on the instrument panel – usually in the form of a small plastic placard with a spot which will turn dark in the presence of carbon monoxide. These normally have lives of around six months after which they should be replaced with a fresh unit.

A 'CO' (Carbon Monoxide) detector. A dark spot indicates the presence of CO. In general, a CO detector must be changed every 6 months or so

▶ Refuelling Precautions

Whenever an aircraft is being refuelled, safety is of paramount importance. Nobody should be smoking around the refuelling installation (smoking is normally banned on the apron and in the hangars in any case) and it is wise to know the location of the nearest fire extinguisher. Mobile telephones should not be used in the vicinity either. To avoid a dangerous static electricity discharge (e.g. a spark), the aircraft should be 'bonded' to the fuelling installation before refuelling starts to prevent a difference in electrical charge between the aircraft and the refuelling unit. This is done using a 'bonding wire', which is a length of wire with a clip, one end is fixed to the re-fuelling machinery and the clip is attached to a metallic part of the aircraft such as an exhaust pipe.

The principal pitfall during refuelling is putting the wrong fuel in. The most common fuels for aircraft engines are AVGAS for piston engines and AVTUR (also known as Jet A-1) for gas turbine (jet) engines. AVTUR is consumed **only** by jet engines and absolutely **cannot** be used in a piston engine designed to run on AVGAS. Many aircraft have so-called 'turboprop' engines which use a gas turbine to drive the propeller. These do require AVTUR, but to add to the potential for confusion, several aircraft with turbocharged piston engines (which use AVGAS) have the word "Turbo" emblazoned on them. This might be mis-interpreted as 'Turbine', meaning a jet engine, leading the refueller to assume that this aircraft requires Jet A-1. There have been several instances of piston-engine aircraft being accidentally re-fuelled with Jet A-1.

The marking of an aviation fuel installation
Note that at a military airfield NATO designations
F18 may be used for AVGAS and F34 or AVTUR
used for JET A-1

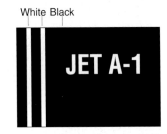

All fuelling installations should clearly indicate the type of fuel they dispense. Check BEFORE allowing the aircraft to be refuelled

Colour coding of the refuelling installation and the aircraft's fuel filler caps is used to distinguish fuel types. All AVGAS notices are red and AVTUR notices are black. Before refuelling the pilot can check the fuel type on the fuelling installation. Just to be sure, the fuel type and grade should also be stated on any fuel receipt. The fuel itself is dyed to indicate fuel type, and each also has a quite individual smell. AVGAS 100LL is dyed blue and smells highly aromatic with a very characteristic 'top note' of benzene. Leaded MOGAS (i.e. standard car petrol) has a heavier and mildly metallic odour; AVTUR/Jet A-1 smells rather like slightly rancid paraffin. The aromas are difficult to describe in writing, but quite characteristic once smelt a few times.

In summary, it is simply not good enough to **assume** that the proper fuel grade will go into the tanks, or just sign off the paperwork without a second glance. If at all possible the pilot should be present at the refuelling, if this is not possible make sure that clear instructions are given as to the fuel grade required (and where it is to go) and see that these instructions are followed through. There is also the question of weight and balance, which on more sophisticated aircraft in particular may dictate how much fuel can go into which tanks. There are few things more frustrating than finding an aircraft has been fuelled in the 'wrong' tanks, so that passengers or baggage have to be unloaded.

Note how this light aircraft compass is deflected by more than 90° by the magnet within an ordinary radio. Headsets can have the same effect if placed near the compass

▶Dangerous Goods

PPL 2 itemises in some detail the dangers of carrying goods that can be hazardous in aircraft. Some of these goods carry obvious dangers – such as flammable or corrosive liquids, compressed gases or substances that give off noxious or poisonous fumes. Other hazards are more subtle, such as strongly magnetic materials or house-hold items (sprays, matches etc.) that may be found in passenger's baggage.

The pilot must also be aware of the hazards presented by portable electronic equipment – personal music systems, mobile phones, laptop PCs, computer games etc. etc. The particular hazard in a light aircraft is that such items are so close to the instruments and radios that they can effect. The simplest solution is not to allow their use at all in-flight and in the case of a mobile phone this prohibition is backed up by the aviation authorities. The pilot may decide to allow the use of other items of electronic equipment, particularly when flying in VMC, but if so must be wary as to any possible effect they may have. Interference with radios, false readings on navigation displays and un-commanded operation of electrical items have all been reported when portable electronic devices are being used in an aircraft. In any event the use of such items should be limited to VMC cruising flight and most specifically not during the key phases of take-off and landing.

▶Revision

150 What type of occupant restraint is normally required for the front seats of a UK-registered aircraft with a Maximum Total Weight Authorised of 2730kg or less?

151 What type of occupant restraint is normally required for the front seats of a UK-registered aircraft if it is to carry-out aerobatic manoeuvres?

152 What type of fire extinguisher(s) can be used on an electrical fire?

153 What action should the pilot take after using a BCF extinguisher with a cockpit or confined space and after the fire has extinguished?

154 For an over-water flight in a single engine aircraft, how should the lifejackets be carried?

155 Where should a liferaft be carried during an over-water flight?

156 What is the inflation system of a standard aviation lifejacket?

157 Why should the cockpit heat control be set to 'off' or 'closed' before engine start?

158 What colour or odour signifies CO (Carbon Monoxide) gas?

159 Name at least three possible symptoms of CO poisoning?

160 What is the colour of the fuel notices of a JET A1 (AVTUR) fuelling pump?

Answers at page fpp72-73

Aircraft General Knowledge

Operational Flight Safety

Aircraft General Knowledge
Operational Flight Safety

▶ Windshear, Gusts and Turbulence

▶ Wake Turbulence

▶ Aquaplaning

▶ Emergency Exits

▶ Passenger Briefing

▶ Revision

Operational Flight Safety

▶Windshear, Gusts and Turbulence

When flying at altitude, above the influence of terrain on the airflow of the atmosphere, changes in wind velocity tend to occur gradually (over a horizontal distance of many miles) or over vertical distances of several hundred or thousand feet. The effect on airspeed is not discernible in most aircraft.

At low level, sudden changes in wind velocity have a far more noticeable effect on airspeed and – particularly in the take-off and landing phase – can present a serious hazard to aircraft.

Imagine an aircraft making an approach to land. The approach speed is 80kts. Initially it is flying into a headwind of 20kts, so its groundspeed is 60kts. It now encounters a strong windshear, so that through a descent of 50ft the wind velocity changes from a headwind of 20kts to a tailwind of 10kts. During this sudden change in wind velocity, inertia means that the groundspeed will stay close to 60kts. However, the airspeed is now just 50kts (airspeed 60kts – 10kts of tailwind). Such a sudden loss of speed means a significant reduction in lift (causing the aircraft to sink), and may even bring the aircraft close to the stall.

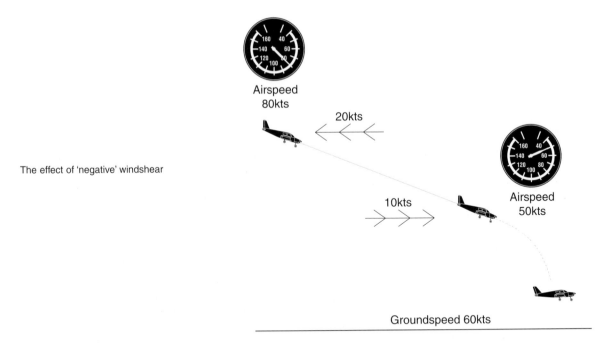

Airspeed
80kts

20kts

The effect of 'negative' windshear

10kts

Airspeed
50kts

Groundspeed 60kts

Given time, the aircraft will overcome inertia and accelerate back to the airspeed of 80kts. However, it is unlikely to do so as quickly as the rapid change in wind velocity that led to the airspeed loss. The heavier the aircraft (and so the greater its inertia) the longer it is likely to take to regain the lost airspeed, and the more vulnerable it is to windshear. The situation described above, causing a sudden reduction in airspeed, would be reported as a negative windshear of 30kts. Such encounters are more likely near the ground, because terrain effects are chiefly responsible for windshear, and are more dangerous at low levels and slow airspeeds – e.g. when aircraft are landing and taking-off.

Gusts are also a potential hazard to aircraft, especially vertical gusts. A vertical gust has the effect of rapidly altering the wing's angle of attack, directly affecting the lift being produced by the wing. This could lead to a stall if the wing is already near the stalling angle of attack, a reduction in lift if the gust reduces angle of attack – or it may overload the aircraft if it is flying at a high airspeed.

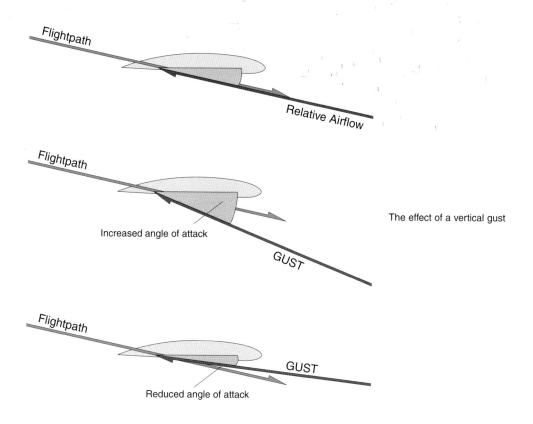

Flightpath

Relative Airflow

Flightpath

Increased angle of attack

GUST

The effect of a vertical gust

Flightpath

Reduced angle of attack

GUST

In gusty conditions, the variation in wind speed will give an idea of the magnitude of the gusts. For example a surface wind of 20kts gusting to 30kts means a gust 'factor' of 10kts. The general advice when taking-off and landing in such conditions is to increase airspeed by half the gust factor, e.g. by 5kts in the example above. This should give protection against an inadvertent stall, but the increased airspeed will also increase take-off and landing distances. As always, a particular power and attitude will result in a specific airspeed, and maintaining the required power and attitude will maintain the desired airspeed *over a period of time*. However, the effect on airspeed of a sudden gust or windshear cannot be ignored if it brings the speed dangerously slow, and the pilot should be prepared to act quickly if the change in airspeed warrants it.

Flight in turbulent conditions also warrants particular attention. If the turbulence is strong enough to require full and rapid control movements, the aircraft should be flying no faster than the manoeuvring speed (Va). Va is the maximum speed at which full and rapid movement of the flying controls (in particular the elevators) can be made without damaging the structure of the aircraft. The POH/FM may state a specific speed for flight in turbulence in which case this should be observed, it is unlikely to be faster than the Va speed. Aside from the other obvious actions, such as tightening seat belts and securing loose objects, flight in turbulence is largely a matter of maintaining the required power and attitude without using excessive control movements, and having to accept certain deviations from the desired flight path. The flaps should be retracted as flight load limitations are usually lower when flap is extended. Consider the source of the turbulence: that caused by being close to a thunderstorm, or just downwind of high ground in strong winds, almost certainly means that the aircraft is in the wrong place at the wrong time.

▶ Wake Turbulence

Wake Turbulence is caused by the movement of an aircraft through the air, and in particular the wing-tip vortices that are shed as a result of the lift produced at the wings. In general, the larger and heavier the aircraft, and the more slowly it is flying, the stronger the wake turbulence it produces. The vortices themselves are areas of rapidly rotating air (velocities of up to 300ft/second are possible) which can, when encountered by an aircraft, cause severe control difficulties.

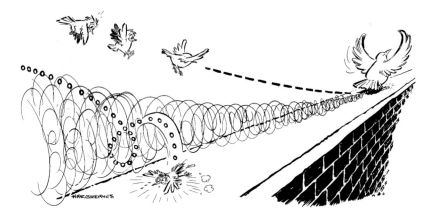

On approach, stay above the leading aircraft's flight path. Aim to touch down well beyond its touch-down point

These vortices become significant as an aircraft rotates for take-off, and last until approximately when the nosewheel touches the ground on landing (in other words, during the period of 'wing-borne' flight). The maximum wake turbulence is likely to be generated at the highest angles of attack, such as during manoeuvring flight and during take-off, approach and landing. As the vortices are shed, they begin to move out from the wingtips (at a horizontal speed of around 5 knots) and sink at a rate of a few hundred feet per minute. It follows that the vortices can persist for some time in gentle wind conditions, and the area to avoid is that behind and below another aircraft. It is also worth knowing that the wake turbulence generated by a helicopter, even one 'hover taxying', is considerably stronger than that for a fixed-wing aircraft of a similar size and weight.

The Air Law section of PPL 2 contains detailed advice on wake turbulence, its avoidance, and the recommended minimum spacing behind large aircraft. It is strongly recommended to revise this material.

▶ Aquaplaning

Aquaplaning can occur when operating on a surface covered in water and is caused by the aircraft's tyres losing contact with the surface. When the tyre is rotating on a water-covered surface, a 'wedge' of water gradually builds up in front of it. Above a certain speed (the aquaplaning speed) a thin film of water can form underneath the tyre, lifting it completely clear of the surface. Once this has happened, all braking action and steering is effectively lost and will only be recovered when the aircraft is travelling at significantly less than the aquaplaning speed. Control is gradually regained as the aircraft slows down, unless of course it reaches part of the surface not covered by water – in which case control and braking may return very suddenly. The aquaplaning speed is a function of tyre pressure; the actual formulae (which is included here for reference only; it does not need to be memorised) is:

Aquaplaning speed (in knots) = $8{\cdot}6\sqrt{P}$, where P is tyre pressure in pounds per square inch.

So a typical light-aircraft tyre with a pressure of 29psi will have an aquaplaning speed of around 46kts. This is, of course, a groundspeed; what is important here is the aircraft's speed relative to the surface.

How aquaplaning occurs

Water film underneath the tyre
Full aquaplane

Water film building up ahead of the tyre
Partial aquaplane

▶ Emergency Exits

Most light aircraft are too small to require specific emergency exits. However, where they do exist it is the pilot's responsibility to know where they are and how to use them. It is possible that the main door(s) or canopy may have emergency opening mechanisms. Often found on aerobatic aircraft, these may include handles attached to the door hinges, that remove them when pulled so that the door falls away; or an emergency jettison mechanism for a canopy. Some aircraft canopies feature 'knock-out' panels.

It should be borne in mind that these emergency mechanisms are designed for a specific purpose, either to aid the rapid in-flight abandoning of the aircraft, or to permit evacuation if the usual exit is blocked or jammed. In a 'normal' forced landing situation, these exits should not be operated before touchdown, as this may weaken the aircraft structure as well as creating an opening in the safety cage surrounding the occupants of the aircraft. The one possible exception to this advice is a ditching situation, where there is a danger that deformation of the airframe during the ditching might jam the exits. In a ditching situation, the common advice is to open the door(s) or canopy before touchdown to prevent such an occurrence. However, this advice is not appropriate to all aircraft types and, once again, the POH/FM of the aircraft being flown should have authoritative guidance.

▶ Passenger Briefing

The pilot-in-command of an aircraft has a moral – as well as a legal – obligation to ensure that all passengers are properly briefed on the use of any safety and emergency equipment in the aircraft and their actions in the event of an emergency.

As part of this briefing, all passengers must know where the main exits are and how to open and close them. They must also know where to find and how to use any emergency exits, and where the fire extinguisher and first-aid kit are located. Passengers must be shown how to use the safety belts and/or harnesses, and they must be able to undo and fasten these unaided. If the seat is adjustable, or if a seat back needs to be moved to give access to rear seats, the passengers must be capable of doing this for themselves. If there is any specialist emergency equipment (life-jackets, dinghies, etc.) on board their use needs to be explained too. All of this will take no more than a few moments, but in an emergency could save lives.

The Pilot In Command is responsible for ensuring that all passengers are properly briefed before flight

Passengers who are new to flying in light aircraft will need to be told not to touch any of the controls or switches without the pilot's permission, and to tell the pilot right away if they move something accidentally. It might be worth showing the passengers the fresh-air vents and how to use them, particularly if these are well away from the main flying controls and instrument panel. If the aircraft is fitted with an intercom and the passengers are wearing headsets, ensure that they are adjusted for comfort. The operation of the intercom needs to be explained, and passengers must realise that they should not talk over any messages the pilot is listening to.

Passengers must also be briefed as to what to do in the event of an emergency. Probably the most crucial point for passengers to appreciate is that in an emergency they will be expected to fasten and tighten-up their own seat-belts or harness as far as possible, and make sure that their seat is secure with the seat back upright. Headsets should be removed before exit (they can get tangled up with seat belts as the wearer tries to leave the cabin) and sharp objects (such as keys and pens) emptied from the pockets. A recommended bracing position has been developed as a result of studies and accident investigations. The lap strap should be fastened tightly and then the upper body bent forward as far as possible to put the chest close to the knees, probably with the head touching the seat back ahead (if there is one). The hands should be placed one above the other on top of the head (i.e. not with interlaced fingers) and the forearms tucked in each side of the face. The lower legs should be pulled back so that they are aft of the vertical, with feet flat on the floor. A jacket or sweater rolled up and placed in front of the face and head might also help. How closely this position can be adopted will largely depend on seating position and individual aircraft design. Nevertheless this 'brace for impact' posture is believed to significantly reduced the risk of injury compared to sitting in an upright position. If the aircraft has rearward-facing passenger seats, those seated in them are also less likely to be injured compared with forward-facing passengers.

In summary, *before* flying with passengers the pilot should ensure that, with the exception of young children, each of them will be able to:

■   open the doors or exits unaided and operate any folding seat backs;

■   fasten and release their seat belts or safety harnesses unaided;

■   know the location of the fire extinguisher and first-aid kit;

■   know how to use any specialist equipment carried (oxygen, life-jackets, dinghies, ELT's, etc.).

▶Revision

161 If the surface wind is reported as gusting between 15 to 25 knots, and the normal approach speed is 65 knots, how should this speed be modified to take account of the gusty conditions?

162 What is the most dangerous position to be in, relative to a larger aircraft, for wake turbulence considerations?

163 As a general rule, does a larger aircraft generate more or less wake turbulence than a smaller one?

164 As tyre pressure is increased, what is the effect on aquaplaning speed?

165 Who is responsible for passenger briefing before flight?

Answers at page fpp73

Flight Performance and Planning Introduction

Incidents and accidents relating to light aircraft have a habit of involving performance and planning-related failures. These failures rarely involve any problem with the aircraft itself; more often than not the aircraft performed exactly as it should. It was just that this performance was not what the pilot wanted at that particular moment. It is only fair to point-out that in the majority of cases, the pilot had not made a calculation of the relevant performance criteria, they no doubt believed – or hoped – that the aircraft would do what they wanted. Such events often take the form of aircraft trying to take-off from, or land on, runways that are too short in the particular circumstances; aircraft being overloaded or loaded out-of-balance; or aircraft running out of fuel before reaching their destination.

It is no doubt because of the number of such episodes that 'Flight Planning and Performance' now merits an exam in its own right within the JAR PPL and NPPL syllabus, and this section of the PPL Course Series is written for this exam. This section is also written with a view to giving a better understanding of what lies behind the table and graphs in a POH/FM, in particular the principles of flight which govern aircraft performance. With a better understanding of how and why an aircraft performs as it does, you will have a better chance of getting the best from an aircraft, and also knowing when you are asking too much of it.

Although the theory behind performance is explained here in detail, and theoretical principles may be examined, it should be appreciated that the only authoritative information about the performance of a particular aircraft is that aircraft's POH/FM. For example, it is all very well knowing the principle of how approach speed is calculated from stalling speed, but the approach speed to use in real-life is the one in the aircraft's documentation – determining speeds and performance criteria from raw data is the preserve of test pilots and aviation authorities.

So, having looked at the principles behind planning and performance, the emphasis is on the use of POH/FM tables and graphs to determine loading and performance. Here we have used actual examples of such data from real POH/FMs and while they are not especially clear, they are exactly what you can expect to find in 'the real world'. There is a suspicion that many pilots do not use these tables and graphs either because they have forgotten how to use them, or simply because they cannot be bothered. In the former case and answer is training and currency, in the latter a change of mind-set is required – an altogether more difficult matter to address. Either way, the work involved becomes far easier and less daunting after practising a few calculations and there are both worked examples and revision questions at the end of each chapter.

In the end, much about performance comes down to being aware of what the aircraft is capable of and not asking it to do the impossible. No amount of fervent hope will make a runway longer or make an over-loaded aircraft more flyable, but by knowing what the aircraft is capable of and how to get the best from it gives the pilot the best way of utilising the aircraft's capabilities to the full without using up his or her quota of luck!

Flight Performance and Planning

Mass and Balance

Basic a/c = 1150kg

4 x adults = 280kg

Baggage = 100kg

400ltr full fuel = 288kg

1818kg

Maximum permissible weight 1700kg

Flight Performance and Planning
Mass and Balance

▶ Maximum Mass Limits

▶ Centre of Gravity

▶ Loading

▶ Revision

Mass and Balance

▶ Maximum Mass Limits

Before starting this chapter, be prepared to see both the term 'weight' and the term 'mass' used throughout. Although 'mass' is the correct term to use in the context of loading an aircraft on the ground (which is what this chapter is largely about), virtually all the aircraft documents in use at present, and virtually all accepted abbreviations currently used in loading, refer to 'weight'. Therefore, for the purposes of loading, please consider 'weight' and 'mass' to be one and the same.

All aircraft have a specified maximum mass. This limit **must** be respected, whether the aircraft in question is a microlight or a Boeing 747. Attempting to fly an overloaded or overweight aircraft has serious performance and handling penalties: the aircraft will accelerate more slowly on take-off, and because stall speed is increased take-off speeds are increased, all leading to a longer take-off distance; climb performance will be degraded; cruise speed, range and service ceiling will all be reduced; the aircraft will perform badly and is more susceptible to being overstressed, even if the stated load factor limits are not exceeded. Approach and landing speeds will be faster and landing distances will be increased. Put another way, even if you do get airborne there is no guarantee you will be able to climb quickly or high enough to clear obstructions, maintain a reasonable speed, not overstress the aircraft nor make a safe landing at the end of your escapade. Additionally the aircraft's POH/FM limitations are being exceeded, so the aircraft's Certificate of Airworthiness, the aircraft insurance and the pilot's insurance are all invalid. Overloading an aircraft is also an offence under the Air Navigation Order (Pre-flight action by commander of aircraft). So be aware that this is a very serious issue. The final responsibility for checking the aircraft's loading *always* rests with the aircraft commander – regardless of what is said by passengers, co-pilots, operators, handling agents, loadmaster or any other interested parties. "They told me it would be OK" is a phrase high on the list of famous last words.

	WEIGHT LIMITS	Normal	Utility
Weight limits as set out in a POH/FM. These are not recommended, they are mandatory	(a) Maximum Ramp (lbs.)	2558	2138
	(b) Maximum Weight (lbs.)	2550	2130
	(c) Maximum Baggage (lbs.)	200	0

NOTE

Refer to Section 5 (Performance) for maximum weight as limited by performance.

The aircraft's maximum mass can be specified in a number of ways:

■ *Maximum Total Weight Authorised* is the maximum weight for take-off, it is also known as *Maximum All Up Weight (MAUW)* and *Maximum Take-Off Weight (MTOW)*.

■ *Maximum Landing Weight* is the maximum weight for landing.

■ *Maximum Ramp Weight* is the maximum weight of the parked aircraft. The difference between this and Maximum Total Weight Authorised is usually small and is accounted for by the weight of fuel consumed before take-off.

■ *Maximum Zero Fuel Weight* is the maximum weight allowable (of the aircraft and its payload – passengers, baggage etc.) with zero fuel in the tanks. This is primarily a structural load limit to prevent overstressing the aircraft structure. Any weight in excess of the MZFW must be fuel only.

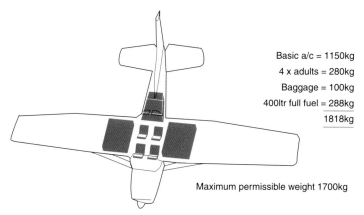

Basic a/c = 1150kg
4 x adults = 280kg
Baggage = 100kg
400ltr full fuel = 288kg
1818kg

The maximum permitted weight of the aircraft is usually more limiting than its capacity in terms of number of seats, baggage area volume, fuel capacity etc. Put another way, in most light aircraft it is simply not possible to fill the fuel tanks to the brim, fill the baggage areas to capacity and put a full-size adult in each seat and still remain within the aircraft's weight limit; some sort of 'trade-off' will be required between the different items of payload

Maximum permissible weight 1700kg

The aircraft mass can be divided into three categories:

- *Basic (Empty) Weight* is the weight of the individual aircraft, taken from the *weight schedule*. The figures in the weight schedule have been obtained by weighing the actual aircraft. A major change in equipment, or a repaint for example, will result in a new weight schedule being calculated. The basic empty weight normally includes unusable fuel and full oil.

- *Variable Load* is the weight of the crew, normally just the pilot in a single-engine light aircraft.

- *Disposable Load* is all other items of 'payload' such as fuel, passengers and baggage. Such items can be dispensed with if weight is a problem.

The **actual** weight of the loaded aircraft, once all these items have been taken into account, is sometimes referred to as the *gross weight*.

Checking whether the aircraft mass is within limits is a question of calculating the appropriate weights and totalling them. Be particularly careful if it is necessary to convert between kilograms and pounds. The conversion can be done with an electronic calculator or with a flight computer. Conversion between units of mass has been covered in the Navigation section of PPL 3, but here is a quick revision.

Example: convert a passenger mass of 160lb into kilograms.

A mental check, based on 2·2lb to the kilogram, says that the answer will be around 70kg.

On the conversions side of the flight computer, locate the 'lbs' line on the outer scale and turn the inner scale to place 160 under this mark. Without moving the scales, find the 'kg' line and use the cursor line to find the number under it on the inner scale. The answer is 72·5kg.

When considering fuel mass, it may be necessary to convert between volume and mass using a known specific gravity (SG). Again this conversion has been covered in the Navigation section of PPL 3 but here is a quick revision.

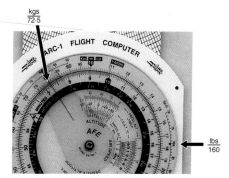

$\frac{kgs}{72·5}$

$\frac{lbs}{160}$

Using a flight computer to convert lb to kg

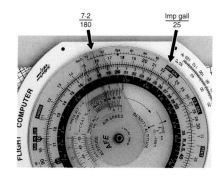

$\frac{7·2}{180}$ $\frac{Imp\ gall}{25}$

Converting fuel volume to weight using a given specific gravity

Example: What is the weight (in pounds) of 25 imperial gallons of AVGAS with a SG of 0.72?

A mental check suggests an answer of around 190lb. On the conversions side of the flight computer, place the fuel volume (25) under the 'Imp Gal' line. Line up the cursor line on 0·72 on the 'Sp.G lbs' scale, and read off the figure on the inner scale – 180lb.

▶ Centre of Gravity

Checking that the aircraft's weight is within the specified limit is only part of the loading calculation. The pilot must also ensure that the weight is distributed in such a way that the *Centre of Gravity* (CG) is within the limits set down by the manufacturer.

If the aircraft could be lifted up and placed on a pivot of some kind, the CG is where the pivot would be placed for the aircraft to balance level. In other words, there is equal mass ahead and behind the CG.

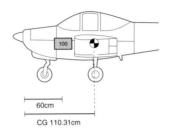 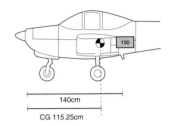

Placing a weight a long way from the 'balance' point can have a marked effect on the new Centre of Gravity position

60cm — CG 110.31cm

140cm — CG 115.25cm

An item of load of a certain mass has two effects on the aircraft. Its mass adds to the aircraft's total mass, and where it is placed affects the balance. A mass of 100lb/45kg has little effect on balance if it is placed very close to the CG. Conversely, if it is placed a long way from the CG it can have a large effect on balance because of the greater leverage.

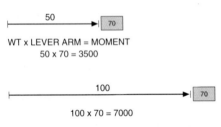

WT x LEVER ARM = MOMENT
50 x 70 = 3500

100 x 70 = 7000

A fixed weight will have a varying moment depending on its distance (lever arm) from the datum. Lever arm x weight = moment

In any aircraft the CG position varies according to where various items are loaded, and will change as fuel consumed during flight and so on. For planning purposes, a fixed point is selected as a datum and the distance from the datum to the location of each item is called the *lever arm* or just *arm*. Multiplying an item's mass by its lever arm gives the item's *moment* (also known as the *moment arm*):

Mass x Lever Arm = Moment.

For example, a piece of baggage weighing 45kg and placed in a baggage compartment where the lever arm is 2m has a moment of 90kg/m (2 x 45).

The aircraft's CG position is found by taking the weight of each item of payload and using its lever arm to calculate the moment for each item. The mass and moments are then totalled and added to the mass and moment of the aircraft itself. The total moment is divided by the total mass to give the CG position. The result will be the CG position in terms of a distance from the datum.

Aircraft loading is most often calculated using a mass-and-balance table that allows both mass and CG position to be calculated at once. This table is the basis for mass and CG calculations:

The aircraft's basic (empty) weight is 650kg, at which the total moment is 620kg/m.

The pilot weighs 75kg and the passenger 80kg and the lever arm for both seats is 0·90m (all lever arms are aft of datum). The fuel weighs 120kg, with a lever arm of 1·05m, and there is 25kg of baggage in the rear baggage compartment, whose lever arm is 2·05m.

Put into a mass and balance table, the above information looks like this:

Item	Mass (kg)	Lever Arm (m)	Moment
Basic (empty) aircraft	650	—	620
Pilot	75	.90	67.5
Passenger	80	.90	72
Fuel	120	1.05	126
Baggage	25	2.05	51.25
TOTAL	950	—	936.75

936.75/950 = 0.986

So the aircraft as loaded has a total mass of 950kg and the CG is positioned 0·986 metres aft of the datum.

Sometimes it is necessary to do a 'what if' calculation to see what effect one item of payload will have on the CG position. For example, an aircraft has been loaded so that its CG is 110cm aft of datum. The acceptable CG range is from 90 to 111cm aft of datum. There is 100kg of cargo to put in the aircraft, which can either go in a forward baggage compartment (whose lever arm is 60) or the rear baggage compartment (whose lever arm is 140). A simplified mass and balance table might look like this:

(Cargo in forward baggage compartment)

Item	Mass (kg)	Lever Arm (cm)	Moment
Aircraft as loaded	1570	–	172700
Baggage (fwd hold)	100	60	6000
TOTAL	1670	–	178700

CG = moment/mass = 107·00cm aft of datum

(Cargo in rear baggage compartment)

Item	Mass (kg)	Lever Arm (cm)	Moment
Aircraft as loaded	1570	–	172700
Baggage (rear hold)	100	140	14000
TOTAL	1670	–	186700

CG = moment/mass = 111·79cm aft of datum

With the cargo in the rear baggage compartment, the CG position too far aft and is outside the permitted range. Hence the cargo can only be placed in the forward compartment, given the existing aircraft loading.

It is usual to calculate the mass and CG based on the loading at take-off, but both mass and CG will alter in flight as fuel is consumed. As a rule the designer will try to place the fuel tanks very close to the mean CG position, so that changes in fuel load do not drastically effect the CG. However, certain aircraft types are more sensitive than others with respect to changing fuel load. An aircraft may have a specified maximum landing weight, and the reduction in fuel weight may move the CG towards the edge of its permitted range, meaning that it may be necessary to do a separate mass and CG calculation for the anticipated loading at landing. So, assuming an aircraft has a mass and CG position at take-off of 950kg and 110cm aft of datum respectively, and a calculated fuel consumption during the flight of 125 litres with a specific gravity (SG) of 0.72; if the fuel has a lever arm of 90cm aft of datum, what will be the mass and CG position for landing?

At take-off, the total moment of the aircraft was (mass x CG) = 104500.

To calculate the weight of fuel burnt, using the flight computer, 125 litres of fuel at an SG of 0.72 equals a weight of 90kg.

Therefore, the fuel burn during flight gives a weight reduction of 90kg, and the total moment is reduced by (90 x 90) = 8100; therefore the landing weight is (950-90) = 860kg and the total moment on landing is (104500 – 8100) = 96400.

So, at landing, dividing the total moment (96400) by the landing weight (860) gives the CG position of 112.09cm aft of datum.

The mass and CG limits are found in the weight schedule and in the POH/FM. Quite often an aircraft may have different mass and CG limits for operations in different categories, e.g. *utility*, *normal* and *aerobatic*. The categories which apply to a particular aircraft type will be clearly noted in the POH/FM. The POH/FM will specify which manoeuvres are permitted for each category, but in general each category has the following meanings:

- **Normal category** Manoeuvres used in normal flight including stalls, lazy eights, chandelles and steep turns where the angle of bank does not exceed 60°. Aerobatic manoeuvres (including spins) are not permitted.

- **Utility category** All manoeuvres permitted in the normal category, together with spins and steep turns with an angle of bank in excess of 60°.

- **Aerobatic category**All the manoeuvres of the Normal and Utility category, together with the aerobatic manoeuvres stated in the POH/FM subject to the declared entry airspeeds and load factor limits.

Where an aircraft is certified to operate in both the normal and utility categories, flight in the latter category often involves a lower mass limit and a smaller CG range. In general the normal category has the lowest load factor limits and the aerobatic category the highest, but the aircraft POH/FM will state the exact limits.

Although the POH/FM may just state the CG limits, those limits may vary according to mass and category. Most POH/FMs therefore display the mass and balance limits in the form of a graph, on to which the pilot can plot the actual values of mass and centre of gravity to see whether they fall within the CG envelope. The mass and centre of gravity is calculated with a table as before, and the information is then plotted on the graph.

Example:

A two-seat training aircraft must be loaded to be within the 'utility' category for a spinning exercise. The pilot weighs 160lb and the instructor weighs 170lb. There is no baggage and the fuel load is presently 140ltr (which at a specific gravity of 0·72 amounts to 222lb)

Item	Mass (lb)	Lever Arm	Moment
Basic (empty) weight	1449·16	86·13	124818·35
Pilot	160	85·5	13680
Instructor	170	85·5	14535
Fuel	222	95	21090
TOTAL	2001·16		174123·35

174123·35/2001·16 = 87·01 inches aft of datum

Plotting these figures on the mass and centre-of-gravity graph, it can be seen that not only is the mass above the 1950lb limit but the CG position is also behind the aft CG limit for the utility category. *So the aircraft is **not** loaded in the utility category.* It is perfectly safe to fly in 'normal' category operations, but the utility-category manoeuvres including spinning must *not* be flown with this loading. Fatal accidents have occurred when even pilots of considerable experience have disregarded this simple dictum.

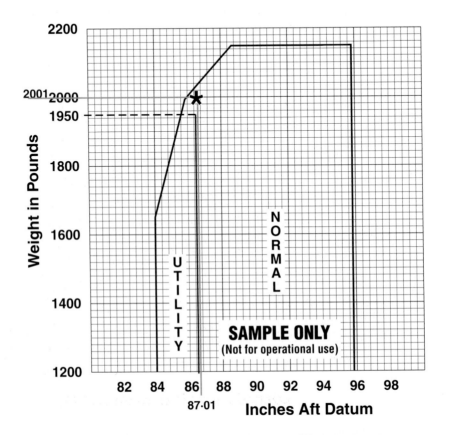

A refinement of the mass and balance calculation is a graph where total mass can be plotted against total moment, to save the calculation of dividing total moment by total mass.

Example:

A touring aircraft has a basic (empty) mass of 654·7kg, at which its moment is 638·57. The pilot weighs 75kg, and he wishes to take the following items of payload:

> One front-seat passenger – 70kg
>
> One rear-seat passenger – 75kg
>
> Baggage Area 1 – 15kg
>
> Baggage Area 2 – 10kg
>
> Full fuel – 109kg

The mass and balance table will look like this:

Item	Mass(kg)	Lever Arm (m)	Moment
Basic aircraft	654·7		638·57
Two front-seat occupants	145	0·94	136·3
Full Fuel	109	1·15	125·35
Rear seat passenger	75	1·85	138·75
Baggage Area 1	15	2·41	36·15
Baggage Area 2	10	3·12	31·2
TOTAL	1008·70		1106·32

A graph for plotting total weight against total moment reduces the mathematics of the weight and balance calculation

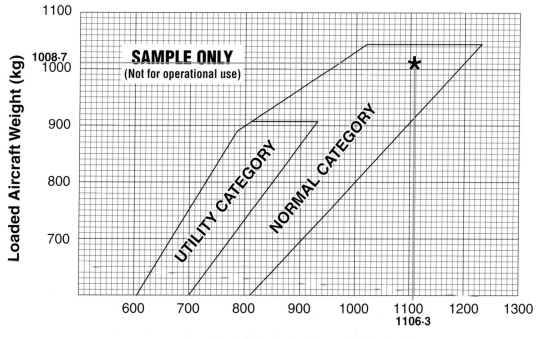

These figures can now be plotted directly on to the mass/moment graph. The aircraft is loaded within the normal category. It is interesting to note, however, that adding a further adult rear-seat passenger (the aircraft has four seats) would certainly take the aircraft over its maximum permitted weight of 1043kg. If this extra passenger is to be carried, some other items of payload – fuel or baggage – will have to be left behind.

Completing the mass and balance table using the lever arms for each item normally involves a calculator of some sort. Some POH/FMs have a 'loading' graph to save time and minimise the possibility of an error. Along one side of the graph is weight and across it are reference lines for each item of load. For each item, simply take a line across from its weight to the reference line and then read off the moment on the bottom of the graph. In essence, this graph is performing the calculation of multiplying item mass by item lever arm.

Example:

Using the figures from the previous example, a simplified mass-and-balance table can be drawn up:

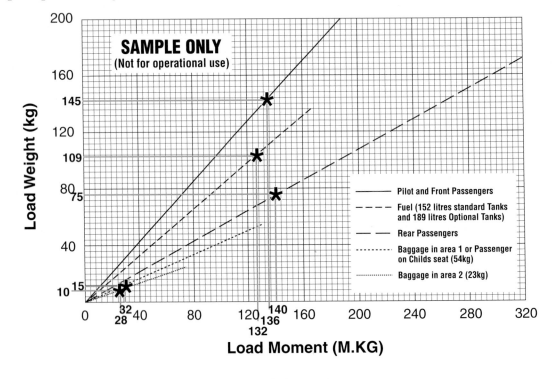

A moment-calculator graph

Item	Mass (kg)	Moment
Basic aircraft	654·7	638·57
Two front-seat occupants	145	136
Full Fuel	109	132
Rear seat passenger	75	140
Baggage Area 1	15	32
Baggage Area 2	10	28
TOTAL	1008·70	1106·57

The total moment figure, slightly different from that in the previous table because of the less exact nature of the loading graph, can be plotted on the mass/moment chart as before.

So far we have assumed a datum at the front of the aircraft, or even some way ahead of it. If the datum is further back – several aircraft use the firewall for the purpose – an item such as a suitcase in a forward luggage bay may be ahead of it. Any item ahead of the datum has a *negative* lever arm. This means that the moment for that item will be negative too, and the total moment is calculated accordingly. However, and to state the obvious, the mass of the item is *not* deducted from the total mass.

▶ Loading

Having looked at the calculation of weight and CG position, it is worth considering some of the practical aspects of aircraft loading. When passengers state their weight, consider the likely accuracy of that information carefully – it is not unknown for humans to underestimate their weight, accidentally or otherwise. Similarly it is by no means unusual for passengers to underestimate the weight of their baggage, or to be economical with the truth. If baggage weight has to be limited (quite a common situation in single-engine aircraft), passengers know that this is a strictly non-negotiable weight limit.

The aircraft's basic empty mass will be stated in the aircraft's documents. However, aircraft (like people) tend to put on weight as they get older. Even without additional equipment, there are many ways an aircraft can become heavier. A re-spray and new gadgets in the cockpit can easily add weight; other and less obvious items include water trapped in poorly drained control surfaces and fuselage sections; ice, which can form inside the propeller spinner and other places where water can collect; and mud and ice inside wheel spats. Aircraft also have a mysterious power of collecting assorted oddments in the cabin over a period of time; wheel chocks, spare cans of oil, a cockpit cover, a towbar, some flight guides, a portable transceiver or GPS, spare microphones or headsets, tie-down equipment, a liferaft and lifejackets etc. It is an interesting exercise to clear out **all** the pockets, baggage compartments, seat backs, glove boxes and other nooks and crannies in an aircraft and weigh the material collected. The result can be surprising.

Having decided that the load is not hazardous in some way, locating and securing it properly is important. A baggage compartment will have its own mass limitation, which *must* be respected. Particular care is required with particularly dense items, whose mass is concentrated in a small area, spreader bars or sheets to spread the load might be required. Ensure also that the load is properly secured, most baggage compartments will have tie-down points and may also feature securing straps or belts.

Although in this section we have concentrated on CG position in the fore-and-aft axis, there is also a CG in the lateral axis. Having one wing fuel-tank full and the other nearly empty will cause the aircraft to fly 'wing-heavy'. This can be compounded by placing people and baggage on just one side too.

▶Revision

1   An aircraft has a Maximum All Up Weight (MAUW) of 2435lbs, and a Maximum Ramp Weight of 2440lbs. What is the maximum permitted weight for take-off?

2   An aircraft has 4 seats, a baggage compartment with a capacity of 75kg and fuel tanks with a capacity of 120kg. Is it necessary to perform a weight and centre of gravity calculation provided that the fuel capacity, seating capacity and baggage compartment limitations are not exceeded?

3   An item weighs 30kg, and is located 2·3 metres aft of the CG datum. What is its moment?

4   An item has a total moment of 100kg/m, and is located 4m from the CG datum. What is its weight?

5   For loading purposes you can accept a maximum of 79kg of AVGAS. Given a specific gravity of 0·72, what is the maximum amount (in litres) that can be uplifted?

6   An aircraft with empty fuel tanks is loaded so that its weight is 750kg and its total moment is 900kg/m. If 150 litres of fuel are added, what is the new weight and total moment, given a specific gravity of 0·72 and a fuel lever arm of 1·2m?

7   The commander (pilot in command) for a short local flight believes that the aircraft loading is outside limits, the legally registered owner of the aircraft believes that loading is within limits. Who is legally responsible for loading in this case?

8   It is intended to carry-out manoeuvres in the utility category. The aircraft weighs 1800lbs, and the CG is located 85.2 inches aft of the datum. Using the graph below, can utility category manoeuvres be carried out?

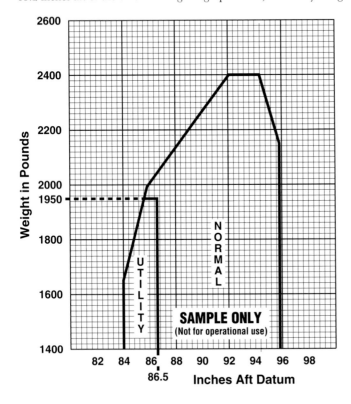

Answers page fpp73

Flight Performance and Planning

Take-off and Climb

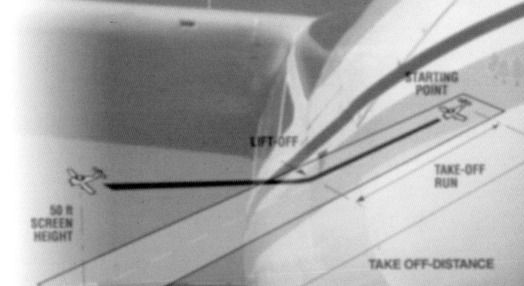

STARTING POINT

LIFT-OFF

TAKE-OFF RUN

50 ft SCREEN HEIGHT

TAKE OFF-DISTANCE

Flight Performance and Planning
Take-off and Climb

▶ Take-off and Climb Performance

▶ Forces in the Take-Off Run

▶ Ground Effect

▶ The Initial Climb

▶ Principles of Climbing

▶ Climb Performance

▶ Calculation of Take-Off Performance

▶ Calculation of Climb Performance

▶ Revision

Take-off and Climb

▶ Take-off and Climb Performance

Before looking in detail at the calculation of take-off and climb performance, it is well-worth considering some of the aerodynamic and handling factors involved, to relate the mathematics of the performance calculation to the real-world consequences. The take-off can be conveniently divided into the *take-off run* (or *take-off roll*) whilst the aircraft is still on the ground, and the initial climb from the moment it gets airborne. For the purposes of what follows we will liberally mix the terms 'weight' and 'mass' as if they are one and the same.

▶ Forces in the Take-Off Run

The take-off run starts with the aeroplane stationary, so to begin with the engine power has to overcome inertia. To accelerate the aircraft once it is moving, the engine power has to overcome both inertia and the rolling friction of the tyres on runway surface. The more powerful the engine and the lighter the aircraft, the more quickly the aircraft will accelerate and the shorter the take-off distance will be. The various yawing effects produced by the engine and propeller combination, notably those due to slipstream and torque, are most pronounced at slow speeds. The rudder is also less effective, so nosewheel steering and differential braking may be needed to maintain directional control. Another effect of power – the *gyroscopic* effect – is experienced by pilots of tailwheel aircraft. The rotating propeller acts as a gyroscope. If a force is applied to it, as happens when the tail is raised during take-off, the force applied to the turning propeller acts through 90° in the direction of rotation (the phenomenon known as *precession*, which has already been described). This means that if the propeller rotates clockwise as seen from the cockpit, gyroscopic precession will cause a yaw to the left as the tail is raised on take-off.

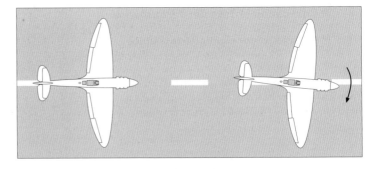

Gyroscopic effect on take-off in a tailwheel aircraft

Whether the aircraft has a nosewheel or a tailwheel, a crosswind on take-off – which will attempt to weathercock the aircraft into the wind – will add to the amount of rudder, steering and differential braking needed to maintain the runway centreline. As airspeed increases, the rudder effectiveness increases and less coarse use of the rudder is possible.

The more slowly the aircraft can get airborne, the shorter its take-off run will be. Therefore, a wing design suited to slow flight and/or high-lift devices such as flaps that lower the stalling speed, can reduce the take-off distance. Lowering flap only improves take-off performance if the recommended flap setting for take-off is used; lowering more flap than this setting will certainly increase lift, but only at the expense of increased drag. This means that using more flap than that recommended in the POH/FM will actually lengthen the take-off distance. Indeed, in many aircraft the use of full flap may even prevent it from getting airborne at all.

55 knots airspeed
55 knots groundspeed

0 airspeed
0 groundspeed

The effect of headwind on take-off run

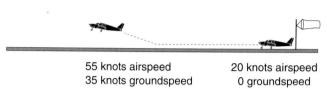

55 knots airspeed
35 knots groundspeed

20 knots airspeed
0 groundspeed

The wind will have a marked effect on take-off performance. Taking-off into wind will not only reduce any crosswind component but will also mean that the aircraft starts the take off with the benefit of some airspeed to start with. If an aircraft has a take-off speed of 55kts in still air (i.e. zero wind) conditions, it must accelerate along the runway to a groundspeed of 55kts to get airborne. However, if the same aircraft starts the take-off into a headwind of 20kts, it effectively has an airspeed of 20kts even when stationary. During the take-off it now only has to accelerate to a groundspeed of 35kts along the runway before getting airborne, and will use less runway than in still air.

▶ Ground Effect

In any take-off, trying to get the aircraft airborne at the slowest possible airspeed is **not** a good idea. Controllability will be limited and moreover the aircraft may be unable to climb above *ground effect*.

Ground effect occurs when the wing is close to the ground. The proximity of the ground alters the downwash behind the wing, which reduces induced drag and makes the wing act as if it has a greater span than is actually the case. Ground effect is at its maximum when the wing is closest to the ground, and decreases in strength until the aircraft is about the equivalent of one wing span above the ground, above which ground effect is negligible. Because ground effect reduces the drag associated with a given amount of lift, an aircraft in ground effect can remain airborne at a slower airspeed than would otherwise be the case because of the reduced power required for level flight. The implication is that even if an aircraft can be hauled off the ground at a very slow airspeed it may be left flying along in ground effect with just a few feet of height. Since the airspeed is on the 'back' of the drag curve (in other words **decreasing** airspeed leads to **increasing** drag), there

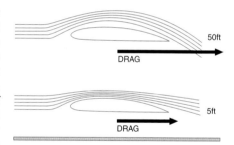

The influence of ground effect alters downwash behind a wing and reduces induced drag

is no excess power to allow a climb. Pitching nose-up will cause a stall, but pitching nose-down to gain airspeed (the best course of action, if possible) may allow the aircraft to descend back to the ground if there is no spare height to trade for airspeed. If sufficient runway remains, the best option is to land back on. If this is not possible, the other option – waiting for the aircraft to accelerate so that it climb out of ground effect – will only work if there are no obstacles in the aircraft's path.

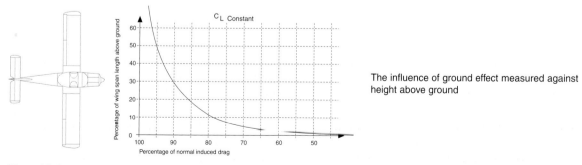

The influence of ground effect measured against height above ground

To avoid the 'ground effect' trap, the proper rotate/lift-off speeds must be used. Furthermore, do not attempt a take-off where there is not enough runway length available to permit an approved (i.e. POH/FM) take-off technique.

▶The Initial Climb

Once safely airborne at the correct airspeed, the aircraft should be established at the appropriate airspeed and configuration for the circumstances. This will normally involve a short period of acceleration, but by the time the aircraft is 50ft above the runway it should be established at the target climb airspeed. If the climb is being made at the best angle-of-climb airspeed for obstacle clearance, this airspeed should be maintained until the aircraft is well clear of obstacles. The aircraft can then be pitched nose-down to accelerate to the best rate-of-climb airspeed. If the climb has been made with flap, retraction should only take place when the 'nil flap' climbing speed is attained. In any case do not retract the flaps suddenly and all at once. Do so in stages, at a safe airspeed – allowing the airspeed and attitude to settle after each flap retraction and re-trimming as required. Whilst using the recommended flap setting will shorten the take-off ground run, the climb performance may be degraded compared with a 'clean' climbing configuration. Therefore a take-off without flap will need a longer take-off run (because of the increased take-off speeds), but the climb after take-off may be better without flap. This principle varies between differing aircraft types so, once again, the POH/FM for the actual aircraft is the authoritative source for this information.

▶ Principles of Climbing

In level flight at a constant airspeed, power set = power required for level flight.

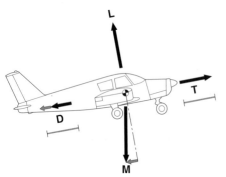

In a sustained climb at a steady airspeed, thrust has to balance drag and a component of mass

To recap:

power set = existing thrust x airspeed;

power required = drag x airspeed;

power available = maximum thrust available x airspeed.

Therefore, to maintain a steady climb at a constant airspeed, an aircraft must firstly produce enough thrust for level flight at that airspeed, and then it must produce enough extra thrust to balance the component of the aircraft's mass which acts in the same direction as drag. The steeper the climb, the greater the component of mass acting alongside drag.

It follows that the climbing performance of the aircraft is dictated by the excess of power available over power required for level flight.

▶ Climb Performance

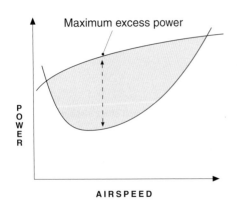

The best **rate** of climb is achieved at the airspeed where there is the greatest available excess power

The standard power-available-versus-power-required diagram, shows that at a certain airspeed there is a maximum excess of power available over power required. So it is at this particular speed that maximum power will produce the maximum rate of climb (ROC). This equates to gaining height in the shortest **time**. Pilots most often make use of this climb speed because it equates to gaining altitude as quickly as possible.

Attaining the best *rate* of climb, however, is not always the prime objective. There are times when obtaining the best *angle* of climb (the maximum climb in the shortest **distance**) is more important – taking-off from a strip with 50ft trees at the end of the runway, for example. In this case, the best angle of climb will give optimum *obstacle clearance*. The best angle-of-climb airspeed is achieved when there is the maximum excess of thrust over drag, which happens at a slower airspeed than the best-rate-of-climb airspeed. You might need to ponder this difference a few times before it sinks in. In simple terms:

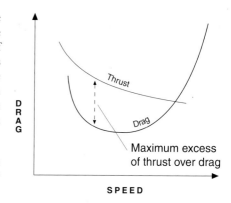

The best **angle** of climb occurs when there is the maximum excess of thrust over drag

- best rate-of-climb speed (the best height gain in a specific **time**) = the speed at which power available exceeds power required by greatest margin.

- best angle-of-climb speed (the best height gain in a specific **distance**) = the speed at which thrust exceeds drag by greatest margin.

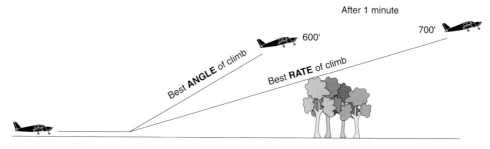

Best angle-of-climb speed is used for obstacle clearance in preference to best rate-of-climb speed

The power, thrust and drag curves needed to determine these speeds, and the interpretation of them, are not the pilot's problem. Instead the aircraft manufacturer does this work and the airworthiness authorities then test these figures to see if they agree. The end result is a set of figures in the POH/FM. The necessary flying technique (in terms of power setting and airspeed) to achieve the quoted performance will be stated, but the principle is simple enough:

Power + Attitude (angle of attack) = Performance.

In the POH/FM the climb airspeeds may be referred to using the 'V' speed code, in which case:

V_y = Best rate-of-climb airspeed,

V_x = Best angle-of-climb airspeed.

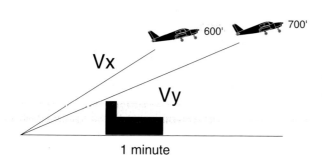

Vy (best rate-of-climb airspeed) and Vx (best angle-of-climb airspeed)

There are several things the pilot can do to maximise climb performance. The simplest is to know the POH/FM recommended speeds and use them. A second and more subtle point is to make sure that the aircraft is flown in balance. There is an increased need to use the rudder to keep the aircraft in balance during the climb, and the extra drag which results if the aircraft is out-of-balance will reduce climb performance.

CLIMB

The climb figures and technique given in a typical POH

The best rate of climb at gross weight will be obtained at 76 KIAS. The best angle of climb may be obtained at 64 KIAS. At lighter than gross weight these speeds are reduced somewhat. For climbing en route, a speed of 87 KIAS is recommended. This will produce better forward speed and increased visibility over the nose during the climb.

Mass is also a factor, and in practical terms reducing the weight of an aircraft (preferably before the flight begins) is a pilot's best way of improving climb performance. The rate of climb (ROC) can be found by the simple formula:

$$\text{ROC (ft/min)} = \frac{\text{excess power}}{\text{weight}} \times 33,000.$$

(The figure 33,000 is a constant which gives an answer in feet per minute).

Since the pilot can do little to increase the amount of excess power available except by flying at the correct ROC airspeed, mass is the only factor over which there is a degree of control. Taking a hypothetical aircraft with 50 excess horsepower available at best ROC airspeed, and weighing 2500lb, rate of climb works out at:

$$\frac{50}{2500} \times 33,000 = 660\text{ft/min}.$$

By reducing weight to 2000lb, climb performance becomes:

$$\frac{50}{2000} \times 33,000 = 825\text{ft/min}.$$

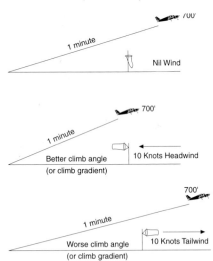

Angle of climb (at a constant climb rate) with zero wind, with a headwind and with a tailwind

Climb *angle* can be improved by flying into the wind. Note that the *rate* of climb remains the same regardless of whether there is a headwind or tailwind. However, the slower groundspeed caused by the headwind component means that more altitude is gained over the same ground distance – giving a steeper *climb gradient*. The higher groundspeed caused by a tailwind gives a more shallow climb angle. This is one of the principal reasons why even the largest and most powerful aircraft take-off into wind. If taking off downwind, the shallow angle of climb caused by climbing with a tailwind will reduce obstacle clearance, which is why taking-off downwind should be avoided.

As the aircraft climbs higher, climb performance reduces. This is because air density reduces with increasing altitude and hence a piston engine without a turbocharger or supercharger produces less power in 'thinner' air. Consequently the excess of power available over power required is less, and climb performance worsens. Ultimately a point will be reached where, even at full power and best rate-of-climb airspeed, the aircraft can do no more than maintain level flight – just! This altitude is the aircraft's *absolute ceiling*. As a limit it is rather meaningless, and a more practical one is the *service ceiling*. This is defined as the altitude at which the rate of climb has reduced to 100ft/min.

In general terms the use of flap reduces rate of climb. Nevertheless, the best-angle-of-climb airspeed is normally quoted with the same flap setting as that recommended for a short-field take-off, not least because it is impractical and dangerous to start retracting flap just as you lift off the ground.

Climbing in a turn is achieved by establishing the wings-level climb, then starting the turn. In a climb, the small loss of airspeed in a turn in more noticeable and more significant. Therefore it is normal to pitch nose-down (reducing the angle of attack) to maintain the normal climbing airspeed. The net result is that the rate of climb is reduced in a climbing turn compared with that in a wings-level climb. In order to keep the loss of airspeed and reduced rate of climb within reasonable limits, most light-aircraft pilots limit climbing turns to 15° angle of bank.

Incidentally, in all this discussion of the climb, there has been no mention of lift. Of course, if a pilot suddenly pitchs-up from level flight (especially at a high airspeed) the aircraft will enter a short-lived 'zoom' climb. However, a steady, sustained climb is achieved solely by the excess power already described. The fact is that in a steady climb, lift is actually less than mass.

▶ Calculation of Take-Off Performance

In thinking about aircraft performance as a whole, the first question has to be "Will this aircraft get airborne from this runway?". If the answer is "no", all other considerations are purely academic.

For the purposes of considering take-off performance, the take-off can be divided into two parts:

- *take-off run* – the distance from the aircraft commencing take-off to getting airborne
- *initial climb* – the distance from lifting-off to reaching 50ft above the runway.

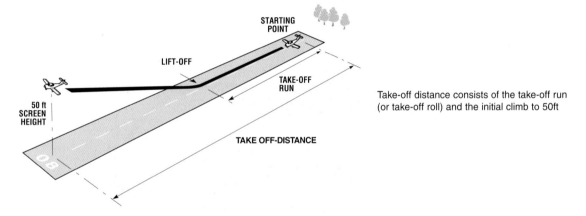

Take-off distance consists of the take-off run (or take-off roll) and the initial climb to 50ft

The total length of these two is known as the *take-off distance*, and take-off should not be attempted if the take-off distance **available** is less than the take-off distance **required**.

In a sense every take-off can be regarded as being different. Even when operating the same aircraft from the same runway on a daily basis, factors such as aircraft weight, wind, air density and runway contamination (snow, ice or standing water) will vary. Each of these will affect the take-off distance required. Furthermore, when using different runways, factors such as obstacles, runway surface and slope have to be considered. Many POH/FMs start with the assumption that the aircraft is operating at maximum weight in zero wind and ISA conditions from a dry, level, paved runway at sea level. So, before looking at the calculation of take-off performance in detail it is considering briefly how 'real-world' factors affect the take-off distance required.

Aircraft mass is a prime issue in take-off performance. In simple terms, the heavier the aircraft, the greater the take-off distance required because of the faster lift-off and climbing speeds needed, the slower acceleration and reduced rate of climb. As a rule of thumb, a 10% increase in weight increases take-off distance by 20%.

The **surface wind** also has a marked impact. Conventionally, all aircraft take-off and land as much as possible into wind. Take-off speeds are based on the aircraft's **air**speed, not **ground**speed. So an aircraft starting a take-off into a 15-knot headwind already has an advantage, it has that much less groundspeed to accelerate to and take-off distance required is consequentially reduced. Furthermore, once airborne a headwind gives a steeper climb gradient for the same airspeed, improving obstacle clearance.

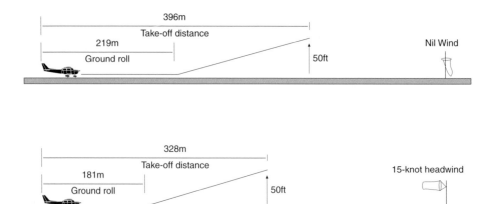

The effect of headwind upon take-off distance, figures based on POH/FM figures for a Cessna 172

Headwind (and crosswind) component can be calculated on the wind side of the flight computer. The technique is discussed in the Navigation section of PPL 3, but here is a short refresher.

Example: the surface wind is 310/15, the runway in use is 02. Assuming the wind direction is magnetic, what is the crosswind and headwind component?

Using a flight computer to calculate headwind and crosswind component

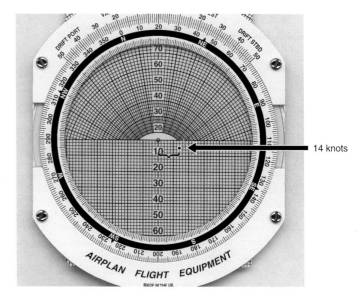

14 knots

As a mental check, the angle between runway and wind is 70°. Using the rules of thumb outlined in PPL 1, the crosswind component will be nearly the full windspeed (15kts) so the headwind component will be no more than a few knots.

On the wind scale side of the flight computer, place the centre dot at the top of the wind grid and rotate the plotting disk until the wind direction is under the index mark. Put a dot or cross on the plotting disk at 15kts. Now rotate the plotting disk until the runway QDM (020°) is under the index. On the wind grid, the vertical distance from the top of the grid to the wind mark is headwind or tailwind component and the distance across to the wind mark from the centreline is the crosswind component. In this case the headwind component is 5kts and crosswind component is 14kts.

Crosswind take-offs are not a problem provided the crosswind is within acceptable limits, but taking off with a tailwind should be avoided if at all possible. The increase in take-off distance can be dramatic, and directional control is more difficult in the early part of the take-off run.

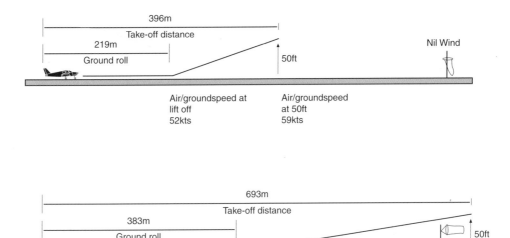

The effect of tailwind upon take-off distance

Air density is influenced by temperature, pressure and humidity. Air density is one of the factors directly related to dynamic pressure and hence the generation of lift. As air density is reduced (for example, with increasing altitude), take-off distances begin to increase quickly. The International Standard Atmosphere has a sea level density of 1·225 kg/m3; by 20,000ft this figure has halved. In aircraft performance the expression *density altitude* is sometimes used. Density altitude is the ISA altitude with the same density as the existing pressure altitude and temperature.

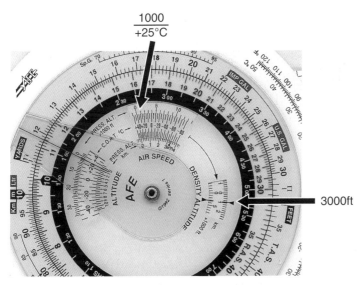

Using the flight computer to calculate air density given air temperature and pressure altitude

Density altitude can be found using the calculator side of the flight computer. For example, the runway elevation is 700ft, the QNH is 1003mb, the temperature is +25°C. What is the density altitude?

Firstly, the runway altitude of 700ft has to be converted into a *pressure altitude*, which is the indicated altitude if the altimeter is set to the standard pressure of 1013mb/hPa. The simple way to do this if you are at the airfield is to go out to the aircraft, set the altimeter to 1013 and read off the altitude. Alternatively, using the approximation 1mb = 30ft, you can adjust the altitude – remembering that pressure **below** 1013 means a **higher** altitude and *vice versa*. With an actual QNH of 1003, a reduction of 10mb below standard pressure (i.e. 300ft) means that the pressure altitude is higher (700 + 300) = 1000ft. Remember, pressure gets lower as you go higher. Now, in the altitude window of the flight computer, the pressure altitude (1000ft) is set over the temperature (+25°C). The density altitude is then read off in the density altitude window and is 3000ft. So on this day at this airfield, the aircraft will perform as it would at 3000ft in the ISA.

In the International Standard Atmosphere there is an ISA temperature for each altitude up to 36,090ft based on the standard lapse rate of 2°C/1000ft. As a rule of thumb, for each 1°C that the actual temperature exceeds the ISA temperature for a particular altitude, the density altitude is increased by 100ft. An airfield is sometimes referred to as 'Hot and High' if its elevation and average temperatures mean that it often has a high density altitude, with a consequent reduction in aircraft performance.

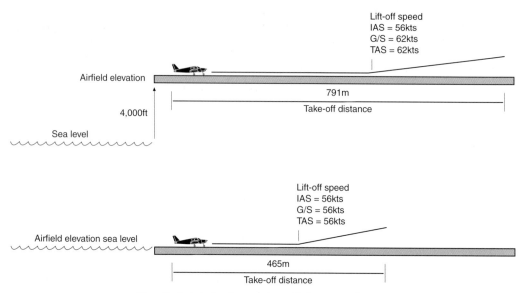

Lift-off speed
IAS = 56kts
G/S = 62kts
TAS = 62kts

Airfield elevation

791m
Take-off distance

4,000ft

Sea level

Lift-off speed
IAS = 56kts
G/S = 56kts
TAS = 56kts

Airfield elevation sea level

465m
Take-off distance

The effect of air density upon take-off distance and groundspeed

The tables or graphs in the POH/FM used for calculating performance usually allow the pilot to input pressure altitude and temperature; in effect calculating the density altitude. Take-off distance increases by around 10% for each extra 1000ft of altitude and another 10% per 10°C increase in temperature. The effect of humidity upon density is less easy to calculate and not normally included as a variable in POH/FM graphs/tables. However, high humidity reduces density and therefore lengthens take-off distance. As a general rule, particularly 'muggy' conditions signifying high humidity can add 10% to the take-off distance required.

Regardless of density altitude, the take-off speeds in terms of indicated airspeed (IAS) will remain the same. Reduced density means that the same indicated airspeed occurs at a higher TAS, implying a longer take-off run, higher groundspeed before becoming airborne and a more shallow climb. All of this can cause visual cues leading the unwary pilot to fly too slowly. In this situation it is even more important to use the proper indicated airspeeds.

Any **contamination** of the runway surface (standing water, slush, ice, snow, etc.) will lengthen the take-off distance as well as making directional control more difficult. The effect differs on different runway surfaces, but a light covering of snow can easily add 25% to the take-off distance required.

Runway surface is an all-important factor. Hard surfaces such as asphalt and concrete allow shorter take-off distances than soft surfaces such as grass. The length of the grass is also significant – the longer the grass, the longer the take-off roll and so the greater the overall take-off distance. In fact, the CAA recommends that if the grass is higher than 10 inches (25cm) a take-off should not be attempted at all.

Some runways are more level than others, and any **runway slope** will affect take-off performance. A downslope allows the aircraft to accelerate more quickly thus reducing take-off roll and so take-off distance; an up-sloping runway increases take-off run and overall take-off distance.

The information for calculating aircraft performance is found in the POH/FM. In its simplest form this information can simply be a known take-off distance for a stated set of conditions (normally Maximum Total Weight Authorised, sea-level ISA conditions, hard runway, nil wind). The technique necessary to achieve this performance should also be stated and used.

A simple form of take-off distance information

TAKE - OFF DISTANCE			FLAPS RETRACTED – HARD SURFACE RUNWAY							
			AT SEA LEVEL & 15°C/59°F.		AT 2500 FT. & 10°C/50°F.		AT 5000 FT. & 5°C/41°F.		AT 7500 FT. & 0°C/32°F.	
GROSS WEIGHT LBS.	IAS 50 FT. MPH	HEAD WIND KNOTS	GROUND RUN	TOTAL TO CLEAR 50 FT. OBS.	GROUND RUN	TOTAL TO CLEAR 50 FT. OBS.	GROUND RUN	TOTAL TO CLEAR 50 FT. OBS.	GROUND RUN	TOTAL TO CLEAR 50 FT. OBS.
		0	735	1385	910	1660	1115	1985	1360	2440
1600	70	10	500	1035	630	1250	780	1510	970	1875
		20	305	730	395	890	505	1090	640	1375

NOTES   1. Increase the distances 10% for each 35°f. increase in temperature above standard for the particular altitude.
            2. For operation on a dry, grass runway, increase distances (both "ground run" and "total to clear 50 ft. obstacle") by 7% of the
                "total to clear 50 ft. obstacle" figure.

For variations from the stated conditions, you will need to apply some kind of correction factor. Where these are noted in the POH/FM, use them. For those not included in the POH/FM, the CAA has produced a table of recommended factors, and the 'raw' take-off distance can be increased by one or more of these factors to allow for various conditions. Unfortunately, it may be necessary to memorise this table for exam purposes (although relying on memory alone is not recommended for real calculations). The table is shown here for reference in the following calculations.

Condition	Percentage increase in take-off distance	Factor
1000ft increase in runway elevation	10%	1·1
10°C increase in temperature	10%	1·1
Runway upslope of 2%	10%	1·1
Tailwind component of 10% of lift-off speed	20%	1·2
10% increase in aircraft weight	20%	1.2
Dry grass on firm soil (grass up to 20cm/8 inches)	20%	1·2
Soft ground or snow	At least 25%	At least 1·25
Wet grass on firm soil (grass up to 20cm/8 inches)	30%	1·3

The required techniques for calculating take-off performance are best explained by example.

Example: The POH states a take-off distance of 410m given Maximum Total Weight Authorised, sea-level ISA conditions, hard runway and nil wind. No information is given for correction factors other than a reduction of 5% in take-off distance for every 5kts of headwind component.

With a headwind component of 10kts, a runway pressure altitude of 500ft, a temperature of +24°C and a dry grass runway surface, find the take-off distance required. Use the CAA table for correction factors not given in the POH/FM.

Firstly the correction factor for each condition is found. Taking the headwind factor, the CAA recommends that for the purposes of performance calculations the pilot should use no more than 50% (factor 0·5) of a headwind component and not less than 150% (factor 1·5) of a tailwind component. Thus the 10-knot headwind component becomes 5kts (0·5 x 10kts), which according to the POH reduces take-off distance by 5% (equivalent to multiplying take-off distance by 0·95).

The pressure altitude of 500ft implies a 5% increase (based on the CAA table) which is a factor of 1·05. The temperature of +24°C is 10°C more than the ISA temperature at 500ft, indicating an increase of 10% – a factor of 1·1. The dry grass is factored at 1·2 (that is, an increase of 20%) as shown in the CAA table.

Each of these correction factors is applied cumulatively, so the calculation will look like this:

'Gross' take-off distance x headwind factor x altitude factor x temperature factor x surface factor = actual take-off distance required;

or

410 x 0·95 x 1·05 x 1·1 x 1·2 = 540 metres (to the nearest metre).

This is not quite the end of the story. This figure does not take account of a final factor, which we might call the real world. In this place, engines and propellers do not give as much power as when brand-new; piloting technique is less than perfect; the headwind decides to stop blowing the moment the take-off commences; the aircraft is heavier than calculated; and so on. For a 'public transport' flight, a safety factor of 33% (1·33) is added to the calculated take-off distance to achieve the final take-off distance required, and the CAA strongly recommends that this factor is used for private flights too. This factor may be included in the POH/FM figures, in which case this will be clearly stated – otherwise add it to the calculated figure.

So 540 x 1·33 = 718m.

This is quite a difference from the original take-off distance required of 410m! And this example isn't particularly extreme; it's a summer day at many European airfields.

Incidentally, although the above calculations are usually done on an electronic calculator, there is no reason why they cannot be performed on a flight computer. Place 1 on the inner scale under the starting figure. Apply the factor, then move 1 on the inner scale to be under the new figure. Repeat this process for each factor. Using the flight computer also allows the user to try-out 'what-if' variations with a much better visual appreciation of how each factor changes the end result.

The POH/FM for a modern light aircraft is most likely to have a table or graph that allows the pilot to input most of the common factors affecting take-off performance. Using a graph, and assuming it states that the headwind and tailwind factors are those recommended by the CAA, let's look at another example.

Example: Given a take-off mass of 2200lb, a pressure altitude of 2000ft, a temperature of +10°C, a 5-knot headwind component and dry tarmac runway with a 2% upslope, find the take-off distance required. Assume that the table *does not* include the CAA recommended safety factor of 1·33.

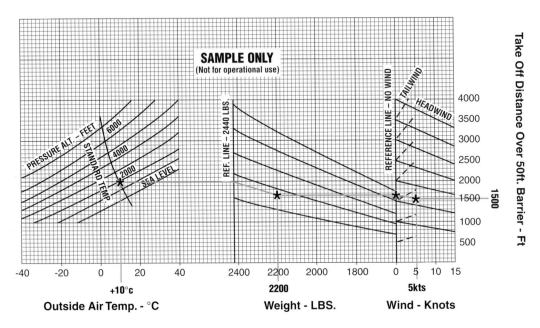

Calculating take-off performance using a POH/FM graph

Start on the left-hand bottom side of the graph, and take a vertical line from the temperature (+10°C) to the pressure altitude (2000ft). From this point, go across horizontally to the first vertical 'reference line'. Now move across parallel to the guide lines until above the aircraft mass (2200lb). From this point go across horizontally to the next reference line. Then move parallel to the headwind guidelines until above the 5-knot point. From here, go horizontally to the far side of the table. If everything has worked, the line should end at a take-off distance required of 1500ft. To allow for the 2% runway upslope, factor this distance by 1·1 (making 1650ft), and finally apply the safety factor of 1·33 to give 2195ft. If the runway distance is given in metres, this can be converted on the flight computer to arrive at a take-off distance required of 670m.

If the POH/FM uses tables instead of graphs, real conditions will almost certainly fall between some of its columns. The pilot can interpolate between figures – a computation best done with the aid of an electronic calculator – or can simply take the next set of figures 'beyond' the exact conditions.

Example: given a pressure altitude of 1000ft, a temperature of +15°C, nil wind and a wet grass runway, find the take-off distance required using the table (the safety factor of 1·33 is not included in the POH/FM table).

WEIGHT LBS.	TAKEOFF SPEED		PRESS ALT FT	0°C		10°C		20°C		30°C		40°C	
	LIFT OFF	AT 50 FT		GROUND ROLL FT	TOTAL FT TO CLEAR 50 FT. OBS.	GROUND ROLL FT	TOTAL FT TO CLEAR 50 FT. OBS.	GROUND ROLL FT	TOTAL FT TO CLEAR 50 FT. OBS.	GROUND ROLL FT	TOTAL FT TO CLEAR 50 FT. OBS.	GROUND ROLL FT	TOTAL FT TO CLEAR 50 FT. OBS.
1670	50	54	S.L.	640	1190	695	1290	755	1390	810	1495	875	1605
	KIAS	KIAS	1000	705	1310	765	1420	825	1530	890	1645	960	1770
			2000	775	1445	840	1565	910	1690	980	1820	1055	1960
			3000	855	1600	925	1730	1000	1870	1080	2020	1135	2185
			4000	940	1775	1020	1920	1100	2080	1190	2250	1285	2440
			5000	1040	1970	1125	2140	1215	2320	1315	2525	1420	2750
			6000	1145	2200	1245	2395	1345	2610	1455	2855	1570	3125
			7000	1270	2470	1375	2705	1490	2960	1615	3255	1745	3590
			8000	1405	2800	1525	3080	1655	3395	1795	3765	1940	4195

Calculating take-off performance using a POH/FM table

Along the row of figures for 1000ft pressure altitude, there is no column for 15°C. So go instead to 20°C (1530). Now factor this figure by 1·3 for the wet grass runway (to give 1990) and then apply the 1·33 safety factor. The final result should be 2645ft or 807m.

To be precise and interpolate between the +10°C figure of 1420 and the +20°C figure of 1530, gives (1420 + 1530) / 2 = 1475. After the other factors have been applied (including the 1·33 safety factor) this gives a result of 2550ft or 777m. This is 95ft or 30m shorter than the first figure calculated, for a fair bit of extra effort. The 'extra' 30m of the first calculation can be considered as an extra safety margin, although technically the second calculation gives a more accurate answer. If the situation is such that 95ft (30m) of runway length is the difference between a successful take-off or not, is it wise to proceed at all?

As a general rule, the POH/FM tables or graphs allow the actual temperature to be used. But temperature is occasionally referred to in terms of ISA – for example ISA +10°C, ISA +20°C and so on. In these cases the pilot must first find the ISA temperature (based on a sea-level temperature of +15°C and a lapse rate of 2°C per 1000ft) then decide how the actual temperature deviates from this.

Example: the temperature at 3000ft pressure altitude is +21°C; what is this in relation to ISA?

In the ISA at 3000ft the temperature is found by: +15°C – (3 x 2) = +9°C. The actual temperature is +21°C so the temperature is 12°C more than standard, or ISA +12°C.

Once the take-off distance required has been calculated, and assuming that the take-off distance available does permit a safe departure (more about runway dimensions later) there are some practical aspects of take-off technique to consider. The first is that old chestnut; to achieve POH performance use POH techniques. If the POH says to use 25° of flap for take-off, do so. In general, a small amount of flap reduces ground run because the stalling and take-off speeds are lowered. However, using more flap than that stated in the POH may result in so much extra drag that there is an increase in the take-off distance. At the other end of the spectrum, some aircraft achieve their best take-off performance with no flap at all. It depends on the aircraft, so read the POH/FM and act on it – that's what it's there for.

Aircraft manufacturers do their very best to obtain the shortest possible take-off distance – it helps to sell aircraft. The certifying authority will verify the figures, disregard any dangerous or impractical techniques and what is left is the POH technique. It's been tested, it's been verified, it's there for the pilot's benefit.

During the take-off itself, a major factor in performance terms is the aircraft's acceleration and the crucial distance is the take-off distance available. Getting airborne a little earlier or later than calculated is immaterial if there is plenty of runway left. There is no instrument to measure acceleration during the take-off, but a quick calculation is all that is needed if the aircraft's recommended lift-off speed is known (it is usually given in the POH). To get airborne in a given distance, the aircraft needs to have reached about 75% of the lift-off speed at the half-way point. If the aircraft has not reached this speed by the time it passes half the take-off distance available (i.e. half-way along the runway) the chances are that something is wrong and the take-off should be abandoned. As a final check, the aircraft should actually be airborne no later that two-thirds of the way along the runway. In most light aircraft it should still be possible to abandon the take-off at this point and stop before the end of the runway, although there may not be too much room to spare if the aircraft is operating near its take-off distance limit. It is also worth knowing that the initial climb speed after take-off is sometimes known as the *take-off safety speed* or V_2. The take-off safety speed is never less than 1·2 x the stalling speed in the take-off configuration.

For a tricycle-undercarriage aircraft, protection of the nosewheel when operating from a rough surface is of the utmost importance because generally the nosewheel assembly is nowhere near as strong as the main undercarriage. The control column should be held back when starting the take-off, the aim being to reduce the weight on the nosewheel rather than actually lifting it clear of the runway – which will ruin the view ahead, make directional control difficult and markedly lengthen the take-off distance.

▶Calculation of Climb Performance

Climb performance is of great interest to the pilot if there is a ridge topped with 50ft trees not far from the end of the runway, and this type of obstruction will be dealt with in the take-off performance tables/graphs. Climb performance to cruising altitude may be dealt with in separate tables and graphs which show rate of climb, distance covered and fuel used. These tables/graphs tend to use the same principles as those used for calculating take-off performance.

Example:

An aircraft will be taking-off from a sea-level airfield, and climbing to a cruising level of FL75 (i.e. 7500ft pressure altitude). How long will the climb take?

A table for calculating climb performance

TIME, FUEL, AND DISTANCE TO CLIMB	MAXIMUM RATE OF CLIMB										
CONDITIONS :			Flaps up		Full throttle			Standard temperature			
Weight	Pressure Altitude		Tempe-rature	Climb Speed IAS		Rate of Climb		From Sea Level				
								Time	Fuel used		Distance	
kg	ft	m	°C	km/h	kts	ft/mn	m/s	mn	US Gal.	Litres	NM	km
726	Sea level		15	135	73	770	3.9	0	0	0	0	0
	1000	305	13	135	73	725	3.7	1	0.3	1.1	2	3.7
	2000	610	11	133	72	675	3.4	3	0.6	2.3	3	5.6
	3000	914	9	133	72	630	3.2	4	0.9	3.4	5	9.3
	4000	1219	7	131	71	580	2.9	6	1.2	4.5	8	14.8
	5000	1524	5	131	71	535	2.7	8	1.6	6.1	10	18.5
	6000	1829	3	130	70	485	2.5	10	1.9	7.2	12	22.2
	7000	2134	1	128	69	440	2.2	12	2.3	8.7	15	27.8
	8000	2438	- 1	128	69	390	2	15	2.7	10.2	19	35.2
	9000	2743	- 3	126	68	345	1.8	17	3.2	12.1	22	40.8
	10,000	3048	- 5	126	68	295	1.5	21	3.7	14	27	50
	11,000	3353	- 7	124	67	250	1.3	24	4.2	15.9	32	59.3
	12,000	3658	- 9	124	67	200	1	29	4.9	18.5	38	70.4

NOTES :
1.   Add 1.1 gallons 4.16 litres of fuel for engine start, taxi and takeoff allowance.
2.   Mixture leaned above 3000 ft - 914 m for maximum RPM.
3.   Increase time, fuel and distance by 10 % for each 10°C above standard temperature.
4.   Distances shown are based on zero wind.

Interpolating between the 7000ft and 8000ft lines gives a time to cruising level of 13·5 minutes, fuel used 9·45 litres, and a distance of 17nm. This calculation is based on 'still air' conditions. If there will be a tailwind averaging 15kts during the climb, the pilot can calculate the distance based on the average groundspeed and time (the time, like the fuel consumption, remains the same as in still air). In the example above, the average TAS in the climb will be around 75kts. Given a 15-knot tailwind, this implies an average groundspeed of 90kts. In 13·5 minutes at 90kts, the distance travelled will be 20·2nm.

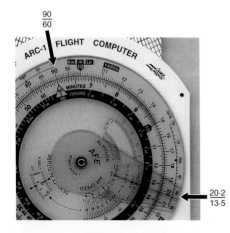

Calculating distance to climb on a flight computer

Unlike some other performance criteria, the best climbing airspeed is obtained at a particular **True** airspeed (TAS). With increasing altitude, TAS gradually diverged from the IAS, such that indicated airspeed has to be reduced to maintain a given TAS. To achieve best climb performance, the rule of thumb is to reduce indicated airspeed by one knot for each 2000ft of altitude above sea level (remembering, however, that the aircraft will still stall at the same indicated airspeed regardless of altitude). Some climb-performance schedules will show the required indicated airspeed for best rate of climb at various altitudes.

The POH/FM will also state the aircraft's *service ceiling* and *absolute ceiling*. The service ceiling is the pressure altitude in the International Standard Atmosphere at which the rate of climb falls to 100ft/min. The absolute ceiling is the pressure altitude at which, even at best-rate-of-climb airspeed, the aircraft will only just fly level – in other words, the excess of power required over power available has reduced to zero.

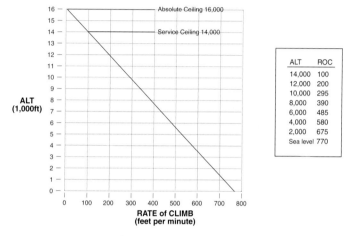

ALT	ROC
14,000	100
12,000	200
10,000	295
8,000	390
6,000	485
4,000	580
2,000	675
Sea level	770

Service ceiling and absolute ceiling

▶ Revision

9   On the 'Power Available versus Power Required' graph, at what airspeed will the aircraft attain the maximum rate of climb?

10   Which *type* of climb airspeed will give the best obstacle clearance?

11   When climbing into a 10 knot headwind, an aircraft has a rate of climb of 650ft/min. If headwind increases to 20 knots, what (approximately) will the rate of climb be?

12   In a steady climb, is lift the same as, greater than or less than, weight?

13   An aircraft has a recommended lift-off airspeed of 50 knots IAS. What will be the correct lift-off airspeed if there is a 15 knot headwind on take-off?

14   The use of the recommended flap setting for take-off will _____ take-off speed and _____ the take-off run compared to take-off without flap (fill in the blanks)

15   Which of the following will *not* increase take-off distance?

An increase in aircraft weight

An increase in air density

An increase in runway upslope

An increase in runway surface grass length

16   Using the table below, calculate the take-off distance required in the following circumstances:

Aircraft weight 1043kg;

Runway 24 – elevation 500ft pressure altitude, temperature +20°C, runway surface dry grass. Surface Wind 310/20.

TAKE OFF DISTANCE			SHORT FIELD									
CONDITIONS :		Flaps up		Full throttle prior to brake release			Paved, Level, Dry runway			Zero wind		
MAXIMUM WEIGHT	IAS		PRESSURE ALTITUDE		0°C / 32°F		10°C / 50°F		20°C / 68°F		30°C / 86°F		40°C / 104°F
	LIFT OFF	AT 15M (50ft)	FT	M	GROUND ROLL M	TOTAL TO CLEAR 15M OBS. M	GROUND ROLL M	TOTAL TO CLEAR 15M OBS. M	GROUND ROLL M	TOTAL TO CLEAR 15M OBS. M	GROUND ROLL M	TOTAL TO CLEAR 15M OBS. M	GROUND ROLL M	TOTAL TO CLEAR 15M OBS. M
1043kg	96km/h	109km/h	Sea Level		219	396	236	424	255	454	273	485	293	518
	52kt	59kt	1000	305	241	433	259	465	279	497	299	532	320	568
	60mph	68mph	2000	610	264	474	283	509	305	546	328	584	352	626
			3000	914	290	521	312	559	335	600	361	645	387	690
			4000	1219	319	573	353	617	369	663	396	712	427	765
			5000	1524	351	632	378	683	407	735	437	791	469	852
			6000	1829	386	703	416	757	450	817	483	882	520	953
			7000	2134	427	782	460	844	497	914	535	989	576	1071
			8000	2438	472	875	511	948	550	1029	593	1119	639	1216
NOTES : 1. 2. 3.		Crosswind limit 15kts											

17   Using the graph below, decide if the runway is long enough to allow a safe take-off in the following circumstances. Assume that the take-off distance safety factor of 1·33 is *not* included in the graph figures:

Aircraft weight 2200lbs;

Runway 32 – elevation 1000ft pressure altitude, temperature +10°C, runway surface dry tarmac. Take Off Distance Available 550 metres.

Surface Wind 350/20.

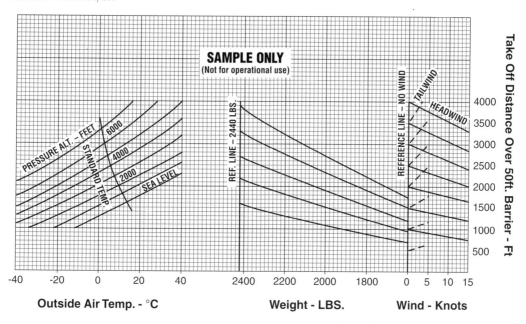

18   Using the graph below, calculate the time required and fuel used (litres) in a climb from sea level to Flight Level (FL) 55, and the climb IAS and rate of climb at FL45.

TIME, FUEL, AND DISTANCE TO CLIMB [MAXIMUM RATE OF CLIMB]

CONDITIONS :   Flaps up   Full throttle   Standard temperature

Weight	Pressure Altitude		Tempe-rature	Climb Speed IAS		Rate of Climb		From Sea Level				
								Time	Fuel used		Distance	
kg	ft	m	°C	km/h	kts	ft/mn	m/s	mn	US Gal.	Litres	NM	km
726	Sea level		15	135	73	770	3.9	0	0	0	0	0
	1000	305	13	135	73	725	3.7	1	0.3	1.1	2	3.7
	2000	610	11	133	72	675	3.4	3	0.6	2.3	3	5.6
	3000	914	9	133	72	630	3.2	4	0.9	3.4	5	9.3
	4000	1219	7	131	71	580	2.9	6	1.2	4.5	8	14.8
	5000	1524	5	131	71	535	2.7	8	1.6	6.1	10	18.5
	6000	1829	3	130	70	485	2.5	10	1.9	7.2	12	22.2
	7000	2134	1	128	69	440	2.2	12	2.3	8.7	15	27.8
	8000	2418	-1	128	69	390	2	15	2.7	10.2	19	35.2
	9000	2743	-3	12n	68	345	1.8	17	3.2	12.1	22	40.8
	10,000	3048	-5	126	68	295	1.5	21	3.7	14	27	50
	11,000	3353	-7	124	67	250	1.3	24	4.2	15.9	32	59.3
	12,000	3658	-9	124	67	200	1	29	4.9	18.5	38	70.4

NOTES :

1. Add 1.1 gallons 4.16 litres of fuel for engine start, taxi and takeoff allowance.
2. Mixture leaned above 3000 ft - 914 m for maximum RPM.
3. Increase time, fuel and distance by 10 % for each 10°C above standard temperature.
4. Distances shown are based on zero wind.

In-flight Performance

Flight Performance and Planning
In-flight Performance

▶ Principles of Cruising Flight

▶ Power + Attitude = Performance

▶ Principles of Manoeuvring Flight

▶ Rate of Turn and Turn Radius

▶ Cruise Performance

▶ Revision

In-flight Performance

▶ Principles of Cruising Flight

In level, unaccelerated flight; **weight** is balanced by an equal amount of **lift**, and **drag** is balanced by an equal amount of **thrust**.

Pilots do not need to know the exact amount of any of these forces. At best, a pilot will only have an approximate idea of the aircraft's weight. But, if the aircraft is flying level, the wings must be producing an equivalent amount of lift; so if the aircraft has a mass of 982·3kg at a particular stage in its flight, the wings will be generating 982·3kg of lift if flying straight and level. What concerns pilots more is the aircraft performance, most often measured in terms of airspeed and height gain/loss. Having decided on the performance required, it is attained by setting an approximate power setting and attitude known from experience to be about right. This set-up is most often done in the order:

- Power
- Attitude
- Trim

which is usually remembered as PAT, and the aerodynamic principle at work can be summed up as:

POWER + ATTITUDE = PERFORMANCE.

Having set up the approximate power and attitude for the required performance, the instruments can be used to check the exact performance in terms of airspeed and altitude. The pilot can then make minor adjustments as required and re-trim if necessary to maintain the desired attitude/angle of attack. Generally, any change in airspeed, power or flap setting will require the pilot to re-trim.

▶ Power + Attitude = Performance

The work output of piston engines, such as those usually found in light aircraft, is best measured and expressed in terms of **power**, a term which is worth a quick revision. Power is *not* the same thing as **thrust**. The amount of power an aircraft piston engine can produce varies with airspeed. For example at 'full power', the actual power output will vary with changing airspeed: power available is equal to (thrust x airspeed). If maximum power attainable is plotted against airspeed, the resulting curve is known as the *power available curve*.

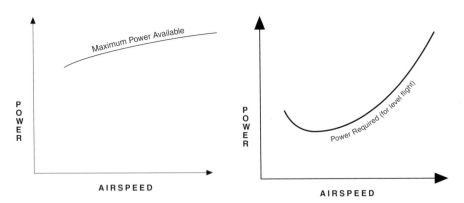

The 'power available' curve, found by multiplying thrust by airspeed

The 'power required' curve, found by multiplying drag by airspeed

To compare this figure with something meaningful, we ought to know the aircraft's *power required*. Power required is found simply by (drag x airspeed) and in this sense power required means the minimum power necessary for the aircraft to maintain level flight. When plotted against airspeed, an average light aircraft's power-required curve looks something like the above.

Attitude is controlled primarily by the control column. Moving the control column back and forwards makes the aircraft pitch up or down, and so the angle of attack of the wings is changed, which changes the lift and drag produced by the aircraft. In short, the control column controls the angle of attack of the wings, and if all other factors remain the same (most especially aircraft weight) **each set angle of attack equates to a set airspeed**.

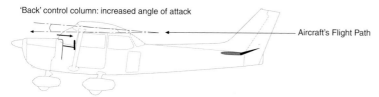

'Back' control column: increased angle of attack

Aircraft's Flight Path

Movement of the elevators alters the angle of attack at the wings

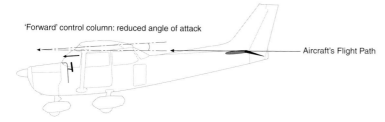

'Forward' control column: reduced angle of attack

Aircraft's Flight Path

There is nothing revolutionary about this notion; aircraft designers and test pilots have known it since the early days of flying. Indeed, many important measures of aircraft performance (the stall, best range and best glide, etc.) occur at a fixed angle of attack. Quite why pilots are not given an angle-of-attack indicator and simply told "Don't exceed 12° angle of attack or it will stall; fly at 4° for best range" and so on is something of a mystery. Instead, we are presented with an airspeed indicator which displays dynamic pressure, $1/2\rho V^2$, and are given indicated airspeeds to fly which will equate to a certain angle of attack under certain conditions – for example, maximum permitted mass. Although the attitude as seen ahead does

not correspond exactly to the angle of attack at the wings, especially near the stalling angle of attack, it is a fact that moving the control column forward always reduces angle of attack and pulling the control column back always increases angle of attack. The maxim of 'Power + Attitude = Performance' works well because the ordinary pilot's usual task is to control the aircraft's performance and flightpath to achieve some set purpose; e.g. to fly level at a certain airspeed, to descend at a set airspeed and rate of descent towards a fixed point, to land and stop within a given distance and so on. So the performance and flightpath required is achieved by setting the wings at a certain angle of attack and setting the power to achieve level flight, or the required rate of descent or rate of climb.

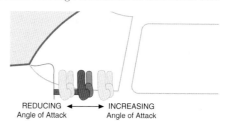

REDUCING ← Angle of Attack   INCREASING → Angle of Attack

How to think of the control column controlling the wing angle of attack

In practice, pilots tend to set power first and then adjust attitude because this leads to more accurate height-keeping. The pilot can try increasing level-flight airspeed by pitching the nose down (thereby reducing the angle of attack) until the target airspeed is reached, then increasing power (because at this higher airspeed more power is required to maintain level flight) until level flight is re-established. After some juggling the aim of flying faster in level flight will be achieved, but at the expense of a loss of altitude. This is not usually a very practical way to fly around.

The airspeed indicator displays dynamic pressure, which is one of the primary factors affecting lift. Dynamic pressure is a function of air density and velocity. As altitude increases, air density reduces; so dynamic pressure will reduce, even if velocity remains the same. This means that with increasing altitude, the airspeed indicator will gradually indicate less than the aircraft's true speed through the air. This discrepancy can be seen in a comparison table:

Altitude (AMSL)	Sea Level	10,000ft	20,000ft	30,000ft
True Airspeed (kts)	100	100	100	100
Dynamic Pressure (lb/sq.ft)	33·9	25	18·1	12·7
Indicated Airspeed (knots)	100	86	73	61

One final point is that at a 'normal' cruise airspeed, the couple between the weight and lift forces usually leaves the aircraft with a residual pitching-down moment. This is 'trimmed' by a lift force acting downwards – a 'download' – at the horizontal tail to maintain the desired attitude. As the CG moves forward, the amount of download required to be produced by the horizontal tail is increased; as the CG moves back, the horizontal tail download decreases. Tail download is altered by moving the elevator position ('up' elevator increases download and *vice versa*) or adjusting the angle of the entire horizontal tail. As an unavoidable consequence of generating lift, any tail download will cause drag and reduce the overall 'positive' lift produced by the aircraft. This small contribution to reducing the aircraft's performance is called *trim drag*, and the effect is most marked with a forward CG. Moving the CG aft (rearwards) reduces trim drag and improves overall lift, perhaps adding a couple of knots to cruise speed or a few miles to range. But regardless of this, an aircraft must **never** be flown with the CG outside the prescribed limits.

▶ Principles of Manoeuvring Flight

To turn an aircraft, it is necessary to provide a force to deflect it from its straight flight-path. This is done by banking in the direction of the desired turn, so that the lift force keeping the aircraft in the air is now also providing the force to turn it. Because the lift now has to provide *both* the turning force and the lift force to oppose aircraft weight, it follows that greater total lift is required to maintain level flight in a turn. For a fairly shallow turn (up to about 30° angle of bank) it is easy enough to increase lift by simply increasing the back pressure on the control column to increase the angle of attack of the wings slightly. At this increased angle of attack, the airspeed will reduce by a knot or two but this is not a problem at normal cruising airspeeds.

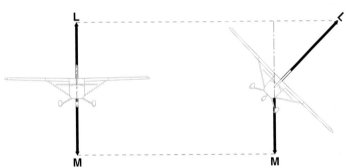

Banking the aircraft provides a component of lift into the direction of the turn

The increase in drag in a turn causes a reduction in airspeed which, if the airspeed is already below the normal cruising figure, can be crucial. It follows that when turning in climbing or descending flight, the attitude will need to be adjusted by pitching nose-down to maintain the required climbing/descending airspeed. The result is that in a climbing turn, the rate of climb (ROC) is reduced, in a descent the rate of descent (ROD) is increased if airspeed is maintained.

As the angle of bank is increased, more and more lift is required to maintain level flight and keep the turn going. The increased angle of attack increases drag, and at some point (usually at around 30° of bank in an average training aircraft) an increase in power becomes prudent. As the angle of bank steepens further, there comes a point where no further increase is possible without incurring a height loss, even with the application of full power. This point is normally governed by the engine power available, but about 60° of bank is the practical limit for most training aircraft.

The steeper the angle of bank, the greater the total lift required to turn the aircraft and maintain level flight

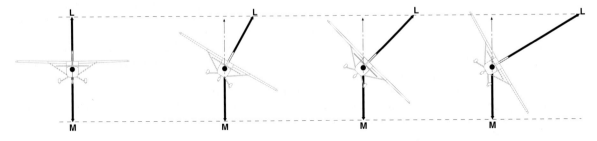

Looking at the diagram of lift forces, it is theoretically impossible to turn at 90° angle of bank without descending. The fact that many aircraft *can* maintain height in a 90° banked turn is chiefly explained by the fact that the fuselage can produce some lift. Also, in such a turn the nose is normally some way above the horizon, which allows a component of thrust to contribute to the overall lift force.

Turning flight, particularly steep turns, also reminds the pilot about the use of rudder. The primary use of the rudder is to maintain balanced flight, which means keeping the balance ball in the centre. Therefore the rudder is there largely to correct unwanted yaw, for example during a change in power setting, and to co-ordinate turns and other manoeuvres when the ailerons are being used. Despite various devices the aircraft designer can try (e.g. differential ailerons and Frise ailerons) it is normally necessary to use the rudder to keep the aircraft in balance when entering or exiting a turn, because the deflection of the ailerons will cause some aileron drag and adverse yaw. As the angle of bank becomes steeper, and as more power is used, more footwork may be required to keep the aircraft in balance during the turn itself. Older aircraft can be quite demanding in this respect. When practising steep turns, note the amount of rudder required in a left turn compared with that required in a right turn. The difference is caused by the various rotational forces – slipstream, torque and so on – of the engine and propeller. To explore the relationship between the movement of the ailerons and the use of rudder to maintain balance, try (under the guidance of an instructor) rolling the aircraft rapidly from side to side with aileron whilst keeping the balance ball in the middle. The effect is at its best, and the footwork required most accurate, in a glider or motor glider.

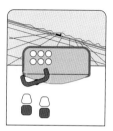 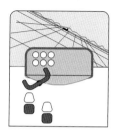 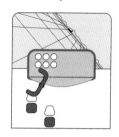

As a general rule, the more aileron applied, the greater the amount of rudder needed in the same direction to maintain balanced flight

The point is that the rudder does *not* turn the aircraft; it is there to remove unwanted yaw and keep the aircraft in balance. It has been that the rudder is only provided to compensate for the designer's mistakes, and in fact several aircraft without any rudder at all have been successfully built and flown.

▶ Rate of Turn and Turn Radius

The *rate of turn* (the number of degrees which the aircraft turns through in a given time) is affected by both angle of bank and airspeed. The faster the airspeed, the steeper the angle of bank necessary to maintain the same rate of turn. As a rule of thumb, to find the angle of bank required for a 'Rate One' turn – i.e. one in which the aircraft passes through 3° per second and therefore makes a full turn in two minutes – divide the airspeed by 10 and add 7. So at 100 knots, a bank angle of 17° will give a rate one turn; at 450 knots a 52° angle of bank is required to achieve a Rate One turn. *Turn radius* also increases with increasing airspeed.

It follows that both the best rate of turn and the minimum radius of turn occur at the slowest airspeed and highest angle of attack that the aircraft (and pilot) can handle safely.

▶ Cruise Performance

The tables or graphs in the POH/FM for various aspects of in-flight performance (climbing, best range or endurance, descent, etc.) tend to use the same principles as those for calculating take-off and climb performance.

Cruising performance is often the principal criterion around which the aircraft is designed – to fly as far and as fast as possible. The trend in aircraft design used to be simply to use a more powerful engine if more performance was required. This did not always work very well. Increasing engine power by, say, 100hp might only translate to an extra 80hp in practice because at least 20% of the engine power is lost between the engine output and the work done by the propeller. The more powerful engine is heavier and will probably consume more fuel, necessitating extra fuel load and adding still more weight whilst possibly reducing the payload. In short, the performance gain may be quite small for a fair amount of extra expense. In recent years the emphasis has changed to making the engine – and particularly the airframe – more efficient. New composite materials, advanced construction techniques and computer-aided design have led to savings in weight and drag in particular. There are now homebuilt and kitplane designs whose cruise performance easily exceeds that of more established designs with the same engine power.

Apart from the highest cruising airspeed, a common design goal is to give an aircraft the maximum possible range. In a propeller-driven aircraft, maximum range occurs at an angle of attack very close to that at which the wing is also producing the minimum drag, (which is also when the aircraft is flying at the best lift/drag ratio, described in more detail shortly). The best range airspeed can also be found using the 'power required' curve as shown here, and in practice is usually just slightly faster than the minimum drag airspeed. It just so happens that the IAS to give the minimum drag is also the airspeed for best glide range, but herein lies a problem. A pilot who buys an expensive fast touring aircraft capable of cruising in excess of 200mph does not want to fly around all day at the best glide speed of 90mph or so. Hence performance figures tend to be constructed around much faster airspeeds than the aerodynamic ideal. Typically, cruise figures may be given for using 75% power (normally the maximum allowable continuous power setting) 65% and maybe 55% power. Indeed, the propeller and engine combination may be optimised for one of these speeds. The performance figures will normally show the manifold pressure/RPM setting necessary to achieve various percentage powers at different altitudes, and the corresponding TAS, fuel consumption and possibly still-air range (i.e. the range without headwind or tailwind).

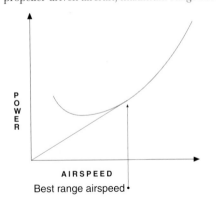

Best range airspeed

Where the tangental line meets the power-required curve, the airspeed for maximum range is found

Cruise performance for a Grumman AA-5. The time/fuel for take-off and climb, and descent and landing, must be allowed for separately

RPM	PRESSURE ALTITUDE 2000 FEET										
	20°C BELOW STD. TEMP				STANDARD TEMP				20°C ABOVE STD. TEMP		
	% BHP	TAS KTS	TAS MPH	FUEL GPH	% BHP	TAS KTS	TAS MPH	FUEL GPH	% BHP	TAS KTS	TAS MPH	FUEL GPH
	−9°C (16°F)				11°C (52°F)				31°C (88°F)			
2700	92	130	150	10.7	87	129	149	10.0	82	129	148	9.5
2600	83	125	143	9.6	79	124	143	9.0	75	123	142	8.6
2500	75	119	137	8.6	71	119	136	8.1	68	118	135	7.7
2400	68	114	131	7.8	65	113	130	7.4	61	111	127	7.0
2300	61	108	124	7.0	58	106	121	6.6	55	103	118	6.3
2200	55	101	116	6.2	52	98	113	5.9	50	96	110	5.7

RPM	PRESSURE ALTITUDE 3000 FEET										
	−11°C (12°F)				9°C (48°F)				29°C (84°F)			
2700	90	130	149	10.4	85	129	149	9.8	80	129	148	9.2
2600	82	125	143	9.4	77	124	142	8.8	73	123	142	8.4
2500	73	119	137	8.4	70	118	136	8.0	66	117	134	7.6
2400	66	113	130	7.6	63	112	129	7.2	60	110	126	6.8
2300	60	107	123	6.8	57	105	121	6.5	54	103	118	6.2
2200	54	100	115	6.1	51	97	112	5.8	50	95	108	5.6

RPM	PRESSURE ALTITUDE 4000 FEET										
	−13°C (9°F)				7°C (45°F)				27°C (81°F)			
2700	88	129	149	10.1	83	129	149	9.6	79	129	148	9.0
2600	80	124	143	9.2	75	124	142	8.6	71	122	141	8.1
2500	72	119	137	8.2	68	118	135	7.8	65	116	133	7.4
2400	65	113	130	7.4	62	111	128	7.0	59	109	125	6.7
2300	59	106	122	6.7	56	103	119	6.3	54	102	117	6.1
2200	52	98	113	5.9	51	96	111	5.7	49	93	107	5.5

Example:

Using the AA-5 table, at 4000ft in ISA conditions (= +7°C), 75% power is achieved at 2600RPM. This gives a TAS of 124kts and a fuel consumption of 8·6 US gal/hr.

As with any other POH figures, the technique necessary to achieve this performance will be stated – including the power settings and fuel-leaning techniques. As usual, to achieve book figures, use book techniques. In some instances failure to use the POH technique can result in fuel consumption 25% greater than the manufacturer's figure.

Here are a few general principles to bear in mind when calculating cruise performance.

Because the POH uses cruising-speed figures which are much faster than aerodynamically ideal, slowing down to somewhere near minimum drag speed will always improve range. This can be useful when, for example, flying at 55% power instead of 75% power may enable a long trip to be completed in one flight rather than having to make a fuel stop. The slower cruise airspeed will be more than compensated for by the time taken to land, refuel and depart at the fuelling stop if using a higher power setting.

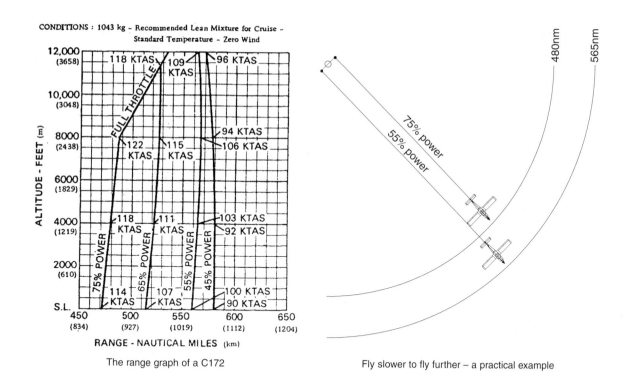

The range graph of a C172

Fly slower to fly further – a practical example

Example:

For a Cessna 172 at 4000ft and 75% power (achieved at 2550RPM and 118kts TAS based on another table in the POH) the still-air range is 480nm. This graph **does** make allowance for taxying, take-off and climb and a 45-minute fuel reserve. Under the same conditions, 55% power (achieved at 2250RPM and 103kts) will give a still-air range of 565nm. So if two identical C172s set-off simultaneously for an airfield 540 nautical miles distant, the one flying at 75% power will have to make a fuel stop and will take at least 5hr 30min to reach the final destination even if the fuel stop is directly *en route*. The aircraft flying at 55% power can make the journey non-stop, completing it in about 5hr 15min and using less fuel.

Leaning technique will make a great difference to fuel consumption. Leaning the mixture has already been discussed in some detail, but it is worth reiterating the fact that leaning to the 'best economy' setting will often decrease fuel consumption significantly whilst reducing speed by only a couple of knots.

Optimum cruising altitude is not merely a case of flying as high as possible to achieve the highest TAS (as a general rule higher altitudes mean a higher TAS for the same IAS). Even with a turbocharged engine capable maintaining maximum power to a much higher altitude than a normally aspirated engine, the fuel consumed in a climb must be considered. And even in still air, increased altitude does not necessarily increase range.

A headwind or tailwind of any significance will have a marked effect on range, which means finding the cruising altitude which offers the greatest tailwind or least headwind. This will vary on a daily basis and can only be found by a survey of the forecast upper winds. A flight computer can be used to find the altitude that will give the fastest groundspeed as follows:

Mark the forecast wind velocity of the possible altitudes on the plotting disk of the flight computer and label them to avoid confusion (no more than three altitudes, separated by at least 2000ft, is best). Now use the POH to find the expected TAS at these altitudes. Place the track at the index mark, and for each altitude place the centre dot over the TAS (wind up) or the wind mark on the TAS line (wind down). One altitude will give the highest groundspeed, assuming that the forecast w/v is accurate! Without a turbocharged engine and oxygen or pressurisation systems, most light aircraft do not fly regularly much above 10,000 feet and the difference in TAS and range for a given power setting is relatively small across the range of usable cruising levels below this level. The difference in headwind or tailwind will usually have a much greater effect on range than the difference in TAS caused by changing cruising altitude by a few thousand feet. Theoretically, the best range airspeed is reduced slightly when flying with a tailwind and increased slightly when flying into a headwind, although this is rarely taken into account in the POH/FM.

As already demonstrated, range increases significantly at a reduced power setting and so a slower cruise airspeed. Anything down to around the best-glide airspeed – that is the best L/D speed – gives the maximum range with or without power. Any other speed reduces range. The choice is with the pilot, but if fuel is short and suitable airfields are far away, flying at best glide airspeed and leaning the mixture as far as possible without rough running will give the maximum range.

When using the POH/FM information to find cruise performance, it is important to check whether or not a suitable fuel reserve is included. The subject of fuel planning and fuel reserves was covered in the Navigation section of PPL 3. Suffice it to say that the best overall move is to carry all the spare fuel possible. It is also wise to adjust cruise performance figures by some sort of safety margin. A good round figure is 10%, so allow for 10% greater fuel consumption than calculated or 10% less range. With this contingency, if a pilot does encounter a stronger than expected headwind, or no tailwind where one was expecting, there is less likelihood of serious problems and wear and tear on the pilot's nerves.

Do, however, check the POH criteria carefully. There is at least one handbook whose graph for range makes no allowance at all for taxying, take-off, climb, descent, landing or reserves! Presumably the pilot is meant to levitate the aeroplane to cruising altitude without using the engine and then complete each flight with a glide approach.

It is also important to appreciate that anything which distorts the shape of the aeroplane – and in particular the wings, can be expected to have an adverse effect on performance. A good example is ice which, if it forms on the aircraft, will reduce lift, increase drag and increase weight. In the vast majority of light aircraft intentional flight in known icing conditions is not permitted. Should the aircaft inadvertently enter icing conditions, descending into warmer air (if safe to do so) is the preferred option. Icing can, of course, also effect the engine in the form of carburettor icing. Most likely to occur at lower power settings, the use of carburettor heat to counter carburettor icing does increase fuel consumption, which might be a factor if flying in carburettor icing conditions and towards the extreme edge of the aircraft's range or endurance.

Occasionally a pilot may wish to fly for maximum endurance – the longest possible *time* spent airborne. Figures for this may be given in the POH/FM, but best endurance airspeed is usually about 25% slower than the best glide-range airspeed. For example, if best glide-range is achieved at 100kts, the best endurance speed will be about 75kts. If this sounds familiar, it is because the minimum-sink glide airspeed (in other words the glide airspeed that allows the aircraft to stay airborne the longest time, even though it doesn't glide as far) is the same. So the maximum endurance airspeed, with or without power, is always the minimum-power-required airspeed and about 75% of the airspeed giving best L/D ratio. The 'endurance' table or graph of a POH/FM is unlikely to recommend flying this slowly, but will instead allow the calculation of endurance at a particular set of conditions.

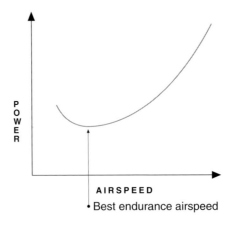

The minimum power-required point marks the airspeed of maximum endurance

P O W E R

AIRSPEED

• Best endurance airspeed

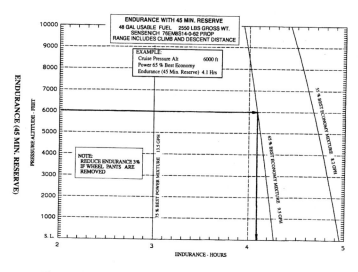

The graph from a POH/FM for calculating maximum endurance

Example:

At 6000ft pressure altitude, and if flying at 65% power with the mixture leaned to best economy setting, the endurance is 4 hours 6 minutes. Reducing to 55% power increases endurance by over 30 minutes, and that the maximum endurance is achieved at the lowest altitude.

There is a story of a radar controller who noticed an unauthorised 'blip' flying around a control zone, obviously lost. Being unable to contact it by radio, he vectored another light aircraft to it to act as a 'shepherd' to lead it to an airfield. The pilot of the shepherd aircraft sighted the lost aircraft and could even tell that it was the same type as he was flying, but even at maximum cruise airspeed he could not catch it. Fortunately the lost aircraft came across an airfield and landed safely. When the pilot was questioned about his turn of speed, he replied that he was flying around at full throttle in order to find somewhere to land quickly before he ran out of fuel! Having appreciated the principles of flying for best range and best endurance, the reader should understand the fundamental flaw in this thinking.

▶ Revision

19   If the control column is moved back, how will angle of attack change?

20   A 'conventional' aircraft in the cruise is producing a download at the horizontal tail. If the CG is moved rearwards, how will this download change to maintain the original flight condition?

21   Why is it normally necessary to apply rudder in the same direction as aileron when rolling into or out-of a turn?

22   If airspeed remains constant, how does rate of descent (ROD) differ between a wings-level descent and a turning descent?

23   On the graph below, describe points 1 and 2

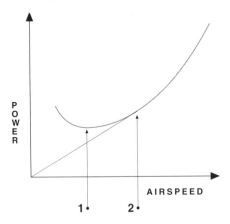

24   An aircraft has a maximum range airspeed of 80 knots. What, approximately, will the maximum endurance airspeed to be?

25   If an aircraft has a minimum drag airspeed of 65 knots, what will the maximum range airspeed to be in relation to this?

26   Using the table below, and assuming a pressure altitude of 3000ft and a temperature of +9°C, find the RPM setting necessary to maintain a minimum groundspeed of 105 knots given a 7 knot headwind component. At this power setting, how much fuel (in litres) will be consumed in the cruise whilst covering a distance of 270 nautical miles. *Do not* include climb/descent allowances, *do not* factor in a 10% safety figure.

RPM	PRESSURE ALTITUDE 2000 FEET											
	20°C BELOW STD. TEMP				STANDARD TEMP				20°C ABOVE STD. TEMP			
	% BHP	TAS KTS	TAS MPH	FUEL GPH	% BHP	TAS KTS	TAS MPH	FUEL GPH	% BHP	TAS KTS	TAS MPH	FUEL GPH
	−9°C (16°F)				11°C (52°F)				31°C (88°F)			
2700	92	130	150	10.7	87	129	149	10.0	82	129	148	9.5
2600	83	125	143	9.6	79	124	143	9.0	75	123	142	8.6
2500	75	119	137	8.6	71	119	136	8.1	68	118	135	7.7
2400	68	114	131	7.8	65	113	130	7.4	61	111	127	7.0
2300	61	108	124	7.0	58	106	121	6.6	55	103	118	6.3
2200	55	101	116	6.2	52	98	113	5.9	50	96	110	5.7
	PRESSURE ALTITUDE 3000 FEET											
	−11°C (12°F)				9°C (48°F)				29°C (84°F)			
2700	90	130	149	10.4	85	129	149	9.8	80	129	148	9.2
2600	82	125	143	9.4	77	124	142	8.8	73	123	142	8.4
2500	73	119	137	8.4	70	118	136	8.0	66	117	134	7.6
2400	66	113	130	7.6	63	112	129	7.2	60	110	126	6.8
2300	60	107	123	6.8	57	105	121	6.5	54	103	118	6.2
2200	54	100	115	6.1	51	97	112	5.8	50	95	108	5.6
	PRESSURE ALTITUDE 4000 FEET											
	−13°C (9°F)				7°C (45°F)				27°C (81°F)			
2700	88	129	149	10.1	83	129	149	9.6	79	129	148	9.0
2600	80	124	143	9.2	75	124	142	8.6	71	122	141	8.1
2500	72	119	137	8.2	68	118	135	7.8	65	116	133	7.4
2400	65	113	130	7.4	62	111	128	7.0	59	109	125	6.7
2300	59	106	122	6.7	56	103	119	6.3	54	102	117	6.1
2200	52	98	113	5.9	51	96	111	5.7	49	93	107	5.5

Fuel consumption is given in US gallons per hour (GPH)

Answers page fpp74

Flight Performance and Planning

Descent and Landing Performance

L/D Ratio
10:1

Flight Performance and Planning
Descent and Landing Performance

▶ Principles of Descending

▶ Gliding Performance

▶ Sideslipping

▶ The Powered Descent

▶ Minimum Sink Glide

▶ 'Stretching' the Glide

▶ Controlling the Approach

▶ The Landing

▶ Ground Effect

▶ Calculating Landing Performance

▶ Revision

Descent and Landing Performance

▶ Principles of Descending

An aircraft will fly level when power set is equal to power required for that airspeed. It will climb when power set is greater than power required. It follows that if power set is less than power required, the aircraft will descend.

In this discussion of descending we will look primarily at gliding – which for training purposes means descending with the engine throttled right back to idle. As thrust has been reduced or removed altogether, the aircraft must descend so that a component of mass acts in the same direction as thrust would, to overcome drag. The higher the airspeed required, the steeper the descent must be to provide a greater component of mass along the thrust line.

In a glide descent, a component of mass replaces thrust

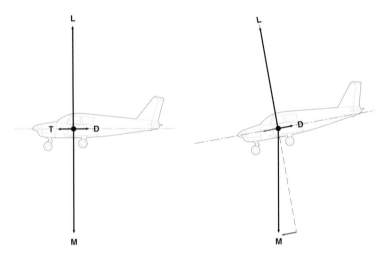

▶ Gliding Performance

The gliding efficiency of an aircraft is based on its aerodynamic efficiency, in particular a figure known as the lift/drag (L/D) ratio. This is found by dividing the coefficient of lift (CL) by the coefficient of drag (CD) at each angle of attack. The wing is most efficient at the angle of attack which gives the maximum ratio of lift to drag. On the graph below, the maximum L/D ratio is 10. This means that at this angle of attack the wing is producing 10 units of lift for every one unit of drag. In this particular case, this 'peak' occurs at 5° angle of attack. At any other angle of attack, the wing is operating less efficiently.

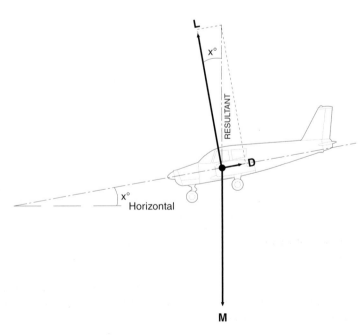

In the glide, the ratio of lift to drag determines the glide angle

When operating at the best L/D ratio, the aircraft will have the shallowest glide angle and thus the maximum glide range. A pilot does not usually have an angle-of-attack indicator in the cockpit. Instead the POH/FM will state an airspeed at which the best L/D ratio occurs under certain conditions (including, usually, maximum mass).

A knowledge of the L/D ratio can be used to predict gliding performance. For example, a L/D ratio of 10:1 means that the aircraft will travel 10 units forward for every one unit descent, i.e. for every 10 feet travelled horizontally it will descend one foot. So in this particular case, if the aircraft were at 1000ft AGL in still-air conditions, it could glide 10,000ft forward (a little less than two nautical miles assuming 6082ft to a nautical mile) before reaching the ground.

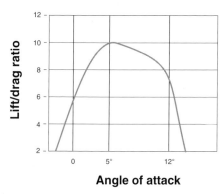

The Lift/Drag ratio plotted against angle of attack

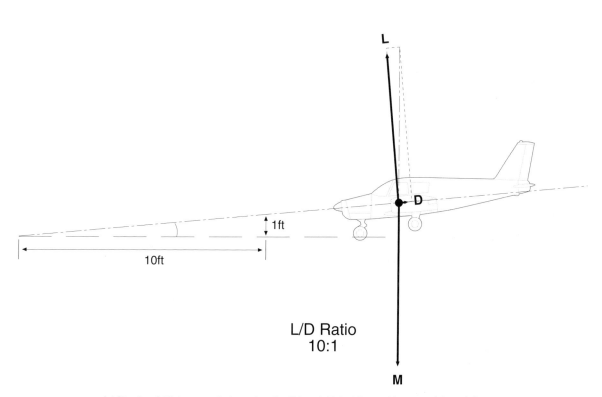

A L/D ratio of 10:1 means that an aircraft will travel 10 feet forward for every 1 foot of descent

Of course, still air conditions are a rarity and probably the most significant factor in glide range is the wind. A tailwind makes the glide angle more shallow, increasing gliding range. A headwind makes the glide angle steeper, reducing gliding range. In neither case does the rate of descent (ROD) change, so the aircraft still reaches the ground in the same time. But the overall distance covered will differ significantly. For example, a typical general-aviation tourer with a still-air glide range of 3nm from 2000ft (implying a L/D ratio of 9:1, based on 6000ft in a nautical mile) would have a glide range of 2·2nm if gliding into a 20-knot headwind, or 3·75nm with a 20-knot tailwind. In principle, glide performance can be improved by increasing speed slightly when flying into a headwind and decreasing speed slightly when gliding with a tailwind. However, POH/FMs rarely give the necessary figures and very few powered-aircraft pilots adopt this practice except in very strong winds.

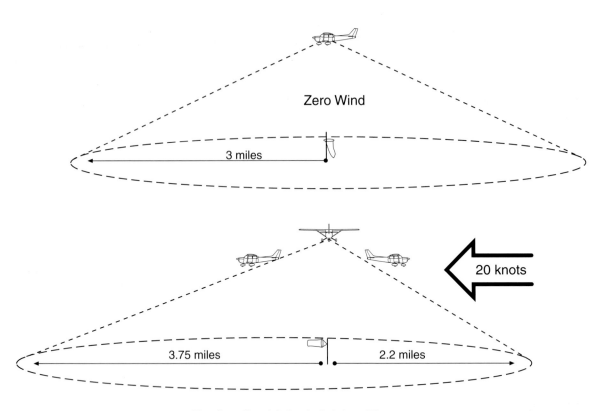

The effect of headwind and tailwind on glide range

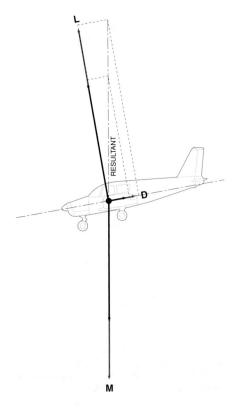

Aircraft mass, surprisingly, does not affect gliding range. The L/D ratio is achieved at a specific angle of attack: provided the pilot flies at that angle of attack, the aircraft will fly just as far whether it weighs 1000kg or 10,000kg. What does change is the glide airspeed; a heavier aircraft will have a higher airspeed at a given angle of attack than a lighter one. In practice, given the small range of practical weights for a General Aviation (GA) aircraft, the difference is not measurable. For this reason, gliding airspeed is usually quoted for just the maximum weight. Glide performance is dictated purely by L/D ratio, and in fact a modern airliner weighing hundreds of tonnes can glide further from the same altitude than an average club tourer by virtue of its greater aerodynamic efficiency. However, the airliner will be flying at a much higher airspeed.

Weight affects glide airspeed but not the L/D ratio and so glide range is unchanged. However, the heavier aircraft must fly faster to attain the same L/D ratio

Lowering flap in the descent increases lift, at the expense of increased drag. Most aircraft achieve their best glide performance with a 'clean' wing – in other words with no flap lowered. Unless the aircraft's POH/FM specifically states otherwise, assume that the maximum glide range is obtained without using any flap. Where flap is useful in a descent is to steepen the glide angle without increasing airspeed; in effect flaps are used to worsen the lift/drag ratio. Thus flaps come into their own when landing on a short runway, and/or a runway with obstacles on the approach. As more flap is lowered, the glide angle becomes steeper without the airspeed increasing. Some aircraft POH/FMs recommend different gliding speeds for a 'clean' glide or a glide with flap, invariably the 'flaps lowered' gliding speed is slower, and the glide range is reduced.

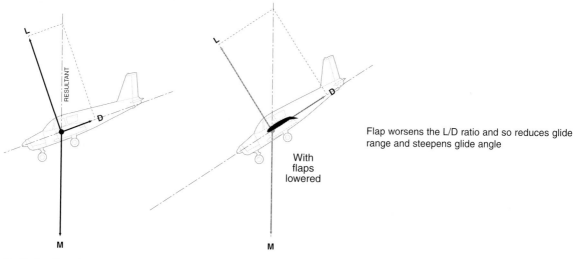

With flaps lowered

Flap worsens the L/D ratio and so reduces glide range and steepens glide angle

▶ Sideslipping

Early aircraft types, and indeed many modern light aircraft, have no flaps. This leaves the pilot with the problem of steepening the glide without incurring excessive airspeed – which as extra kinetic energy has to be bled-off when the aircraft levels out (e.g. in the flare for landing). The solution is a much-neglected manoeuvre known as the *sideslip*. Sideslipping basically amounts to flying sideways. In a descent it implies deliberately flying the aircraft grossly out of balance, usually by applying bank in one direction and then 'opposite' or 'top' rudder so that the aircraft descends in a straight line (although slipping turns are also possible, and can be extremely useful for losing a lot of height very quickly). The extra drag caused by flying the aircraft out-of-balance worsens the L/D ratio, so the glide angle will steepen without the airspeed increasing. Sideslipping is a simple manoeuvre well worth practising with an instructor, but a few points should be borne in mind:

- ■ check the aircraft's POH/FM to ensure that sideslipping, particularly with flaps lowered, is permitted.

- ■ avoid steep angles of bank and excessive slipping, which will lead to a very high rate of descent. When recovering to balanced flight, the energy of the aircraft in a steep descent may translate into extra airspeed – which can be embarrassing on a short runway.

- ■ out-of-balance flight can cause significant errors in the airspeed indicator (ASI) reading. It is normally necessary to pitch down in a sideslip to maintain a safe airspeed.

- ■ if fuel levels are low, an excessive slip or skid could uncover the inlet pipe in a fuel tank, leaving the engine without fuel.

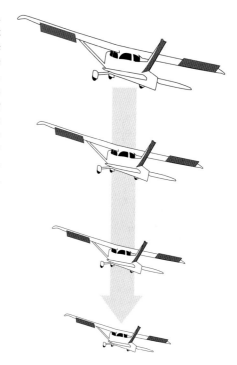

Using a sideslip to worsen the L/D ratio and so steepen the glide angle without increasing airspeed. Some aircraft have restrictions regarding sideslipping – especially with flap extended

▶The Powered Descent

So far we have considered the descent in terms of gliding, with no significant engine power applied. If engine power is used in the descent, it has the effect of reducing the angle of descent if the best glide airspeed (angle of attack) is maintained. The more power applied, the more shallow the descent – until the aircraft reaches level flight. Most descents are, in fact, carried out with a degree of power set. This is not only kinder to the engine (and passengers) but also a more practical way of flying the aircraft because it gives the pilot more control over the aircraft's flightpath. Typically, you might be approaching the destination airfield and wish to descend to circuit height. By reducing the power by about 20% from the normal cruising setting, and pitching down to maintain the cruising airspeed, the pilot should achieve a reasonable rate of descent without sacrificing speed or allowing the engine to cool too quickly – sudden cooling is exceedingly bad for air-cooled engines. As a rule of thumb for a typical 'cruise' descent, the point to start the descent (known as 'top-of-descent') is found by taking the amount of descent in thousands of feet and multiplying by three to give distance in nautical miles required to make a cruise descent. For example, to descend from 6000ft to 1000ft is a total descent of 5000ft. Five times three is 15, so the descent should be started 15nm from where the pilot wants to be at 1000ft. It is important to remember the effect of wind. A tailwind will cause a more shallow descent, so start the descent earlier; a headwind will cause a steeper descent, requiring the descent to be started later. If working in minutes, take the descent required in thousands of feet, then multiply by 2 (for a 500ft/min ROD) to give the time required for the descent. The result is the number of minutes at which to start the descent before ETA at the destination.

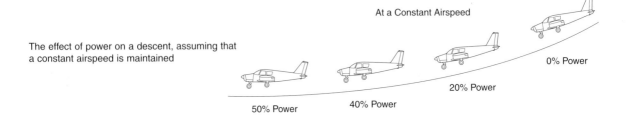

At a Constant Airspeed

The effect of power on a descent, assuming that a constant airspeed is maintained

0% Power

20% Power

50% Power   40% Power

▶Minimum Sink Glide

Occasionally a pilot might want to glide for the minimum rate of descent (i.e. maximum time airborne) rather than the best range. The minimum sink will occur at the minimum-power-required airspeed, which will normally be about 25% slower than the normal glide airspeed. At the minimum-sink airspeed, the aircraft will have the minimum ROD at the expense of reduced glide range. This is an important point, worth repeating. Maximum glide range will **only** occur at the best glide-angle airspeed (this is usually the *only* glide airspeed quoted in a light aircraft POH/FM). An airspeed slower than this may reduce the *rate* of descent, but only at the expense of a steeper glide angle, and hence a reduced gliding range.

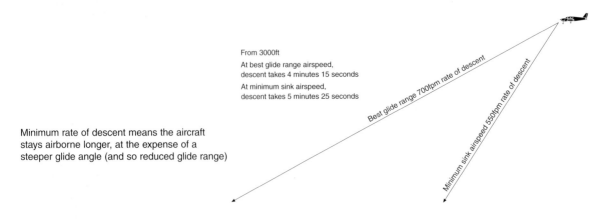

From 3000ft
At best glide range airspeed,
descent takes 4 minutes 15 seconds
At minimum sink airspeed,
descent takes 5 minutes 25 seconds

Best glide range 700fpm rate of descent

Minimum sink airspeed 550fpm rate of descent

Minimum rate of descent means the aircraft stays airborne longer, at the expense of a steeper glide angle (and so reduced glide range)

▶ 'Stretching' the Glide

Attempting to 'stretch' a glide – by pitching the aircraft nose up and so reducing airspeed below the best glide-range speed – is a classic aerodynamic trap. At the increased angle of attack, the L/D ratio is actually worse, the aircraft descends more steeply and slows down; pitching nose up further only steepens the glide more. Eventually the aircraft either reaches the surface short of its target or (worse still) the wing reaches the stalling angle of attack and stalls – at which point an excessive rate of descent is inevitable, and loss of control of the aircraft in a spin is possible.

It is worth restating here that the basic maxim of Power + Attitude = Performance still applies for a normal powered descent. If there is no power (i.e. the aircraft is in a pure glide) it is all the more important to fly at the correct angle of attack (seen by the pilot as indicated airspeed) in order to obtain the maximum possible performance. Despite their name, the elevators cannot 'elevate' the aircraft. Their primary purpose is to control the angle of attack of the wing.

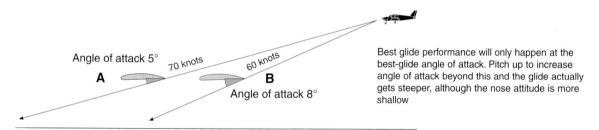

Best glide performance will only happen at the best-glide angle of attack. Pitch up to increase angle of attack beyond this and the glide actually gets steeper, although the nose attitude is more shallow

▶ Controlling the Approach

The approach is merely a descent, usually with flap and power. However, the need to reach the ground at a specific point adds an extra requirement to control of the aircraft's performance and airspeed and flightpath control has to be more precise than at other stages of flight, particularly if the aircraft is landing on a relatively short runway.

We have already established that airspeed is controlled by angle of attack, which is itself controlled through the control column. The maintenance of level flight – or rate of climb or descent – is governed by power, set by means of the throttle. The problem is that trying to control an aircraft by making these two operations into totally separate actions is not a practical approach to flying smoothly, not least when aiming to control both airspeed and flightpath to a high standard of accuracy.

Let's go back to straight and level flight. From a stable cruise, pitch the aircraft nose-up. Naturally the airspeed will reduce. What will also happen is that the aircraft will start to climb, because at the slower airspeed there is now an excess of power set over power required for level flight. This is perfectly normal and, and for altering altitude in the cruise by less than 100ft or so, a perfectly acceptable way to maintain a constant level. Much more so, in fact, than making constant power changes to adjust the level. Likewise, if the airspeed in the cruise in a little slower than target and the aircraft is flying at a constant level, the power is below the 'nominal' setting (and that the angle of attack and nose attitude are a little higher than normal). The first action should be to increase the power setting to that required. This will cause the aircraft to climb, so the pilot selects a lower nose attitude (meaning a reduced angle of attack) to stay at the chosen level and allow the aircraft to accelerate to the target airspeed.

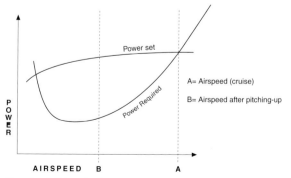

From level flight, pitching up will cause a climb because at the lower airspeed there is an excess of power set over power required for level flight

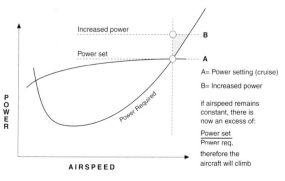

From level flight an increase in power will lead to a higher airspeed only if the angle of attack is reduced, otherwise the aircraft will climb

After a while this becomes an almost sub-conscious series of actions to maintain accurate flight. Minor excursions in level and airspeed are not significant when there is plenty of both to spare. But the clear message is that **both** power **and** attitude alter **both** flightpath **and** airspeed, even if the change lasts only a few seconds. In other words, **power + attitude = performance**.

In basic training, an instructor will say that a certain power setting and attitude will give the correct airspeed and rate of descent for example:

power (1600RPM) + **attitude** (nose 15cm/6in below the horizon with one stage of flap) = **performance** (descent at 500 feet per minute and airspeed 65 knots).

One of the basic properties of this simple formula is that to maintain the desired performance, an alteration in *either* power *or* attitude will necessitate an alteration in the other as well. So now imagine an aircraft on final approach. It is on the desired glidepath at the correct rate of descent, but the airspeed is 10 knots too slow. So:

■ the pilot pitches the aircraft nose-down to a lower attitude (implying a reduced angle of attack) to accelerate to the correct airspeed. This is vital.

However, now the aircraft will have an increased rate of descent, and will descend below the desired glidepath. So:

■ this increased rate of descent needs to be corrected by increased power, the pilot increases the throttle setting.

Again: Power + Attitude = Performance.

In the early stages of training, a student pilot will probably carry out the first action followed a short while later by the second. An instructor – by virtue of greater experience – will do the two things simultaneously, and probably won't wait for a large-scale reduction in airspeed either. Which action, if any, comes first in this case is academic. However, instructors are prone to say "stick (control column) for airspeed, power for height"

There are three principal reasons why light aircraft instructors are so keen this mantra.

The first is that at the slower airspeed of the approach, good speed control is more important than it is in the cruise. If the airspeed is critically slow, pitching nose-down is a safe option as it reduces the wing loading (thereby reducing the stalling speed) in addition to reducing angle of attack and increasing airspeed. Conversely a sudden increase in power could destabilise the aircraft, especially in yaw, which this is not a good thing at slow airspeed. Moreover, an aircraft can stall irrespective of power setting, whereas it can **only** stall at the stalling angle of attack (e.g. usually with the control column too far back).

A second reason for controlling airspeed with the control column is that in the event of a problem with the engine, or a total power loss, the control column is the only influence the pilot has over airspeed. In emergency situations, pilots tend to revert to the behaviour they have trained for and know best. If a pilot has been trained to increase airspeed by increasing power, he will probably instinctively push in the throttle forwards, even if he knows that the engine has failed. Additionally, most light aircraft are relatively low-powered and may not have enough available to fly out of a critically slow-airspeed situation (on the back of the power curve) using throttle alone.

Finally, it is worth mentioning that in a situation of slow airspeed, instinctively pitching nose-down is also consistent with the standard stall recovery learned by most pilots in Exercise 10.

All in all, 'Attitude for Airspeed, Power for Height' is considered the safe technique when flying a powered approach in a light aircraft. However, considered in terms of power plus attitude equals performance, the pilot should come to regard the attitude and the power as factors to be adjusted together in order to achieve the desired performance (airspeed and flightpath), rather than two totally separate operations in flying the aircraft. One essential ingredient in making the technique work is *anticipation*. This means making small adjustments of power and attitude as soon as a minor airspeed/flightpath excursion is apparent rather than waiting until a major correction is required. Experience is a great aid in recognising when the aircraft is no longer in the right place and making a correction whilst the power/attitude change needed is still minor.

▶The Landing

A good approach should lead to an aircraft arriving over the runway at the correct airspeed and on the desired flightpath. From here the objectives are simple; to decelerate the aircraft to the point where it can land safely, to touch down in a controlled manner and proper attitude, to bring the aircraft to a stop or safe taxying speed, and to do all this within the confines of the runway!

The flare and hold-off

The first phase of the landing is the *flare*, in which the aircraft transitions from the descent to a flightpath parallel to the runway and a few feet above it. Now the throttle is closed, but the aircraft is pitched nose up (increasing angle of attack) to keep it airborne. This stage is the *hold-off*, during which the pilot slowly pitches the aircraft nose-up (increasing the angle of attack) to keep the aircraft flying level above the runway. Angle of attack increases and airspeed decreases until the aircraft sinks gently on to the runway a few knots above the stall speed, the mainwheels contacting first with the nosewheel still clear of the ground. As the nosewheel is lowered to the runway (to allow steering and improve the view ahead) the rolling friction of the wheels and the brakes slow the aircraft to a safe speed. It is worth noting that at light-aircraft landing speeds the aerodynamic drag from flaps etc. is not as effective at slowing the aircraft as braking.

▶Ground Effect

In the flare and hold-off stage of the landing, ground effect becomes evident again. By reducing drag, ground effect reduces the aircraft's deceleration to touchdown speed. The reduced power required also permits the aircraft to fly down to a slower airspeed than if outside ground effect. Ground effect is not really noticeable as such because it occurs during every landing, so the pilot's reflexes naturally adjust to it. Beware, however, of not reducing power enough in the flare, or of not using full flap when landing on a short runway. At average light-aircraft landing speeds, an extra five seconds of 'float' in ground effect can easily consume an extra 150m of runway.

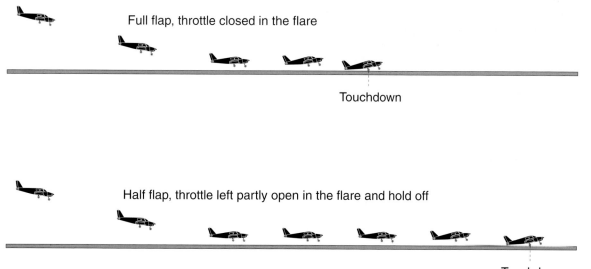

Leaving excess power set during the flare, and using less than full flap, will lengthen the landing distance markedly

▶Calculating Landing Performance

Rather like take-off performance, landing performance can be divided into two parts:

- the *initial approach* – the point from 50ft above the runway to touchdown, and
- the *ground roll* (or *ground run*) – the point from touchdown to reaching a full stop.

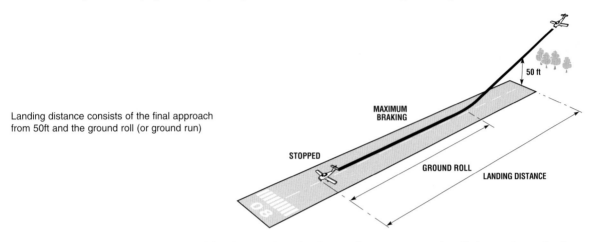

Landing distance consists of the final approach from 50ft and the ground roll (or ground run)

In general terms, somewhat similar considerations apply to landing performance as to take-off. Attempting to land an aircraft on a runway where the landing distance **available** is shorter than the landing distance **required** will sooner or later lead to broken aircraft and holes in airfield boundary fences.

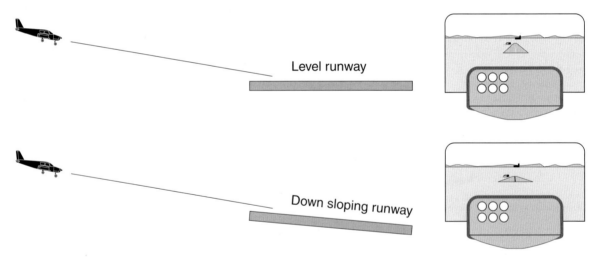

The visual illusion when approaching a downsloping runway, despite being on the correct glidepath, the aircraft appears to be low approaching the downsloping runway

An important determinant of landing distance is braking effectiveness. Any factor that reduces the efficiency of the brakes or makes directional control more difficult (crosswinds, slippery runways, soft ground etc.) will increase landing distance significantly. One factor well worth considering in more detail is runway slope. When landing, runway downslope increases landing distance and upslope reduces landing distance. Moreover, a sloping runway gives a visual illusion to a pilot on approach that the aircraft is higher or lower than is actually the case. To the pilot, an approach to an upsloping runway appears to be too high even if on the correct glideslope; the approach to a downsloping runway appears too low. This can lead to the aircraft arriving over the runway too high, at the wrong airspeed or at the wrong descent angle, with a consequent increase in landing distance. The effect of such an optical illusion is a common feature of 'over-run' accidents.

Aircraft mass (weight) is a determinant of stall speed (a lighter aircraft stalls more slowly than a heavier one), and as approach speeds are set by reference to stall speed in the landing configuration, this has a bearing on landing performance. Once again we are back to the POH/FM: know the recommended approach and landing speeds and configurations and use them. Approaching too fast leads to longer landing distances; approaching too slowly leads to the graveyard. As a general guide, the approach speed is usually around 1.3 x Vso (Vso = the stall speed in the landing configuration). So a Vso stall speed of 50 knots infers an approach speed of around 65 knots (50 x 1.3). The approach speed can go under various pseudonyms, including Vref, Vapp and even Vat (Velocity at Threshold).

As with take-off performance, POH/FMs vary in the amount of information they give for calculating landing performance and in particular the factors to be used for variable conditions. In the absence of a factor for a specific condition, the landing-distance factor table published by the CAA gives some guidance. Again, it may be necessary to memorise this table for exam purposes, but in real life the table (published in an Aeronautical Information Circular – AIC) should be consulted.

Condition	Percentage increase in landing distance	Factor
1000ft increase in runway elevation	5%	1·05
10°C increase in temperature	5%	1·05
10% increase in aircraft weight	10%	1·1
Runway downslope 2%	10%	1·1
A wet, paved runway	15%	1.15
Dry Grass on firm soil (grass up to 20cm/8in)	15%	1·15
Tailwind component 10% of landing speed	20%	1·2
Soft ground or snow	At least 25%	At least 1·25
Wet Grass on firm soil (grass up to 20cm/8in)*	35%	1·35

*If the grass is very short, the surface may become slippery and landing distance may be increased by up to 60%, giving a factor of 1·6.

The methods of calculating landing performance are the same as those for working out take-off and cruise performance. In the case of landing, the overall safety factor (mandatory for public-transport flights and highly recommended for private flights) is 43%, or 1·43.

Example: The aircraft's POH/FM gives a landing distance of 900ft on a dry, level hard runway in nil wind and ISA sea-level conditions. If no other variables are accounted for in the POH/FM, find the landing distance when the pressure altitude is 760ft, the temperature is +20°C and the runway has a 1% downslope.

Clearly some of the variables do not exactly fit into those in the CAA table. A calculator can be used to average the figures or they can be 'rounded-up' to the variable to the nearest figure in the table. Rounding up to the nearest figure in the CAA table would produce a calculation like this:

> 900 x 1·05 (1000ft pressure altitude) x 1·05 (ISA temperature +10°C) x 1·1 (2% downslope) x 1·.43
> (safety factor) = 1560ft or 475m.

Using a calculator to average the variables produce a calculation like this:

A 1000ft increase in pressure altitude increases landing distance by 5%. (5/1000) = 0·005%; multiplying this by 760 gives 3·8%. Therefore multiplying the landing distance given by 1·038 to find the exact factor at 760ft pressure altitude. Continuing in this vein;

> 900 x 1·038 (760ft pressure altitude) x 1·0325 (ISA temperature + 6.5°C) x 1·05 (1% downslope) x 1·43
> (safety factor) = 1448ft or 441m.

This final result is just 34m less than the figure obtained by rounding-up to the nearest variable. It is best to regard this 34m as a little extra safety margin for the sake of a much easier calculation.

As for take-off performance, the POH/FM may include a graph for calculating landing performance:

Example:

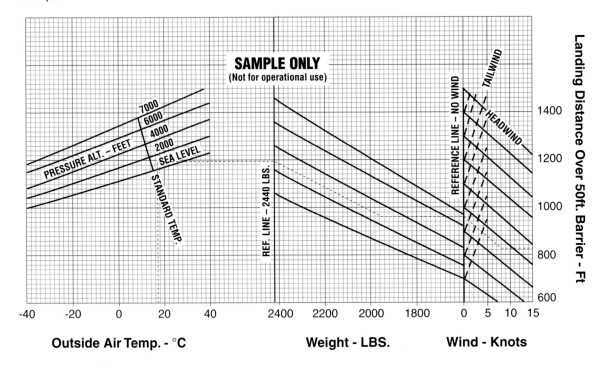

Given a pressure altitude of 1250ft, a temperature of +17°C, a weight of 1950lb and a headwind of 8kts (assume the headwind/tailwind *has* been factored as recommended by the CAA), find the landing distance.

Starting at the temperature of +17°C, go vertically to the 1250ft pressure altitude. From this point go horizontally to the weight reference line, then move parallel to the guide lines until over the weight of 1950lb. From this point, go horizontally to the wind reference line, then parallel the headwind guidelines until over the 8-knot headwind point. Go from here horizontally to the far side and read off the landing distance of 830ft. Multiplying this by the safety factor of 1·43 to give the final figure of 1187ft or 362m.

The POH/FM may also give landing performance as a table.

Example:

Using the table below, find the landing distance on a dry, grass runway, at 1000ft and temperature 10°C, with a 4-knot headwind component.

LANDING DISTANCE				FLAPS LOWERED TO 40° – POWER OFF HARD SURFACE RUNWAY – ZERO WIND					
GROSS WEIGHT	APPROACH SPEED,	AT SEA LEVEL & 15°C/59°F		AT 2500 FT. & 10°C/50°F.		AT 5000 FT. & 5°C/41°F.		AT 7500 FT. & 0°C/32°F.	
		GROUND ROLL	TOTAL TO CLEAR 50 FT. OBS.	GROUND ROLL	TOTAL TO CLEAR 50 FT. OBS.	GROUND ROLL	TOTAL TO CLEAR 50 FT. OBS.	GROUND ROLL	TOTAL TO CLEAR 50 FT. OBS.
1600	60	445	1075	470	1135	495	1195	520	1255

NOTES 1. Decrease the distances shown by 10% for each 4 knots of headwind.
2. Increase the distance by 10% for each 60°F. temperature increase above standard.
3. For operation on a dry, grass runway, increase distances (both "ground roll" and "total to clear 50 ft. obstacle") by 20% of the "total to clear 50 ft. obstacle" figure.

The runway altitude and temperature do not fall exactly into the table, so the next highest figure (that for 2500ft and 10°C) is taken – 1135ft.

1135ft is decreased by 10% for the headwind (see Notes): 1135 x 0·90 = 1021·5ft

1021·5ft is increased by 20% for the dry grass surface (see Notes):
1021·5 x 1.2 = 1225·8ft

1225·8ft x 1·43 (safety factor) = 1753ft or 531m

The practical aspects of obtaining the best landing performance begin with the usual advice that to achieve book figures, the pilot must use book techniques. In particular, the flap setting and airspeed stated are crucial to achieving the best landing performance. Invariably the POH will recommend using full flap for best landing performance – this allows a steeper approach, more drag (and so greater deceleration) and the slowest touchdown speed. Using anything less than full flap will increase landing distance required.

A common error is to approach at too fast an airspeed. The POH/FM will give the approach airspeed; this will be based on the stalling airspeed in the landing configuration and the usual factor is 1·3 x the stalling speed in the landing configuration, although the exact figure will be given in the POH/FM. The pilot may find a speed called the V_{AT} (Velocity At Threshold), or more correctly V_{REF}, or more colloquially the 'speed over the hedge' or 'speed over the numbers'. The V_{REF} speed may be quoted in the POH/FM, but in a light aircraft it is often very close to the approach speed. In any case, the aircraft should be stabilised at this V_{REF} airspeed before reaching the point 50ft above the runway, and this is particularly important for a 'short field' landing. Landing-performance calculations allow for a controlled deceleration from this airspeed to the touchdown speed in the remaining 50ft of height. If an aircraft arrives at the 50ft point with excess speed, it is in effect carrying excess kinetic energy. Kinetic energy increases as the square of speed, so a final approach speed 10% faster than expected will increase landing distance by at least 21%.

The other common piloting error is to arrive over the threshold too high. The landing distance required assumes that the aircraft arrives over the landing runway at 50ft. At an average descent gradient, every 1ft above this ideal adds about 20ft to the landing distance. Clearly no pilot is perfect, and flying to within a foot of altitude at a specified point is not a practical proposition – hence the need for the safety margin. Nevertheless, in the last few hundred feet of the approach, most pilots can make a good guess at their likely touchdown point. As a rule of thumb, when landing on a short runway the pilot should aim to touch down well within the first third of it. Any later than this and there is no guarantee that the brakes will be able to stop the aircraft before the end of the runway.

When landing on a 'short' runway, aim to touch down no later than one third into the runway

Aim to touchdown no later than in the first third of the runway

'Over-run' accidents on runways long enough for the aircraft are far more common on landing than on take-off, because of the greater number of variables introduced by piloting technique. In many over-run accidents, the aircraft was high and/or fast on approach, and landed fast and well beyond the one-third point of the runway. Clearly an early decision to go around would have averted such accidents. Moreover, a great number of over-run accidents – perhaps the majority – occur on runways which are simply too short for the aircraft attempting to land.

Once on the ground, braking technique is all-important. Ensure that the throttle is fully closed – there may be some residual power at touchdown – and apply the brakes evenly to the maximum extent possible without locking the wheels. If necessary, modulate the braking pressure to keep the wheels turning. Braking pressure can usually be increased as speed reduces, again as far as possible without locking the wheels. A locked wheel gives *less* deceleration than one under full, proper braking. It is usually safe to allow the nosewheel to contact the runway quite early in the landing run to aid steering, although the control column should still be used to keep pressure off the nosewheel. This will help protect it from damage on a rough surface and keep the maximum force pressing down on the mainwheels, improving the braking action.

It is sometimes said that raising the flaps on landing increases brake effectiveness by reducing the wing lift and putting more weight on the wheels. This may be true to a small extent, but raising the flaps also reduces drag which has some effect in slowing the aircraft. More importantly, fiddling about with the flap lever can detract from the primary task of controlling the aircraft, and if the machine has a retractable undercarriage it is remarkably easy to raise the undercarriage instead of the flaps! This type of accident happens to impatient pilots every year.

Above all, having established that the runway is long enough for the aircraft, the key to successful landings on short runways is *practice and currency*. A pilot who usually operates from 2000m tarmac runways and hasn't done a short-field landing for years, is asking for trouble by planning to land on a sloping 400m wet grass runway surrounded by obstacles. Likewise, some aircraft are better than others at dealing with short and rough runways; the closer to the aircraft's performance limits, the less margin for error in piloting technique.

▶ Revision

27   When gliding at the angle of attack for maximum glide range, an aircraft has a L/D ratio of 9 (i.e. it is producing 9 units of lift for every 1 unit of drag). What (approximately) will its still-air glide range be from a height of 6000ft AGL?

28   How does aircraft weight affect glide range?

29   During the landing, at what height will ground effect become significant for an aircraft with a wing span of 35ft?

30   In the absence of a POH/FM figure, if an aircraft has a stalling speed in the landing configuration of 50kts, what will the anticipated approach speed be?

31   If landing on wet grass (up to 20cm/8in long), what CAA factor should be applied to the landing distance required?

32   According to CAA figures, what will be the effect of a tailwind of 10% of lift-off speed upon landing distance?

33   Using the table below, decide if a safe landing can be made in the following circumstances:

LANDING DISTANCE					SHORT FIELD						
CONDITIONS :	Flaps 40°	Power off		Maximum braking		Paved, Level, Dry runway		Zero wind			
WEIGHT	IAS	PRESSURE ALTITUDE		0°C / 32°F		10°C / 50°F		20°C / 68°F		30°C / 86°F		40°C / 104°F	
	At 15M (50ft)	FT	M	GROUND ROLL M	TOTAL TO CLEAR 15M OBS. M	GROUND ROLL M	TOTAL TO CLEAR 15M OBS. M	GROUND ROLL M	TOTAL TO CLEAR 15M OBS. M	GROUND ROLL M	TOTAL TO CLEAR 15M OBS. M	GROUND ROLL M	TOTAL TO CLEAR 15M OBS. M
1043kg	111km/h	Sea Level		151	367	155	376	162	386	166	395	172	405
	60kt	1000	305	155	376	162	386	168	396	172	405	178	416
	69mph	2000	610	162	386	168	396	174	407	180	418	186	428
		3000	914	168	396	174	407	180	418	186	428	192	439
		4000	1219	174	407	183	418	187	430	194	440	200	451
		5000	1524	180	418	187	431	194	442	200	453	207	465
		6000	1829	187	431	195	443	201	454	209	468	215	479
		7000	2134	195	443	201	456	209	468	216	480	223	492
		8000	2438	203	457	210	469	216	482	224	494	232	507

NOTES :
1.
2.
3.

Aircraft weight 1043kg;

Runway 24 – elevation 1500ft pressure altitude, temperature +15°C, runway surface dry grass, 2% downslope, Landing Distance Available 700m

Surface Wind calm.

Use CAA figures for any factors not found in the table. Assume that the table does not include the recommended 1·43 landing distance safety factor.

34   The runway is 1050ft long, it is paved, dry and level. Temperature is +20°C, pressure altitude is 1000ft. The aircraft weighs 2400lbs. Assuming that the table below *does* include the recommended safety factor of 1·43, what is the minimum headwind component required to make a safe landing on this runway?

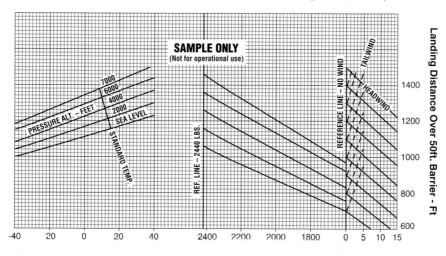

Answers at page fpp74

Flight Performance and Planning
Runway Dimensions

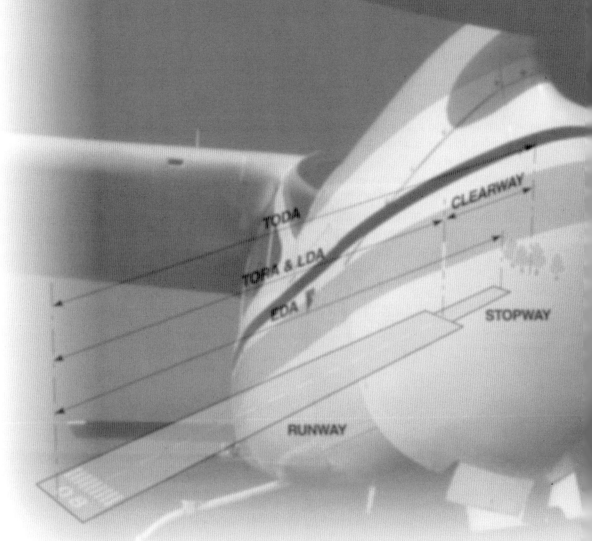

Flight Performance and Planning
Runway Dimensions

▶ Runway Dimensions

▶ Revision

Runway Dimensions

▶ Runway Dimensions

If an airfield is listed in an Aeronautical Information Publication (AIP) its runways will probably have been measured and inspected by authority personnel. They will be interested not just in the runway itself, but also the area surrounding the runway, and in particular the surface and obstacles in the undershoot and overrun areas. Additionally, at licensed airfields in the UK, CAA specify dimensions for the areas to each side of the runway as well as the undershoot and overrun areas. The basic concepts are important.

The length of runway available for the take-off run is the *Take-Off Run Available (TORA)*. This distance often coincides with actual length of the runway itself.

Beyond the end of TORA may be a *stopway*. A stopway is an area of ground where the aircraft can be safely brought to a halt in an emergency. The stopway should be clear of obstructions that could damage the aircraft.

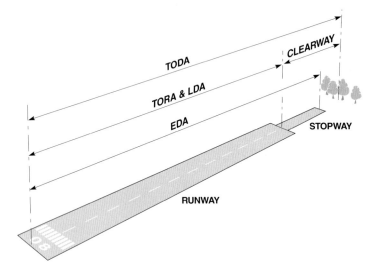

The definitions of the runway and surrounds

The area beyond the TORA over which the aircraft can climb to 50ft is the *clearway*. The clearway will include the stopway and any additional surface cleared of obstructions over which the aircraft can safely climb. As a general rule, the clearway will only extend as far as the airfield boundary and in any case the maximum clearway accounted for is no more than 50% of the TORA distance.

The TORA plus the stopway distance is the *Emergency Distance Available (EDA)*

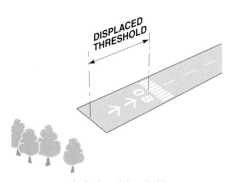

A displaced threshold

The TORA plus the clearway distance (which includes the stopway) is known as the *Take-Off Distance Available (TODA)*. The calculated take-off distance required should never be more than the TODA if a safe take-off is to be made.

The length of runway available for the landing run is the *Landing Distance Available (LDA)*. The LDA is calculated assuming that the landing aircraft arrives over the runway threshold at 50ft. If there is some obstacle high enough to endanger a landing aircraft in the area approaching the landing runway, the runway threshold will be *displaced* and the LDA will be reduced accordingly. A displaced threshold allows the landing aircraft to make an approach high enough to clear obstacles in the approach path.

RWY	Surface	TORA	LDA	Lighting
03/21	Grass	480	480	Nil
14	Grass	598	598	Nil
32	Grass	610	540	Nil

Runway distances as listed in the UK VFR Flight Guide

The TORA, TODA, EDA and LDA for a runway will be listed in the AIP, and this document (as updated and amended) is the primary reference for runway length information. Commercially produced flight guides will also list some or all of these distances. The situation is not so well defined at the small airfields and airstrips not listed in the AIP. Here a pilot may have to rely on very basic information concerning runway lengths and there may be slopes, poor surfaces and obstructions which would not be acceptable at licensed airfields. Pilot's planning to use such a strip should seek to gather all possible information beforehand, and include plenty of safety margin in performance planning. It is not unknown for a strip to be 'one-way' – i.e. take-off and landing must be made in opposite directions, normally because of runway slope and/or obstructions at the end of the runway.

To establish the length of a runway 'on site', it can be 'paced', working on the assumption that each step is about 2·5 feet. Runway slope can be established by taking the altitude or elevation at each end of the runway (using the altimeter) and dividing the difference by runway length to give a percentage. Remember to work in the same units, which will usually require knowing the runway length in feet. So, for example, if a runway has an elevation at one end of 412ft, and an elevation at the other of 470ft, and it is 3000ft long, the gradient is found by taking the difference in elevation (472 – 412 = 60ft) and dividing this by the runway length (60/3000) = 2%.

▶Revision

35 What is the definition of TORA?

36 What is a stopway?

37 If a 4000ft runway has an elevation of 590ft at the lower end and an upslope of 1·5%, what is the elevation of the higher end?

Answers at page fpp75

Appendices

Appendix 1
Energy Management

Flight
Performance
and Planning

fpp63

▶ Energy Management

Some pilots, particularly those who fly aerobatics or simulated combat on a regular basis, talk about manoeuvring an aircraft in terms of 'energy management'. Although the concept is not a mandatory part of the PPL syllabus, a basic understanding can be particularly useful for those thinking of flying some form of aerobatics.

Imagine for a moment a ball, placed quite still at the top of a slope. It has a mass, and if it were pushed on to the slope it would begin to roll down – drawn by gravity. It would roll faster and faster. The higher the slope, the greater the speed the ball could eventually reach.

Sitting at the top of the slope, the ball is said to have *potential* energy. The higher the slope, the greater the potential energy the ball has.

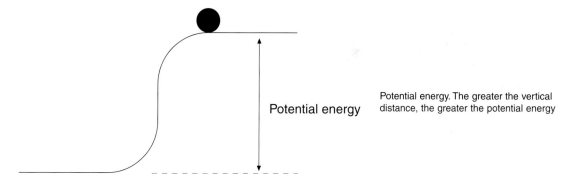

Potential energy

Potential energy. The greater the vertical distance, the greater the potential energy

Once the ball is moving, it has *kinetic* energy; the faster it is moving, the greater its kinetic energy. Kinetic energy increases as the square of speed, so doubling speed from 100kts to 200kts quadruples the kinetic energy.

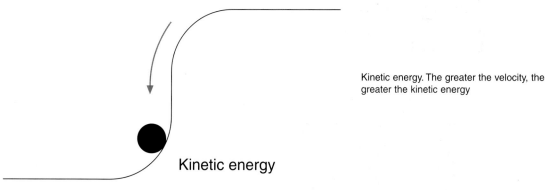

Kinetic energy. The greater the velocity, the greater the kinetic energy

Kinetic energy

Aerobatics are most often a matter of exchanging one type of energy for another. For example, let's look at a loop; for simplicity we'll consider that the manoeuvre is being flown by a glider. The loop begins by the aircraft building up airspeed (often requiring a shallow dive) until the recommended speed for entering the manoeuvre is reached. At this point of the manoeuvre the aircraft possesses maximum kinetic energy. The pilot then pitches the aircraft nose-up into the first half of the loop. The speed begins to reduce as the aircraft climbs – in a sense the pilot is trading speed for height. Speed continues to reduce until the minimum airspeed is reached, right at the top of the loop. At this point the pilot has converted nearly all the kinetic energy from the start of the manoeuvre into potential energy; he has traded nearly all his speed for height. What the aircraft now has is a lot of potential energy. Gravity will accelerate the aircraft in the second half of the loop and the greater the height of the aircraft, the greater the potential energy available for the pilot to turn into kinetic. As the aircraft speed increases in the descent, potential energy is changed back into kinetic as height is traded for speed.

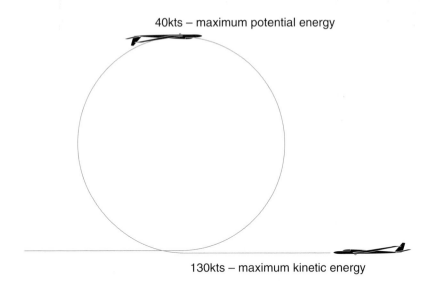

40kts – maximum potential energy

130kts – maximum kinetic energy

A loop flown by a glider, turning kinetic energy into potential and back into kinetic

For practical purposes, energy management can be thought of in terms of speed and height. Leaving aside the factors of engine power and aviation law for a moment, a pilot can either fly low and fast, with the option to pull up and convert excess speed into height in a 'zoom' climb; or fly high and slow, with the option to lower the nose and allow gravity to convert height into speed. What the pilot cannot do without engine power is fly low and slow and still have excess energy for the unexpected.

Think of excess energy (be it height or speed) as a safety margin, money in the bank or whatever, and the practical use of this concept is quite straightforward: airspeed is safety, height is safety. This can be summed-up in the phrase:

Speed is life, Height is life insurance!

Appendix 2
Wind, movement of the atmosphere and the downwind turn

▶ Wind, movement of the atmosphere and the downwind turn

For the most part, it is convenient to consider airspeed and groundspeed as two quite different attributes possessed by an aircraft in flight.

A particular power setting and attitude will result in a specific airspeed; the speed of the aircraft through the air. This gives the aircraft its fundamental aerodynamic properties in terms of performance, controllability etc. To keep an aircraft flying, keep the airspeed within a safe range. The groundspeed, on the other hand, has no aerodynamic effect on the aircraft. An aircraft with an airspeed of 50kts will handle just the same whether in still air, with a 50-knot headwind or a 100-knot tailwind. Groundspeed in these cases is merely a factor in navigation calculations.

In isolation, both statements are quite correct and indisputable. However, an aircraft in flight, like any moving object, has inertia (it resists changes in its velocity) and momentum (as a result of its mass and velocity). So it cannot change speed instantly, whether relative to the ground or relative to the air. There has to be a period of acceleration or deceleration. This is basic physics – and we cannot change the laws of physics. To see what this has to do with the real business of flying aeroplanes, let's look at an aircraft turning in a strong wind.

Imagine an aircraft with an airspeed of 90kts, flying into a headwind of 40kts. Its groundspeed is 50kts (90 – 40). If it turns through 180°, the same airspeed of 90kts will give a groundspeed of 130kts (90 + 40). The change in groundspeed means that, relative to the ground, the aircraft has accelerated by 80kts. If this acceleration in groundspeed takes place through the course of a wide, gentle turn, at high altitude, it will go unnoticed by the pilot. And, in any case, as long as the airspeed is maintained at 90kts, the aircraft will still handle in the same way. Nevertheless, many pilots claim that when they turn downwind, the aircraft loses *airspeed*. A scientist can use maths and physics to prove that this is not the case – the centripetal force of the turn supplies the difference in momentum. Apparently. However, a less than perfect turn, a sudden change in wind velocity, or the extra drag in a turn (which can reduce airspeed) might still leave the pilot and scientist with a difference of opinion.

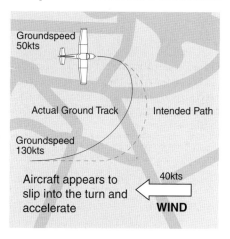

Groundspeed
50kts

Actual Ground Track   Intended Path

Groundspeed
130kts

Aircraft appears to
slip into the turn and
accelerate

40kts

WIND

Turning downwind

What is not disputed, however, is that any minor change in airspeed when turning downwind, whatever the cause, is insignificant compared with the **apparent change** in speed caused by the visual illusion when turning close to the ground. Taking the figures above, a pilot turning quickly from a 40-knot headwind to a 40-knot tailwind will see the rapid acceleration in groundspeed (from 50kts to 130kts), together with an apparent 'slip' into the turn. This can lead the unwary pilot to raise the nose and/or reduce power (even though the *airspeed* is not too fast) and use 'top' rudder, even though the aircraft is in balance. The end result is an out-of-balance aircraft at slow airspeed close to the ground in turning flight (which itself increases the stalling airspeed). This combination adds up to a very dangerous situation.

Aircraft have been known to come to earth in downwind turns, and the following two facts are indisputable:

■ aircraft stall because of a lack of *airspeed*, not a lack of *groundspeed*

■ downwind turns at low level are dangerous for unwary pilots

So above all, when turning downwind at low level and in a strong wind, watch the airspeed and the balance ball. And where possible, make all turns gentle ones.

Revision
Answers

Principles of Flight

▶The Atmosphere and Properties of the Air

1   – 1·98°C per 1000ft up to 36,090ft

2   +1°C

3   +3°C

4   – air density will be reduced (less dense)

5   – air density is inversely proportional to humidity; i.e. as humidity increases, air density reduces and vice versa.

6   – 21%

7   – nitrogen and water vapour

8   – the percentage of water vapour the air is holding, compared with the amount it could hold before becoming saturated

9   – as dynamic pressure increases, static pressure reduces

▶The four Forces

10   – aircraft A (whose wing loading is 22·2lb/sq.ft)

11   – thrust is increased

12   – less than

13   – the distance across the wing from the trailing edge to leading edge (i.e. the wing's width)

14   – the angle between the chord line and the relative airflow

15   – the wing will stall (with marked airflow separation)

16   – the centre of pressure moves forward

17   – drag

18   – 100kg (parasite drag increases as the square of airspeed, doubling airspeed quadruples parasite drag)

19

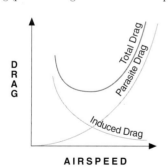

Total Drag
(eg. Parasite Drag + Induced Drag)

20   – a downforce

21   – the aircraft pitches nose-down

▶ Stability and Control

22   – positive stability

23   – the longitudinal axis

24   – the horizontal tail (tailplane)

25   – the aircraft will become more stable in pitch

26   – NO!

27   – as airspeed increases, the elevators will feel more effective

28   – to aid stability in roll (lateral stability)

29   – roll and yaw

30   – the right-hand aileron (on the down-going wing) will be deflected up through a greater angle than the left aileron is deflected down

31   – expect the aircraft to yaw to the right with an increase in power

32   – a mass balance

▶ Trimming Controls

33   – the trimmer is used to maintain the angle of attack

34   – down (this type of question can be best worked out by sketching the relative control positions)

35   – up

36   – it does not, the trim tab maintains a constant angle relative to the control surface until the trimming control is operated by the pilot

37   – the anti-balance or anti-servo tab

38   – it moves in the opposite direction to the control surface it is attached to, to aid the movement of that flying control

▶ Flaps and Slats

39   – the maximum coefficient of lift ($C_{L\,max}$) is increased

40   – lesser

41   – a slat is formed by part of the wing leading edge moving in and out, a slot is a permanent 'gap' in the wing structure

42   – a slot or slat effect *increases* stalling angle of attack

▶ The Stall

43   – an increase in power

44   – the maximum available power

45   – reducing the angle of attack (which means moving the control column forward unless the aircraft is inverted)

46   – as CG moves forward, stall airspeed increases, and vice versa

47   – YES! Any airframe icing will increase stalling airspeed

48   – 50 knots IAS (*indicated* airspeed is not affected by altitude)

49   – a small strip, usually fitted to the wing leading edge, which encourages airflow separation (and hence buffeting and eventually the stall) at that part of the wing

50   – 70 knots (50 x 1·41)

▶Avoidance of Spins

51   – the right-hand (down-going) wing

52   – Check throttle closed and ailerons neutral (flaps up),

Confirm direction of spin, apply full opposite rudder,

Move the control column forward until rotation stops,

Centralise the rudder and recover from the ensuing dive.

53   – the turn indicator or turn co-ordinator

▶Load Factor and Manoeuvring Flight

54   – as angle of bank increases, load factor increases; in a 60° angle of bank turn load factor will be around 2

55   – the operating airspeed range permitted with flaps extended

56   – VNE, the never exceed speed

57   – Va, the manoeuvring speed

Aircraft General Knowledge

▶The Airframe

58   – A spar, B rib, C stringer

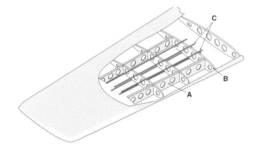

59   – a structure which carries all or most of the stresses in its outside skin

60   – aircraft A (aspect ratio 10)

61   – washout is a decrease in angle of incidence from the wing root to wing tip. It is used to encourage the inner part of the wing to reach the stall before the wing tips

62   – turbulent boundary layer

63   – A bulkhead, B longeron

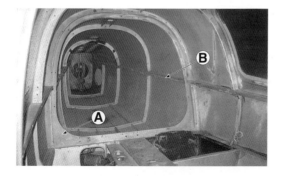

64   – a 'T-tail'

65   – Yes, it may indicate serious damage to the aircraft structure

66   – an anti-balance or anti-servo tab

67   – to help prevent stalling of the fin/rudder in a sideslip

68   – the V_{fe} speed

69   – To prevent damage to the flying controls on the ground as a result of them being moved around forcefully

70   – side-load or sideways force

71   – by cables or rods

72   – No

73   – 2mm

74   – No

75   – no more than 'half' a width split across the creep marks

▶Aero Engines

76   – induction, compression, expansion (or power) and exhaust

77   – the crankshaft

78   – once

79   – the total cylinder volume

80   – the compression ratio

81   – the camshaft

▶The Fuel System

82   – fuel starvation (i.e. fuel in the tank but not reaching the engine)

83   – blue

84   – increased risk of detonation

85   – in a CAA Airworthiness Notice

▶The Induction System

86   – to control the ratio of fuel to air entering the engine

87   – to prevent a 'lean cut' when the throttle is opened rapidly

88   – closed throttle (i.e. idling engine power)

▶The Ignition System

89   – from rotation of its electro-magnets, which are driven by a linkage to engine rotation, *not* the aircraft's electrical system

90   – the spark can be said to be *retarded*

91   – no

92   – pre-ignition

▶The Cooling System

93   – to direct airflow over the engine

94   – open

▶The Oil System

95   – the oil reservoir is the sump itself (located under the engine in this case)

96   – before entering the hot sections of the engine

97   – just downstream of the oil pump

98   – 'straight' mineral oil

99   – because the oil needs time (at least ten minutes) to flow down through the engine and return to the oil sump (where the dipstick measures oil level)

▶The Propeller

100 – to maintain a constant angle of attack along the rotating propeller blade

101 – engine RPM will increase

102 – the aircraft will try to roll anti-clockwise (to the left).

103 – for maximum slow speed performance a fine pitch propeller is required

▶Engine Handling

104 – if the starter warning light remains on after engine start, the engine should be shut down immediately

105 – 30 seconds

106 – a reduction in propeller RPM

107 – the fuel-air mixture will become richer (due to the reducing air density)

108 – set the mixture control to the position which corresponds with the 'peak' RPM

109 – overheating and detonation

110 – carburettor icing and shock cooling

▶Aircraft Systems

111 – 12 volts and 40 amps

112 – 24 volts and 20 amps

113 – an alternator

114 – Direct Current (DC)

115 – 10 amps

116 – once only

117 – A discharge, the alternator is **NOT** charging the battery

118 – A positive flow of current from the alternator

119 – to operate properly, the alternator must draw some electricity from the battery to power the rectifier. Thus, if the battery is not connected to the system, the alternator cannot produce DC electricity

120 – No, the suction flow will bypass the instruments

121 – the Heading Indicator and Attitude Indicator

122 – No, it is usually slightly less

123 – when flying at a large angle of attack

▶ Instruments

124 – the altimeter and Vertical Speed Indicator (VSI)

125 – the airspeed indicator (ASI)

126 – the altimeter will read 4000ft altitude (i.e. the altitude at which the blockage occurred; the VSI will read zero regardless of the rate of climb or descent

127 – 160ft to 260ft amsl

128 – 59 knots IAS in both cases

129 – static and dynamic pressure

130 – it is the caution range, from the maximum normal operating airspeed (VNO) to the never exceed air speed (VNE)

131 – Va airspeed is the *manoeuvring speed*, and is the maximum speed at which full and rapid movement of the flying controls can be made without damaging the structure of the aircraft

132 – VNO – the maximum Normal Operating or structural cruising speed, only to be exceeded with caution and in smooth flying conditions

133 – position error and instrument error

134 – more than, TAS is usually more than IAS, the difference increasing with increased altitude and increased temperature

135 – the ASI will overread – indicating that the airspeed is faster than it actually is

136 – rigidity and precession

137 – any two of: increasing gyro spin speed; increasing the mass of the gyro or increasing the effective radius of the gyro

138 – the turn indicator (or turn co-ordinator)

139 – the turn co-ordinator aircraft symbol will show a turn to the left, whilst the balance ball would be displaced to the right

140 – airspeed indicator, compass, altimeter

141 – apparent wander is caused by the earth's rotation, and causes the Heading Indicator to apparently move away from a fixed heading, when in fact it is staying aligned with a fixed point in space – not the surface of the earth

142 – a series of magnets, a magnet assembly, fluid and a compass rose card

143 – magnetic, deviation, compass

144 – 000° on the HI, and 330° on the compass

145 – the compass will show an apparent turn to the north

▶ Airworthiness

146 – the CAA supplement

147 – the period stated on the certificate

148 – the person who has carried-out the work must record it in the aircraft's logbook(s), and sign and date the entry

149 – an engineer, or a pilot qualified on type

▶ Aeroplane Flight Safety

150 – a safety belt with diagonal shoulder strap, or a safety harness

151 – a safety harness

152 – a Carbon Dioxide, Dry Powder or BCF extinguisher

153 – ventilate the area well to disperse the fumes

154 – the lifejackets should be worn but not inflated

155 – within easy reach of the occupants

156 – the lifejacket is inflated from a Carbon Dioxide (CO_2) bottle, with a back-up oral inflation tube

157 – because the heating pipework runs from the engine compartment to the cockpit. In the event of a fire in the engine compartment, the fire could spread into the cockpit if the heater vent was open. Closing the vent seals the firewall

158 – CO itself is both colourless and odourless. That said, it is found in exhaust fumes which can usually be smelt and sometimes seen as light smoke

159 – dizziness, headaches, nausea, dizziness, blurred vision, drowsiness, impairment of mental functions, unconsciousness and death

160 – black

▶ Operational Flight Safety

161 – the pilot could add half the gust factor (in this case, half of 10 knots) to the approach speed, making 70 knots (65 + 5)

162 – close in below and behind

163 – a larger aircraft generates more wake turbulence

164 – aquaplaning speed increases

165 – the pilot-in-command

Flight Performance and Planning

▶ Mass and Balance

1 – 2435lbs. The Maximum Ramp Weight is the maximum weight for manoeuvring on the ground. The difference between this and Maximum All Up Weight is the weight of fuel expected to be used during start, taxying and pre-take-off checks.

2 – YES!

3 – 69kg/m (i.e. 30 x 2·3)

4 – 25kg (i.e. 100/4)

5 – 110 litres

6 – weight 858kg, total moment 1030kg/m

7 – the Pilot In Command. The aircraft commander (i.e. the pilot in command) is ALWAYS legally responsible for loading.

8 Yes

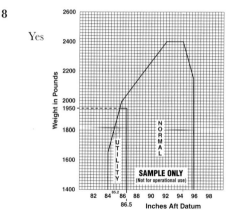

▶Take-off and Climb

9   – at the point at which there is the maximum excess of Power Available over Power Required

10   – the best angle of climb (Vx), i.e. the best height gain in a specific **distance**

11   – 650ft/min. Headwind/tailwind will effect climb angle (i.e. climb gradient), but *rate* of climb is not altered

12   – in a steady climb, lift is less than weight

13   – 50 knots IAS. The headwind does not affect the required *airspeed*, only the groundspeed

14   – reduce, reduce

15   – an increase in air density will *reduce* take-off distance

16   – take-off distance required is irrelevant in these circumstances, as the crosswind component (18 knots) is outside the limit stated.

17   – from graph, take-off distance required is 1300ft. 1300 x 1·33 = 1729ft. 1729ft = 527 metres. Therefore, the runway *is* long enough to allow a safe take-off.

18   – 9 minutes, 6.7lt, 71kts, 558fpm

▶In-flight Performance

19   – angle of attack will increase

20   – the download will reduce

21   – because of aileron drag/adverse yaw, which tends to yaw the aircraft in the opposite direction to that in which it is rolling

22   – in turning flight the ROD will increase

23   – 1= best endurance airspeed, 2= best range airspeed

24   – 60 knots

25   – slightly faster

26   – to maintain 105 knots groundspeed, a TAS of 112 knots is required, which in the table equates to a RPM setting of 2400 (which is producing 63% power in this instance). At this power setting fuel consumption is 7·2 US gallons per hour.

The distance of 270nm will be covered in 2 hours and 35 minutes, consuming 18·5 US gallons, which converts to 70 litres

▶Descent and Landing Performance

27   – 54000ft (i.e. around 8.8 nautical miles)

28   – aircraft weight does not in itself alter glide range, however a heavier aircraft must be flown at a faster airspeed to maintain the angle of attack for best glide range

29   – 35ft

30   – 65kts (i.e. 1·3 x 50)

31   – at least 35% or 1·35

32   – an increase of 20% (factor 1·2)

33   – landing distance required is 747m (including the 1·43 safety factor). Therefore the runway is not long enough to make a safe landing

34   – 5 knots

▶Runway Dimensions

35 – TORA (Take-Off Run Available) is the length of runway available for the take-off run

36 – a stopway is an area of ground beyond the runway where the aircraft can be safely brought to a halt in an emergency

37 – 650ft (4000 x 1·5% = 60ft. 590 + 60 = 650ft)

Index

150 hour check gen138
50 hour check gen138

A

Absolute ceiling fpp18, fpp27
Accelerated stall pf64-65
Acceleration error (of compass)..gen130
Acceleration pf11
Accelerator pump gen53, gen88
Accelerometer pf81
Adverse yaw pf33, pf55, gen18
Aerobatic category..fpp5
Aerodynamic centre (AC) pf29-30
Aerofoil section gen4
Aerofoil pf12
Aeronautical Information Publication (AIP) fpp60
Aileron drag pf55, fpp35
Aileron pf33, gen18
Aileron, use in stall recovery pf61
Air filter gen52
Air intake gen52
Airbrakes pf51, gen19
Air-cooling...gen66-67
Airfield elevation gen116
Airframe gen2-28
Airspeed and control effectiveness pf31, pf33, pf36, pf50, fp55
Airspeed Indicator (ASI) checks gen123
Airspeed Indicator (ASI) gen119-123
Airspeed indicator markings pf56
Airspeed ....pf15, et seq
Airworthiness Directive (AD) gen139
Airworthiness notices gen47, gen139
All-moving tailplane gen16
Alternate induction air gen55
Alternate static source gen109, gen123, gen147
Alternating current (AC) gen102
Alternator gen102-103
Altimeter checks..gen117
Altimeter errors gen116-117
Altimeter gen114-117
Altitude gen114
Ammeter gen104-105
Amphere-hour...gen102
Angle of attack pf15-16, pf28, pf50, pf54-64, fpp33-35, fpp36,
....fpp44-45, fpp49
Angle of bank – effect on stall pf57, pf59
Angle of bank, load factor pf78
Angle of climb fpp17-19
Angle of incidence gen7
Anhedral pf32
Annual check gen138
Annunciator panel gen105
Anti-balance tab pf44, gen16
Anti-servo tab pf44, gen16
Apparent drift gen127

Apparent wander gen127-128
Approach to land fpp49-50
Aquaplaning gen158
Artificial horizon gen125
Aspect ratio gen5-6
Asymmetric blade effect gen77-78
Atmosphere pf2-3
Attitude indicator (AI)..gen125-126
Autorotation pf70
AVGAS...gen47, gen150-151
AVTUR gen150-151
Axisymmetric air inlets gen66

B

Baffle..gen66
Balance indicator gen124
Balance tab pf44
Barometric error gen116
Basic weight fpp3
Batteries...gen100-102, gen105
Bernoulli's theorem pf4-5, pf18, gen52
Big-end bearing gen35
Biplane gen2
Blade angle...gen76
Bottom Dead Centre (BDC)..gen33
Boundary layer pf20, gen8-10, gen13
Bracing position..gen159
Brake pad gen24
Braking technique fpp56
Brakes...gen24-27
Bulkheads gen11
Busbar gen103
Butterfly tail gen16-17
Butterfly valve gen52, gen55

C

CAA supplement (to POH) gen136
Caging (of gyro)...gen127
Calibrated airspeed (CAS) gen121-122
Camber pf13-14, pf30, pf33, pf36, pf48
Camshaft...gen35
Canard..gen2, gen13
Cantilever wing gen4
Carbon Monoxide gen149
Carburettor heat control gen54-55, gen88
Carburettor icing gen54-55, gen90
Carburettor gen34, gen52-55, gen88
Castellated nut gen21
Centre of gravity (CG) pf9, pf22, pf29-30, pf35, fpp4-9, fpp34
Centre of pressure pf17
Centrifugal force pf71, gen77
Centripetal force fpp65
Certificate of airworthiness...gen136-137, fpp2
Certificate of approval of radio installation...gen137
Certificate of maintenance review gen137
Certificate of release to service gen137

CG – effect on stall pf59
CG – lateral pf34
Check A gen138
Chocks gen27
Chord line pf15, pf60
Circuit Breaker gen104
Circulation force pf13
Clearance volume gen33
Clearway fpp60
Climb gradient fpp18
Climb performance fpp16-19, fpp26-27
Climbing engine checks gen89
Cockpit fire gen107, gen145
Coefficient of drag fpp44
Coefficient of lift pf16-18, gen6
Compass checks gen131, gen151
Compass north gen129
Compass swing gen131
Compass gen129-131, gen151
Composite materials gen4, gen15-16
Compressibility error gen122
Compression ratio gen33
Conrod gen35
Constant speed unit (CSU) gen78-80
Constituents of the atmosphere pf2
Contamination (of runway) fpp19, fpp22
Control column pf30, pf33, pf37, pf50, pf55, pf64
Control in pitch pf30-31
Control in yaw pf36-37
Control locks gen20
Conversion, weight fpp3
Cooling drag pf20, gen66
Cooling gen66-67
Cowl flap gen66
Cowling gen66
Crankshaft gen32-33, gen60, gen88
Creep marks gen27
Critical altitude (for turbocharged engine) gen39
Critical angle of attack pf16
Crosswind component calculation fpp20
Cruise descent fpp48
Cruise - engine handling gen90-93
Cruise performance fpp32, fpp35-39
Cylinder Head Temperature (CHT) gauge gen67, gen93
Cylinder gen32-33

D

Dangerous goods gen151
Deceleration error (of compass) gen130
De-icing equipment gen147-148
Density altitude fpp21-22
Density error gen121-122
Departure stall pf65
Descending performance fpp44-50
Descent engine checks gen95

Detonation gen34, gen92
Deviation card gen129
Deviation gen129
Differential ailerons pf33
Differential braking gen25
Dihedral...pf31-32, pf35
Dip gen129
Direct current (DC) gen102
Direct Vision (DV) window gen148
Direction Indicator (DI) gen127
Directional gyro indicator gen127
Directional gyro gen127
Disc brakes gen24
Disposable load fpp3
Dorsal fin gen17
Downwash pf13, pf20-21, fpp15
Downwind turn fpp65
Drag curve pf21, fpp15
Drag pf8, pf12, pf19-22, pf31, pf33, pf48-49, pf51, pf54, pf70-71
Drum brakes gen24
Duplicate control inspection gen140
Dynamic pressure pf3-4, pf13, pf14, pf15, pf17-18, pf31, pf55, pf56, gen119, gen121, fpp33
Dynamic stability pf26-27

E

'E' Type compass gen129
Earth gyro...gen125
Earthing...gen100
Electrical bonding..gen106
Electrical circuits gen100-101
Electrical failure...gen106
Electrical fire gen107
Electrolyte...gen101
Elevator pf30-31, gen16-17
Elevator trim pf42-43
Emergency Distance Available (EDA) fpp60
Emergency exits...gen159
Empty weight...fpp3
Endurance fpp38-39
Energy fpp63-64
Engine design gen34-36
Engine designators gen40
Engine fire gen94-95
Engine handling...gen84-96
Engine mounting gen36
Equilibrium pf8, pf26
Equivalent airspeed (EAS)..gen122
Exhaust gas temperature (EGT) gauge gen93
Exhaust system...gen35
Exhaust valve gen32-33
External power socket..gen107

F

Fabric-covered structure gen15
Fairings..pf19
Feathering gen80

Fin pf32, pf34-36, gen12, gen17
Fire extinguishers gen145
Fire on starting gen86
Fire types gen145
Firewall gen36, gen149
First Aid Kits gen145
Fixed-pitch propeller gen77-78
Flap and coefficient of lift pf60
Flap, effect on pitch control pf31, pf48
Flap – effect on stall pf58
Flap pf17, pf48-50, gen19
Flap, use on take-off fpp14, fpp25
Flap – effect on glide fpp47
Flare fpp51
Flight level gen114
Float chamber gen52
Flooded engine gen86
Flutter pf38
Flying control balance pf37-38
Form drag pf19
Four stroke cycle gen32-33
Fowler flap pf49-50
Frise ailerons pf33, gen18
Frost pf59
Fuel bladder gen44
Fuel cell gen44
Fuel contents gauge gen45-46
Fuel drain.. gen45
Fuel flow computer gen46
Fuel grades gen47
Fuel injection gen55
Fuel pressure gauge gen46
Fuel pump gen45
Fuel sampling gen47-48
Fuel selector gen45
Fuel starvation gen45
Fuel system management gen48-49
Fuel system gen44-49
Fuel tank venting gen44-45
Fuse gen103-104
Fuselage design gen11-13
Fuselage structure gen11

G

'g' pf57, pf78-81
'g' meter pf81
'g'-break pf60, pf63
Generator gen102
Gimbals gen123, gen124, gen125, gen127
Gliding.. fpp44-49
Gravity-feed fuel system gen44
Gross weight fpp3
Ground effect fpp15, fpp51
Ground roll fpp52
Ground run fpp52

Grounding (of electrical circuits) gen100
Gusts gen156-157
Gyro horizon gen125
Gyroscope..gen123
Gyroscopic force pf71, fpp14

H

Hand-swinging propeller gen85
Hanger rash gen16
Harnesses...gen144
Heading Indicator (HI) gen127-128
Heading Indicator checks gen128
Headwind component calculation fpp20
Heating system gen148-149
Height gen114
High-tension leads gen34, gen60, gen61, gen62
Hold-off fpp51
Horizontally opposed engine gen36
Horn balance...pf38, gen18
Humidity pf2, gen54-55, fpp22
Hydraulic lock gen96
Hydraulic system gen25

I

Icing (airframe)..pf59, fpp38
Idle Cut Off (ICO)...gen86, gen96
Idling jet gen53
Ignition system gen34, gen60-62
Impact icing gen54
Impulse coupling gen62
Indicated airspeed (IAS) gen119-120
Indicated stall airspeed pf19, gen119
Induced drag pf19-21, gen5, fpp15
Induction system gen34, gen52-56
Inertia fpp14, fpp65
In-line engine gen35
Instantaneous Vertical Speed Indicator (VSI) gen118-119
Instrument error..gen116, gen118, gen121
Intake valve gen32-33
Interference drag pf20
International Standard Atmosphere (ISA) pf2, pf18, gen115, fpp21
Isogonals gen129

J

Jet A-1 ....gen150-151

K

Kinetic energy fpp55, fpp63-64
Kitplanes gen13
Known icing gen54

L

Laminar flow..gen8, gen13
Landing Distance Available...fpp60
Landing performance fpp52-56
Landing technique fpp51
Laptop PC gen151
Lateral axis...pf27
Lateral CG pf34, fpp9

Latitude nut gen128
Leading edge devices pf50
Leading edge pf14, gen10
Lead-acid battery gen101
Left-centre ammeter gen105
Lever arm fpp4-9
Lifejackets gen146-147
Liferaft gen147
Lift dumpers pf50
Lift formulae pf17
Lift pf4, pf8-9, pf12-18, pf22, pf28, pf30, pf32, pf33, pf34,
 ....pf36, pf48-50, pf55, pf57-58, pf70-71, pf78, fpp32-34
Lift/Drag ratio fpp32-34, fpp44-47
Lift/mass couple pf22
Lift-dependant drag pf21
Light Aircraft Maintenance Scheme (LAMS) gen137-138
Liquid-cooled engines gen35, gen67
Load ammeter gen105
Load factor – effect on stall pf63
Load factor pf11, pf57, pf78-81
Loading fpp8-9
Loadmeter gen105
Logbooks gen140
Longerons gen11
Longitudinal axis pf27
Longitudinal stability..pf28
Low Voltage (LV) light gen105

M

Magnetic compass..gen129-131, gen151
Magnetic north gen129
Magnetic goods gen151
Magneto switch gen84
Magnetos gen34, gen60-62, gen88
Magnus effect pf13
Manifold pressure gen38-39, gen79-80
Manoeuvre-induced error gen110, gen116, gen118
Manoeuvring flight..fpp34-35, fpp63
Manoeuvring speed pf79-80, gen157
Mass – effect on stall pf57
Mass balance pf37-38, gen18
Mass...pf8-pf11, pf22, pf29, pf57, pf71, pf78, fpp2, fpp19, fpp46
Master switch gen105
Maximum All Up Weight (MAUW) fpp2
Maximum Landing Weight fpp2
Maximum mass limit fpp2
Maximum Ramp Weight fpp2
Maximum Take-Off Weight (MTOW) fpp2
Maximum Total Weight Authorised (MTWA) fpp2
Maximum weight limit fpp2
Maximum Zero Fuel Weight fpp2
Metal-covered structure...gen14-15
Minimum drag airspeed fpp36
Minimum rate of descent fpp48
Minimum-power-required airspeed..pf54

Mixture control gen34, gen90-93
Mixture gen53, gen90-93
Mobile phones gen151
Modifications gen141
MOGAS gen47, gen151
Moment..pf28-29, fpp4
Momentum fpp65
Monocoque structure gen4, gen11
Monoplane gen2

N

Normal axis pf27
Normal category..fpp5
Nosewheel steering gen23

O

Obstacle clearance fpp16-18
Octane gen47
Oil breather pipe gen72
'Oil canning' gen44
Oil cooler...gen70
Oil dipstick gen72
Oil filter gen70
Oil grades gen71
Oil pressure gauge gen70
Oil pressure gen70-71
Oil sump gen70
Oil system gen35, gen70-72
Oil temperature gauge gen70
Oil temperature gen70-71
Oleo undercarriage leg gen22-23
Otto cycle gen32-33

P

Parallel electrical circuit gen102
Parasite drag pf19-21
Parking brake gen25
Passenger briefing gen159-160
Payload pf9, pf29, fpp5
Pendulous unit gen125
Permit to fly gen137, gen139
Phugoid pf27
Pilot maintenance...gen140
Pilot's Operating Handbook/Flight Manual (POH/FM) pf11, pf29, pf56, pf72, pf79,
....pf80, gen136, fpp2 et seq
Piston engines...gen32-34
Piston rings...gen70
Piston gen32-33
Pitch angle gen76
Pitch control pf30-31
Pitch lever...gen78-80
Pitch stability pf28-30
Pitot heat gen109, gen123
Pitot pressure gen119
Pitot tube gen109, gen123
Pitot-static head...gen109
Pitot-static system gen108, gen110

Plain flap pf49
Pneumatic de-icing boots gen148
Position error gen110, gen116, gen118, gen121
Potential energy fpp63-64
Power – effect on stall pf58
Power + Attitude = Performance.........................fpp17, fpp32-33, fpp49-50
Power available curve fpp32
Power checks gen87-88
Power curve..pf54, fpp32
Power required curve fpp32
Precession gen123, fpp14
Pre-flight check...gen14-16, gen20-21
Pre-ignition gen60
Pressure altitude gen115, fpp21
Pressure carburettor gen53
Pressure drag pf19
Primer gen84
Propeller angle of attack gen76
Propeller...pf12, gen76-81
Pusher propeller gen11, gen14

Q

QFE..gen114, gen117
QNH gen114, gen117
Quasi stall pf60, gen13

R

Radial engine gen35-36
Radiator gen35, gen67
Radius of turn..fpp35
Range fpp36-38
Rate gyro gen124
Rate of climb...fpp16-19
Rate of turn fpp35
Real drift gen127
Real wander...gen127
Reciprocating piston engines gen32-37
Rectified airspeed (RAS)...gen121
Rectifier gen102
Refuelling precautions gen150
Relative airflow..pf15
Resistance torque gen76
Rib gen3-4
Ribbed tyre tread...gen24
Rigidity gen123
Roll stability...pf31-32
Rotary engine gen35
Rotating combustion engine gen38
Rudder pf36, gen17-18, fpp35
Rudder trim pf42-43
Rudder – use in stall recovery pf61
Runway dimensions fpp60-61
Runway slope fpp22-23, fpp52-53, fpp61
Runway surface fpp22-23, 53

S

Saturated pf2
Seat belts gen144
Seats gen144
Secondary effect of roll pf33
Secondary effect of rudder...pf36
Secondary effect of yaw pf35
Semi-cantilever wing..gen4
Semi-monocoque structure gen4, gen11
Series electrical circuit gen102
Service bulletins..gen138
Service ceiling fpp18, fpp27
Shimmy damper gen23
Simple flap fp49
Shock cooling...gen67, gen95
Shoulder strap gen144
Sideslipping fpp47
Skin friction drag pf19-20, gen4
Slats pf50, gen19
Slaved Heading Indicator (HI)..gen128
Slipstream pf12, pf31, pf35, pf36
Slot pf50, gen19
Slotted flap...pf49
Slow flight pf54-55
Slow-running jet gen53
Small-end bearing gen35
Snow pf59
Span loading gen5
Spar gen3-4
Spark plugs gen32-33, gen60-62
Spark timing gen61
Specific gravity...fpp3
Spin accidents pf74
Spin forces pf71
Spin recovery pf71-72
Spinner gen77
Spinning...pf70-74
Spiral dive pf73
Split flap pf49
Spoilers...pf50, gen19
Spring-leaf undercarriage leg gen22
Stabilator...gen16
Stability in pitch..pf28-30
Stability in roll..pf31-32
Stability in yaw pf35-36
Stability pf26-37
Stability-definition pf26
Stagnation pressure...gen119
Stall accidents pf63-65
Stall airspeed pf56-59
Stall and wing design gen6-7
Stall recovery pf60-62
Stall strips pf62-63, gen7
Stall symptoms pf59-60

Stall warners pf62
Stall pf16, pf54-65
Stalling angle of attack pf16
Stalling in a turn pf62
STAR annual..gen138
Starter ring gen84
Starter warning light gen85
Static electricity gen106
Static port gen109, gen117, gen119, gen123
Static pressure pf3-4, pf13, pf14, pf18, pf20, gen109, gen117, gen118-119, gen123
Static stability pf26-27
Static wicks gen106
Stopway..fpp60
Storage gen96
Streamlining pf19
Stressed skin construction gen4
Stringer gen3-4
Suction gauge gen108, gen126
Suction pump gen108, gen126
Suction system gen107-108, gen129
Suction failure..gen126
Supercharging gen38-39
Supplemental type certificate gen141
Surface friction drag pf19
Swept wing..gen8, gen14
Switch gen101

T

'T'-tail gen12
Tachometer...gen78
Tailplane pf22, pf28-29, pf32, gen12
Tailwheel undercarriage gen3
Take-Off Distance Available (TODA) fpp60
Take-off performance fpp14-16, fpp19-26
Take-off roll fpp14
Take-Off Run Available (TORA) fpp60
Take-off run fpp14, fpp19
Take-off safety speed fpp25
Tapered wing gen6
Taxying gen87
Technical log gen138
Temperature deviation...pf2
Temperature error gen116
Throttle gen52-53
Thrust bending force gen77
Thrust pf8, pf12, pf22, pf58, gen76-77, fpp32
Thrust/drag couple...pf22
Time lag gen116, gen118, gen121
Tip clearance pf12
Tip tanks gen44
Toe brakes gen26
Top Dead Centre (TDC) gen33, gen60
Torque link gen23
Torque..gen76-78
Total cylinder volume gen33

Towbar gen28
Tractor propeller gen11
Trailing edge pf14
Trailing vortex drag pf21
Transport wander gen128
Tricycle undercarriage gen3
Trim drag fpp34
Trim tab...pf42-44
Trimmer controls pf42-44
Trimmer pf42-44, gen16, gen18
True airspeed (TAS) gen121-122, fpp27
True altitude...gen115
True north gen129
Turbocharger gen38-39
Turbulence gen156-157
Turbulent flow gen8, gen13
Turn and slip gen124
Turn co-ordinator checks gen125
Turn co-ordinator gen124
Turn indicator gen124
Turn on to final spin pf74
Turn radius fpp35
Turn rate fpp35
Turning downwind fpp65
Turning error (of compass) gen130
Turning flight fpp34-35
Two-stroke engines gen37
Tyre inflation gen26-27
Tyre tread gen26-27
Tyres gen24

U

Undercarriage checks...gen26-28
Undercarriage gen22-28
Unusable fuel gen46
Upwash pf13
Usable fuel gen46
Utility category...fpp5-6

V

V2...fpp25
'V'-tail gen16-17
'V-type' engine gen36
Va..pf79-80, gen120, gen157
Vacuum pump...gen107
Vacuum system gen107
Valves gen32-33, gen35
Variable load..fpp3
Variable pitch propeller..gen78-80
Variation gen129
Vat fpp55
Ventilation gen148
Ventral strake gen12
Venturi pf4, pf13, pf14, gen52, gen53, gen54
Vertical Speed Indicator (VSI) checks gen119
Vertical Speed Indicator (VSI) errors gen118-119

Vertical Speed Indicator (VSI) gen118-119
Vertical stabiliser pf34, gen11-12
Vfe pf80, gen19
V-n envelope pf79-80
VNE pf80, gen120
VNO...pf80, gen120
Volt gen102
Voltmeter gen105
Vortex generator gen10
Vortices pf20-pf21, gen9-10, gen158
Vortilons gen10
Vref fpp55
Vs1 ....pf56, pf80, gen120
Vso pf56, pf80, gen120
Vx fpp17
Vy fpp17

W

Wake turbulence gen158
Wankel engine gen38
Washout...gen7
Wastegate gen39
Water vapour pf2
Weight and centre of gravity schedule gen137
Weight schedule gen137
Weight pf9-pf11, pf18, pf28, pf57, pf71, pf78, pf80, fpp2-3
Wet wings gen44
Wheel spats gen27
Windmilling propeller gen80
Windshear gen156-157
Wing chord pf14, gen6
Wing construction gen3-5
Wing design gen5-10
Wing drop pf61
Wing fences gen10
Wing loading pf9-11
Wing planform...gen6-7
Wing root pf14
Wing section pf14
Wing span pf14
Wing stall characteristics gen8-10
Wing tip pf14, gen8-9
Wing sweep gen7, gen14
Winglet...gen9-10

Y

Yaw control pf36-37
Yaw stability pf34-35

Z

Zero-centre ammeter gen104